Good Housekeeping

Best-Loved Desserts

More Than 250 Scrumptious Recipes

HEARST BOOKS

A division of Sterling Publishing Co., Inc.

New York / London
www.sterlingpublishing.com

This book was previously published as a hardcover.

Good Housekeeping

Rosemary Ellis	Editor in Chief
Sara Lyle	Lifestyle Editor
Susan Westmoreland	Food Director
Samantha Cassetty	Nutrition Director
Sharon Franke	Food Appliances Director

Cover design by: Roberto de Vicq de Cumptich

The hardcover edition of this title was cataloged by the Library of Congress as follows:
Good Housekeeping best-loved desserts / editors of Good Housekeeping Magazine.
    p. cm.
  Includes index.
  ISBN 978-1-58816-550-3
1. Desserts. I. Good Housekeeping Institute (New York, N.Y.).
  TX773.G646 2006
  641.8'6--dc22

                                2006009750

10 9 8 7 6 5 4 3 2 1

The Good Housekeeping Cookbook Seal guarantees that the recipes in this cookbook meet the strict standards of the Good Housekeeping Research Institute. The Institute has been a source of reliable information and a consumer advocate since 1900, and established its seal of approval in 1909. Every recipe has been triple-tested for ease, reliability, and great taste.

First Paperback Edition 2010
Published by Hearst Books
A division of Sterling Publishing Co., Inc.
387 Park Avenue South, New York, NY 10016

Good Housekeeping and Hearst Books are trademarks of Hearst Communications, Inc.

www.goodhousekeeping.com

For information about custom editions, special sales, premium and corporate purchases, please contact Sterling Special Sales Department at 800-805-5489 or specialsales@sterlingpublishing.com.

Distributed in Canada by Sterling Publishing
c/o Canadian Manda Group, 165 Dufferin Street
Toronto, Ontario, Canada M6K 3H6

Distributed in Australia by
Capricorn Link (Australia) Pty. Ltd.
P.O. Box 704, Windsor, NSW 2756 Australia

Manufactured in China

Sterling ISBN 978-1-58816-779-8

The Good Housekeeping Triple-Test Promise

At *Good Housekeeping*, we want to make sure that every recipe we print works in any oven, with any brand of ingredient, no matter what. That's why, in our test kitchens at the **Good Housekeeping Research Institute**, we go all out: We test each recipe at least three times and, often, several more times after that.

When a recipe is first developed, one member of our team prepares the dish and we judge it on these criteria: it must be **delicious, family-friendly, healthy,** and **easy to make.**

1. The recipe is then tested several more times to fine-tune the flavor and ease of preparation, always by the same team member, using the same equipment.

2. Next, another team member follows the recipe as written, **varying the brands of ingredients** and **kinds of equipment.** Even the types of stoves we use are changed.

3. A third team member repeats the whole process **using yet another set of equipment** and **alternative ingredients.**

BY THE TIME THE RECIPES APPEAR ON THESE PAGES, THEY ARE GUARANTEED TO WORK IN ANY KITCHEN, INCLUDING YOURS. WE PROMISE.

Very Blueberry Pie (page 157)

Contents

~~~~~~~~~~~~~~~~~~~~~~~~~~~~~~~~~~~~~

Introduction

~~~~~~

DESSERTS MAKE PEOPLE HAPPY. There's hardly anyone anywhere who can resist digging into a luscious, sweet dessert, be it a mile-high cake; a warm and bubbling peach cobbler; or a creamy, rich chocolate pudding.

So what is it about desserts that everyone finds so appealing? Maybe it's that sweet foods connect us to the comforts of family and home. They magically transport grown-ups back to the innocence and security of childhood while making childhood a bit more magical for kids. Every spoon- or forkful evokes pleasant memories: the fragrance of mom's holiday baking wafting over you as you entered the kitchen; the excitement of birthday parties with fancy layer cakes; the challenge of eating ice cream cones before they melted during summers at the beach; and the anticipation of after-school milk and home-baked brownies, among others. If it's true that the secret ingredient in a wonderful dish is love, then perhaps we equate sweets with the love that was lavished on us in an unforgettable time and place, by the people we hold dear. In the South, when people say "Give me some sugar," they mean "give me some love." *Good Housekeeping Best-Loved Desserts* has both in abundance.

Between the covers of this book are recipes for more than 250 heavenly desserts and confections that promise to put a smile on the faces of all those lucky people who sit at your table. There are enough cookies, cakes, pies, tarts, and pastries to supply several bakeshops as well as lots of other sweet temptations, such as frozen and fruit desserts, soufflés, custards, puddings, meringues, and candies. Whether you're planning for a backyard barbecue or other special event, a lunch-box treat, family dinner, or holiday gala, you'll find yourself reaching for *Good Housekeeping Best-Loved Desserts* again and again. So get ready to make your reputation as a dessert diva.

Before you begin, however, it's a good idea to become familiar with some of the culinary basics that will help you turn out many a grand finale. Then, when dinner is served, be sure to tell everyone to save room for dessert!

BAKING ESSENTIALS

When you cook up a stew or casserole, in the right order, a "little of this and a pinch of that" won't drastically affect the outcome, but baking requires strict attention to details: measurements, adding ingredients in the right order, pan size, oven temperature, and timing. Using the right tools and equipment and, of course, the best and freshest ingredients will make the job easier and more enjoyable and the results delectable. The following rundown of the basic equipment and ingredients is a good introduction to what you'll find in our recipes. When you're ready to begin, read the recipe carefully, assemble all ingredients and equipment, set oven racks in position, and preheat.

TOOLS AND EQUIPMENT

In our great-grandmothers' kitchens, baking was an all-day affair. Her *batterie de cuisine* consisted of not much more than a few bowls and knives, a wooden spoon or two, and a rolling pin. Today, with the help of electrical kitchen appliances and a few well-chosen tools and gadgets, you can start to bake while dinner is in the oven and serve a fresh-from-the-oven dessert that same evening.

Appliances

BLENDER Useful for pureeing fruits for sauces, mixing liquid batters, and chopping small quantities of nuts. A pulse button will help get the precise results. For larger quantities, use a food processor.

ELECTRIC MIXERS A heavy-duty stand-mounted machine, with its powerful motor, can handle everything from beating delicate meringues to mixing stiff cookie doughs with speed and efficiency. Stand mixers come with an assortment of bowls and attachments for a number of mixing chores. For small jobs, such as whipping cream, use a hand-held mixer.

FOOD PROCESSOR For chopping, grinding, grating, kneading, and mixing in a flash. A 6-cup processor bowl can knead a dough made with up to 6 cups of flour; an 8-cup bowl can handle a dough made with up to 8 cups.

Baking Pans, Dishes, And Sheets

Take an inventory of your baking pans and be sure that they are in good shape and that you have enough of each shape and size for the type of baking you'll be doing.

BAKING DISHES A large, coverless rectangular dish that is usually glass or ceramic, with sides about 2 inches high. Most frequently used sizes: 13" by 9", 15" by 10", and 11" by 7".

BAKING PANS Same as baking dish but made of metal, with sides 1½ to 2 inches high. Essential are 8- and 9-inch square pans and a 13" by 9" rectangular pan.

BUNDT PAN One-piece tube pan, curved on the bottom and deeply fluted so it turns out cakes that are decorative even without frosting. Available in 6- and 12-cup sizes.

COOKIE SHEETS Flat metal sheets with slightly raised edges on one or more sides. Keep several on hand for baking cookies (they have to cool down before reusing) and for placing under tarts and pies, which may leak during baking. Cookie sheets should fit your oven rack with 2 inches to spare on all sides.

COOLING RACKS Round racks are for cooling cake layers; rectangular racks are good for cookies. A rack is also useful when glazing or icing cakes, cookies, or pastries (with a sheet of waxed paper underneath), because it allows the drips to fall through instead of puddling around the cake.

CUPCAKE PAN Usually referred to as a muffin pan. The standard size, which measures 2½ inches across each individual cup, holds about ⅓ cup of batter. For easy removal of finished baked goods, use fluted paper cup liners.

CUSTARD CUPS Individual ovenproof porcelain, stoneware, or glass dishes with a capacity of 4 to 6 ounces. Ramekins, which resemble miniature soufflé dishes, can be substituted.

JELLY-ROLL PAN A 15½" by 10½" rectangular metal pan with low sides for baking sheets of sponge cake that will become rolled cakes.

LAYER-CAKE PANS Medium-weight aluminum are best. Have three 8-inch and three 9-inch round pans, at least 1½ inches deep; 8- and 9-inch square pans about 2 inches deep for square layer cakes and bar cookies.

LOAF PANS Deep rectangular pans, both metal and glass, used for loaf cakes and quick breads. A loaf baked in a glass pan will bake faster than one baked in a metal pan. Standard sizes are 8½" by 4½" and 9" by 5".

PIE PLATES Made of ovenproof glass, metal, or ceramic, pie plates come in 8-, 9-, and 10-inch sizes. Disposable foil pie pans have a smaller capacity than standard pie plates.

SHEETCAKE PAN A versatile 13" by 9" by 2" rectangular pan, in either metal or glass, is used for single-layer cakes and large batches of bar cookies. It can also be used as a water bath for custards.

SOUFFLÉ DISHES Round ovenproof dishes with straight sides to help the soufflé rise. They range in capacity from 3½ ounces to 2 quarts. Cold dessert soufflés require a paper or foil collar placed around the rim to support the sides of the mixture while it sets.

SPRINGFORM PAN A round, deep, two-piece pan used for baking cheesecakes and other cakes that are too delicate to be turned out. The side unlatches so that it can be removed from the cake for serving.

TART PANS Available in a variety of sizes and shapes. Choose a removable-bottom pan, which comes in two parts.

TUBE PAN For baking sponge cakes and angel food cakes. The "tube" in the middle gives the batter a surface to adhere to as it rises. Useful sizes are 9- and 10-inch round. They come in one piece or with a removable bottom.

HOW TO MEASURE PANS

Use a ruler to measure across the top of a baking pan or dish, from inside edge to inside edge. Measure the depth on the inside as well, from the bottom to the top of the pan.

Utensils, Gadgets, And Accoutrements

BOWLS A set of three mixing bowls in sizes ranging from 1- to 3-quart will get you through most baking projects.

COOKIE CUTTERS In assorted shapes and sizes for cutting out rolled dough and pastry sheets in different shapes. Also used for cutting chocolate shapes.

COOKIE PRESS A cylindrical tube with interchangeable perforated metal plates fitted to a nozzle at the end, through which the dough is pressed to make variously shaped spritz, or molded, cookies from buttery dough.

FLOUR SIFTER OR FINE-MESH SIEVE To aerate the flour and eliminate lumps before mixing.

GRATER Most versatile is a box grater with different-size perforations on each side for shredding chocolate, cheese, nutmeg, citrus zest, carrots, etc.

KNIVES Most useful are an 8-inch chef's knife for chopping, a 4-inch paring knife for peeling and cutting fruit, and a long knife with a serrated blade for cutting cake layers. It's essential that knives be sharp and well balanced.

MEASURING CUPS *Dry measuring cups* for measuring flour, sugar, cornmeal, cocoa, and other dry ingredients come in sets of graduated sizes from ¼- to 1-cup. *Liquid measuring cups* are clear beaker-shaped cups with an easy-pour lip and measurements marked on the side. Liquid measures in 1- and 2-cup sizes will serve most purposes.

MEASURING SPOONS Sets of ⅛, ¼, ½, and 1 teaspoon, plus 1 tablespoon that are joined by a ring. They can be used for both dry and wet ingredients.

PASTRY BAG AND ASSORTED TIPS For making cream puffs and éclairs, shaping meringue, and decorating cakes with whipped cream or frosting.

PASTRY BRUSH A 1-inch-wide natural-bristle brush is best for smoothing on glazes; a wider brush works well for brushing off crumbs or excess flour.

ROLLING PIN For evenly rolling out dough to the desired thickness for pies, tarts, and cookies. Choose the American-style hardwood free-spinning roller with ball bearing or the one-piece tapered European-style wooden pin.

SPATULAS A variety of spatulas in different sizes are a must for baking. *Nylon and rubber spatulas* are used to fold in flour mixtures, whipped cream and beaten egg whites as well as to scrape bowls. A *wide metal spatula* or pancake turner is used to remove hot cookies from cookie sheets. Frosting the top and sides of cakes requires *narrow metal spatulas:* one about 10 inches long and one about 4 inches long. *Offset Spatulas* (the blade is lower than the handle) are handy for applying frosting; their angled shape keeps hands in a comfortable position for smoother application. Use a small one for hard-to-reach spots.

SPOONS *Long-handled wooden spoons* are nonreactive, gentle on food, and won't burn your fingers when stirring hot liquids. They're excellent for mixing butters, stirring sauces, and pushing purees through a sieve. A large *metal basting spoon* is good for spooning sauces or poaching liquid over fruit. A *metal slotted spoon* is useful for lifting poached fruit out of the poaching liquid.

WIRE WHISKS Ideal for stirring sauces, whisking mixtures together, and beating eggs and cream. Available in many sizes, with the largest, the balloon whisk, used for beating egg whites until stiff.

THE BAKER'S LARDER

Most baking ingredients can be kept on hand in the cabinet, refrigerator, or freezer. All should be the freshest and best quality possible. Buy your baking ingredients in a store with a good turnover, and check the packages for freshness dates. Because baking requires the proper combination of specific ingredients, use only those listed in the recipes.

Dairy Products

- BUTTERMILK Use only when specified, it balances sugar's sweetness amd reacts with baking soda to give baked goods a fine crumb.
- CREAM Heavy or whipping cream for toppings, fillings, and frostings.
- CREAM CHEESE For cheesecakes and some frostings.
- EGGS Our recipes call for large eggs, about 2 ounces each.
- MILK Use plain whole milk to achieve the desired richness of baked goods, or substitute 2 percent reduced-fat milk.
- SOUR CREAM Full-fat sour cream is best, but the "light" version can be substituted in some recipes where indicated.
- YOGURT Lowfat, but not nonfat, can be substituted for full-fat yogurt in most recipes.

Fats

- BUTTER Butter brings a rich, sweet taste to baked goods that nothing can else can match. The recipes in this book were developed using salted butter.
- MARGARINE If you prefer to bake with margarine (some of our recipes suggest it as an acceptable alternative), use the solid stick form with at least 80 percent fat. Avoid "diet" margarines and those that come in a tub or squeeze bottle.

- **OIL** For baking, use a flavorless vegetable oil such as corn, safflower, sunflower, canola, or soybean. Do not substitute oil for solid shortening in any baking recipe.
- **VEGETABLE SHORTENING** The all-fat content makes it ideal for pie and tart crusts (butter and margarine contain some milk solids). Store in refrigerator.

Flavorings

- **CHOCOLATE**

  Unsweetened, or bitter or baking, chocolate contains 50 to 58 percent cocoa butter and no sugar. Do not substitute semisweet.

  Bittersweet chocolate is at least 35 percent chocolate liquor. It has some sugar added together with butterfat, lecithin, and flavorings.

  Semisweet chocolate can be used interchangeably with bittersweet but has more sugar, therefore a less intense chocolate flavor.

  Dark sweet chocolate, like that used in German chocolate cake, is a sweet, edible chocolate that contains no milk.

  Milk chocolate is very sweet and soft-textured and is sold for eating. It shouldn't be substituted for other chocolates to flavor a cake batter or cookie dough, but it can be cut up and used instead of semisweet chocolate chips.

  White chocolate is not truly chocolate because it lacks cocoa butter (although the best brands do contain some cocoa butter) and should be used only when white chocolate is specified.

  Unsweetened cocoa is a powder made by removing most of the fat from chocolate. Do not substitute instant cocoa mix and use Dutch-process cocoa only if specified.

- **EXTRACTS** Use pure, not imitation, extracts whenever possible to obtain the truest flavor. Vanilla is most commonly used, but almond, orange, lemon, and peppermint are also good to have on hand.
- **PEPPER** For pepper at its most flavorful, use a peppermill to grind whole black or white peppercorns as needed.
- **SALT** Without salt, sweet baked goods can taste flat. Use table salt for the recipes in this book unless otherwise specified.
- **SPICES** Keep in a cool, dark place—away from heat and moisture. To maintain freshness, buy spices such as nutmeg and cardamom whole and crush or grind them as needed.

Flours And Meals

- **WHEAT FLOUR** *All-purpose* flour is a blend of high-gluten hard wheat and low-gluten soft wheat, producing a balance of protein and starch that works well in most recipes. *Cake flour* is made from finely ground soft wheat and is low in protein and high in starch; it produces very tender cakes and pastries. To substitute all-purpose flour for cake flour: For every cup of cake flour, put 2 tablespoons of cornstarch into a 1-cup dry measure and fill the cup with all-purpose flour, then level off.
- **CORNMEAL** Although yellow and white cornmeal are ground from different types of corn, choosing one over the other will affect only the color, not the taste, of the finished product.
- **CORNSTARCH** Used in combination with flour for very fine-textured cakes and cookies; also used as a thickening agent for puddings, sauces, and fruit filling for pies.

Dried Fruits And Nuts

- COCONUT Flaked, sweetened coconut is sold in bags, ready to use; refrigerate leftovers. Do not substitute fresh coconut unless the recipe calls for it.
- DRIED FRUITS Store dried fruits in ziptight bags or jars with tight-fitting lids; they'll keep longer if refrigerated. To soften fruit that has become too dry and hard, place in a shallow bowl, sprinkle with water, cover, and microwave for about 30 seconds. To keep dried fruit from sticking to a knife or kitchen shears when chopping, lightly oil the blade.
- NUTS AND SEEDS Their high fat content makes them perishable. Nuts keep longest in the shell or buy shelled (not chopped) nuts in airtight containers. Store nuts and seeds in the freezer in airtight freezer bags.

Leavenings

- BAKING POWDER (DOUBLE-ACTING) When mixed with a liquid, baking powder releases carbon dioxide gas bubbles, which cause a cake to rise. As it is very perishable, keep in a cool, dark place with the container tightly closed. Never let moisture enter the container. To test for freshness, stir ½ teaspoon into ½ cup warm water: It should foam up immediately. Discard any baking powder you've had longer than a year.
- BAKING SODA Combined with baking powder when an acidic ingredient such as yogurt or molasses is used. Always mix baking soda with the other dry ingredients before any liquid is added. Once dry and wet ingredients are combined, place batter in oven quickly.
- CREAM OF TARTAR Sometimes added to egg whites while they're being beaten to help stabilize them, which makes them a more effective leavening, particularly for angel food cakes.

NOTES ON NUTS

Nut yields: As a rule of thumb, 4 ounces of most nuts equal 1 cup chopped nuts.

Toasting nuts intensifies their flavor and in the case of nuts such as hazelnuts, allows the skins to be removed (see Tip on page 256). Toasted nuts aren't as likely as untoasted nuts to sink in cakes, breads, and other batter-based foods. To toast almonds, pecans, walnuts, or hazelnuts, preheat the oven to 350°F. Spread the shelled nuts in a single layer on a cookie sheet. Bake, stirring occasionally, until lightly browned and fragrant, about 10 minutes.

Nuts are easier to chop when warm. Either heat in microwave oven at High (100 percent power) for 1 minute or in a preheated conventional oven at 325°F for 5 minutes.

To keep chopped nuts from sinking in batters you can also toss them with 1 or 2 tablespoons of the flour used in the recipe.

Chop nuts quickly in the food processor fitted with a metal blade. Process by using quick on/off pulses until the nuts are of the desired texture. Keep a sharp eye on the mixture; you don't want nut butter.

To add flavor and texture to pie crusts, once the dough is in the pan and fluted, sprinkle the bottom and sides with about ¼ cup ground or finely chopped, toasted nuts. Press the nuts gently into the crust; bake or fill as the recipe directs.

When using chopped nuts as a garnish, put them in a strainer and toss them a few times to remove bits of nuts and skin that would spoil the look of your decorated dessert.

- YEAST A one-celled microscopic organism that, as it grows, converts its food (sugar and starch) into alcohol and carbon dioxide. Yeasts used for baking are *active dry* yeast (tiny dehydrated granules) and *compressed fresh* yeast, which comes in tiny cakes and is highly perishable. One cake of fresh yeast can be substituted for 1 envelope of dry yeast. To *proof* yeast, to see if it is still active, dissolve it in warm water and add a pinch of sugar; set aside for 5 to 10 minutes. If it begins to swell and foam, it is active and capable of leavening. Yeast should be stored in a cool, dry place. It can also be refrigerated or frozen. Use by the expiration date on the package or label. Bring to room temperature before using.

Sweeteners

- CORN SYRUP Made from cornstarch, it comes in light and dark versions, the latter having a strong caramel flavor. Corn syrup helps cookies stay moist and is used in frostings and icings, candy, jams, and jellies to prevent sugar from crystallizing.
- HONEY In baking, it is used for sweetening, flavoring, and moisture retention. Honey varies in color and flavor, depending on the nectar the bees favor. Generally, the darker the color the stronger the flavor. To reliquify honey that has crystallized in the refrigerator, microwave the opened jar at 100 percent power for about 30 seconds or place the opened jar in a pan of water and cook over low heat for 10 to 15 minutes.
- MAPLE SYRUP Buy only pure maple syrup, not pancake syrup, which may not contain any maple. Grades AA or Fancy are the palest in color and most delicate in flavor. For more maple flavor opt for a darker and less expensive grade, such as Grade B.

- MOLASSES The best molasses (unsulfured) is a very thick, brown syrup with tangy undertones. The lighter the molasses, the milder and sweeter its flavor. Baked goods made with molasses tend to brown quickly, so check them as they bake.
- SUGAR More than a sweetener, sugar helps batters and doughs to rise by allowing more air to be incorporated as the mixture is beaten. It also helps keep cakes and cookies tender and moist.

   Granulated white sugar is the form used most in baking.

   Superfine sugar is more finely granulated and, because it dissolves almost instantly, is perfect for meringues and sweetening cold liquids. It can be substituted for regular granulated sugar cup for cup.

   Confectioners', or *powdered*, sugar is granulated sugar that's been crushed to a fine powder, sifted, and mixed with a bit of cornstarch to prevent lumping. The designation 10X, often seen on the package, indicates the finest possible texture. It is used to make frostings and icings, and, by itself, as a decorative dusting on desserts.

   Brown sugar is simply granulated white sugar with molasses added. Dark brown sugar contains more molasses than does light brown sugar. Hardened brown sugar can be softened by placing it in a plastic bag with a slice of apple and sealing the bag tightly for 1 to 2 days.

MEASURING INGREDIENTS

Accurate measurements are essential to getting good results. To measure small amounts of liquids or dry ingredients, use a set of measuring spoons. For large amounts of *liquids*, use a 1-cup or larger measuring cup with a pouring lip. Read the measurements at eye level on a flat surface. For *dry ingredients*, use a set of graduated measuring cups and level off with the straight edge of a knife or metal spatula.

Measuring Butter, Margarine, or Shortening

Butter and margarine are generally sold in boxes containing four ¼-pound sticks. Each stick equals ½ cup or 8 tablespoons. The wrapper is usually marked off in tablespoons, so, following the guidelines on the wrapper, cut off the number of tablespoons needed. If not using sticks, spoon shortening into a graduated measuring spoon or cup. With the back of a spoon, pack it firmly into the cup, adding more to fill if necessary. Level off with the edge of a knife or metal spatula.

Measuring Flour

Measure all flours straight from the package or canister, stirring the flour to aerate it before measuring. Never pack flour into a measuring cup or spoon or shake or tap the sides of the measure. Lightly spoon flour from the package into a graduated measuring cup or spoon. Level off the surplus with the edge of a knife or metal spatula. If the recipe calls for 1 cup sifted flour, sift first, then measure. If it says 1 cup flour, sifted, you should measure, then sift.

Measuring Sugar

Spoon *granulated* or *confectioners'* sugar into a graduated measuring cup or spoon; level off with the edge of a knife or metal spatula. To measure *brown* sugar, pack it down firmly into a graduated dry measuring cup with the back of a spoon, then level off.

Measuring Syrups

Lightly coat the inside of a liquid measuring cup or spoon with vegetable oil before pouring in honey, molasses, maple syrup, corn syrup, etc., and the syrup will pour out easily.

Cookies and Confections

CHEWY AND MOIST OR LIGHT AND CRISP, cookies are the one sweet treat no one can pass up. Because they're small, completely totable, and easy to eat on the go, they're the perfect snack anytime your sweet tooth starts nagging for a quick fix. You'll be hard-pressed to select a favorite from among this irresistible collection of cookies.

If you're partial to brownies, you'll want to try any or all of our *bar cookies*—just mix, spread in a pan, and bake. Yummy ice-cream–filled Brownie Sundae Cups (page 30), offer a new take on brownies à la mode. Rich chocolate and creamy almond cheesecake meld beautifully in Cheesecake Swirl Brownies (page 20). And for a fund-raiser or special luncheon, Macadamia Triangles (page 24) or our buttery Lemon Bars (page 32) are sure to impress.

Drop cookies are fun to bake—spoonfuls of dough dropped onto cookie sheets spread out as they bake into perfect, round cookies. Classic Whoopie Pies (page 36) have always been a childhood favorite, now you get to choose chocolate cake or spicy gingerbread to sandwich the fluffy marshmallow filling. Remember those lacy, chocolate-filled Florentines (page 40) that were a bakeshop specialty? They can be a specialty of yours. So too can the White Chocolate–Macadamia Jumbos (page 35)—bursting with cherries, chocolate, and nuts.

As a child, you probably helped mom cut shapes from rolled-out dough using cookie cutters. These *rolled cookies* are a bit more sophisticated, but the roll/cut/shape principle is the same. You'll still enjoy making Pinwheels (page 42) with jam filling; crescent-shaped Apricot-Raspberry Rugelach (page 43), layered with preserves, dried fruit, and walnuts; and Cinnamon Twists (page 44) made from a cream-cheese dough.

Molded cookies, shaped either before or after baking, include some longtime favorites: Curled, wafer-thin Almond Tuiles (page 54), are draped over a rolling pin while warm; crisp Brandy Snaps (page 53) are rolled around the handle of a wooden spoon to get their characteristic cigar shape; and the five versions of twice-baked biscotti are shaped into logs, baked, sliced, then baked again.

Sometimes referred to as slice-and-bake cookies, *refrigerator cookies* are sliced or shaped from dough that has been chilled in the fridge first. For melt-in-your-mouth Cinnamon Bun Cookies (page 49), a layer of cinnamon-flavored dough is rolled with plain cream-cheese dough jelly-roll fashion, chilled, then sliced before baking. The dough for Almond Crescents (page 50) is refrigerated before it is worked by hand into the familiar half-moon shapes.

And what better way to finish up this chapter than with time-honored recipes for several delicious chocolate and nut candies. Whether you're drawn to truffles, pralines, or dipped fruit, these elegant palate pleasers are just right when you want to serve "a little something sweet" with after-dinner coffee.

Black-and-White Cookies (page 33)

Almond Lattice Brownies

A rich almond-paste topping is piped over brownie batter before it is baked.

PREP 25 minutes plus cooling • BAKE 25 minutes • MAKES 24 brownies.

BROWNIE
1¼ cups all-purpose flour
½ teaspoon salt
½ cup butter or margarine (1 stick)
4 squares (4 ounces) unsweetened chocolate, chopped
4 squares (4 ounces) semisweet chocolate, chopped
1½ cups sugar
2 teaspoons vanilla extract
3 large eggs, lightly beaten

ALMOND LATTICE TOPPING
1 tube or can (7 to 8 ounces) almond paste, crumbled
1 large egg
¼ cup sugar
1 tablespoon all-purpose flour
1 teaspoon vanilla extract

1 Preheat oven to 350°F. Grease 13" by 9" baking pan.

2 Prepare brownie: In small bowl, with wire whisk, mix flour and salt. In 3-quart saucepan, melt butter and unsweetened and semisweet chocolates over low heat, stirring frequently, until smooth. Remove from heat; stir in sugar and vanilla. Add eggs; stir until well mixed. Stir flour mixture into chocolate mixture just until blended. Spread batter evenly in prepared pan.

3 Prepare topping: In food processor with knife blade attached, pulse almond paste, egg, sugar, flour, and vanilla until mixture is smooth, scraping bowl with rubber spatula. Transfer almond mixture to small ziptight plastic bag. With scissors, cut bottom corner of bag on diagonal, ¼ inch from edge. Pipe topping over brownie batter to make 10 diagonal lines, spacing them 1 inch apart. Pipe remaining topping diagonally across first set of lines to make 10 more lines and create a lattice design.

4 Bake until toothpick inserted 2 inches from edge comes out almost clean, 25 to 30 minutes. Cool completely in pan on wire rack.

5 When cool, cut brownie lengthwise into 4 strips, then cut each strip crosswise into 6 pieces.

EACH BROWNIE About 220 calories, 4g protein, 28g carbohydrate, 11g total fat (5g saturated), 46mg cholesterol, 100mg sodium.

Almond Lattice Brownies

Cheesecake Swirl Brownies

A ribbon of creamy almond cheesecake winds its way through the middle of these super-chocolate brownies.

PREP 30 minutes • **BAKE** 35 to 40 minutes • **MAKES** 24 brownies.

½ cup butter or margarine (1 stick)
4 squares (4 ounces) unsweetened chocolate, chopped
4 squares (4 ounces) semisweet chocolate, chopped
2 cups sugar
5 large eggs
2½ teaspoons vanilla extract
1¼ cups all-purpose flour
¾ teaspoon baking powder
½ teaspoon salt
1½ packages (8 ounces each) cream cheese, chilled
¾ teaspoon almond extract

1 Preheat oven to 350°F. Grease 13" by 9" baking pan.

2 In 4-quart saucepan, melt butter and unsweetened and semisweet chocolates over low heat, stirring frequently, until smooth. Remove from heat. With wooden spoon, beat in 1½ cups sugar. Add 4 eggs and 2 teaspoons vanilla; beat until well blended. Stir in flour, baking powder, and salt.

3 In small bowl, with mixer at medium speed, beat cream cheese until smooth; gradually beat in remaining ½ cup sugar. Beat in almond extract, remaining egg, and remaining ½ teaspoon vanilla just until blended.

4 Spread 1½ cups chocolate batter in prepared pan. Spoon cream-cheese batter in 6 large dollops on top of chocolate mixture (cream-cheese mixture will cover much of chocolate batter). Spoon remaining chocolate batter in 6 large dollops over and between cream-cheese batter. With tip of knife, cut and twist through mixtures to create marble design.

5 Bake until toothpick inserted in center comes out almost clean with a few crumbs attached, 35 to 40 minutes. Cool completely in pan on wire rack.

6 When cool, cut lengthwise into 4 strips, then cut each strip crosswise into 6 pieces.

EACH BROWNIE About 240 calories, 4g protein, 26g carbohydrate, 14g total fat (8g saturated), 70mg cholesterol, 160mg sodium.

Cheesecake Swirl Brownies

Mochaccino Brownies

Mocha is a combination of coffee and chocolate, whereas a mochaccino is a cappuccino with chocolate syrup added.

PREP 25 minutes plus cooling • **BAKE** 25 minutes • **MAKES** 24 brownies.

BROWNIE
1 cup all-purpose flour
¼ teaspoon salt
2 tablespoons instant coffee or espresso powder
1 tablespoon very hot water
½ cup butter or margarine (1 stick)
1 package (8 ounces) unsweetened chocolate squares, chopped
2 cups granulated sugar
4 large eggs, lightly beaten
1 teaspoon vanilla extract

MOCHACCINO GLAZE
4 teaspoons instant coffee or espresso powder
2 tablespoons butter or margarine, melted and kept hot
2 cups confectioners' sugar
3 tablespoons milk
1 teaspoon vanilla extract

1 Preheat oven to 350°F. Grease 13" by 9" baking pan.

2 Prepare brownie: In small bowl, with wire whisk, mix flour and salt. In cup, dissolve coffee in water; set aside. In 3-quart saucepan, melt butter and chocolate over low heat, stirring frequently, until smooth. Remove from heat; stir in granulated sugar. Add eggs, vanilla, and coffee mixture; stir until blended. Stir flour mixture into chocolate mixture just until blended. Spread batter evenly in prepared pan.

3 Bake until toothpick inserted 2 inches from edge comes out almost clean, 25 to 30 minutes. Cool in pan on wire rack.

4 When brownie is cool, prepare glaze: In medium bowl, with wire whisk, stir coffee and hot melted butter until coffee dissolves. Stir in confectioners' sugar, milk, and vanilla until smooth.

5 With small metal spatula, spread glaze over cooled brownie. Cut lengthwise into 4 strips, then cut each strip crosswise into 6 pieces.

EACH BROWNIE About 230 calories, 3g protein, 33g carbohydrate, 11g total fat (9g saturated), 59mg cholesterol, 78mg sodium.

 A CAVALCADE OF COOKIES

BAR COOKIES are made by mixing up a dough, spreading it out in a pan, then baking, cooking, and cutting.

DROP COOKIES are made by dropping spoonfuls of soft dough onto cookie sheets.

ROLLED COOKIES are made from a stiff dough that is rolled out and then cut into shapes with cookie cutters.

PRESSED COOKIES are made by squeezing a semistiff dough onto cookie sheets through a cookie press or pastry bag to create specific shapes.

MOLDED COOKIES are made from a stiff dough that is hand-formed into balls, logs, twists, or other shapes, or baked in individual molds.

REFRIGERATOR COOKIES begin with a stiff dough that is chilled, then cut into even slices and baked.

Plenty-of-Peanuts Bars

The combination of chocolate, peanuts, and peanut butter makes a decadently delicious bar. For an extra-special treat, cut them into twelve or sixteen rectangles and sandwich a generous scoop of vanilla ice cream between two of them.

PREP 30 minutes • BAKE 55 minutes • MAKES 48 bars.

CRUST
⅓ cup quick-cooking oats, uncooked
1 cup all-purpose flour
⅓ cup light brown sugar
4 tablespoons butter or margarine (½ stick), softened
3 tablespoons chunky peanut butter

PEANUT TOPPING
3 large eggs
4½ teaspoons light molasses
1½ cups packed light brown sugar
⅓ cup chunky peanut butter
4 tablespoons butter or margarine (½ stick), softened
⅔ cup all-purpose flour
2 teaspoons baking powder
½ teaspoon salt
1 cup salted cocktail peanuts, chopped
1 package (6 ounces) semisweet chocolate chips (1 cup)

confectioners' sugar (optional)

1 Preheat oven to 350°F. Grease 13" by 9" baking pan.

2 Prepare crust: In large bowl, with mixer at low speed, beat oats, flour, brown sugar, butter, and peanut butter until blended. Pat dough evenly onto bottom of prepared pan. Bake 15 minutes.

3 Meanwhile, prepare filling: In large bowl, with mixer at medium speed, beat eggs, molasses, brown sugar, peanut butter, and butter until well combined, constantly scraping bowl with rubber spatula. Reduce speed to low; add flour, baking powder, and salt and beat until blended, occasionally scraping bowl. With spoon, stir in peanuts and chocolate chips. Spread mixture evenly over hot crust.

4 Bake until golden, about 40 minutes longer. Cool completely in pan on wire rack.

5 When cool, sprinkle with confectioners' sugar, if you like. Cut lengthwise into 4 strips, then cut each strip crosswise into 12 pieces.

EACH BAR About 125 calories, 3g protein, 16g carbohydrate, 6g total fat (2g saturated), 18mg cholesterol, 94mg sodium.

Macadamia Triangles

This elegant special-occasion cookie owes its fine flavor to macadamia nuts. Native to Australia, macadamia trees were planted in Hawaii near the end of the nineteenth century. The nuts are a little pricier than others, but very delicious.

PREP 15 minutes plus cooling • **BAKE** 35 minutes • **MAKES** 32 triangles.

1 cup all-purpose flour
¼ cup granulated sugar
⅛ teaspoon salt
6 tablespoons cold butter or margarine
3 tablespoons cold water
1 jar (7 ounces) macadamia nuts
⅔ cup packed light brown sugar
1 large egg
2 teaspoons vanilla extract

1 Preheat oven to 425°F. Grease 9-inch square baking pan. Line pan with foil, (see Tip, below); grease foil.

2 In medium bowl, with wire whisk, mix flour, sugar, and salt. With pastry blender or two knives used scissor-fashion, cut in butter until mixture resembles coarse crumbs. Sprinkle in water, about 1 tablespoon at a time, mixing lightly with fork after each addition, until dough is just moist enough to hold together. With lightly floured hand, press dough evenly onto bottom of prepared pan. With fork, prick dough at 1-inch intervals to prevent puffing and shrinking during baking.

3 Bake crust until golden, 15 to 20 minutes (crust may crack slightly during baking). Cool completely in pan on wire rack. Turn oven control to 375°F.

4 Coarsely chop ½ cup macadamia nuts; reserve for topping. In food processor with knife blade attached, pulse remaining macadamia nuts and brown sugar until nuts are finely ground. Add egg and vanilla. Pulse until just combined.

5 Spread macadamia filling evenly over cooled crust. Sprinkle reserved chopped macadamia nuts on top. Bake until filling has set, 20 minutes. Cool completely in pan on wire rack.

6 When cool, lift foil with pastry out of pan and place on cutting board; peel foil away from sides. Cut into 4 strips, then cut each strip crosswise into 4 squares. Cut each square diagonally in half.

EACH TRIANGLE About 105 calories, 1g protein, 10g carbohydrate, 7g total fat (2g saturated), 12mg cholesterol, 35mg sodium.

> **Test Kitchen Tip**
>
> **LINING PAN WITH FOIL** To line a pan with foil the easy way, invert the baking pan so it is bottom side up. Mold a length of foil, shiny side facing out, over the pan, pressing the foil firmly to set the shape. Lift up the foil. Turn the pan right side up. Lower the foil "pan" into the baking pan; smooth it to create a tight fit.

Malted Milk Bars

Milkshake fans will adore these superlative bars. The frosting is made with malted milk powder and sprinkled with chopped malted milk balls.

PREP 15 minutes • **BAKE** 25 minutes • **MAKES** 32 bars.

CHOCOLATE BASE

1½ cups all-purpose flour
½ teaspoon baking powder
½ teaspoon salt
¾ cup butter or margarine (1½ sticks)
4 squares (4 ounces) semisweet chocolate, chopped
2 squares (2 ounces) unsweetened chocolate, chopped
1½ cups granulated sugar
1 tablespoon vanilla extract
4 large eggs, beaten

MALTED MILK TOPPING

¾ cup malted milk powder
3 tablespoons milk
1 teaspoon vanilla extract
3 tablespoons butter or margarine, softened
1 cup confectioners' sugar
1½ cups malted milk ball candies (about 5 ounces), coarsely chopped

1 Preheat oven to 350°F. Grease 13" by 9" baking pan. Line pan with foil, extending it over rim; grease foil.

2 Prepare chocolate base: In small bowl, with wire whisk, mix flour, baking powder, and salt. In heavy 3-quart saucepan, melt butter and semisweet and unsweetened chocolates over low heat, stirring frequently, until smooth. Remove from heat. With wooden spoon, stir in granulated sugar and vanilla. Beat in eggs until well blended. Add flour mixture to chocolate mixture; stir until blended. Spread batter evenly in prepared pan.

3 Bake 25 to 30 minutes, until toothpick inserted 1 inch from edge of pan comes out clean. Cool in pan on wire rack.

4 Prepare topping: In small bowl, stir malted milk powder, milk, and vanilla until blended. Stir in butter and confectioners' sugar until blended. With small spatula, spread topping over cooled bars; top with chopped malted milk ball candies. Allow topping to set.

5 When topping is firm, lift foil with pastry out of pan and place on cutting board. Cut lengthwise into 4 strips, then cut each strip crosswise into 8 pieces.

EACH BAR About 200 calories, 3g protein, 27g carbohydrate, 10g total fat (5g saturated), 42mg cholesterol, 155mg sodium.

Mississippi Mud Bars

Mississippi Mud Bars

Dense as mud, rich as millionaires, and they freeze well. Don't tell anyone, but they taste great frozen.

PREP 20 minutes plus cooling • **BAKE** 35 minutes • **MAKES** 32 bars.

MUD CAKE
¾ cup butter or margarine (1½ sticks)
1¾ cups granulated sugar
¾ cup unsweetened cocoa
4 large eggs
2 teaspoons vanilla extract
½ teaspoon salt
1½ cups all-purpose flour
½ cup pecans, chopped
½ cup flaked sweetened coconut
3 cups mini marshmallows

FUDGE TOPPING
5 tablespoons butter or margarine
1 square (1 ounce) unsweetened chocolate,
  chopped
⅓ cup unsweetened cocoa
⅛ teaspoon salt
¼ cup evaporated milk (not sweetened
  condensed milk) or heavy or
  whipping cream
1 teaspoon vanilla extract
1 cup confectioners' sugar
½ cup pecans, coarsely broken
¼ cup flaked sweetened coconut

1 Preheat the oven to 350°F. Grease and flour 13" by 9" baking pan.

2 Prepare cake: In 3-quart saucepan, melt butter over low heat. With wire whisk, stir in granulated sugar and cocoa. Remove from heat. Beat in eggs, one at a time. Beat in vanilla and salt until well blended. With wooden spoon, stir in flour just until blended; stir in pecans and coconut. Spread batter evenly in prepared pan (batter will be thick).

3 Bake 25 minutes. Remove from oven. Sprinkle marshmallows in even layer on top of cake. Return to oven and bake until marshmallows are puffed and golden, about 10 minutes longer. Cool completely in pan on wire rack.

4 When cake is cool, prepare topping: In heavy 2-quart saucepan, melt butter and chocolate over low heat, stirring frequently, until smooth. With wire whisk, stir in cocoa and salt until smooth. Stir in evaporated milk and vanilla (mixture will be thick); beat in confectioners' sugar until smooth and blended. Pour hot topping over cake.

5 Cool fudge-topped cake 20 minutes, then sprinkle with pecans and coconut. Serve at room temperature or chilled. To store, leave cake in pan and wrap. To serve, cut lengthwise into 4 strips, then cut each strip crosswise into 8 pieces.

EACH BAR About 204 calories, 3g protein, 26g carbohydrate, 11g total fat (5g saturated), 44mg cholesterol, 125mg sodium.

Brownie Sundae Cups

A new presentation for an old-fashioned dessert. Brownies baked in muffin pans are scooped out in the center to make room for your favorite ice cream and our hot fudge sauce.

PREP 20 minutes plus cooling • BAKE 30 minutes • MAKES 6 servings.

BROWNIE CUPS
1 cup all-purpose flour
½ cup unsweetened cocoa
1 teaspoon baking powder
¼ teaspoon salt
¾ cup butter or margarine (1½ sticks)
1½ cups sugar
3 large eggs, lightly beaten
2 teaspoons vanilla extract

HOT FUDGE SAUCE
½ cup sugar
⅓ cup unsweetened cocoa
¼ cup heavy or whipping cream
2 tablespoons butter or margarine
1 teaspoon vanilla extract

1 pint vanilla ice cream

1 Preheat oven to 350°F. Grease 6 jumbo muffin-pan cups (about 4" by 2" each) or six 6-ounce custard cups.

2 Prepare brownie cups: In medium bowl, with wire whisk, mix flour, cocoa, baking powder, and salt. In 3-quart saucepan, melt butter over medium-low heat. Remove from heat; stir in sugar. Add eggs and vanilla; stir until well mixed. Stir in flour mixture just until blended. Spoon batter evenly into muffin-pan cups.

3 Bake until toothpick inserted in center comes out almost clean, 30 to 35 minutes. Cool in pan on wire rack 5 minutes. Run tip of thin knife around edge of brownies to loosen. Invert brownies onto rack and cool 10 minutes longer to serve warm, or cool completely to serve later.

4 While brownie cups cool, prepare hot fudge sauce: In heavy 1-quart saucepan, heat sugar, cocoa, cream, and butter to boiling over medium-high heat, stirring frequently. Remove from heat; stir in vanilla. Serve sauce warm, or cool completely, then cover and refrigerate for up to 2 weeks. Gently reheat before using. Makes about ⅔ cup.

5 Assemble brownie sundaes: With small knife, cut a 1½- to 2-inch circle in center of each brownie; remove top and set aside. Scoop out brownie centers, without scooping through bottom of brownies. Transfer centers to small bowl and reserve for another use. Place each brownie cup on a dessert plate. Scoop ice cream into cups and drizzle with hot fudge sauce; replace tops.

EACH SERVING WITHOUT SAUCE About 500 calories, 7g protein, 61g carbohydrate, 28g total fat (16g saturated), 152mg cholesterol, 355mg sodium.

EACH TABLESPOON SAUCE About 80 calories, 1g protein, 10g carbohydrate, 5g total fat (3g saturated), 14mg cholesterol, 25mg sodium.

Brownie Sundae Cups

Lemon Bars

Our recipe for this timeless classic is very straightforward, but its sweet/tart flavor and rich texture are sensational—literally.

PREP 25 minutes plus cooling • **BAKE** 40 minutes • **MAKES** 32 lemon bars.

¾ cup butter (1½ sticks), softened
   (do not use margarine)
2¼ cups all-purpose flour
⅔ cup plus 1 tablespoon confectioners' sugar
3 to 4 large lemons
6 large eggs
2 cups granulated sugar
1 teaspoon baking powder
¾ teaspoon salt

1 Preheat oven to 350°F. Grease 13" by 9" baking pan. Line pan with foil, extending foil over rim; lightly grease foil.

2 In food processor with knife blade attached, pulse butter, 2 cups flour, and ⅔ cup confectioners' sugar until mixture is moist but crumbly. Dough should hold together when pressed between two fingers. Sprinkle mixture into prepared pan. With fingertips, press dough evenly onto bottom of pan. Bake until lightly browned, 20 to 25 minutes.

3 While crust bakes, prepare filling: From lemons, grate 2½ teaspoons peel and squeeze ⅔ cup juice. In large bowl, with wire whisk, beat eggs. Add lemon peel and juice, granulated sugar, baking powder, salt, and remaining ¼ cup flour; whisk until well blended.

4 Whisk filling again and pour onto hot crust. Bake until filling is just set and golden around edges, 18 to 22 minutes. Transfer pan to wire rack. Sift remaining 1 tablespoon confectioners' sugar over warm filling. Cool completely in pan on wire rack.

5 When cool, lift foil with pastry out of pan and place on cutting board; carefully peel foil away from sides. If you like, trim edges. Cut lengthwise into 4 strips, then cut each strip crosswise into 8 pieces.

EACH BAR About 146 calories, 2g protein, 23g carbohydrate, 5g total fat (3g saturated), 51mg cholesterol, 126mg sodium.

> **Test Kitchen Tip** **MAKE-AHEAD TREATS** If you like, prepare lemon bars up to a day ahead: Prepare through Step 4, but do not top with confectioners' sugar. Refrigerate until ready to serve. Sprinkle with confectioners' sugar before cutting into bars.

Lemon Bars

Black-and-White Cookies

These giant sugar cookies with half chocolate and half vanilla frosting are popular in New York City bakeries. You can also enjoy them the way they do across the Hudson in New Jersey by just eliminating the frosting. See photo on page 16.

PREP 20 minutes plus cooling • **BAKE** 15 minutes • **MAKES** about 12 cookies.

2 cups all-purpose flour
½ teaspoon baking soda
¼ teaspoon salt
10 tablespoons butter or margarine
    (1¼ sticks), softened
1 cup granulated sugar
2 large eggs
2 teaspoons vanilla extract
½ cup buttermilk

WHITE AND CHOCOLATE GLAZES
1¾ cups confectioners' sugar
2 tablespoons light corn syrup
8 to 10 teaspoons warm water
¼ cup unsweetened cocoa

1 Preheat oven to 350°F. In small bowl, with wire whisk, mix flour, baking soda, and salt.

2 In large bowl, with mixer at medium speed, beat butter and granulated sugar until creamy. Beat in eggs and vanilla until blended. Reduce speed to low, add flour mixture alternately with buttermilk, beginning and ending with flour mixture. Beat just until combined, scraping bowl occasionally with rubber spatula.

3 Drop dough by ¼ cups, about 3 inches apart, on two ungreased large cookie sheets. Bake until edges begin to brown and tops spring back when lightly touched with finger, 15 to 17 minutes, rotating sheets between upper and lower racks halfway through baking. With wide metal spatula, transfer cookies to wire racks to cool completely.

4 When cookies are cool, prepare white glaze: In medium bowl, mix 1¼ cups confectioners' sugar, 1 tablespoon corn syrup, and 5 to 6 teaspoons water, 1 teaspoon at a time, until spreadable. Turn cookies over, flat side up. With small metal spatula, spread glaze over half of each cookie. Allow glaze to set 20 minutes.

5 Meanwhile, prepare chocolate glaze: In small bowl, stir remaining ½ cup confectioners' sugar, the cocoa, remaining 1 tablespoon corn syrup, and remaining 3 to 4 teaspoons water, 1 teaspoon at a time, until spreadable. With clean small metal spatula, spread chocolate glaze over unglazed half of each cookie. Let glaze set completely, at least 1 hour.

EACH COOKIE About 280 calories, 3g protein, 46g carbohydrate, 9g total fat (6g saturated), 53mg cholesterol, 190mg sodium.

Triple-Chocolate Chubbies

We added more chocolate, walnuts, and pecans to a dense brownielike batter to create a big, fat cookie that became an instant tradition in our test kitchen.

PREP 25 minutes plus cooling • **BAKE** 12 minutes per batch • **MAKES** about 24 cookies.

¼ cup all-purpose flour
¼ cup unsweetened cocoa
½ teaspoon baking powder
¼ teaspoon salt
8 squares (8 ounces) semisweet chocolate, chopped
6 tablespoons butter or margarine, cut into pieces
1 cup sugar
2 teaspoons vanilla extract
2 large eggs
1 package (6 ounces) semisweet chocolate chips (1 cup)
½ cup pecans, chopped
½ cup walnuts, chopped

1 Preheat oven to 350°F. In small bowl, with wire whisk, mix flour, cocoa, baking powder, and salt.

2 In 3-quart saucepan, melt chopped chocolate and butter over low heat, stirring frequently, until smooth. Pour into large bowl; cool to lukewarm. Stir in sugar and vanilla until blended. Stir in eggs, one at a time, until well blended. Add flour mixture and stir until combined (batter will be thin). Stir in chocolate chips, pecans, and walnuts.

3 Drop batter by heaping tablespoons, 1½ inches apart, on ungreased large cookie sheet. Bake until set, 12 to 14 minutes. Cool on cookie sheet on wire rack 2 minutes. With wide metal spatula, carefully transfer cookies to wire rack to cool completely.

4 Repeat with remaining batter.

EACH COOKIE About 180 calories, 2g protein, 21g carbohydrate, 11g total fat (5g saturated), 26mg cholesterol, 70mg sodium.

Test Kitchen Tip

SHIPPING COOKIES

Chewy, soft drop, or bar cookies are best for mailing; avoid mailing crisp cookies.

Line a sturdy cardboard box or tin with waxed paper or bubble wrap. Wrap cookies individually or in pairs, back to back, with plastic wrap. Cushion each layer with crumpled paper. Fill any empty spaces with crumpled paper or bubble wrap. Mark wrapped package FRAGILE.

White Chocolate–Macadamia Jumbos

Chock-full of cherries, white chocolate, and macadamia nuts, just one of these cookies is a dessert by itself. But when you sandwich a scoop of your favorite ice cream between two, it's a party waiting to happen. The recipe came to us from Joanne Steinback.

PREP 30 minutes plus cooling • BAKE 15 minutes per batch • MAKES about 24 cookies.

2½ cups all-purpose flour
¾ cup butter or margarine (1½ sticks), softened
¾ cup granulated sugar
½ cup packed dark brown sugar
3 tablespoons corn syrup
2 teaspoons vanilla extract
1 teaspoon baking soda
1 teaspoon salt
2 large eggs
12 squares (12 ounces) white chocolate, coarsely chopped
1 jar (7 ounces) macadamia nuts, chopped (about 1⅓ cups)
1½ cups dried tart cherries

1 Preheat oven to 325°F. In large bowl, with mixer at medium speed, beat flour, butter, granulated and brown sugars, corn syrup, vanilla, baking soda, salt, and eggs until blended, occasionally scraping bowl with rubber spatula. With spoon, stir in white chocolate, nuts, and dried cherries.

2 Drop dough by slightly rounded ¼ cups, 3 inches apart, on ungreased large cookie sheet. Bake until lightly browned, 15 to 17 minutes. With wide metal spatula, transfer cookies to wire rack to cool.

3 Repeat with remaining dough.

EACH COOKIE About 310 calories, 4g protein, 37g carbohydrate, 16g total fat (7g saturated), 37mg cholesterol, 275mg sodium.

> **Test Kitchen Tip** FLATTENING STIFF COOKIE DOUGH
> A stiff cookie dough will bake more evenly if flattened slightly with a small metal spatula after it is dropped onto the cookie sheet.

Whoopie Pies

We discovered these soft, marshmallow-filled, chocolate sandwiches at a farmers' market and just loved them. So we re-created the recipe, and now you can bake them at home.

PREP 30 minutes plus cooling • BAKE 12 minutes • MAKES 12 whoopie pies.

COOKIES
2 cups all-purpose flour
1 cup granulated sugar
½ cup unsweetened cocoa
1 teaspoon baking soda
6 tablespoons butter or margarine, melted
¾ cup milk
1 large egg
1 teaspoon vanilla extract
¼ teaspoon salt

MARSHMALLOW FILLING
6 tablespoons butter or margarine, slightly
 softened
1 cup confectioners' sugar
1 jar (7 ounces) marshmallow creme
 (about 1½ cups)
1 teaspoon vanilla extract

1 Preheat oven to 350°F. Grease two large cookie sheets.

2 Prepare cookies: In large bowl, stir flour, granulated sugar, cocoa, and baking soda. Stir in melted butter, milk, egg, vanilla, and salt until smooth.

3 Drop 12 heaping tablespoons dough, 2 inches apart, on each prepared cookie sheet. Bake until puffy and toothpick inserted in center comes out clean, 12 to 14 minutes, rotating sheets between upper and lower racks halfway through baking. With wide metal spatula, transfer cookies to wire racks to cool completely.

4 When cookies are cool, prepare filling: In large bowl, with mixer at medium speed, beat softened butter until smooth, occasionally scraping bowl with rubber spatula. At low speed, gradually beat in confectioners' sugar, marshmallow creme, and vanilla until smooth.

5 Spread 1 rounded tablespoon filling on flat side of 12 cookies. Top with remaining cookies. Cover and refrigerate if not serving within 2 hours.

EACH WHOOPIE PIE About 365 calories, 4g protein, 59g carbohydrate, 14g total fat (8g saturated), 51mg cholesterol, 290mg sodium.

Test Kitchen Tip

FREEZING WHOOPIE PIES
Bake these cookies up to 1 month ahead, wrap individually in plastic wrap, and freeze in freezer-weight ziptight plastic bags. Once made, marshmallow filling can be stored, covered, in the refrigerator up to 1 week. Let filling come to room temperature, about 30 minutes, to soften to spreading consistency.

Gingerbread Whoopie Pies

This holiday-spiced variation of the traditional childhood treat keep the same delicious marshmallow filling.

PREP 30 minutes plus cooling • **BAKE** 12 minutes • **MAKES** 12 whoopie pies.

COOKIES

2 cups all-purpose flour
¾ cup light (mild) molasses
¼ cup granulated sugar
6 tablespoons butter or margarine, melted
2 teaspoons ground ginger
1 teaspoon ground cinnamon
½ teaspoon baking soda
½ teaspoon salt
1 large egg

MARSHMALLOW FILLING

6 tablespoons butter or margarine, slightly
   softened
1 cup confectioners' sugar
1 jar (7 ounces) marshmallow creme
   (about 1½ cups)
1 teaspoon vanilla extract

1 Preheat oven to 350°F. Grease two large cookie sheets.

2 Prepare cookies: In large bowl, with spoon, mix flour, molasses, granulated sugar, butter, ginger, cinnamon, baking soda, salt, and egg until smooth. Drop 12 heaping tablespoons batter, 2 inches apart, on each prepared cookie sheet.

3 Bake until puffy and toothpick inserted in center comes out clean, about 12 minutes, rotating cookie sheets between upper and lower racks halfway through baking. With wide metal spatula, transfer cookies to wire racks to cool completely.

4 When cookies are cool, prepare filling: In large bowl, with mixer at medium speed, beat softened butter until smooth, occasionally scraping bowl with rubber spatula. At low speed, gradually beat in confectioners' sugar, marshmallow creme, and vanilla until smooth.

5 Spread 1 rounded tablespoon filling on flat side of 12 cookies. Top with remaining cookies. Cover and refrigerate if not serving within 2 hours.

EACH WHOOPIE PIE About 345 calories, 3g protein, 57g carbohydrate, 12g total fat (7g saturated), 49mg cholesterol, 289mg sodium.

Gingerbread Whoopie Pies

Coconut Macaroons

Though a traditional Passover dessert, these chewy flourless cookies are good any time of the year.

PREP 10 minutes • **BAKE** 25 minutes
MAKES about 42 cookies.

3 cups flaked sweetened coconut
¾ cup sugar
4 large egg whites
¼ teaspoon salt
1 teaspoon vanilla extract
⅛ teaspoon almond extract

1 Preheat oven to 325°F. Line two cookie sheets with parchment or foil.
2 In large bowl, stir coconut, sugar, egg whites, salt, vanilla, and almond extract until well combined.
3 Drop batter by rounded teaspoons, 1 inch apart, on prepared cookie sheets. Bake until set and lightly golden, about 25 minutes, rotating cookie sheets between upper and lower oven racks halfway through baking. Cool 1 minute on cookie sheets; with wide metal spatula, transfer cookies to wire racks to cool completely.

EACH COOKIE About 41 calories, 1g protein, 6g carbohydrate, 2g total fat (2g saturated), 0mg cholesterol, 32mg sodium.

Chocolate-Hazelnut Macaroons

The fabulous combination of chocolate and toasted hazelnuts tastes even better when added to a macaroon. You can whip these up quickly and easily in the food processor.

PREP 30 minutes • **BAKE** 10 minutes per batch
MAKES about 30 cookies.

1 cup hazelnuts (filberts)
1 cup sugar
¼ cup unsweetened cocoa
1 square (1 ounce) unsweetened chocolate, chopped
⅛ teaspoon salt
2 large egg whites
1 teaspoon vanilla extract

1 Preheat oven to 350°F. Toast and skin hazelnuts (see page 256). Line two large cookie sheets with foil.
2 In food processor with knife blade attached, pulse hazelnuts, sugar, cocoa, chocolate, and salt until nuts and chocolate are finely ground. Add egg whites and vanilla and process until blended.
3 Drop dough by rounded teaspoons, using another spoon to release batter, 2 inches apart on prepared cookie sheets. Bake until tops feel firm when pressed lightly, 10 minutes, rotating sheets between upper and lower racks halfway through baking. Cool on cookie sheets on wire racks.
4 Repeat with remaining cookie dough.

EACH COOKIE About 60 calories, 1g protein, 8g carbohydrate, 3g total fat (1g saturated), 0mg cholesterol, 15 mg sodium.

Chocolate-Hazelnut Macaroons

Florentines

A pastry-shop favorite, these elegant cookies are easily made at home. The only tricky part is knowing when to remove them from the cookie sheet as they are very sticky. If you do it too soon, the cookies are too soft; if you wait until they're completely cool, they'll stick. So let them cool slightly, just until you can handle them, then move them to a rack. Always use parchment paper. Surprisingly, these ship very well: just sandwich two with the chocolate as a filling in the middle.

PREP 40 minutes plus cooling • **BAKE** 10 minutes per batch • **MAKES** about 48 cookies.

6 tablespoons butter, cut into pieces
    (do not use margarine)
¼ cup heavy or whipping cream
1 tablespoon light corn syrup
½ cup sugar
2 tablespoons all-purpose flour
1 cup slivered almonds, finely chopped
½ cup candied orange peel, finely chopped
8 squares (8 ounces) semisweet chocolate,
    melted

1 Preheat oven to 350°F. Line large cookie sheet with parchment.

2 In 1-quart saucepan, combine butter, cream, corn syrup, sugar, and flour and heat to boiling over medium heat, stirring frequently. Remove pan from heat; stir in almonds and candied orange peel.

3 Drop batter by rounded teaspoons, 3 inches apart, on prepared cookie sheet. (Do not place more than 6 cookies on sheet.) Bake just until set, about 10 minutes. Cool on cookie sheet on wire rack 1 minute. With wide metal spatula, transfer cookies to wire racks to cool completely. If cookies become too hard to remove, return sheet to oven briefly to soften. Repeat with remaining batter.

4 With small metal spatula or butter knife, spread flat side of each cookie with melted chocolate. Return to wire racks, chocolate side up, and let stand until chocolate has set.

EACH COOKIE About 70 calories, 1g protein, 8g carbohydrate, 5g total fat (2g saturated), 6mg cholesterol, 15mg sodium.

> **Test Kitchen Tip**
>
> ## STORING COOKIES
> Always cool cookies before storing in airtight containers.
>
> Store soft and crisp cookies in separate containers with tight-fitting lids. Crisp cookies that become soft can be recrisped in a 300°F oven for 3 to 5 minutes. To keep soft cookies soft or soften cookies that have hardened, add a piece of apple or bread to the container and change it every other day.
>
> Store bar cookies in the pan they were baked in, tightly covered with foil or plastic wrap.

Biscochitos

These flaky, rich Mexican cookies are traditionally made with lard. We substituted half butter and half shortening, with delicious results.

PREP 20 minutes • BAKE 11 minutes per batch • MAKES about 76 cookies.

3 cups all-purpose flour
1½ teaspoons baking powder
¼ teaspoon salt
½ cup butter or margarine (1 stick), softened
½ cup vegetable shortening
1 cup sugar
2 teaspoons anise seeds
1 large egg yolk
¼ cup sherry or sweet wine
4 teaspoons ground cinnamon

1 Preheat oven to 375°F. In large bowl, with wire whisk, mix flour, baking powder, and salt.
2 In separate large bowl, with mixer at medium speed, beat butter, shortening, and ½ cup sugar until light and fluffy. Beat in anise seeds and egg yolk until well combined. Beat in sherry until smooth. Reduce speed to low and beat in flour mixture until well combined.
3 Divide dough into 4 equal pieces. On lightly floured surface, roll out 1 piece of dough, ¼ inch thick.

4 In small bowl, stir remaining ½ cup sugar and cinnamon. Sprinkle one-fourth of cinnamon-sugar mixture over dough. With 2-inch decorative cookie cutter, cut out as many cookies as possible. (Cut cookies as close to each other as possible; do not reroll scraps.)
5 Place cookies, 1 inch apart, on two ungreased large cookie sheets. Bake until set, about 11 minutes, rotating sheets between upper and lower racks halfway through baking. Cool on cookie sheets on wire racks 1 minute. With wide metal spatula, transfer to wire racks to cool completely.
6 Repeat with remaining dough and cinnamon-sugar.

EACH COOKIE About 50 calories, 1g protein, 6g carbohydrate, 3g total fat (1g saturated), 6mg cholesterol, 30mg sodium.

Pinwheels

You'll be surprised at how easy it is to shape these pretty treats. For variety in both flavor and color, try using several different kinds of jam.

PREP 35 minutes plus chilling • **BAKE** 9 minutes per batch • **MAKES** 24 cookies.

1⅓ cups all-purpose flour
¼ teaspoon baking powder
⅛ teaspoon salt
6 tablespoons butter or margarine, softened
½ cup sugar
1 large egg
1 teaspoon vanilla extract
¼ cup Damson plum, seedless raspberry,
  or other jam

1 In small bowl, with wire whisk, mix flour, baking powder, and salt.

2 In large bowl, with mixer at medium speed, beat butter and sugar until light and fluffy. Beat in egg and vanilla until combined. Reduce speed to low and beat in flour mixture just until combined. Divide dough in half. Wrap each half in waxed paper and refrigerate until firm enough to roll, at least 1 hour or overnight. (If using margarine, freeze overnight.)

3 Preheat oven to 375°F. On floured surface, with floured rolling pin, roll 1 piece of dough into 10" by 7½" rectangle; keep remaining dough refrigerated. With fluted pastry wheel or sharp knife, cut into twelve 2½-inch squares. Place 1 square at a time, 1 inch apart, on ungreased cookie sheet. Make a 1½-inch cut from each corner toward center. Spoon ½ teaspoon jam in center of each square. Fold every other tip in to center. Repeat with remaining squares.

4 Bake until edges are lightly browned and cookies are set, about 9 minutes. With wide metal spatula, transfer to wire racks to cool completely.

5 Repeat with remaining dough and jam.

EACH COOKIE About 80 calories, 1g protein, 12g carbohydrate, 3g total fat (2g saturated), 17mg cholesterol, 50mg sodium.

Pinwheels

Apricot-Raspberry Rugelach

The classic cream-cheese dough with a tangy fruit filling.

PREP 1 hour plus chilling • BAKE 35 minutes • MAKES 48 rugelach.

1 cup butter or margarine (2 sticks), softened
1 package (8 ounces) cream cheese, softened
¾ cup granulated sugar
1 teaspoon vanilla extract
¼ teaspoon salt
2 cups all-purpose flour
1 cup walnuts (4 ounces), chopped
¾ cup dried apricots, chopped
¼ cup packed light brown sugar
1½ teaspoons ground cinnamon
½ cup seedless raspberry preserves
1 tablespoon milk

1 In large bowl, with mixer at low speed, beat butter and cream cheese until creamy. Beat in ¼ cup granulated sugar, vanilla, and salt. Beat in 1 cup flour. With wooden spoon, stir in remaining 1 cup flour just until blended. Divide dough into 4 equal pieces; flatten each into a disk. Wrap each disk in waxed paper and refrigerate until firm, at least 2 hours.

2 In medium bowl, combine walnuts, apricots, brown sugar, ¼ cup plus 2 tablespoons granulated sugar, and ½ teaspoon cinnamon until well mixed. Line two large cookie sheets with foil; grease foil.

3 On lightly floured surface, with floured rolling pin, roll 1 disk of dough into 9-inch round; keep remaining dough refrigerated. Spread 2 tablespoons preserves over dough. Sprinkle with ½ cup walnut mixture; gently press to adhere. With pastry wheel or sharp knife, cut dough into 12 equal wedges. Starting at curved edge, roll up each wedge, jelly-roll fashion. Place cookies, point side down, ½ inch apart, on prepared cookie sheets; shape into crescents. Repeat with remaining dough, 1 disk at a time.

4 Preheat oven to 325°F. In cup, combine remaining 2 tablespoons granulated sugar and remaining 1 teaspoon cinnamon. With pastry brush, brush rugelach with milk. Sprinkle evenly with cinnamon-sugar.

5 Bake until golden, 35 to 40 minutes, rotating cookie sheets between upper and lower oven racks halfway through baking. With wide metal spatula, immediately transfer rugelach to wire racks to cool completely.

EACH RUGELACH About 116 calories, 1g protein, 12g carbohydrate, 7g total fat (4g saturated), 16mg cholesterol, 67mg sodium.

̒non Twists

Good Housekeeping *reader Carrie Deegan of Glen Cove, New York, sent us this recipe for tender cream-cheese cookies coated with walnut-and-cinnamon sugar. She created the recipe for her homemade-cookie business.*

PREP 1 hour plus chilling • **BAKE** 15 minutes per batch • **MAKES** 66 cookies.

1 package (8 ounces) cream cheese, softened
1 cup butter or margarine (2 sticks), softened
2½ cups all-purpose flour
¾ cup walnuts
1 cup sugar
2 teaspoons ground cinnamon
1 large egg, beaten

1 In large bowl, with mixer at low speed, beat cream cheese and butter until blended, constantly scraping bowl with rubber spatula. Increase speed to high; beat until light and creamy, about 2 minutes. With mixer at low speed, gradually add 1 cup flour and beat until blended. With wooden spoon, stir in remaining 1½ cups flour until smooth.

2 On lightly floured sheet of plastic wrap, pat dough into 9-inch square. Wrap in the plastic and refrigerate until dough is firm enough to roll, about 2 hours.

3 Meanwhile, in food processor with knife blade attached, pulse walnuts and ¼ cup sugar until walnuts are finely ground. In small bowl, stir cinnamon, remaining ¾ cup sugar, and walnut mixture until well blended; set aside.

4 Preheat oven to 400°F. Grease large cookie sheet. On lightly floured sheet of waxed paper, with floured rolling pin, roll dough square into 11" by 10½" rectangle. With pastry brush, brush dough with some beaten egg. Sprinkle with half of walnut mixture; gently press into dough. Invert dough rectangle, nut side down, onto another sheet of lightly floured waxed paper. Brush with beaten egg, sprinkle with remaining walnut mixture, and gently press nut mixture into dough.

5 Cut dough lengthwise into three 3½-inch-wide bars, then cut each bar crosswise into ½-inch-wide strips to make sixty-six 3½" by ½" strips in all. Twist each strip twice, then place, about 1 inch apart, on prepared cookie sheet.

6 Bake twists until lightly browned, 15 to 17 minutes. With wide metal spatula, gently loosen twists from cookie sheet and transfer to wire rack to cool.

7 Repeat with remaining strips.

EACH COOKIE About 75 calories, 1g protein, 7g carbohydrate, 5g total fat (1g saturated), 7mg cholesterol, 50mg sodium.

Test Kitchen Tip

SOFTENING CREAM CHEESE

You can use the microwave to quickly soften cream cheese. Remove all wrappings and place cream cheese in a microwave-safe bowl. For a 3-ounce package, microwave on High for 10 to 15 seconds. For a 8-ounce package, microwave on High for 30 seconds to 1 minute.

Sugar Twists

Children will love to help shape these sparkly cookies. For variety, you can use different-colored sugars or a drizzle of melted white chocolate in place of the white sugar crystals.

PREP 1 hour plus chilling • **BAKE** 11 minutes per batch • **MAKES** 120 cookies.

1⅓ cups all-purpose flour
½ teaspoon baking soda
½ teaspoon salt
4 large eggs
1 cup butter (2 sticks), softened (do not use margarine)
1½ cups granulated sugar
2 teaspoons vanilla extract
white sugar crystals (optional)

1 In small bowl, with wire whisk, mix flour, baking soda, and salt. Separate 2 of the eggs, placing yolks in small bowl and whites in another. Cover and refrigerate whites; reserve for brushing on cookies later.

2 In large bowl, with mixer at medium speed, beat butter and granulated sugar until creamy, occasionally scraping bowl with rubber spatula. Beat in the 2 whole eggs, egg yolks, and vanilla. Reduce speed to low; gradually beat in flour mixture until blended.

3 Divide dough into 4 equal pieces. Wrap each piece in plastic wrap and refrigerate until dough is firm enough to roll, at least 2 hours. (Or place dough in freezer for 30 minutes.)

4 Preheat oven to 350°F. Grease large cookie sheet.

5 On lightly floured surface with floured hands, press 1 piece of dough into 6" by 3" by ¾" rectangle; keep remaining dough refrigerated. Cut rectangle into 30 equal pieces. Roll each piece into a 6-inch-long rope. Transfer 1 rope at a time to prepared cookie sheet; gently shape into a loop, with ends overlapping. Repeat with remaining ropes, placing cookies 1 inch apart. Lightly beat the reserved egg whites. Brush cookies with egg whites; sprinkle with sugar crystals, if you like.

6 Bake until lightly browned, 11 to 12 minutes. With wide metal spatula, transfer cookies to wire rack to cool.

7 Repeat with remaining dough, egg whites, and sugar crystals, if using.

EACH COOKIE: About 41 calories, 1g protein, 5g carbohydrate, 2g total fat (1g saturated), 12mg cholesterol, 36mg sodium.

Fortune Cookies

With our homemade fortune cookies, you can have fun personalizing the fortunes for special occasions. The secret to shaping the cookies is to bake only two at a time and to fold them quickly while still hot.

PREP 45 minutes • **BAKE** 4 minutes per batch • **MAKES** about 14 cookies.

2 tablespoons butter (do not use margarine)
¼ cup confectioners' sugar
1 large egg white
1 teaspoon vanilla extract
pinch salt
¼ cup all-purpose flour
14 strips paper (3" by ½" each) with fortunes

1 Preheat oven to 375°F. Grease two small cookie sheets.

2 In 1-quart saucepan, heat butter over low heat until melted. Remove saucepan from heat. With wire whisk, beat in confectioners' sugar, egg white, vanilla, and salt until blended. Beat in flour until batter is smooth.

3 Drop 1 heaping teaspoon batter onto cookie sheet. Repeat with another teaspoon batter, at least 4 inches away from first. With small metal spatula or back of spoon, spread batter evenly to form two 3-inch rounds.

4 Bake until cookies are lightly golden, about 4 minutes. Loosen both cookies with metal spatula. Working with 1 cookie at a time, place a fortune across center of hot cookie. Fold hot cookie in half, forming a semicircle, and press edges together. Quickly fold semicircle over edge of small bowl to create fortune-cookie shape. Repeat with remaining cookie. Let shaped cookies cool completely on wire rack.

5 Repeat with remaining batter and strips of fortune paper to make 14 cookies in all, cooling cookie sheets between batches and regreasing sheets as necessary.

EACH COOKIE About 35 calories, 1g protein, 4g carbohydrate, 2g total fat (1g saturated), 4mg cholesterol, 30mg sodium.

Jumbo Gingersnaps

We like our soft, chewy gingersnaps extra big, but you can make them smaller if you prefer. Be sure to cool the cookies briefly on the cookie sheet before moving them to racks, as they are very moist and soft when hot and could fall apart.

PREP 20 minutes • **BAKE** 15 minutes • **MAKES** 10 giant cookies or about 30 small cookies.

2 cups all-purpose flour
2 teaspoons ground ginger
1 teaspoon baking soda
½ teaspoon ground cinnamon
½ teaspoon salt
¼ teaspoon ground black pepper (optional)
¾ cup vegetable shortening
½ cup plus 2 tablespoons sugar
1 large egg
½ cup dark molasses

1 Preheat oven to 350°F. In medium bowl, combine flour, ginger, baking soda, cinnamon, salt, and pepper if using.

2 In large bowl, with mixer at medium speed, beat shortening and ½ cup sugar until light and fluffy. Beat in egg until blended; beat in molasses. Reduce speed to low; beat in flour mixture just until blended.

3 Place remaining 2 tablespoons sugar on waxed paper. Roll ¼ cup dough into ball; roll in sugar to coat evenly. Repeat with remaining dough to make 10 balls in all. Place balls, 3 inches apart, on ungreased large cookie sheet. Or, for small cookies, roll dough by slightly rounded tablespoons into balls and place 2 inches apart on two ungreased cookie sheets.

4 Bake until set, about 15 minutes for large cookies or 9 to 11 minutes for smaller cookies, rotating cookie sheets between upper and lower oven racks halfway through baking. Cookies will be very soft and may appear moist in cracks. Cool 1 minute on cookie sheets on wire racks; with wide spatula, transfer cookies to wire racks to cool completely.

EACH COOKIE: About 323 calories, 3g protein, 42g carbohydrate, 16g total fat (4g saturated), 21mg cholesterol, 258mg sodium.

Brandy Snaps (page 53) and Cinnamon-Bun Cookies

Cinnamon-Bun Cookies

Nothing could equal the mouth-watering flavor and aroma of fresh-baked cinnamon buns, but these melt-in-your-mouth cookies come close. And, unlike buns, they keep well.

PREP 45 minutes plus chilling and cooling • **BAKE** 15 minutes per batch • **MAKES** 66 cookies.

2¾ cups all-purpose flour
½ teaspoon baking powder
¼ teaspoon salt
¾ cup butter or margarine (1½ sticks), softened
1 package (8 ounces) cream cheese, softened
2 teaspoons vanilla extract
2¾ cups confectioners' sugar
2 teaspoons ground cinnamon
3 tablespoons milk

1 In medium bowl, with wire whisk, mix flour, baking powder, and salt.

2 In large bowl, with mixer at medium speed, beat butter, cream cheese, vanilla, and 1¾ cups confectioners' sugar until creamy. Reduce speed to low; gradually beat in flour mixture just until blended, occasionally scraping bowl with rubber spatula. Remove 2 cups dough; set aside. To dough remaining in large bowl, add cinnamon; beat on low speed just until blended.

3 Between two 20-inch-long sheets of waxed paper, roll cinnamon dough into 14" by 10" rectangle. (If paper wrinkles during rolling, peel it off, then replace it to remove wrinkles.) Transfer dough rectangle, with waxed paper, to large cookie sheet. Repeat with plain dough, transferring it to cookie sheet with cinnamon-dough rectangle. Refrigerate doughs until chilled but still pliable, about 10 minutes.

4 Transfer plain dough to work surface with long side facing you; remove top sheet of waxed paper. Remove top sheet of waxed paper from cinnamon dough; invert onto plain dough so that edges of rectangles line up evenly. Remove top sheet of waxed paper. Starting from one long side, tightly roll rectangles together jelly-roll fashion, lifting bottom sheet of waxed paper as you roll. Wrap log in plastic wrap and refrigerate until dough is firm enough to slice, at least 4 hours or overnight. (Or place dough in freezer 1 hour 30 minutes if using butter, 2 hours if using margarine.)

5 Preheat oven to 350°F. Remove log from freezer. With sharp knife, cut log crosswise into scant ¼-inch-thick slices. Place slices, 1 inch apart, on ungreased large cookie sheet. Bake until lightly browned around edges, 15 to 16 minutes.

6 Meanwhile, prepare glaze: In small bowl, with fork, stir milk and remaining 1 cup confectioners' sugar until smooth.

7 Transfer cookies to wire rack set over waxed paper. With spoon, drizzle glaze in circular motion over warm cookies. Let cookies cool completely on rack. Cover glaze to prevent drying out.

8 Repeat with remaining dough and glaze. Layer cookies between waxed paper in airtight container. Store at room temperature up to 2 weeks, or in freezer up to 3 months.

EACH COOKIE About 70 calories, 1g protein, 9g carbohydrate, 4g total fat (2g saturated), 10mg cholesterol, 45mg sodium.

Almond Crescents

A classic holiday favorite, these crescents also make a welcome gift. Butter is essential to the exquisite texture and flavor.

PREP 45 minutes plus chilling • **BAKE** 20 minutes per batch • **MAKES** about 72 cookies.

1 cup blanched whole almonds (4 ounces),
    lightly toasted (page 13)
½ cup granulated sugar
¼ teaspoon salt
1 cup butter (2 sticks), softened (do not
    use margarine)
2 cups all-purpose flour
1 teaspoon almond extract
½ teaspoon vanilla extract
¾ cup confectioners' sugar

1 In food processor with knife blade attached, pulse almonds, ¼ cup granulated sugar, and salt until almonds are very finely ground.

2 In large bowl, with mixer at low speed, beat butter and remaining ¼ cup granulated sugar until blended, occasionally scraping bowl with rubber spatula. Increase speed to high; beat until light and fluffy, about 3 minutes. Reduce speed to low. Gradually add flour, ground-almond mixture, almond extract, and vanilla and beat until blended. Divide dough in half; wrap each piece and refrigerate until dough is firm enough to handle, about 1 hour, or freeze about 30 minutes.

3 Preheat oven to 325°F. Working with one piece of dough at a time, with lightly floured hands, shape rounded teaspoons of dough into 2" by ½" crescents. Place crescents, 1 inch apart, on two ungreased cookie sheets.

4 Bake until lightly browned around edges, about 20 minutes, rotating cookie sheets between upper and lower oven racks halfway through baking. With spatula, transfer cookies to wire racks set over waxed paper. Immediately dust cookies with confectioners' sugar until well coated; cool completely.

5 Repeat with remaining dough.

EACH COOKIE About 58 calories, 1g protein, 6g carbohydrate, 4g total fat (2g saturated), 7mg cholesterol, 34mg sodium.

WALNUT OR PECAN CRESCENTS
Prepare crescents as directed but substitute *1 cup walnuts or pecans* (not toasted) for almonds and omit almond extract.

HAZELNUT CRESCENTS
Prepare crescents as directed but substitute *1 cup toasted, skinned hazelnuts (filberts),* see page 13, for almonds and omit almond extract.

Almond Crescents

Raspberry Linzer Cookies

Our hazelnut cookies topped with raspberry jam deliver all the flavor of the traditional Austrian linzertorte without the fuss.

PREP 45 minutes • **BAKE** 20 minutes per batch • **MAKES** about 48 cookies.

1⅓ cups hazelnuts (filberts)
½ cup sugar
¾ cup butter or margarine (1½ sticks),
   cut into pieces
1 teaspoon vanilla extract
¼ teaspoon salt
1¾ cups all-purpose flour
¼ cup seedless red-raspberry jam

1 Preheat oven to 350°F. Toast and skin 1 cup hazelnuts (see page 256); set aside remaining ⅓ cup.

2 In food processor with knife blade attached, pulse 1 cup toasted hazelnuts and sugar until nuts are finely ground. Add butter, vanilla, and salt and process until blended. Add flour and process until evenly combined. Remove knife blade and press dough together with hands.

3 Finely chop remaining ⅓ cup hazelnuts; spread on sheet of waxed paper. With hands, shape dough, 2 teaspoons at a time, into 1-inch balls (dough may be slightly crumbly). Roll balls in nuts, gently pressing nuts into dough. Place balls, about 1½ inches apart, on ungreased large cookie sheet. With tip of spoon, make small indentation in center of each ball. Fill each indentation with ¼ teaspoon jam.

4 Bake until lightly golden around edges, about 20 minutes. With wide metal spatula, transfer cookies to wire racks to cool completely.

5 Repeat with remaining balls and jam.

EACH COOKIE About 75 calories, 1g protein, 7g carbohydrate, 5g total fat (2g saturated), 8mg cholesterol, 40mg sodium.

Brandy Snaps

These lacy cookies are a welcome addition to any homemade cookie assortment. Make them in dry weather or they will be sticky. See photo on page 48.

PREP: 25 minutes • BAKE: 5 minutes per batch • MAKES about 24 cookies.

½ cup butter (1 stick, do not use margarine)
3 tablespoons light (mild) molasses
½ cup all-purpose flour
½ cup sugar
1 teaspoon ground ginger
¼ teaspoon salt
2 tablespoons brandy

1 Preheat oven to 350°F. Grease large cookie sheet.

2 In 2-quart saucepan, melt butter with molasses over medium-low heat, stirring occasionally, until smooth. Remove from heat. With wooden spoon, stir in flour, sugar, ginger, and salt until blended and smooth; stir in brandy. Set saucepan in bowl of hot water to keep warm.

3 Drop 1 teaspoon batter on prepared cookie sheet; with small metal spatula, spread in circular motion to make 4-inch round (during baking, batter will spread and fill in any thin areas). Repeat to make 4 rounds in all, placing them 2 inches apart. (Do not place more than 4 cookies on sheet.)

4 Bake until golden brown, about 5 minutes. Cool on cookie sheet on wire rack just until edges have set, 30 to 60 seconds, then, with wide spatula, quickly flip cookies over.

5 Working as quickly as possible, roll up each cookie around handle (½-inch diameter) of wooden spoon or dowel. If cookies become too hard to roll, return to oven briefly to soften. As each cookie is shaped, slip off spoon handle and cool completely on wire racks.

6 Repeat with remaining batter.

EACH COOKIE: About 72 calories, og protein, 8g carbohydrate, 4g total fat (2g saturated), 10mg cholesterol, 64mg sodium.

Almond Tuiles

Our delicate almond cookies are curved to resemble terra-cotta roof tiles (tuiles), *but you can make them flat, too.*

PREP 30 minutes • **BAKE** 5 minutes per batch • **MAKES** about 30 cookies.

3 large egg whites
¾ cup confectioners' sugar
½ cup all-purpose flour
6 tablespoons butter, melted (do not use margarine)
¼ teaspoon salt
¼ teaspoon almond extract
⅔ cup sliced almonds

1 Preheat oven to 350°F. Grease large cookie sheet.

2 In large bowl, with wire whisk, beat egg whites, confectioners' sugar, and flour until blended and smooth. Beat in melted butter, salt, and almond extract until blended.

3 Drop 1 heaping teaspoon batter on prepared cookie sheet; with small metal spatula, spread in circular motion to make 3-inch round. Repeat to make 4 cookies in all, placing them 3 inches apart. (Do not place more than 4 cookies on sheet.) Sprinkle each cookie with some almonds (do not overlap).

4 Bake until golden around edges, 5 to 7 minutes. With wide spatula, quickly lift cookies, one at a time, and drape over rolling pin to curve cookies. When firm, transfer to wire racks to cool completely. (If you like, omit shaping and cool cookies flat.) If cookies become too firm to shape, briefly return to oven to soften.

5 Repeat with remaining batter and almonds. (Batter will thicken slightly upon standing.)

EACH COOKIE About 56 calories, 1g protein, 5g carbohydrate, 4g total fat (2g saturated), 6mg cholesterol, 48mg sodium.

Madeleines

The classic shell-shaped sponge cakes extolled by French writer Marcel Proust must be baked in a special pan but they taste so good you'l want to consider buying one. A madeleine pan makes a nice butter and candy mold as well.

PREP 25 minutes • **BAKE** 10 minutes per batch • **MAKES** 24 madeleines.

1 cup all-purpose flour
½ teaspoon baking powder
10 tablespoons butter (1¼ sticks), softened
    (do not use margarine)
¾ cup sugar
3 large eggs
1 large egg yolk
1½ teaspoons vanilla extract

1 Preheat oven to 400°F. Generously grease and flour madeleine pan. In small bowl, with wire whisk, mix flour and baking powder.

2 In large bowl, with mixer at medium speed, beat butter and sugar until creamy, about 2 minutes. Add eggs, egg yolk, and vanilla. Increase speed to high and beat until pale yellow, about 3 minutes. Reduce speed to low and beat in flour mixture just until blended, scraping bowl with rubber spatula.

3 Spoon batter by rounded tablespoons into prepared pan. Bake until edges are browned and tops spring back when lightly pressed, 10 to 12 minutes. Let madeleines cool in pan 1 minute. With tip of table knife, release onto wire rack to cool completely.

4 Wash, grease, and flour pan. Repeat with remaining batter.

EACH COOKIE About 105 calories, 2g protein, 11g carbohydrate, 6g total fat (3g saturated), 48mg cholesterol, 65mg sodium.

Test Kitchen Tip

SEPARATING EGGS

Many recipes call for egg whites or egg yolks, which means the eggs must be separated. Eggs separate most easily when cold. You can use an egg separator, but the half-shell method works just as well.

To separate an egg, on the side of a bowl, sharply tap the eggshell along its middle to make a crosswise crack. With your thumbs, gently pull open the shell along the crack, letting some of the white run into the bowl. Slowly transfer the yolk back and forth from one half-shell to the other, being careful not to break the yolk on any sharp shell edges, until all the white has run into the bowl. The smallest trace of fat from the yolks will keep the whites from foaming properly when beaten, so be very careful. If any yolk does get into the whites, it can sometimes be removed with a small spoon or the edge of an eggshell, but be sure to remove it all.

Cover leftover unbroken egg yolks with cold water (to prevent a skin from forming on the surface) and refrigerate for up to two days; drain before using. Store leftover egg whites for up to five days in an airtight container in the refrigerator.

Almond-Anise Biscotti

Soaking the anise seeds in liqueur softens them and releases their delicious flavor. Store in an airtight container at room temperature up to 3 weeks or in freezer up to 6 months.

PREP 25 minutes plus cooling • **BAKE** 55 minutes • **MAKES** about 84 biscotti.

1 tablespoon anise seeds, crushed
1 tablespoon anise-flavored apéritif or liqueur
2 cups all-purpose flour
1 cup sugar
1 cup whole almonds (4 ounces), toasted and coarsely chopped (page 13)
1 teaspoon baking powder
⅛ teaspoon salt
3 large eggs

1 Preheat oven to 325°F. In medium bowl, with fork, stir anise seeds and anise-flavored apéritif; let stand 10 minutes.

2 Grease large cookie sheet. In large bowl, with wire whisk, mix flour, sugar, chopped almonds, baking powder, and salt. With wire whisk, beat eggs into anise mixture. With wooden spoon, stir egg mixture into flour mixture until blended.

3 Divide dough in half. On prepared cookie sheet, with floured hands, shape each half into 15-inch-long log, placing them 3 inches apart (dough will be sticky). Bake until golden and toothpick inserted in center comes out clean, about 40 minutes. Cool on cookie sheet on wire rack 10 minutes.

4 Transfer logs to cutting board. With serrated knife, cut each log crosswise on diagonal into ¼-inch-thick slices. Place slices, cut side down, on two ungreased cookie sheets. Bake 15 minutes, turning slices over once and rotating cookie sheets between upper and lower oven racks halfway through baking. With spatula, transfer biscotti to wire racks to cool completely.

EACH COOKIE About 33 calories, 1g protein, 5g carbohydrate, 1g total fat (0g saturated), 8mg cholesterol, 12mg sodium.

Test Kitchen Tip **FREEZING COOKIES** Always cool baked cookies completely before freezing them.

Place in sturdy airtight containers, cushioned with crumpled wax paper. If cookies are decorated, freeze them first in a single layer on a cookie sheet, then pack for freezing, separating the layers with waxed paper.

To thaw cookies, unwrap them and let them stand at room temperature for about 10 minutes.

Double-Chocolate Biscotti

These crunchy twice-baked "biscuits" will satisfy purists as well as the many chocoholics among us.

PREP 30 minutes plus cooling • **BAKE** 50 minutes • **MAKES** about 32 biscotti.

1 teaspoon instant espresso-coffee powder
1 teaspoon hot water
2½ cups all-purpose flour
¾ cup unsweetened cocoa
1 tablespoon baking powder
½ teaspoon salt
1⅓ cups sugar
½ cup butter or margarine (1 stick), softened
3 large eggs
2 squares (2 ounces) semisweet chocolate, melted
¾ cup semisweet-chocolate mini chips

1 Preheat oven to 350°F. Grease and flour large cookie sheet. In cup, dissolve espresso-coffee powder in water; set aside.

2 In large bowl, with wire whisk, mix flour, cocoa, baking powder, and salt.

3 In another large bowl, with mixer at medium speed, beat sugar and butter until creamy. Reduce speed to low. Beat in eggs, one at a time, then add melted chocolate, and beat until mixed. Beat in espresso mixture. Add flour mixture and beat just until blended. With hand, knead in chocolate chips until combined.

4 Divide dough in half. On floured surface, with floured hands, shape each half into 12" by 3" log. Place logs, about 3 inches apart, on prepared cookie sheet. Bake 30 minutes. Cool on cookie sheet on wire rack until easy to handle, about 10 minutes.

5 Transfer logs to cutting board. With serrated knife, cut each log crosswise on diagonal into ¾-inch thick slices. Place slices, cut side down, on same cookie sheet. Bake 20 to 25 minutes, turning slices over once and rotating cookie sheets between upper and lower oven racks halfway through baking. With spatula, transfer biscotti to wire racks to cool completely. (Biscotti will harden as they cool.)

EACH COOKIE About 115 calories, 2g protein, 19g carbohydrate, 4g total fat (2g saturated), 25mg cholesterol, 97mg sodium.

Cherry and Ginger Biscotti

Dried tart cherries and chopped crystallized ginger may not be traditional, but these tart/sweet/spicy biscuits are absolutely luscious.

PREP 35 minutes plus cooling • **BAKE** 50 minutes • **MAKES** about 52 biscotti.

3¼ cups all-purpose flour
1 tablespoon baking powder
1 teaspoon ground ginger
½ teaspoon salt
¾ cup butter or margarine (1½ sticks),
   cut into pieces
1¼ cups sugar
3 large eggs
1 jar (2 ounces) diced crystallized ginger
   (⅓ cup), coarsely chopped
¾ cup dried tart cherries, chopped

1 Preheat oven to 350°F. In large bowl, with wire whisk, mix flour, baking powder, ground ginger, and salt.

2 In microwave-safe large bowl, heat butter in microwave oven on High until butter has melted, about 1 minute. With wire whisk, stir in sugar and eggs until smooth. With spoon, stir flour mixture, crystallized ginger, and cherries into egg mixture until dough forms.

3 Divide dough in half. On ungreased large cookie sheet, with floured hands, shape 1 piece of dough into 14" by 4" log (about ¼ inch high).

Repeat with remaining dough on second cookie sheet. Bake until golden and toothpick inserted in center comes out clean, 25 to 30 minutes, rotating cookie sheets between upper and lower racks halfway through baking. Cool on cookie sheets on wire racks 20 minutes. Reset oven to 325°F.

4 Transfer 1 log to cutting board. With serrated knife, cut log crosswise on diagonal into ½-inch-thick slices. Place slices, cut side down, on same cookie sheet. Repeat with remaining log. Bake 25 to 30 minutes, until golden on bottom, turning slices over once and rotating cookie sheets between upper and lower racks halfway through baking. Transfer biscotti to wire racks to cool completely.

EACH COOKIE About 80 calories, 1g protein, 13g carbohydrate, 3g total fat (2g saturated), 19mg cholesterol, 75mg sodium.

Spice-Nut Biscotti

These spicy, fragrant biscotti are perfect with coffee or tea for a light afternoon pick-me-up.

PREP 45 minutes plus cooling • **BAKE** 1 hour • **MAKES** about 66 cookies.

- 3 cups all-purpose flour
- 1 tablespoon baking powder
- 1 teaspoon ground ginger
- 1 teaspoon ground cinnamon
- ½ teaspoon salt
- 3 large eggs
- 1 cup sugar
- ½ cup butter or margarine (1 stick), melted
- 1 teaspoon vanilla extract
- 1 jar (2 ounces) diced crystallized ginger, finely chopped
- 1 cup pecans, coarsely chopped
- 1 cup walnuts, coarsely chopped

1 Preheat oven to 325°F. Grease 2 large cookie sheets.

2 In medium bowl, with wire whisk, mix flour, baking powder, ground ginger, cinnamon, and salt.

3 In large bowl, with mixer at medium speed, beat eggs and sugar 1 minute, occasionally scraping bowl with rubber spatula. Add butter and vanilla; beat until mixed. Reduce speed to low; gradually add flour mixture and beat just until blended, occasionally scraping bowl. With spoon, stir in crystallized ginger, pecans, and walnuts until evenly mixed.

4 Divide dough into thirds. On 1 prepared cookie sheet, 3 inches apart, shape 2 pieces of dough into 12" by 2" logs (about ¾ inch high). Repeat with remaining piece of dough on second cookie sheet. Bake until firm, 28 to 30 minutes, rotating cookies sheets between upper and lower racks halfway through baking. Cool logs on cookies sheets on wire racks 30 minutes. Reset oven temperature to 275°F.

5 Place logs on cutting board. With serrated knife, cut logs crosswise on diagonal into ½-inch-thick slices. Place slices, cut side down, ½ inch apart, on same cookie sheets. Bake 30 minutes, rotating cookie sheets halfway through baking. Cool biscotti completely on cookie sheets on wire racks. (Biscotti will harden as they cool.)

EACH COOKIE About 75 calories, 1g protein, 9g carbohydrate, 4g total fat (1g saturated), 14g cholesterol, 55mg sodium.

OPPOSITE: Cherry and Ginger Biscotti

Mandelbrot

An Eastern European cookie, mandelbrot, *or almond bread, is baked in logs, sliced, and rebaked just like biscotti. There are many variations on the classic recipe: some feature nuts; others dried fruit, chocolate pieces, or a swirl of cocoa.*

PREP 30 minutes plus cooling • **BAKE** 37 minutes • **MAKES** about 48 cookies.

3¾ cups all-purpose flour
2 teaspoons baking powder
½ teaspoon salt
3 large eggs
1 cup sugar
¾ cup vegetable oil
2 teaspoons vanilla extract
¼ teaspoon almond extract
1 teaspoon freshly grated orange peel
1 cup blanched almonds, coarsely chopped
  and toasted (page 13) until golden

1 Preheat oven to 350°F. In large bowl, with wire whisk, mix flour, baking powder, and salt.
2 In separate large bowl, with mixer at medium speed, beat eggs and sugar until light lemon-colored. Add oil, vanilla and almond extracts, and orange peel and beat until blended. With wooden spoon, beat in flour mixture until combined. Stir in almonds.

3 Divide dough in half. Drop each half by spoonfuls down length of ungreased large cookie sheet. With lightly floured hands, shape each half into 12-inch-long log, leaving 4 inches between logs (dough will be slightly sticky). Bake until lightly colored and firm, 30 minutes. Cool on cookie sheet on wire rack 10 minutes.
4 Transfer logs to cutting board. With serrated knife, cut each log crosswise into ½-inch-thick slices. Place slices, cut side down, on two ungreased cookie sheets. Bake until golden, 7 to 8 minutes, turning slices over and rotating sheets between upper and lower racks halfway through baking. With wide metal spatula, transfer cookies to wire racks to cool completely.

EACH COOKIE About 105 calories, 2g protein, 12g carbohydrate, 5g total fat (1g saturated), 13mg cholesterol, 50mg sodium.

Mandelbrot

Chunky Black-and-White Chocolate Bark

A crunchy homemade chocolate candy loaded with dried cranberries and pistachio nuts makes a festive holiday treat.

PREP 20 minutes plus chilling • **MAKES** about 1 ¾ pounds.

1 cup shelled pistachios (about 8 ounces in shells)

12 squares (12 ounces) semisweet chocolate, chopped

8 squares (8 ounces) white chocolate, or use Swiss confectionery bar or white baking bar, chopped

¾ cup dried cranberries

1 Preheat oven to 350°F. Place pistachios in 13" by 9" metal baking pan and toast in oven, stirring occasionally, until lightly browned, 10 to 15 minutes. Cool in pan on wire rack.

2 Meanwhile, in 2-quart saucepan, melt semisweet chocolate over low heat. In 1-quart saucepan, melt white chocolate over low heat. Remove both pans from heat.

3 In small bowl, combine pistachios and cranberries. Stir half of nut mixture into semisweet chocolate. On large cookie sheet, with small metal spatula, spread semisweet-chocolate mixture into ¼-inch-thick layer. Drop white chocolate by tablespoons onto semisweet-chocolate mixture. With tip of knife, swirl chocolates together for marbled look. Sprinkle with remaining nut mixture.

4 Refrigerate until firm, about 1 hour. Break bark into pieces. Store in waxed paper–lined airtight container. Refrigerate up to 1 month.

EACH OUNCE About 140 calories, 2g protein, 16g carbohydrate, 9g total fat (4g saturated), 1mg cholesterol, 10mg sodium.

Chocolate and Hazelnut Truffles

Use the best chocolate to give these truffles European flair. If you wish, add two tablespoons of coffee-, orange-, or almond-flavored liqueur to the melted-chocolate mixture.

PREP 25 minutes plus chilling • **MAKES** 32 truffles.

8 squares (8 ounces) bittersweet chocolate or
    6 squares (6 ounces) semisweet chocolate
    plus 2 squares (2 ounces) unsweetened
    chocolate, coarsely chopped
½ cup heavy or whipping cream
3 tablespoons butter, cut into pieces and
    softened (do not use margarine)
⅓ cup hazelnuts (filberts), toasted, skinned
    (page 256), and finely chopped
3 tablespoons unsweetened cocoa

1 Line 8½" by 4½" loaf pan with plastic wrap, extending plastic wrap over rim. In food processor with knife blade attached, pulse chocolate until finely ground.

2 In 1-quart saucepan, heat cream to simmering over medium-high heat. With food processor running, add hot cream to chocolate and process until smooth. Add butter and process until smooth.

3 Pour chocolate mixture into prepared pan; spread evenly. Refrigerate until cool and firm enough to handle, about 3 hours.

4 Place hazelnuts in small bowl; place cocoa in separate small bowl. Remove chocolate mixture from pan by lifting edges of plastic wrap. Invert chocolate block onto cutting board; discard plastic wrap. Cut chocolate lengthwise into 4 strips, then cut each strip crosswise into 8 pieces. (To cut chocolate neatly and easily, occasionally dip knife in hot water and wipe dry.)

5 With cool hands, quickly roll each square into ball. Roll 16 truffles in chopped hazelnuts and remaining 16 truffles in cocoa. Layer between waxed paper in waxed paper–lined airtight container. Refrigerate up to 1 week, or freeze up to 1 month. Remove from freezer 5 minutes before serving.

EACH TRUFFLE About 66 calories, 1g protein, 5g carbohydrate, 6g total fat (3g saturated), 8mg cholesterol, 13mg sodium.

OPPOSITE: Chunky Black-and-White Chocolate Bark

Amaretto Truffles

This recipe is so easy to prepare, you'll be able to make many batches to give to all your friends and family for the holidays. Place each truffle in a fluted foil or paper cup.

PREP 25 minutes plus chilling • **MAKES** 64 truffles.

10 squares (10 ounces) semisweet chocolate, coarsely chopped

2 squares (2 ounces) unsweetened chocolate, coarsely chopped

¾ cup heavy or whipping cream

5 tablespoons unsalted butter, cut into pieces and softened (do not use margarine)

¼ cup almond-flavor liqueur

⅓ cup blanched almonds, toasted (page 13) and finely chopped

¼ cup unsweetened cocoa

1 Grease 8" by 8" metal baking pan; line with plastic wrap, extending plastic wrap over rim. In food processor, with knife blade attached, pulse semisweet and unsweetened chocolates until very finely ground.

2 In 1-quart saucepan, heat cream to boiling over medium-high heat. With food processor running, add hot cream, butter, and liqueur to chocolate, and process until smooth.

3 Pour chocolate mixture into prepared pan; spread evenly. Refrigerate until cool and firm enough to handle, at least 3 hours, or freeze 1 hour.

4 Place chopped almonds in small bowl; place cocoa in separate small bowl. Invert chocolate block onto cutting board; discard plastic wrap. Cut chocolate into 8 strips, then cut each strip crosswise into 8 squares. (To cut chocolate neatly and easily, occasionally dip knife in hot water and wipe dry.)

5 With cool hands, working with one square at a time, quickly roll half the squares in chopped almonds to coat; roll remaining squares in cocoa. Layer between waxed paper in waxed paper–lined airtight container. Refrigerate up to 2 weeks, or freeze up to 2 months. Remove from freezer 5 minutes before serving.

EACH TRUFFLE About 55 calories, 1g protein, 4g carbohydrate, 4g total fat (2g saturated), 6mg cholesterol, 1mg sodium.

Amaretto Truffles

Peanut Brittle

Around the turn of the twentieth century, recipes for peanut brittle began appearing; it didn't take long for Americans to embrace it as a favorite. In the original recipe, raw peanuts are slowly poached in hot sugar syrup, which infuses the candy with lots of peanut flavor. In our recipe, roasted peanuts are stirred into the candy just before it is removed from the heat. The bubbling-hot mixture is poured onto a cookie sheet and stretched into a thin rectangle. Confectioners traditionally use a slab of marble for this step, as the cool temperature of the marble gives more time to stretch the hot mixture before it turns to brittle. Once it hardens, the brittle is broken into pieces just right for eating out of hand.

PREP 5 minutes plus cooling • **COOK** 30 minutes • **MAKES** about 1 pound.

1 cup sugar
½ cup light corn syrup
¼ cup water
2 tablespoons butter or margarine
1 cup salted peanuts
½ teaspoon baking soda

1 Lightly grease large cookie sheet.
2 In heavy 2-quart saucepan, combine sugar, corn syrup, water, and butter; cook over medium heat, stirring constantly, until sugar has dissolved and syrup is bubbling.
3 Set candy thermometer in place and continue cooking, stirring frequently, until temperature reaches 300° to 310°F, 20 to 25 minutes. (Once temperature reaches 220°F, it will rise quickly, so watch carefully.) Stir in peanuts.
4 Remove saucepan from heat and stir in baking soda (mixture will bubble vigorously); immediately pour onto prepared cookie sheet. With two forks, quickly lift and stretch peanut mixture into 14" by 12" rectangle.
5 Cool brittle completely on cookie sheet on wire rack. With hands, break brittle into small pieces. Layer between waxed paper in airtight container. Store at room temperature up to 1 month.

EACH OUNCE About 146 calories, 2g protein, 22g carbohydrate, 6g total fat (2g saturated), 4mg cholesterol, 103mg sodium.

GOLD RUSH NUT BRITTLE
Prepare as directed but use only ¾ *cup salted peanuts; stir in ¾ cup sliced blanched almonds and ¾ cup pecans,* coarsely broken, with peanuts. Makes about 1¼ pounds.

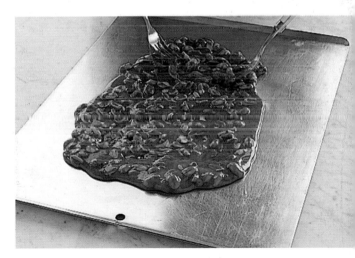

Peanut Brittle

Pralines

This is the classic pecan candy from the South. Use dark brown sugar if you prefer a richer flavor.

PREP 15 minutes • **COOK** 25 minutes • **MAKES** about 40 pralines.

½ cup butter (1 stick), cut into pieces
   (do not use margarine)
2 cups granulated sugar
1 cup packed light brown sugar
1 cup heavy or whipping cream
2 tablespoons light corn syrup
2 cups pecans (8 ounces), toasted (page 13)
   and coarsely chopped
1 teaspoon vanilla extract

1 Grease 2 or 3 cookie sheets.

2 In heavy 3-quart saucepan, combine butter, granulated and brown sugars, cream, and corn syrup; cook over medium heat, stirring occasionally, until sugars have dissolved and syrup is bubbling.

3 Set candy thermometer in place and continue cooking, without stirring, until temperature reaches 230° to 234°F, about 8 minutes.

4 Add pecans and vanilla; stir until bubbling subsides. Heat to boiling. Continue cooking until candy temperature reaches 244° to 248°F or firm-ball stage (when small amount of syrup forms a firm ball after standing in very cold water for about 30 seconds).

5 Remove pan from heat and stir vigorously until syrup thickens and turns opaque, about 3 minutes.

6 Working quickly, drop mixture by tablespoons, at least 1 inch apart, on prepared cookie sheets (stir briefly over low heat if mixture gets too thick). Cool pralines completely. Layer between waxed paper in airtight container. Store at room temperature up to 1 week, or freeze up to 3 months.

EACH PRALINE About 144 calories, 1g protein, 17g carbohydrate, 9g total fat (3g saturated), 14mg cholesterol, 29mg sodium.

 Test Kitchen Tip

SUGAR SYRUP TEMPERATURES

Many candies are made with sugar syrup. As the syrup cooks, its temperature rises and the liquid begins to evaporate. In general, a syrup that is cooked to a high temperature makes candy with a harder texture because it contains less liquid than one cooked to a lower temperature.

Accurate temperature readings are crucial in candy making. For the best results, always use a candy thermometer. When attaching the thermometer to the pan, be sure the tip of the thermometer doesn't touch the bottom of the pan, or you may get an inaccurate reading. We don't recommend the old-fashioned "cold water" test.

When cooking a sugar syrup, as the liquid evaporates and the amount of syrup decreases, sugar crystals form on the side of the saucepan. These crystals must be dissolved, or they can make candy grainy. Dip a pastry brush into cold water; rub the brush firmly against the sugar crystals to wash the crystals into the cooking syrup. Repeat this procedure all around the inside of the saucepan until no sugar crystals remain.

Do not make sugar syrup-based candies in rainy or humid weather. Sugar syrup attracts the moisture in the air, so the candy will either not set properly or be sticky.

Chocolate-Dipped Dried Fruit

This recipe can be easily doubled for a crowd. We found the most efficient way of coating was to dip larger pieces of fruit into chocolate before smaller ones. For our dried fruit, we used 4 pineapple rings, 5 pear halves, 7 apple slices, 8 apricot halves, and 9 large slices of crystallized ginger.

PREP 10 minutes plus cooling • **COOK** 5 minutes • **MAKES** about 1¼ pounds or 33 pieces.

4 squares (4 ounces) semisweet chocolate, chopped
1 teaspoon vegetable shortening
1 pound dried fruit, such as apricots, apples, pears, and pineapple
3 ounces crystallized ginger (optional)

1 Place sheet of waxed paper under large wire rack. In top of double boiler or in small stainless-steel bowl set over 2-quart saucepan with 1 inch simmering water (double-boiler top or bowl should be 2 inches above water), heat chocolate and shortening, stirring, until melted.

2 With fingers, dip fruit, 1 piece at a time, halfway into chocolate. Shake off excess chocolate or gently scrape fruit across rim of double-boiler, being careful not to remove too much chocolate. Place dipped fruit on wire rack until chocolate has set, at least 1 hour.

3 When set, layer fruit between waxed paper in airtight container. Store at room temperature up to 1 week.

EACH PIECE About 55 calories, 1g protein, 12g carbohydrate, 1g total fat (1g saturated), 0mg cholesterol, 1mg sodium.

Chocolate-Dipped Dried Fruit

r-Nut Toffee Crunch

This crunch is also delicious without the chocolate topping.

PREP 15 minutes plus cooling and standing • COOK about 25 minutes • MAKES about 1 ¾ pounds.

1¾ cups sugar
⅓ cup light corn syrup
¼ cup water
1 cup butter or margarine (2 sticks)
2 cups walnuts (8 ounces), lightly toasted
(page 13)

CHOCOLATE GLAZE

2 squares (2 ounces) unsweetened chocolate,
chopped
2 squares (2 ounces) semisweet chocolate,
chopped
1 teaspoon vegetable shortening

1 In heavy 2-quart saucepan, combine sugar, corn syrup, and water; heat to boiling over medium heat, stirring occasionally. Stir in butter.
2 Set candy thermometer in place and continue cooking, stirring frequently, until temperature reaches 300°F, about 20 minutes. (Once temperature reaches 220°F, it will rise quickly, so watch carefully.)
3 Meanwhile, lightly grease 15½" by 10½" jelly-roll pan. Finely chop walnuts.
4 Remove saucepan with syrup from heat. Reserve ⅓ cup walnuts; stir remaining walnuts into hot syrup. Immediately pour hot mixture into prepared jelly-roll pan. Working quickly, with spatula, spread evenly. Cool candy completely in pan on wire rack.
5 Meanwhile, prepare chocolate glaze: In heavy 1-quart saucepan, melt unsweetened and semisweet chocolates and shortening over low heat, stirring until smooth. Remove from heat; cool slightly.

6 Lift candy out of pan in one piece, and place on cutting board. With narrow metal spatula, spread warm chocolate evenly over candy; sprinkle with reserved ⅓ cup walnuts. Let stand until chocolate has set, about 1 hour.
7 Use sharp knife to break hardened candy into serving-size pieces. Layer between waxed paper in airtight container. Store at room temperature up to 2 weeks.

EACH OUNCE About 195 calories, 2g protein, 18g carbohydrate, 14g total fat (6g saturated), 19mg cholesterol, 75mg sodium.

DECORATING GIFTS

Half the appeal of specialty-shop gifts lies in their charming presentation. These tricks will make your creations look equally lovely.

- Use containers with interesting shapes.
- Dress up cans or boxes with self-sticking wallpaper, shelf liner, or spray paint.
- Trim covers and lids with remnants from a fabric store.
- Use butcher's twine or painted kitchen string in place of ribbon.
- Create your own gift tags by cutting up old cards. Punch a hole in a corner, and thread twine or ribbon through it.

Butter-Nut Toffee Crunch

Frozen Desserts

WHEN WE THINK "FROZEN DESSERTS," most of us immediately envision a big dish of ice cream. While it's true that ice cream is certainly America's favorite frozen treat, it is only the tip of the iceberg, so to speak. So if dessert isn't dessert without a scoop of something frozen and delicious, this is the chapter for you.

Just imagine dipping a spoon into the creamy simplicity of homemade Raspberry Ice Cream (page 73) or Orange Sherbet (page 85), the fresh fruit flavors recharging your palate and the silky texture bursting with pieces of real fruit. Or bite into a Frozen Mochaccino Bar (page 75) and experience the heavenly mingling of coffee and vanilla ice cream between chocolate cookie–crumb layers. And when the kids are looking for a quick lick on a hot summer's day, have a batch of ice cream sandwiches at the ready in the freezer. They're so easy to make with packaged cookies, ice cream, and a few add-ins or go-withs.

Looking for something with less fat and fewer calories to satisfy your craving for a frozen treat? Do as they do in Italy: Indulge in the dairy-free goodness of fruit granitas. These icy mixtures of pureed seasonal fruit and a simple syrup are dished out from the same pan in which they're frozen. Or serve one of many smooth-textured fruit sorbets, a favorite end-of-meal refreshment in many parts of the world. The pureed fruit mixture can be frozen in an ice cream maker or chilled until firm in the freezer. Both granitas and sorbets capture the essence of tree-ripe fruit in a frozen dessert.

And let's not forget those special occasions when nothing less than a decadent dessert will do. That's when it's time for a composed frozen dessert to take center stage. Combining ice cream or sorbet with a sweet crust, fruits, and chopped nuts, then dressing it up with whipped cream or a sweet sauce produces a frozen creation of contrasting tastes and textures that is greater than the sum of its parts. The composition could be as simple yet elegant as a scoop of ice cream in a delicate Tulipe cookie bowl (page 94) drizzled with your favorite dessert sauce or as dramatic and fun as our Banana Split Cake (page 92), composed of three different layers of ice cream separated by fudge sauce and sliced bananas, topped with whipped cream, nuts, and maraschino cherries, all in a chocolate-cookie crust. If a less extravagant approach is your preference, Cool Lime Pie (page 80)—a frosty version of Key Lime Pie—or Banana-Caramel Tart (page 83)—a south-of-the-border marriage of shortbread, *dulce de leche* ice cream, bananas, and pecans—definitely will not disappoint.

In addition to winning applause from family and guests, frozen desserts offer a wonderful benefit for the busy cook: They're made ahead of time and left to chill until ready to serve. All a host has to do is let the dessert temper a few minutes to reach optimum consistency before making the show-stopping presentation.

Raspberry Ice Cream (page 73) and Cantaloupe Sorbet (page 90)

Rich Vanilla-Bean Ice Cream

Using a vanilla bean instead of vanilla extract makes this classic extra-special. The yolks in the custard base make it sinfully rich.

PREP 5 minutes plus chilling and freezing • **COOK** 15 minutes • **MAKES** about 5 cups or 10 servings.

1 vanilla bean or 1 tablespoon vanilla extract
¾ cup sugar
3 cups half-and-half or light cream
4 large egg yolks
⅛ teaspoon salt
1 cup heavy or whipping cream

1 Chop vanilla bean, if using, into ¼-inch pieces. In blender, pulse vanilla bean and sugar until vanilla bean is very finely ground. If using vanilla extract, add with heavy cream in Step 4.
2 In heavy 3-quart saucepan, heat half-and-half to boiling over medium-high heat.

3 Meanwhile, in medium bowl, with wire whisk, whisk egg yolks, vanilla-sugar mixture, and salt until smooth. Gradually whisk half-and-half into egg-yolk mixture. Return mixture to saucepan and cook over medium heat, stirring constantly, just until mixture coats back of spoon as in photo (do not boil, or it will curdle). Remove from heat.
4 Strain custard through sieve into large bowl; add heavy cream and vanilla extract, if using. Press plastic wrap directly onto surface of custard to prevent skin from forming. Refrigerate until well chilled, at least 2 hours or up to overnight.
5 Freeze in ice-cream maker as manufacturer directs.

EACH SERVING About 261 calories, 4g protein, 19g carbohydrate, 19g total fat (11g saturated), 144mg cholesterol, 71mg sodium.

NO-COOK VANILLA ICE CREAM
In large bowl, stir *2 cups half-and-half or light cream, 2 cups heavy or whipping cream, ¾ cup sugar, 1 tablespoon vanilla extract,* and *⅛ teaspoon salt* until sugar has completely dissolved. Freeze in ice-cream maker as manufacturer directs.

Chocolate Ice Cream

A delightfully intense chocolate experience.

PREP 25 minutes plus chilling and freezing
MAKES about 6 cups or 12 servings.

Rich Vanilla-Bean Ice Cream (opposite) or
   No-Cook Vanilla Ice Cream (opposite)
3 squares (3 ounces) unsweetened chocolate,
   chopped
2 squares (2 ounces) semisweet chocolate,
   chopped

1 Prepare Rich Vanilla-Bean Ice Cream as directed in Steps 1 through 4, reserving ¼ cup heavy cream.
2 In heavy 2-quart saucepan, heat unsweetened and semisweet chocolates with reserved cream over low heat, stirring, until chocolates have melted and mixture is smooth; remove from heat.
3 Stir 1 cup ice-cream mixture into chocolate mixture; stir back into ice-cream mixture. Freeze in ice-cream maker as manufacturer directs.

EACH SERVING About 277 calories, 4g protein, 21g carbohydrate, 21g total fat (13g saturated), 120mg cholesterol, 61mg sodium.

Raspberry Ice Cream

Top with Raspberry Sauce (page 95) for a double dose of berry flavor. See photo on page 70.

PREP 10 minutes plus chilling and freezing
MAKES about 4 cups or 8 servings.

4 cups fresh (about 3 half-pints) or frozen,
   thawed raspberries
¾ cup sugar
⅛ teaspoon salt
1 cup heavy or whipping cream
1 cup milk

1 In blender or in food processor with knife blade attached, puree raspberries until smooth. With spoon, press puree through sieve into large bowl; discard seeds.
2 With wire whisk, stir sugar and salt into raspberry puree until sugar has completely dissolved. Whisk in cream and milk. Cover and refrigerate until well chilled, about 1 hour or up to 4 hours.
3 Freeze in ice-cream maker as manufacturer directs.

EACH SERVING About 224 calories, 2g protein, 28g carbohydrate, 12g total fat (7g saturated), 45mg cholesterol, 63mg sodium.

 Test Kitchen Tip

AVOIDING FROZEN DESSERT PITFALLS

LUMPY MIXTURE Make sure the mixture is completely cooled before the freezing process begins to maintain a smooth texture.

GRITTY TEXTURE This can result if measuring is not accurate, the mixture is churned too slowly, or the finished ice cream is stored in the freezer too long.

BLAND TASTE Taste the mixture before freezing and sweeten as necessary. If you're making sorbet, add a bit more lemon juice to brighten the flavor. Allow the flavor to ripen in the freezer for at least four hours before serving.

ICE CRYSTALS Don't store ice cream too long or refreeze partially melted ice cream. It keeps best in the freezer at 0°F or lower. Use within one month if stored in refrigerator freezer or up to two months if stored in home freezer.

Frozen Mochaccino Bars

Your favorite blended coffee drink, frozen on a chocolate-cookie base and capped with whipped cream and a dusting of cinnamon. If you're a real java lover, seek out espresso or other rich coffee-flavored ice cream.

PREP 30 minutes plus freezing • **MAKES** 16 servings.

CHOCOLATE COOKIE CRUST
1 package (9 ounces) chocolate wafer cookies
1 tablespoon ground cinnamon
4 tablespoons butter or margarine, melted

ICE CREAM FILLING
1 quart coffee ice cream, softened
1 quart vanilla ice cream, softened

1 Prepare crust: In food processor with knife blade attached, pulse cookies and cinnamon until cookies are very finely ground. With food processor running, drizzle in butter until blended. With hand, pat 1 cup cookie-crumb mixture evenly onto bottom of 9" by 9" metal pan or glass baking dish. Place pan in freezer to firm crust, about 15 minutes.

2 Prepare filling: Spoon coffee ice cream over cookie crust. Place plastic wrap on ice cream; press down to spread evenly and to eliminate any air pockets. Remove plastic wrap. Sprinkle remaining crumb mixture over ice cream. Return pan to freezer for 15 minutes.

3 Spoon vanilla ice cream over crumb layer. Place plastic wrap on ice cream and spread evenly; remove plastic wrap. Cover pan and freeze until firm, at least 6 hours. If not serving bars same day, wrap and freeze up to 2 weeks.

4 To serve, remove cover and let stand at room temperature to soften slightly for easier slicing, about 10 minutes. Cut into 16 squares.

EACH SERVING About 365 calories, 6g protein, 33g carbohydrate, 23g total fat (14g saturated), 128mg cholesterol, 210mg sodium.

Test Kitchen Tip

ICE CREAM AND COMPANY

ICE CREAM is made from a combination of milk products and a sweetening agent; sometimes pieces of chocolate, nuts, or fruit are added. Most quality ice creams are prepared with an egg-custard base, which gives the product its silky smoothness.
ICES are also made from sweetened fruit purees or juices and beaten with a mixer after an initial freezing to incorporate air and produce a lighter texture. It is then frozen again until firm.
GRANITA is an Italian fruit ice and has the same ingredients as sorbet but is chilled in a baking pan and stirred frequently during freezing to achieve a granular, icy texture.
SHERBET is a combination of fruit juice, sugar, and milk, cream, or egg whites.
SORBET is usually made from a sweetened fruit puree without the addition of dairy products.

Frozen Mochaccino Bars

Banana Icebox Cake

We've added bananas to this favorite mixture of chocolate wafer cookies and whipped cream to make it even more luscious.

PREP 30 minutes plus chilling • **MAKES** 10 servings.

2 cups heavy or whipping cream
3 tablespoons confectioners' sugar
1 teaspoon vanilla extract
2 small ripe bananas, finely chopped
35 chocolate wafer cookies (part of 9-ounce package)
¼ cup semisweet chocolate chips

1 In large bowl, with mixer at medium speed, beat cream, confectioners' sugar, and vanilla until stiff peaks form. Spoon half of whipped cream into separate bowl; cover and refrigerate. With rubber spatula, gently fold bananas into remaining whipped cream.

2 On one side of each of 6 chocolate wafers, spread about 2 heaping teaspoons banana whipped cream. Stack wafers on top of one another. Top with plain wafer. Repeat with remaining wafers and remaining banana cream until all wafers are used, making 5 stacks of 7 wafers each.

3 Turn each stack on its side; place stacks, side by side, on serving platter (see photo, left). Cover with reserved whipped cream and sprinkle with chocolate chips. Cover and refrigerate 5 hours or up to overnight to soften wafers. To serve, slice cake on diagonal for striped effect.

EACH SERVING About 302 calories, 3g protein, 26g carbohydrate, 22g total fat (12g saturated), 66mg cholesterol, 140mg sodium.

Banana Icebox Cake

Quick Licks: Ice Cream Sandwiches

When the kids have eaten their broccoli, serve them one of these quick treats. They're easy to make with a package of cookies, ice cream, and a few little extras. They also freeze well—just wrap individually in plastic wrap and store in a freezer-weight bag or container.

PB&J Spread *peanut butter* and *jelly* on a big, soft *oatmeal-raisin cookie*. Top with *vanilla ice cream* and *another cookie*.

S'MORE Spread *marshmallow cream* on a *chocolate-covered* or *cinnamon graham cracker*. Cover with *chocolate ice cream*, then *another cracker*.

CHOCOLATE-CHERRY Place a scoop of *cherry-vanilla ice cream* between *2 large, soft chocolate cookies*.

PISTACHIO SHORTBREAD Scoop some *pistachio ice cream* onto a small *shortbread cookie*. Top with *another cookie*, then dip side into toasted, *finely chopped pistachio nuts*.

CHOCOLATE CHIPPER Place a scoop of *chocolate* or *vanilla ice cream* between *2 chocolate-chip cookies*. Roll side in *toffee bits*.

TUTTI-FRUTTI Scoop *rainbow sherbet* onto a *crisp sugar cookie*. Top with a *second cookie*. Roll in *chopped candied cherries or oranges*.

CARAMEL CRUNCH Press a scoop of *caramel-swirl ice cream* between *2 amaretti cookies*.

RASPBERRY–WHITE CHOCOLATE WAVE Spread a scoop of *raspberry gelato* on a *white-chocolate macadamia cookie*. Top with *another cookie*.

BURIED MINT Place a scoop of *mint chocolate-chip ice cream* on a *chocolate cookie*. Push a *soft, chocolate-covered mint candy* into the middle of the ice cream. Top with *another cookie*.

NEAPOLITAN Scoop *strawberry ice cream* onto a *soft chocolate chocolate-chip cookie*. Press a *soft vanilla cookie* on top.

MINI CONFETTI TREAT Spread your favorite *ice cream* between *2 lemon cookies*, then roll side in *multicolored décors*.

GINGER GEM Fill *2 large, soft ginger-molasses cookies* with *lemon sherbet*. Sprinkle side with a little finely grated *lemon peel*.

And for the grown-ups . . .

TIRAMISÙ TREAT Brush 1 side of a *crisp Italian-style ladyfinger* (also called *savoiardi*) with *coffee-flavored liqueur*, then spread with *coffee ice cream*. Brush side of *second ladyfinger* with liqueur and place, liqueur-side down, over ice cream. Sprinkle top with *ground cinnamon*.

Test Kitchen Tip

STORING ICE CREAM

To ensure heavenly ice cream:

- Check the temperature of your freezer: Ice cream keeps best at 0°F or lower.
- Store ice cream in the main freezer compartment (not on the freezer door), preferably toward the back, where it's the coldest.
- Before returning ice cream to freezer, press plastic wrap directly on surface of ice cream, then put on lid. This will help prevent a skin from forming (caused by evaporation) and minimize the development of ice crystals (caused by condensation in container).
- Don't refreeze partially melted ice cream.

Rocky Road Ice Cream Cake

This ooey-gooey treat is like a big sundae in a springform pan. It's made with chocolate ice cream, our secret homemade Fudge Sauce (also delicious served hot over a bowl of vanilla ice cream), cookies, peanuts, and mini marshmallows. If you don't have time to make the sauce, a jar from the store will do just fine.

PREP 30 minutes plus chilling and freezing • **COOK** 8 minutes • **MAKES** 14 servings.

FUDGE SAUCE
1 cup heavy or whipping cream
¾ cup sugar
4 squares (4 ounces) unsweetened chocolate
2 tablespoons light corn syrup
2 tablespoons butter or margarine
2 teaspoons vanilla extract

ROCKY ROAD CAKE
2 pints chocolate ice cream, softened
14 chocolate sandwich cookies
2 cups miniature marshmallows
1 cup salted peanuts, coarsely chopped

1 Prepare fudge sauce: In heavy 2-quart saucepan, heat cream, sugar, chocolate, and corn syrup over medium heat, stirring occasionally, until mixture boils. Cook, stirring constantly, until sauce thickens slightly (mixture should be gently bubbling), about 4 minutes. Remove from heat; add butter and vanilla, stirring until sauce is smooth and glossy. Place plastic wrap directly on surface of sauce to prevent skin from forming; refrigerate until cool, about 2 hours. Makes about 1⅔ cups.

2 When sauce is cool, assemble cake: Wrap bottom and side of 9" by 3" springform pan with heavy-duty foil. Spoon 1 pint chocolate ice cream into pan. Place plastic wrap on ice cream and press down to spread evenly and eliminate air pockets; remove plastic wrap. Insert cookies, standing upright, into ice cream to form ring around side of pan, making sure to press cookies all the way to pan bottom. Sprinkle 1 cup marshmallows and ½ cup peanuts over ice cream; press in gently with hand.

3 Spoon remaining ice cream over marshmallows and peanuts. Place plastic wrap on ice cream and spread evenly; remove plastic wrap. Spread ⅔ cup fudge sauce over ice cream (if sauce is too firm, microwave briefly to soften but not heat); reserve remaining sauce to serve later. Sprinkle remaining marshmallows and peanuts over sauce; press in gently with hand. Cover and freeze until firm, at least 6 hours.

4 To serve, remove cover and foil from pan. Wrap towels dampened with warm water around side of pan for about 20 seconds to slightly soften ice cream. Remove side of pan and place cake on cake stand or plate. Let stand at room temperature to soften for easier slicing, about 10 minutes.

5 Meanwhile, place remaining fudge sauce in microwave-safe bowl. Microwave sauce, uncovered, on High, stirring once, until hot, 30 to 40 seconds. Serve hot sauce to spoon over cake, if you like.

EACH SERVING WITH SAUCE About 365 calories, 7g protein, 36g carbohydrate, 23g total fat (11g saturated), 77mg cholesterol, 220mg sodium.

Rocky Road Ice Cream Cake

Cool Lime Pie

In this frosty version of Key lime pie, we swirled vanilla ice cream into a condensed-milk mixture. You'll need lots of fresh lime juice (zap limes for about ten seconds in the microwave so they're easier to squeeze) and a store-bought graham-cracker crust.

PREP 20 minutes plus freezing • **MAKES** 10 servings.

4 to 5 limes
1 can (14 ounces) fat-free sweetened
   condensed milk
1 pint vanilla ice cream, softened
1 ready-to-use graham-cracker piecrust
   (6 ounces)
½ cup heavy or whipping cream
lime-peel slivers for garnish

1 From limes, finely grate 4 teaspoons peel and squeeze ⅔ cup juice. In large bowl, with wire whisk, stir undiluted condensed milk, lime peel, and lime juice until blended. Whisk ice cream into condensed-milk mixture until evenly blended (mixture will be the consistency of sour cream). Pour ice-cream mixture into piecrust. Freeze until firm, at least 6 hours. If not serving pie same day, wrap and freeze up to 1 week.

2 To serve, remove cover from pie and let stand at room temperature to soften slightly for easier slicing, about 10 minutes.

3 Meanwhile, in small bowl, with mixer at medium speed, beat cream until stiff peaks form. Top each serving of pie with a dollop of whipped cream and sprinkle with grated lime peel.

EACH SERVING About 300 calories, 5g protein, 42g carbohydrate, 12g total fat (6g saturated), 33mg cholesterol, 160mg sodium.

Test Kitchen Tip

CUTTING FROZEN DESSERTS

To cut ice cream cakes or pies, dip a thin knife into hot water. Plunge the point into the center of the dessert, cutting all the way through. Using an up-and-down sawing motion, cut through to the outside edge

Cool Lime Pie

Banana-Caramel Tart

Dulce de leche is a sweet Latin dessert made by slowly cooking milk (usually sweetened condensed milk) until it's thick and almost caramelized. Traditionally, it's spread on bread or crackers or used in pastries and cakes. But now you can get the dulce de leche *flavor in luscious ice cream, which we layered with fresh bananas in a no-bake pecan cookie crust.*

PREP 30 minutes plus freezing • **MAKES** 12 servings.

SHORTBREAD COOKIE CRUST
18 pecan shortbread cookies (about 14 ounces)
1 cup pecans, toasted (page 13)
2 tablespoons butter or margarine, melted

ICE-CREAM FILLING
2 pints dulce de leche ice cream, softened
4 ripe medium bananas

1 Prepare crust: In food processor with knife blade attached, pulse cookies and ½ cup pecans until very finely ground. With food processor running, drizzle in butter until mixture is moistened. With hands, press cookie mixture evenly onto bottom and up side of 11" by 1" round tart pan with removable bottom. Freeze until crust is firm, about 15 minutes.

2 Meanwhile, coarsely chop remaining ½ cup pecans; set aside.

3 Prepare filling: Spread 1 pint ice cream evenly over crust. Cut 3 bananas crosswise into ¼-inch-thick slices and arrange them in single layer over ice cream. Cover tart with plastic wrap and freeze 30 minutes.

4 Spread remaining pint ice cream over banana layer. Slice remaining banana. Arrange banana slices on ice cream overlapping slightly, in a ring 2 inches from edge of tart pan. Sprinkle top of tart with chopped pecans. Cover and freeze until firm, at least 6 hours. If not serving tart same day, wrap and freeze up to 2 weeks.

5 To serve, remove cover from tart and let stand at room temperature to soften slightly for easier slicing, about 10 minutes. Remove side of pan and place tart on serving plate.

EACH SERVING About 490 calories, 6g protein, 47g carbohydrate, 31g total fat (12g saturated), 75mg cholesterol, 200mg sodium.

Banana-Caramel Tart

Tartufo

*These chocolate-coated ice-cream balls are intended to resemble truffles (*tartufo *means "truffle" in Italian).*

PREP 30 minutes plus freezing • **MAKES** 6 servings.

1 pint chocolate or vanilla ice cream
2 tablespoons brandy
6 maraschino cherries, stems removed
1 cup fine amaretti cookie crumbs (20 cookies)
1½ cups semisweet chocolate chips
4 tablespoons butter or margarine, cut into pieces
2 tablespoons light corn syrup

1 Place ice cream in refrigerator to soften slightly, about 30 minutes. Line small cookie sheet with waxed paper and place in freezer. Meanwhile, in cup, pour brandy over cherries. Place amaretti crumbs on waxed paper.

2 Working quickly, with large ice-cream scoop (⅓ cup), scoop ball of ice cream. With ice cream still in scoop, gently press 1 cherry deep into center of ball; reshape ice cream around cherry. Release ice-cream ball on top of amaretti crumbs and roll to coat well. Place on prepared cookie sheet in freezer. Repeat to make 6 ice-cream balls. Freeze until firm, at least 1 hour 30 minutes.

3 In medium bowl set over saucepan of simmering water, heat chocolate chips, butter, and corn syrup, stirring occasionally, until chocolate and butter have melted and mixture is smooth. Remove pan from heat, but leave bowl in place to keep chocolate warm for easier coating.

4 Remove 1 ice-cream ball from freezer; place in slotted spoon and slip ice-cream ball into melted chocolate, turning quickly to coat thoroughly. Return to cookie sheet. Repeat with remaining ice-cream balls. Freeze until chocolate is firm, about 1 hour. If not serving right away, wrap in foil and freeze up to 1 day.

5 To serve, let tartufo stand at room temperature until slightly softened, about 10 minutes.

EACH SERVING About 476 calories, 5g protein, 59g carbohydrate, 27g total fat (15g saturated), 36mg cholesterol, 133mg sodium.

 QUICK ICE-CREAM TREATS

WAFFLES AND ICE CREAM

Lightly toast 1 frozen Belgian waffle; top with vanilla ice cream or frozen yogurt and frozen (thawed) strawberries or raspberries in syrup.

ICE CREAM PARFAITS

Pour some almond-flavored liqueur over 1 scoop coffee ice cream; top with whipped cream and crushed amaretti cookies.

ICE CREAM DRINK

In blender, combine 2 tablespoons orange-flavored liqueur with 2 scoops peach or vanilla ice cream; blend until smooth. Pour into tall glass; top with whipped cream.

S'MORE SUNDAE

Spoon 1 tablespoon fudge sauce over graham cracker; top with 1 scoop chocolate ice cream and marshmallow topping.

Orange Sherbet

No need to pull out your ice-cream machine for this rich and creamy sherbet.

PREP 10 minutes plus chilling and freezing
COOK 10 minutes
MAKES about 4 cups or 8 servings.

1½ cups milk
½ cup sugar
5 large oranges
⅛ teaspoon salt

1 In heavy 2-quart saucepan, heat milk and sugar over medium-high heat, stirring occasionally, until bubbles form around edge and sugar has completely dissolved, about 2 minutes. Pour into medium bowl; press plastic wrap directly onto surface. Refrigerate until well chilled, about 1 hour or up to 4 hours.
2 From oranges, grate 1 teaspoon peel and squeeze 2 cups juice. Stir orange peel and juice and salt into chilled milk mixture. Pour into 9-inch square metal baking pan; cover and freeze until firm, at least 4 hours.
3 With spoon, scoop sherbet into food processor with knife blade attached; process sherbet until smooth but still frozen. Return mixture to pan; cover and freeze until firm, 1 to 2 hours longer.
4 To serve, let sherbet stand at room temperature until just soft enough to scoop, about 10 minutes.

EACH SERVING About 104 calories, 2g protein, 21g carbohydrate, 2g total fat (1g saturated), 6mg cholesterol, 60mg sodium.

Five-Minute Frozen Peach Yogurt

A food processor makes quick work of this dessert. Try it with strawberries, blueberries, or your favorite combination of flavorful frozen fruits.

PREP 15 minutes plus standing
MAKES about 4 cups or 8 servings.

1 bag (20 ounces) frozen unsweetened peach slices
1 container (8 ounces) plain lowfat yogurt
1 cup confectioners' sugar
1 tablespoon fresh lemon juice
⅛ teaspoon almond extract

1 Let frozen peaches stand at room temperature 10 minutes. In food processor with knife blade attached, process peaches until fruit resembles finely shaved ice, occasionally scraping down side with rubber spatula.
2 With processor running, add yogurt, confectioners' sugar, lemon juice, and almond extract; process until mixture is smooth and creamy, occasionally scraping down side. Serve the yogurt immediately.

EACH SERVING About 107 calories, 2g protein, 25g carbohydrate, 1g total fat (0g saturated), 2mg cholesterol, 20mg sodium.

MAKING GRANITA

Cover and freeze the granita mixture until it is partially frozen, about 2 hours. Stir with a fork to break up the chunks. Cover and freeze until the mixture is completely frozen, at least 3 hours or up to overnight. To serve, let the granita stand at room temperature until slightly softened, about 15 minutes. Use a metal spoon to scrape across the surface of the granita, transferring the ice shards to chilled dessert dishes or wine goblets without packing them.

Raspberry or Blackberry Granita

Berries make a richly colored granita that tastes like summer.

> **PREP** 15 minutes plus cooling and freezing
> **COOK** 5 minutes
> **MAKES** about 8 cups or 16 servings.

> 1 cup sugar
> 1¼ cups water
> 3 pints raspberries or blackberries
> 2 tablespoons fresh lime juice

1 In 2-quart saucepan, heat sugar and water to boiling over high heat, stirring until sugar has dissolved. Reduce heat to medium and cook 1 minute. Set saucepan in bowl of ice water until syrup has cooled.

2 Meanwhile, in blender or in food processor with knife blade attached, puree raspberries until smooth. With spoon, press puree through sieve into medium bowl; discard seeds.

3 Stir sugar syrup and lime juice into puree; pour into 9-inch square metal baking pan. Cover, freeze, and scrape as directed for granitas (this page, left).

> **EACH SERVING** About 71 calories, 0g protein, 18g carbohydrate, 0g total fat, 0mg cholesterol, 0mg sodium.

Strawberry Granita

Make this granita with flavorful ripe strawberries for the quintessential early-summer dessert.

PREP 10 minutes plus cooling and freezing
COOK 8 minutes
MAKES about 6 cups or 12 servings.

½ cup sugar
1 cup water
2 pints strawberries, hulled
1 tablespoon fresh lemon juice

1 In 2-quart saucepan, heat sugar and water to boiling over high heat, stirring until sugar has dissolved. Reduce heat to medium and cook 5 minutes. Set saucepan in bowl of ice water until syrup has cooled.
2 Meanwhile, in blender or in food processor with knife blade attached, purée strawberries until smooth.
3 Stir strawberry puree and lemon juice into sugar syrup; pour into 9 inch square metal baking pan. Cover, freeze, and scrape as directed for granitas (see page 86).

EACH SERVING About 49 calories, 0g protein, 12g carbohydrate, 0g total fat, 0mg cholesterol, 1mg sodium.

Lemon Granita

This simple, zesty granita has an invigorating citrus tang.

PREP 10 minutes plus cooling and freezing
COOK 10 minutes
MAKES about 4 cups or 8 servings.

1 cup sugar
2 cups water
4 large lemons

1 In 2-quart saucepan, heat sugar and water to boiling over high heat, stirring until sugar has dissolved. Reduce heat to medium and cook 5 minutes. Set saucepan in bowl of ice water until syrup has cooled.
2 Meanwhile, from lemons, grate 2 teaspoons peel and squeeze ¾ cup juice.
3 Stir lemon peel and juice into sugar syrup; pour into 9-inch square metal baking pan. Cover, freeze, and scrape as directed for granitas (see page 86).

EACH SERVING About 103 calories, 0g protein, 27g carbohydrate, 0g total fat, 0mg cholesterol, 1mg sodium.

Watermelon Granita

The ultimate hot-weather refreshment.

PREP 15 minutes plus cooling and freezing
COOK 5 minutes
MAKES about 9 cups or 18 servings.

1 cup sugar
¾ cup water
1 piece watermelon (5½ pounds), rind and
   seeds removed and flesh cut into bite-size
   pieces (9 cups)
2 tablespoons fresh lime juice

1 In 2-quart saucepan, heat sugar and water to boiling over high heat, stirring until sugar has dissolved. Reduce heat to medium and cook 1 minute. Set saucepan in bowl of ice water until syrup has cooled.

2 Meanwhile, in blender or in food processor with knife blade attached, in batches, puree watermelon until smooth. With spoon, press watermelon puree through sieve into large bowl; discard watermelon fibers.

3 Stir sugar syrup and lime juice into watermelon puree; pour into 9-inch square metal baking pan. Cover, freeze, and scrape as directed for granitas (see page 86).

EACH SERVING About 69 calories, 0g protein, 17g carbohydrate, 0g total fat, 0mg cholesterol, 2mg sodium.

Coffee Granita

A Neapolitan tradition. If you like, use decaffeinated espresso.

PREP 10 minutes plus cooling and freezing
MAKES about 5 cups or 10 servings.

⅔ cup sugar
2 cups hot espresso coffee (see Tip, below)
unsweetened whipped cream (optional)

In medium bowl, stir sugar and espresso until sugar has completely dissolved. Pour into 9-inch square metal baking pan; cool. Cover, freeze, and scrape as directed for granitas (see page 86). Serve granita with whipped cream, if you like.

EACH SERVING About 53 calories, 0g protein, 14g carbohydrate, 0g total fat, 0mg cholesterol, 1mg sodium.

Test Kitchen Tip

MAKING ESPRESSO

If you do not have an espresso maker, use 3 cups water and 1⅓ cups ground espresso coffee in an automatic drip coffeemaker.

Pink Grapefruit Sorbet

A welcome change from the usual flavors; serve it with a splash of vodka or dark rum.

PREP 20 minutes plus cooling and freezing
COOK 15 minutes
MAKES about 5 cups or 10 servings.

3 large pink or red grapefruit
1 cup sugar
4 cups water
¼ cup light corn syrup
drop red food coloring (optional)

1 From grapefruit, with vegetable peeler, remove 3 strips peel (4" by ¾" each); squeeze 2 cups juice.

2 In 2-quart saucepan, heat sugar, water, corn syrup, and grapefruit peel to boiling over high heat, stirring until sugar has dissolved. Reduce heat to medium and cook 2 minutes. Set saucepan in bowl of ice water until syrup has cooled; discard peel.

3 Strain grapefruit juice through sieve into large bowl. With spoon, press pulp to extract juice; discard pulp. Stir in sugar syrup and food coloring, if using. Pour into 9-inch square metal baking pan; cover and freeze, stirring occasionally, until partially frozen, about 4 hours.

4 In food processor with knife blade attached, process sorbet until smooth but still frozen, stopping processor frequently to scrape down side. Return to pan; cover and freeze until almost firm, 3 to 4 hours.

5 To serve, process sorbet in food processor until smooth.

EACH SERVING About 120 calories, 0g protein, 31g carbohydrate, 0g total fat, 0mg cholesterol, 11mg sodium.

Peach Sorbet

Fragrant, fully ripe peaches are a must for this sorbet.

PREP 15 minutes plus chilling and freezing
COOK 6 minutes
MAKES about 7½ cups or 15 servings.

1¼ cups sugar
½ cup water
3 tablespoons fresh lemon juice
3 pounds fully ripe peaches, peeled, pitted, and sliced (7 to 8 cups)

1 In 2-quart saucepan, heat water and sugar to boiling over high heat, stirring until sugar has dissolved. Reduce heat to medium and cook 3 minutes. Set saucepan in bowl of ice water until syrup has cooled; stir in lemon juice.

2 In blender or in food processor with knife blade attached, in batches, puree peaches with sugar syrup until smooth; pour into large bowl. Cover and refrigerate until well chilled, about 2 hours.

3 Freeze peach mixture in ice-cream maker as manufacturer directs.

EACH SERVING About 95 calories, 0g protein, 25g carbohydrate, 0g total fat, 0mg cholesterol, 0mg sodium.

Cantaloupe Sorbet

If your ice-cream maker is large enough, the recipe can easily be doubled. This sorbet is best eaten the day it's made. See photo on page 70.

PREP 15 minutes plus chilling and freezing
COOK 8 minutes • **MAKES** about 3 ½ cups or 7 servings.

1 lemon
½ cup sugar
½ cup water
1 ripe cantaloupe (3 to 3½ pounds), rind and seeds removed and flesh chopped (4 cups)

1 From lemon, with vegetable peeler, remove 2 strips (3" by 1" each) peel; squeeze 1 tablespoon juice. In 2-quart saucepan, heat lemon peel, sugar, and water to boiling over high heat, stirring until sugar has dissolved. Reduce heat to medium and cook 5 minutes. Set saucepan in bowl of ice water until syrup has cooled; stir in lemon juice. Strain syrup through sieve into large bowl.
2 In blender or in food processor with knife blade attached, in batches, puree cantaloupe until smooth. Stir puree into sugar syrup. Cover and refrigerate until well chilled, 2 to 4 hours.
3 Freeze in ice-cream maker as manufacturer directs.

EACH SERVING: About 88 calories, 1g protein, 22g carbohydrate, 0g total fat, 0mg cholesterol, 8mg sodium.

CANTALOUPE CREAM SHERBET
Prepare as directed, adding *½ cup heavy or whipping cream* to cantaloupe mixture.

EACH SERVING About 128 calories, 1g protein, 20g carbohydrate, 6g total fat (3g saturated), 20mg cholesterol, 13mg sodium.

Berry Sorbet

Cool off with this refreshing sorbet. Four easy-to-find ingredients and a food processor are all you need. No ice-cream maker required.

PREP 5 minutes • **MAKES** about 4 cups or 6 servings.

1 package (20 ounces) frozen strawberries or raspberries
1 container (8 ounces) plain lowfat yogurt
1 cup confectioners' sugar
1 tablespoon fresh lemon juice

1 In food processor with knife blade attached, pulse frozen berries until fruit resembles finely shaved ice, stopping processor occasionally to scrape down side with rubber spatula.
2 With processor running, add yogurt, sugar, and lemon juice and puree, stopping processor and scraping down side occasionally, until mixture is smooth and creamy. Serve immediately for creamy texture or freeze and serve later for a firmer sorbet.

EACH SERVING About 135 calories, 2g protein, 31g carbohydrate, 1g total fat (0g saturated), 2mg cholesterol, 29mg sodium.

Chocolate Sorbet

An alternative to rich ice cream, with lots of chocolate flavor.

> **PREP** 10 minutes plus chilling and freezing
> **COOK** 12 minutes • **MAKES** about 4 cups
> or 8 servings.

¾ cup sugar
2 ½ cups water
2 squares (2 ounces) unsweetened chocolate, chopped
¼ cup light corn syrup
1 ½ teaspoons vanilla extract

1 In 2-quart saucepan, combine sugar and water; heat to boiling over high heat, stirring until sugar has dissolved. Reduce heat to medium and cook 3 minutes. Remove from heat.
2 In heavy 1-quart saucepan, combine chocolate and corn syrup; heat over low heat, stirring frequently, until chocolate is melted and smooth.
3 With wire whisk, stir 1 cup sugar syrup into chocolate mixture until well blended. Stir chocolate mixture into remaining sugar syrup in saucepan; stir in vanilla. Pour into medium bowl; cover and refrigerate until well chilled, about 1½ hours.
4 Freeze chocolate mixture in ice-cream maker as manufacturer directs.

EACH SERVING About 141 calories, 1g protein, 29g carbohydrate, 4g total fat (2g saturated), 0mg cholesterol, 14mg sodium.

OPPOSITE: Berry Sorbet

Frozen Peanut Butter Pie

Serve this treat with Hot Fudge Sauce (page 95).

> **PREP** 30 minutes plus cooling and freezing
> **BAKE** 10 minutes • **MAKES** 16 servings.

Chocolate Wafer–Crumb Crust (page 139)
1 package (8 ounces) Neufchâtel, softened
1 cup creamy peanut butter
1 cup plus 2 tablespoons confectioners' sugar
2 tablespoons milk
2 teaspoons vanilla extract
1 cup heavy or whipping cream
¼ cup salted peanuts, chopped
Hot Fudge Sauce (page 95; optional)

1 Prepare and bake crust as directed; cool completely.
2 In large bowl, with mixer at medium speed, beat Neufchâtel, peanut butter, and 1 cup confectioners' sugar until well blended. Add milk and vanilla; beat until smooth.
3 In small bowl, with clean beaters and mixer at medium speed, beat cream and remaining 2 tablespoons confectioners' sugar until stiff peaks form. With rubber spatula, gently fold whipped cream, half at a time, into peanut-butter mixture until blended. Spoon filling into cooled crust; sprinkle with peanuts. Cover pie with plastic wrap and freeze at least 6 hours or up to 24 hours.
4 Prepare Hot Fudge Sauce.
5 Let pie stand at room temperature to soften slightly for easier slicing, about 10 minutes. Serve with Hot Fudge Sauce if you like.

EACH SERVING WITHOUT HOT FUDGE SAUCE
About 298 calories, 8g protein, 19g carbohydrate, 22g total fat (9g saturated), 39mg cholesterol, 233mg sodium.

Banana-Split Cake

A fabulous freeze-ahead finale for your next party.

PREP 35 minutes plus softening, chilling, and freezing • **BAKE** 12 minutes • **MAKES** 16 servings.

Hot Fudge Sauce (page 95)
14 chocolate sandwich cookies
3 tablespoons butter or margarine, melted
1 pint vanilla ice cream
4 ripe medium bananas
1 pint chocolate ice cream
1 pint strawberry ice cream
½ cup heavy or whipping cream
¼ cup walnuts, broken into small pieces
maraschino cherries

1 Preheat oven to 350°F. Prepare Hot Fudge Sauce; let stand until completely cool. In plastic bag, with rolling pin, finely crush cookies.

2 In 9" by 3" springform pan, with fork, stir cookie crumbs and melted butter until evenly moistened. With hand, press cookie mixture firmly onto bottom of pan. Bake until crust is slightly darker at edge, 12 to 14 minutes. Place crust in freezer until well chilled, about 30 minutes.

3 Meanwhile, place vanilla ice cream in refrigerator to soften slightly, about 30 minutes. With narrow metal spatula, evenly spread vanilla ice cream over crust; cover and freeze until firm, about 45 minutes.

4 Cut 3 bananas lengthwise in half. Pour cooled fudge sauce over vanilla ice cream; arrange bananas on top. Cover and freeze cake until fudge sauce is firm, about 1 hour. Meanwhile, place chocolate ice cream in refrigerator to soften slightly, about 30 minutes.

5 Evenly spread chocolate ice cream over fudge sauce and bananas. Cover and freeze until firm, about 20 minutes. Meanwhile, place strawberry ice cream in refrigerator to soften slightly.

6 Spread strawberry ice cream evenly over chocolate ice cream. Cover and freeze until firm, about 3 hours or up to 2 days.

7 To serve, in small bowl, with mixer at medium speed, beat cream until soft peaks form. Cut remaining banana crosswise on diagonal into ½-inch-thick slices. Dip small knife in hot water, shaking off excess; run knife around edge of pan to loosen cake. Remove side of pan; place cake on platter. With narrow metal spatula, spread whipped cream on top of cake. Arrange banana slices over whipped cream; sprinkle with walnuts and top with cherries. Let stand at room temperature to soften slightly for easier slicing, about 10 minutes.

EACH SERVING About 324 calories, 4g protein, 38g carbohydrate, 19g total fat (10g saturated), 52mg cholesterol, 158mg sodium.

Banana-Split Cake

Tulipes

For an elegant ending to a dinner party or other occasion, serve your favorite ice cream in these delicate cookie shells.

PREP 30 minutes • **BAKE** 5 minutes per batch • **MAKES** about 12 tulipes.

3 large egg whites
¾ cup confectioners' sugar
½ cup all-purpose flour
6 tablespoons butter, melted (do not use margarine)
½ teaspoon vanilla extract
¼ teaspoon salt
1 quart ice cream or sorbet

1 Preheat oven to 350°F. Grease large cookie sheet.

2 In large bowl, with wire whisk, beat egg whites, confectioners' sugar, and flour until well blended. Beat in melted butter, vanilla, and salt.

3 Make 2 cookies by dropping batter by heaping tablespoons, 4 inches apart, on prepared cookie sheet. With narrow metal spatula, spread batter to form 4-inch rounds. Bake cookies until golden around edges, 5 to 7 minutes.

4 Place two 2-inch-diameter glasses upside down on surface. With spatula quickly lift 1 hot cookie and gently shape over bottom of glass.

Shape second cookie. When cookies are cool, transfer to wire rack. (If cookies become too firm to shape, return them to cookie sheet and place in oven to soften slightly.)

5 Repeat Steps 3 and 4 with remaining batter. (Batter will become slightly thicker upon standing.) Store tulipes in single layer in airtight container at room temperature. To serve, place on dessert plates and fill with ice cream.

EACH SERVING WITH ICE CREAM About 192 calories, 3g protein, 22g carbohydrate, 11g total fat (7g saturated), 35mg cholesterol, 155 mg sodium.

Tulipes

Hot Fudge Sauce

Use this rich chocolaty sauce as a topping for ice cream or other desserts. Unsweetened cocoa powder makes it easy to prepare.

PREP 5 minutes • **COOK** 5 minutes
MAKES about 1¼ cups.

¾ cup sugar
½ cup unsweetened cocoa
½ cup heavy or whipping cream
4 tablespoons butter or margarine, cut into pieces
1 teaspoon vanilla extract

In heavy 1-quart saucepan, heat sugar, cocoa, cream, and butter to boiling over high heat, stirring frequently. Remove saucepan from heat; stir in vanilla. Serve warm, or cool completely, then cover and refrigerate up to 2 weeks. Gently reheat before using.

EACH TABLESPOON About 75 calories, 1g protein, 9g carbohydrate, 5g total fat (3g saturated), 14mg cholesterol, 26mg sodium.

Butterscotch Sauce

An old fashioned favorite—divine in an ice-cream sundae but also wonderful with apple pie.

PREP 5 minutes • **COOK** 5 minutes
MAKES 1⅓ cups.

1 cup packed brown sugar
½ cup heavy or whipping cream
⅓ cup light corn syrup
2 tablespoons butter or margarine
1 teaspoon distilled white vinegar
⅛ teaspoon salt
1 teaspoon vanilla extract

In heavy 3-quart saucepan, heat brown sugar, cream, corn syrup, butter, vinegar, and salt to boiling over high heat, stirring occasionally. Reduce heat and simmer 2 minutes. Remove saucepan from heat; stir in vanilla. Serve warm, or cover and refrigerate up to 1 week.

EACH TABLESPOON About 84 calories, 0g protein, 14g carbohydrate, 3g total fat (2g saturated), 11mg cholesterol, 38mg sodium.

Raspberry Sauce

Bright in color and tart in flavor, this red sauce dresses up cakes from Chocolate Truffle (page 315) to Angel Food (page 324), as well as tarts, puddings, ice cream, and fresh fruit.

PREP 5 minutes • **COOK** 5 minutes
MAKES 1 cup.

1 package (10 ounces) frozen raspberries in syrup, thawed
2 tablespoons red currant jelly
2 teaspoons cornstarch

1 With back of spoon, press raspberries through fine sieve into nonreactive 2-quart saucepan; discard seeds. Stir in jelly and cornstarch. Heat to boiling over high heat, stirring constantly; boil 1 minute.
2 Serve sauce at room temperature, or cover and refrigerate up to 2 days.

EACH TABLESPOON About 26 calories, 0g protein, 7g carbohydrate, 0g total fat, 0mg cholesterol, 1mg sodium.

Fruit Desserts

FRUITS ARE THE MOST VERSATILE OF ALL OF NATURE'S BOUNTY. No other food offers such a variety of colors, textures, scents, and flavors to choose from: the deep jewel tones of berries and plums; the sweet perfume of a perfectly ripe peach; the toothsome crispness of an autumn apple; the juicy bite of an orange, or the summer sweetness of a slice of cold watermelon. And all that beauty and goodness come in health-giving packages bursting with natural vitamins, minerals, fiber, energy-providing sugars, and hydrating water while measuring low in fat and calories.

While most fruits can be eaten out of hand, they can all be cooked into an amazing array of desserts, such as those in this chapter. They range from the simple—succulent baked apples, mixed-fruit compotes, and crisps and cobblers—to the festive—berry-topped shortcakes and Blueberry Lemon Tiramisù (page 107). And for drama it's hard to beat flaming Cherries Jubilee (page 109) and Flambéed Bananas (page 103). Additionally, throughout this book you'll find fruits as the featured ingredient in pies, puddings, cakes, frozen treats, mousses, and soufflés.

Thanks to modern harvesting and shipping methods, fruits from just about every part of the world are now available year round. But for the ultimate in flavor, follow the calendar, just like previous generations of home cooks did. Practically every fruit has a season when it's at its flavorful peak and its most reasonable price. There is nothing that can compare to the just-picked taste of locally grown fruits in season. What is a summertime get-together without a Peach Cobbler (page 112) with vanilla ice cream? Autumn's harvest paves the way for warm old-fashioned Apple Strudel (page 100). Winter's dark days are made just a bit brighter with individual Brown-Sugar Pear Shortcakes (page 117); and Rhubarb-Apple Crumble (page 126) nods good-bye to winter as it welcomes spring.

However, if you have the overwhelming desire to have berries in January or plums in May, for example, don't despair. The freezer department of your supermarket will likely have bags of berries and cut fruits that were flash-frozen at their peak of flavor, ready to be turned into glorious desserts anytime the mood strikes.

Berries-and-Cream Shortcake (page 106)

Vermont Baked Apples

Choose a sweet apple that holds its shape when baked, such as Rome Beauty or Cortland. If you like, serve with whipped cream.

PREP 10 minutes • BAKE 1 hour 45 minutes
MAKES 6 servings.

6 large cooking apples (7 to 8 ounces each)
3 tablespoons butter or margarine
1 cup maple syrup or maple-flavored syrup

1 Preheat oven to 350°F. Remove apple cores; beginning at stem, peel one-third of way down. Stand apples in shallow 13" by 9" baking dish. Place 1½ teaspoons butter into cavity of each apple. Pour maple syrup over and around apples.
2 Bake apples, basting occasionally with syrup in baking dish, until tender, about 1 hour and 45 minutes. Serve hot, or cover and refrigerate to serve chilled.

EACH SERVING About 288 calories, 0g protein, 61g carbohydrate, 6g total fat (4g saturated), 16mg cholesterol, 63mg sodium.

FASTEST BAKED APPLES

Microwaved apples are ready in minutes. Remove cores from *large cooking apples (10 ounces each)*, such as Romes, but don't cut through to bottom. Peel one-third of the way down. Stand apples in small individual bowls or 8-inch square baking dish. Place *1 teaspoon butter* and *1 tablespoon brown sugar* into cavity of each apple. Cover and cook on medium-high (70% power) until tender, about 9 minutes, turning halfway though cooking. Cover and let stand 5 minutes.

Apple-Oatmeal Crisp

The ultimate autumn dessert. Substitute Golden Delicious apples for the Granny Smiths if you prefer a sweeter dessert.

PREP 20 minutes • BAKE 30 minutes
MAKES 6 servings.

2¾ pounds Granny Smith apples (7 medium), peeled, cored, and cut into ¼-inch-thick slices
2 tablespoons fresh lemon juice
¾ cup packed brown sugar
2 tablespoons plus ⅓ cup all-purpose flour
½ cup old-fashioned oats, uncooked
¼ teaspoon ground cinnamon
6 tablespoons butter or margarine, cut into pieces

1 Preheat oven to 425°F. In 1½-quart baking dish, toss apples with lemon juice; add ½ cup brown sugar and 2 tablespoons flour and toss to coat.
2 In small bowl, combine oats, cinnamon, remaining ⅓ cup flour, and remaining ¼ cup brown sugar. With pastry blender or two knives used scissor-fashion, cut in butter until mixture resembles coarse crumbs. Sprinkle over apple mixture.
3 Bake until apples are tender and topping is lightly browned, 30 to 35 minutes. Cool slightly on wire rack to serve warm.

EACH SERVING About 368 calories, 2g protein, 65g carbohydrate, 13g total fat (7g saturated), 31mg cholesterol, 128mg sodium.

Vermont Baked Apples

Apple Strudel

Layer upon layer of delicate phyllo surround a tender apple filling. Try one of the variations, too.

PREP 1 hour plus cooling • **BAKE** 35 minutes • **MAKES** 10 servings.

8 tablespoons butter or margarine (1 stick)
4 pounds Granny Smith apples (8 large),
    peeled, cored, and cut into ½-inch pieces
½ cup dark seedless raisins
⅔ cup plus ¼ cup granulated sugar
¼ cup walnuts, toasted (page 13)
    and ground
¼ cup plain dried bread crumbs
½ teaspoon ground cinnamon
¼ teaspoon ground nutmeg
8 sheets (16" by 12" each) fresh or frozen
    (thawed) phyllo
confectioners' sugar

1 Prepare filling: In 12-inch skillet, heat 2 tablespoons butter over medium heat until melted. Add apples, raisins, and ⅔ cup granulated sugar. Cook, stirring occasionally, 15 minutes. Increase heat to medium-high and cook until

liquid has evaporated and apples are soft and golden, about 15 minutes longer. Remove from heat; let filling cool completely.

2 Meanwhile, in small bowl, stir ground walnuts, bread crumbs, remaining ¼ cup granulated sugar, cinnamon, and nutmeg until thoroughly combined.

3 Preheat oven to 400°F. In 1-quart saucepan, heat remaining 6 tablespoons butter until melted. Cut two 24-inch lengths of waxed paper. Overlap two long sides by about 2 inches. On waxed paper, place 1 phyllo sheet; lightly brush with some melted butter. Sprinkle with scant 2 tablespoons bread-crumb mixture. Repeat layering with remaining phyllo, melted butter, and crumb mixture; reserve about 1 tablespoon melted butter.

4 Spoon cooled apple filling along one long side of phyllo, leaving ¾-inch borders and covering about one-third of phyllo. Starting from filling side, roll up phyllo, jelly-roll fashion, using waxed paper to help lift roll. Place roll, seam side down, on diagonal, on ungreased large cookie sheet. Tuck ends of roll under; brush with reserved 1 tablespoon melted butter.

5 Place two foil sheets under cookie sheet; crimp edges to form rim to catch any overflow during baking. Bake strudel until phyllo is golden and filling is heated through, 35 to 40 minutes. If necessary, cover strudel loosely with foil during last 10 minutes of baking to prevent overbrowning. Cool on cookie sheet on wire rack about 20 minutes. To serve, dust with confectioners' sugar and cut into thick slices.

EACH SERVING About 338 calories, 2g protein, 58g carbohydrate, 13g total fat (6g saturated), 25mg cholesterol, 192mg sodium.

CHEESE STRUDEL

In large bowl, with mixer at medium speed, beat *1 package (8 ounces) cream cheese,* softened, *¼ cup sugar,* and *1 tablespoon cornstarch* until thoroughly blended. With rubber spatula, fold in *1 cup ricotta cheese, 1 teaspoon freshly grated lemon peel,* and *½ teaspoon vanilla extract* until well combined. Cover and refrigerate filling while preparing phyllo. Prepare and fill strudel as directed, but substitute cheese filling for apple filling. Bake and cool as directed.

EACH SERVING About 301 calories, 6g protein, 23g carbohydrate, 21g total fat (12g saturated), 56mg cholesterol, 255mg sodium.

DRIED-FRUIT STRUDEL

In 2-quart saucepan, combine *2 cups mixed dried fruit,* cut into 1-inch pieces; *1 cup dried figs,* cut into 1-inch pieces; *2 strips (3" by 1" each) lemon peel; 1 cinnamon stick (3 inches);* and *1¾ cups water.* Heat to boiling over high heat, stirring occasionally. Reduce heat to medium; cook until all liquid has been absorbed and fruit is tender, about 20 minutes. Remove saucepan from heat; cool completely. Prepare and fill strudel as directed, but substitute dried-fruit filling for apple filling. Bake and cool as directed.

EACH SERVING About 285 calories, 3g protein, 49g carbohydrate, 10g total fat (5g saturated), 19mg cholesterol, 175mg sodium.

APPLE-CRANBERRY STRUDEL

In 12-inch skillet, heat *4 tablespoons butter* over medium heat until melted. Add *3 pounds Golden Delicious apples (about 6 large),* peeled, cored, and cut into ½-inch pieces, *1½ cups cranberries, ½ cup dark seedless raisins, ½ cup sugar,* and *½ teaspoon ground cinnamon.* Cook, uncovered, stirring occasionally, 12 minutes.

Increase heat to medium-high and cook until liquid has evaporated and apples are tender but not brown, about 10 minutes longer. Remove skillet from heat; cool completely. Prepare and fill strudel as directed, but substitute apple-cranberry filling for apple filling. Bake and cool as directed.

EACH SERVING About 285 calories, 2g protein, 44g carbohydrate, 13g total fat (7g saturated), 31mg cholesterol, 190mg sodium.

PEAR STRUDEL

Prepare filling as directed, but substitute *4 pounds Bartlett pears,* peeled, cored, and cut into ½-inch pieces, for apples and use only *½ cup sugar.* In Step 1, cook pear filling 35 minutes in all; cool completely. Prepare and fill strudel as directed, but substitute pear filling for apple filling. Bake and cool as directed.

EACH SERVING About 320 calories, 3g protein, 52g carbohydrate, 13g total fat (6g saturated), 25mg cholesterol, 190mg sodium.

CHERRY STRUDEL

In 4-quart saucepan, heat *2 cans (16 ounces each) tart cherries packed in water,* drained (½ cup liquid reserved), *1 cup sugar, ¼ cup cornstarch, 1 tablespoon fresh lemon juice,* and *¼ teaspoon ground cinnamon* to boiling over medium-high heat, stirring occasionally. Reduce heat to medium-low; boil 1 minute. Remove saucepan from heat; stir in *¼ teaspoon vanilla extract.* Cool completely. Prepare and fill strudel as directed, but substitute cherry filling for apple filling. Bake and cool as directed.

EACH SERVING About 230 calories, 2g protein, 40g carbohydrate, 8g total fat (4g saturated), 19mg cholesterol, 150mg sodium.

Apple Brown Betty

A betty is fruit baked under a bread-crumb topping. Be indulgent: Pour a little heavy cream over each serving.

PREP 35 minutes • **BAKE** 1 hour 5 minutes (including toasting) • **MAKES** 8 servings.

8 slices firm white bread, torn into
    ½-inch pieces
½ cup butter or margarine (1 stick), melted
1 teaspoon ground cinnamon
2½ pounds Granny Smith apples (6 medium),
    peeled, cored, and thinly sliced
⅔ cup packed brown sugar
2 tablespoons fresh lemon juice
1 teaspoon vanilla extract
¼ teaspoon ground nutmeg

1 Preheat oven to 400°F. Grease shallow 2-quart baking dish.

2 Place bread pieces in jelly-roll pan; bake, stirring occasionally, until very lightly toasted, 12 to 15 minutes.

3 In medium bowl, combine melted butter and ½ teaspoon cinnamon. Add toasted bread pieces, tossing gently until evenly moistened.

4 In large bowl, combine apples, brown sugar, lemon juice, vanilla, nutmeg, and remaining ½ teaspoon cinnamon; toss to coat.

5 Place ½ cup toasted bread pieces in baking dish. Cover with half of apple mixture; top with 1 cup toasted bread pieces. Place remaining apple mixture on top and sprinkle evenly with remaining bread pieces, leaving 1-inch border around edges.

6 Cover with foil and bake 40 minutes. Remove foil and bake until apples are tender and bread pieces have browned, about 10 minutes longer. Let stand 10 minutes before serving.

EACH SERVING About 319 calories, 3g protein, 51g carbohydrate, 13g total fat (7g saturated), 31mg cholesterol, 277mg sodium.

Test Kitchen Tip

BUYING APPLES
The peak season for apples is October through March, but apples are available year-round. Look for firm, crisp, well-shaped fruit. Avoid apples that are soft or have brown bruise spots. There are many varieties of apples, but if you are planning to cook apples, be sure to choose a variety that will work will in the particular recipe. Cooking apples are preferred for baking and pies. They include Gala, Golden Delicious, Granny Smith, Jonagold, Macoun, and Newtown Pippin.

Flambéed Bananas

In this classic dessert, be sure to use dark Jamaican rum; it gives the bananas an incomparable flavor.

PREP 5 minutes • **COOK** 8 minutes • **MAKES** 8 servings.

3 tablespoons butter or margarine
¾ cup packed brown sugar
1 tablespoon fresh lemon juice
4 ripe medium bananas, each peeled,
    cut crosswise in half, and then
    lengthwise in half
⅓ cup dark Jamaican rum or brandy
vanilla ice cream (optional)

1 In 12-inch skillet, heat butter over medium heat until melted. Stir in brown sugar and lemon juice. Place bananas in single layer in skillet; cook until just slightly softened, about 2 minutes per side. Reduce heat to low.

2 In 1-quart saucepan, heat rum over low heat. With long match, carefully ignite rum; pour over bananas. Spoon rum over bananas until flames die out. Serve with ice cream, if you like.

EACH SERVING About 179 calories, 1g protein, 34g carbohydrate, 5g total fat (3g saturated), 12mg cholesterol, 53mg sodium.

Test Kitchen Tip

RIPENING FRUITS

Whether fresh fruits are used alone or in combination with other foods, they should always be firm, ripe, and in season. The heavier the fruit is, the juicier and better tasting it will be. Use the sniff test: No sweet fruit aroma means there will be little flavor.

Ripe and ready to use at purchase: apples, berries, cherries, citrus fruits, grapes, pineapples, pomegranates, rhubarb.

Soft fruits: apricots, nectarines, peaches, pears, plums. To speed ripening of these soft fruits, place them in a loosely closed paper bag, at room temperature and away from direct sunlight. They will absorb the natural ethylene gas that ripening fruit produces. Putting a ripe banana or apple in the bag with them steps things up even more.

Fruits to peel: bananas, kiwifruit, mangoes, melons, papayas, and persimmons. Let fruit stand at room temperature, uncovered and away from sunlight, for a few days, to allow for the changes in sugar and juice content that signal ripening.

The ripening process stops when fruit is refrigerated, so once completely ripe, store in the refrigerator.

Three-Berry Charlotte

Ladyfingers enclose a delectable berry filling in this tempting do-ahead dessert. Make it when berries are at their peak of flavor.

PREP 45 minutes plus chilling • **MAKES** 8 servings.

2 tablespoons fresh orange juice
1 tablespoon orange-flavored liqueur
1 package (3 ounces) sponge-type
   ladyfingers, split
1 pint strawberries, hulled and cut in half
⅓ cup sugar
3 tablespoons fresh lemon juice
1 envelope unflavored gelatin
¼ cup cold water
1 cup heavy or whipping cream
1 cup raspberries
1 cup blackberries
1½ cups mixed berries (optional)

1 Line 9" by 5" loaf pan with plastic wrap, allowing plastic wrap to extend over sides of pan. In cup, combine orange juice and liqueur. With pastry brush, lightly brush flat side of ladyfingers with juice mixture. Line long sides and bottom of loaf pan with ladyfingers, placing rounded side against pan.

2 In blender, puree strawberries with sugar and lemon juice until smooth.

3 In 2-quart saucepan, evenly sprinkle gelatin over water; let stand 2 minutes to soften slightly. Cook over low heat, stirring frequently, until gelatin has completely dissolved, 2 to 3 minutes. Remove saucepan from heat; stir in strawberry puree. Set saucepan in large bowl of ice water. With rubber spatula, stir just until mixture forms mound when dropped from spatula, 10 to 15 minutes. Remove saucepan from bowl of water.

4 In large bowl, with mixer at medium speed, beat cream until stiff peaks form. Fold one-third of whipped cream into strawberry mixture; fold strawberry mixture into remaining whipped cream. Gently fold in raspberries and blackberries. Spoon mixture into ladyfinger-lined pan. Cover and refrigerate at least 4 hours or up to overnight.

5 To serve, unmold charlotte onto serving plate; remove plastic wrap. Garnish with mixed berries if you like.

EACH SERVING About 225 calories, 3g protein, 26g carbohydrate, 12g total fat (7g saturated), 80mg cholesterol, 29mg sodium.

RASPBERRY CHARLOTTE

Prepare as directed, but substitute *2 packages (10 ounces each) frozen raspberries in syrup,* thawed, for strawberries and use only *¾ cup sugar.* In blender, puree raspberries with lemon juice and sugar until smooth; press through sieve and stir into dissolved gelatin.

EACH SERVING About 278 calories, 3g protein, 40g carbohydrate, 12g total fat (7g saturated), 80mg cholesterol, 30mg sodium.

Strawberry Shortcake

No seasonal dessert is awaited with more anticipation than luscious strawberry shortcake, and this biscuit-based version is the classic.

PREP 30 minutes • **BAKE** 20 minutes • **MAKES** 10 servings.

2 cups all-purpose flour
¾ cup sugar
2 teaspoons baking powder
¼ teaspoon salt
⅓ cup cold butter or margarine, cut into pieces
⅔ cup milk
2 pints strawberries
1 cup heavy or whipping cream

1 Preheat oven to 425°F. Grease 8 inch round cake pan.

2 In medium bowl, with wire whisk, mix flour, 3 tablespoons sugar, baking powder, and salt. With pastry blender or two knives used scissor-fashion, cut in butter until mixture resembles coarse crumbs. Stir in milk just until mixture forms soft dough that leaves side of bowl.

3 On lightly floured surface, knead dough 10 times. With floured hands, pat evenly into prepared pan and sprinkle with 1 tablespoon sugar. Bake until golden, 20 to 22 minutes. Cool 10 minutes.

4 Meanwhile, reserve 4 whole strawberries for garnish; hull remaining strawberries and cut in half, or into quarters if large. In medium bowl, toss strawberries with remaining ½ cup sugar until sugar has dissolved.

5 Run thin knife around edge to loosen short-cake from pan; invert onto work surface. With long serrated knife, cut warm shortcake horizontally in half. In bowl, with mixer at medium speed, beat cream just until soft peaks form.

6 Place bottom half of shortcake, cut side up, on cake plate; top with half of strawberry mixture and half of whipped cream. Place remaining shortcake, cut side down, on strawberry mixture. Top with remaining strawberry mixture and remaining whipped cream. Garnish with reserved whole strawberries.

EACH SERVING About 321 calories, 4g protein, 41g carbohydrate, 16g total fat (10g saturated), 51mg cholesterol, 235mg sodium.

> **Test Kitchen Tip**
> **BUYING STRAWBERRIES**
> Choose bright red berries with fresh green stems still attached: Pale or yellowish white strawberries are unripe and sour. Locally grown strawberries are available from April to July, but strawberries are found year round.

Berries-and-Cream Shortcake

A tender cake, instead of a baking-powder biscuit, is the base for this showstopper. Assemble just before serving. See photo on page 96.

PREP 40 minutes • **BAKE** 25 minutes • **MAKES** 10 servings.

½ cup butter or margarine (1 stick), softened
1 cup plus 1 tablespoon sugar
1½ cups cake flour (not self-rising)
1½ teaspoons baking powder
¼ teaspoon salt
½ cup milk
2 large eggs
1 teaspoon vanilla extract
1 pint blueberries
½ pint strawberries, hulled and cut in half
½ pint raspberries
½ pint blackberries
½ cup seedless strawberry jam
1 cup heavy or whipping cream

1 Preheat oven to 350°F. Grease and flour two 8-inch round cake pans.

2 In large bowl, with mixer at low speed, beat butter and 1 cup sugar just until blended. Increase speed to high; beat until light and fluffy, about 5 minutes. Reduce speed to low. Add flour, baking powder, salt, milk, eggs, and vanilla; beat, frequently scraping bowl with rubber spatula, until well mixed. Increase speed to high; beat 2 minutes.

3 Spoon batter into prepared pans. Bake until toothpick inserted in center of each layer comes out clean, 25 to 30 minutes. Cool in pans on wire racks 10 minutes. Run thin knife around edges to loosen layers from sides of pans. Invert on wire racks to cool completely.

4 Meanwhile, in large bowl, gently combine blueberries, strawberries, raspberries, blackberries, and strawberry jam.

5 In small bowl, with mixer at medium speed, beat cream with remaining 1 tablespoon sugar until stiff peaks form when beaters are lifted.

6 Place 1 cake layer on cake plate; spread with half of whipped cream and top with half of fruit mixture. Place second cake layer on fruit mixture; top with remaining whipped cream and remaining fruit.

EACH SERVING About 415 calories, 4g protein, 56g carbohydrate, 21g total fat (12g saturated), 102mg cholesterol, 261mg sodium.

> *Test Kitchen Tip* **STORING BERRIES**
> Berries are very perishable and can deteriorate within twenty-four hours of purchase. You can store them in their baskets for a brief period, but to keep them for two or three days, place the (unwashed) berries in a paper towel-lined jelly-roll or baking pan in a single layer; cover loosely with paper towels, and refrigerate.

Blueberry-Lemon Tiramisù

A summer alternative to traditional tiramisù, this rendition is light, fruity, and refreshing.

PREP 1 hour plus chilling • **MAKES** 12 servings.

LEMON CURD
2 large lemons
3 large egg yolks
2 large eggs
⅓ cup sugar
6 tablespoons butter or margarine,
    cut into pieces

double recipe Best Blueberry Sauce
1 lemon
¼ cup sugar
¼ cup water
1 package (7 ounces) Italian-style ladyfingers
8 ounces mascarpone cheese
½ cup heavy or whipping cream

1 Prepare lemon curd: From 2 lemons, finely grate 1 tablespoon peel and squeeze ⅓ cup juice. In heavy nonreactive 2-quart saucepan, whisk grated lemon peel and juice, egg yolks, whole eggs, and sugar just until mixed. Add butter and cook over low heat, stirring constantly, until mixture coats spoon (do not boil, or mixture will curdle). Pour lemon curd through sieve into bowl; press plastic directly wrap onto surface and refrigerate until cool, about 15 minutes.

2 Meanwhile, prepare Best Blueberry Sauce; cool to room temperature.

3 From lemon, peel 3 strips (3" by ¾" each) peel. In nonreactive, 1-quart saucepan, heat peel, sugar, and water over medium heat, stirring occasionally, until sugar dissolves and mixture boils. Pour sugar syrup into bowl; cool to room temperature.

4 Line bottom and short sides of 13" by 9" baking dish with ladyfingers. Remove lemon peel from syrup and discard. Brush ladyfingers with syrup. Spread blueberry sauce over ladyfingers in bottom of dish.

5 In large bowl, whisk cooled lemon curd, mascarpone, and cream until smooth. Spoon mascarpone mixture evenly over blueberry sauce, spreading to cover completely. Cover and refrigerate until well chilled, at least 6 hours or up to overnight.

EACH SERVING About 386 calories, 5g protein, 47g carbohydrate, 21g total fat (12g saturated), 133mg cholesterol, 129mg sodium.

BEST BLUEBERRY SAUCE

Perfect with vanilla ice cream for a cooling, easy summer dessert.

PREP 5 minutes • **COOK** 10 minutes
MAKES about 2 cups.

3 cups blueberries
½ to ¾ cup confectioners' sugar
3 tablespoons water
1 to 2 teaspoons fresh lemon or lime juice

1 In nonreactive 2-quart saucepan, heat blueberries, ½ cup confectioners' sugar, and water to boiling over medium-high heat. Reduce heat to medium and cook, stirring occasionally, until berries have softened and sauce has thickened slightly, 5 to 8 minutes.

2 Remove saucepan from heat; stir in 1 teaspoon lemon juice. Taste and stir in additional lemon juice and sugar, if desired. Serve warm, or cover and refrigerate up to 1 day. Reheat to serve, if you like.

EACH TABLESPOON About 17 calories, 0g protein, 4g carbohydrate, 0g total fat, 0mg cholesterol, 1mg sodium.

Sugar-and-Spice Blueberry Crisp

You can put this together really fast. Try it warm, with a scoop of vanilla ice cream on top.

PREP 20 minutes • BAKE 35 minutes • MAKES 8 servings.

½ cup granulated sugar
2 tablespoons cornstarch
3 pints blueberries
1 tablespoon fresh lemon juice
1 cup all-purpose flour
¾ cup quick-cooking or old-fashioned oats
½ cup packed light brown sugar
½ cup cold butter or margarine (1 stick),
    cut into pieces
¾ teaspoon ground cinnamon

1 Preheat oven to 375°F. In large bowl, with wire whisk, mix granulated sugar and cornstarch until blended. Add blueberries and lemon juice; toss to coat evenly. Spoon blueberry mixture into shallow 2-quart baking dish; spread evenly.
2 In same bowl, with fingers, mix flour, oats, brown sugar, butter, and cinnamon until coarse crumbs form. Crumble flour mixture over blueberry mixture.

3 Place baking dish on foil-lined cookie sheet to catch any overflow during baking. Bake crisp until top is browned and fruit is bubbly at edges, 35 to 40 minutes. Cool crisp on wire rack 1 hour to serve warm, or cool completely to serve later. Reheat, if desired.

EACH SERVING About 390 calories, 5g protein, 64g carbohydrate, 14g total fat (8g saturated), 33mg cholesterol, 135mg sodium.

Test Kitchen Tip BUYING BLUEBERRIES
The silvery "bloom" on this berry is a natural protective coating and a sign of freshness. Only buy berries that still have their bloom. Blueberry varieties range in color from purplish blue to almost black. Wild blueberries, also called lowbush berries, are pea-sized and quite tart; they hold their shape well in baked in goods. Look for cultivated berries from June through August. Wild berries, most easily found along the coasts, are available in August and September.

Cherries Jubilee

Cherries Jubilee was created in 1887 by the famous chef Auguste Escoffier in honor of Great Britain's Queen Victoria. The queen was celebrating her golden jubilee, and cherries were her favorite fruit. The original dessert was made with sweet cherries cooked in a slightly thickened sugar syrup and then poured into fireproof dishes; hot brandy was added and the dessert was flambéed at the moment of serving. However, soon after, Escoffier began serving Cherries Jubilee with vanilla ice cream, and that's when the dessert really took off.

PREP 15 minutes • **COOK** 10 minutes • **MAKES** 6 servings.

1 pound dark sweet cherries (about 3 cups),
   stems removed and pitted
½ cup sugar
1 pint vanilla ice cream, slightly softened
½ cup brandy

1 In 10-inch skillet, cook cherries and sugar over medium heat, stirring frequently, until mixture simmers and sugar has dissolved, about 8 minutes.

2 Divide ice cream among 6 dessert bowls

3 In small saucepan, heat brandy over medium-high heat 30 seconds. With long match, carefully ignite brandy. Pour flaming brandy into cherry mixture in skillet. To serve, spoon flaming cherries with their syrup over ice cream.

EACH SERVING About 255 calories, 3g protein, 38g carbohydrate, 9g total fat (5g saturated), 30mg cholesterol, 30mg sodium.

 PREPARING FRUITS FOR COOKING

To remove pesticides, wax coatings, and bacteria, wash fruits under gently running water. Berries should be refrigerated (unwashed) as soon as you get them home; just before using, rinse in a large bowl of cold water (never under running water); then drain on paper towels.

Individual fruits can vary in sweetness, so taste before cooking and adjust the amount of sugar called for in the recipe as necessary.

To prevent peeled or cut apples, pears, peaches, and bananas from oxidizing and turning brown, dip them in a bowl filled with 1 quart cold water to which 2 tablespoons lemon juice have been added, or rub fruit with a cut lemon.

If using fruit pieces in a batter, toss them first with flour until well coated to prevent them from sinking as they bake.

Don't throw out soft, overripe fruit! Peel if necessary, cut off any bruised spots, then puree or finely chop and use as topping for ice cream, waffles or pancakes, or shortcake.

Grapes with Sour Cream and Sugared Tortillas

A quick and easy light dessert that goes perfectly with a southwestern-style meal like fajitas. It's also a great way to use up any leftover flour tortillas.

PREP 10 minutes • **BAKE** 5 minutes • **MAKES** 4 servings.

1 tablespoon butter or margarine
¼ teaspoon ground cinnamon
2 tablespoons sugar
2 (6- to 7-inch) flour tortillas
1 cup reduced-fat sour cream
½ teaspoon vanilla extract
2 cups red and/or green seedless grapes

1 Preheat oven to 425°F. In microwave-safe cup, melt butter in microwave oven on High 30 seconds. In small bowl, with fork, mix cinnamon and 1 tablespoon sugar. On cutting board, brush 1 side of each tortilla with some butter, then sprinkle evenly with cinnamon-sugar mixture.
2 Cut each tortilla into 8 wedges; place on large cookie sheet. Bake until golden, 5 to 7 minutes.
3 Meanwhile, in medium bowl, mix sour cream, vanilla, and remaining 1 tablespoon sugar.
4 Cut each grape in half; divide among 4 dessert bowls. To serve, top grapes with sour-cream mixture and tortilla wedges.

EACH SERVING About 240 calories, 4g protein, 32g carbohydrate, 12g total fat (6g saturated), 31mg cholesterol, 131mg sodium.

FIVE-MINUTE GINGERED CREAM AND GRAPES
Serve halved red and green seedless grapes with a dollop of sour cream topped with coarsely chopped crystallized ginger or preserved ginger in syrup.

Test Kitchen Tip   **BUYING GRAPES**
Bunches of grapes should be plump and fresh-looking, with individual grapes firmly attached to their stems. Avoid dry, brittle stems, shriveled grapes, or fruit leaking moisture.

Table grapes, used for eating rather than winemaking (although a few varieties do double duty), are categorized as seedless or with seeds. Seedless grapes, derived from European varieties, dominate the market and include *Thompson, Perlette, Flame,* and *Ruby Seedless*. Grapes with seeds usually are indigenous American varieties and have a distinct musky flavor. Lambruscas, such as the purple *Concord*, the pale red *Delaware*, and the red-purple *Catawba*, are prized for their pectin-rich juice and make fine jellies. Muscadine grapes, which include the sweet-juiced southern *Scuppernong*, are also great for jellies.

Orange Slices Marinated in Marmalade

You couldn't ask for an easier and more refreshing way to conclude a hearty winter meal than this super-simple dessert with triple orange flavor.

PREP 15 minutes plus chilling
MAKES 4 servings.

5 medium navel oranges, peeled and sliced
   into rounds
½ cup sweet or bitter orange marmalade
1 tablespoon orange-flavored liqueur
   (optional)

Arrange orange slices on platter, overlapping them slightly; brush with marmalade. Sprinkle with liqueur, if you like. Cover and refrigerate at least 30 minutes or up to several hours.

EACH SERVING About 179 calories, 2g protein, 47g carbohydrate, 0g total fat, 0mg cholesterol, 24mg sodium.

Oranges with Caramel

Serve as a light and elegant finale to a rich meal. When the caramel-drizzled orange rounds are refrigerated, the caramel melts into a luscious golden syrup.

PREP 30 minutes plus chilling
COOK 10 minutes • MAKES 6 servings.

6 large navel oranges
2 tablespoons brandy (optional)
1 cup sugar

1 From oranges, with vegetable peeler, remove 6 strips (3" by ¾" each) peel. Cut strips lengthwise into slivers.
2 Cut remaining peel and white pith from oranges. Slice oranges into ¼-inch-thick rounds and place on deep platter, overlapping slices slightly. Sprinkle with brandy, if you like, and orange peel.
3 In 1½-quart saucepan, cook sugar over medium heat, stirring to dissolve any lumps, until sugar has melted and turned deep amber in color. Drizzle caramel over orange slices. Cover and refrigerate until caramel has melted, about 2 hours.

EACH SERVING About 208 calories, 2g protein, 53g carbohydrate, 0g total fat, 0mg cholesterol, 2mg sodium.

Oranges with Caramel

Peach Cobbler

Here's a true summer treat, bursting with the flavor of ripe peaches. To bring out the sweetness of the peaches, we've added a bit of grated lemon peel to the biscuit topping. If calories are not a concern, serve with vanilla ice cream or softly whipped cream.

PREP 45 minutes • **BAKE** 45 minutes • **MAKES** 12 servings.

PEACH FILLING

6 pounds ripe medium peaches (16 to 18),
    peeled, pitted, and sliced (13 cups)
¼ cup fresh lemon juice
⅔ cup granulated sugar
½ cup packed brown sugar
¼ cup cornstarch

LEMON BISCUITS

2 cups all-purpose flour
½ cup plus 1 teaspoon granulated sugar
2½ teaspoons baking powder
¼ teaspoon salt
1 teaspoon freshly grated lemon peel
4 tablespoons cold butter or margarine,
    cut into pieces
⅔ cup plus 1 tablespoon half-and-half or
    light cream

1 Prepare filling: Preheat oven to 425°F. In nonreactive 8-quart saucepot, toss peaches with lemon juice. Add granulated and brown sugars and cornstarch; toss to coat. Heat over medium heat, stirring occasionally, until bubbling; boil 1 minute. Spoon hot peach mixture into 13" by 9" baking dish. Place baking dish on foil-lined cookie sheet to catch any overflow during baking. Bake 10 minutes.

2 Meanwhile, prepare biscuits: In medium bowl, with wire whisk, mix flour, ½ cup granulated sugar, baking powder, salt, and lemon peel. With pastry blender or two knives used scissor-fashion, cut in butter until mixture resembles coarse crumbs. Stir in ⅔ cup half-and-half just until mixture forms soft dough that leaves side of bowl.

3 Turn dough onto lightly floured surface. With lightly floured hands, pat into 10" by 6" rectangle. With floured knife, cut rectangle lengthwise in half; cut each half crosswise into 6 pieces, to make 12 rectangles in all.

4 Remove dish from oven. Arrange biscuits on top of fruit. Brush biscuits with remaining 1 tablespoon half-and-half and sprinkle with remaining 1 teaspoon granulated sugar. Bake until biscuits are golden, about 35 minutes longer. To serve warm, cool cobbler on wire rack about 1 hour.

EACH SERVING About 331 calories, 4g protein, 69g carbohydrate, 6g total fat (3g saturated), 16mg cholesterol, 199mg sodium.

Peach Shortcakes with Ginger Cream

Brown-sugar biscuits are topped with a rosy fruit filling and ginger-spiked cream.

PREP 45 minutes plus standing • **BAKE** 15 minutes • **MAKES** 10 servings.

BISCUITS
2 cups all-purpose flour
⅓ cup packed dark brown sugar
2½ teaspoons baking powder
¾ teaspoon salt
1⅓ cups heavy or whipping cream

FRUIT TOPPING
3 ripe plums (about 8 ounces), pitted and
　coarsely chopped
⅓ cup granulated sugar
5 ripe medium peaches (about 2 pounds),
　peeled, pitted, and sliced

GINGER CREAM
1 cup heavy or whipping cream
3 tablespoons confectioners' sugar
3 tablespoons minced crystallized ginger
slivered crystallized ginger

1 Preheat oven to 425°F. Prepare biscuits: In large bowl, with fork, stir flour and brown sugar, breaking up any lumps of brown sugar. Stir in baking powder and salt. Add cream and stir with fork until mixture forms soft dough that leaves side of bowl.

2 Turn dough onto lightly floured surface; knead 4 times until dough is of uniform consistency throughout. Pat dough into 10" by 6" rectangle. With floured knife, cut rectangle lengthwise in half; cut each half crosswise into 5 pieces to make 10 rectangles in all. With large floured spatula, transfer rectangles to ungreased large cookie sheet. Bake until golden, about 15 minutes. Transfer to wire rack to cool.

3 Meanwhile, prepare topping: In 1-quart saucepan, heat plums and granulated sugar to boiling over medium-high heat. Reduce heat to medium-low; cover and simmer until plums soften and form a sauce, about 5 minutes. Remove cover and simmer until sauce thickens slightly, about 5 minutes longer. Pour sauce into large bowl; set aside to cool slightly.

4 Add peaches to bowl with plums; stir until mixed. Let stand at least 30 minutes to allow flavors to develop.

5 Prepare cream: In bowl, with mixer at medium speed, beat cream, confectioners' sugar, and minced ginger until soft peaks form when beaters are lifted.

6 To serve, split biscuits. Spoon peach mixture onto bottom halves of biscuits; top with ginger cream, then biscuit tops. Garnish each with slivered ginger.

EACH SERVING About 400 calories, 4g protein, 50g carbohydrate, 21g total fat (13g saturated), 77mg cholesterol, 300mg sodium.

Rosy Peach Melba

Less is more! This combination of juicy peaches and berries in a sweet rosé syrup calls for only five basic ingredients.

PREP 15 minutes plus chilling • **COOK** 5 minutes • **MAKES** about 6 cups or 8 servings.

1 cup water
¾ cup sugar
4 ripe large peaches (about 2 pounds), peeled and cut into ½-inch-thick wedges
½ pint raspberries
1½ cups rosé or blush wine
3 tablespoons fresh lemon juice

1 In 1-quart saucepan, heat water and sugar to boiling over high heat. Boil 1 minute. Pour syrup into large bowl; cool to room temperature.

2 To bowl with syrup, add peaches, raspberries, wine, and lemon juice; stir gently to combine. Cover and refrigerate at least 2 hours or overnight.

EACH SERVING About 150 calories, 1g protein, 31g carbohydrate, 0g total fat, 0mg cholesterol, 3mg sodium.

Rosy Peach Melba

Zinfandel-Poached Pears

Easy and light, the poaching liquid is reduced to a spicy syrup.

PREP 20 minutes plus chilling
COOK 45 minutes • MAKES 8 servings.

1 bottle (750 ml) red zinfandel wine (about
   3 cups)
2 cups cranberry-juice cocktail
1¼ cups sugar
1 cinnamon stick (3 inches)
2 whole cloves
½ teaspoon whole black peppercorns
8 medium Bosc pears with stems

1 In nonreactive 5-quart Dutch oven, heat wine, cranberry-juice cocktail, sugar, cinnamon, cloves, and peppercorns just to boiling over high heat, stirring occasionally, until sugar has dissolved.
2 Meanwhile, peel pears, leaving stems on. With melon baller or small knife, remove cores by cutting through blossom end (bottom).
3 Place pears in wine mixture; heat to boiling. Reduce heat; cover and simmer, turning pears occasionally, until tender but not soft, 15 to 25 minutes.
4 With slotted spoon, carefully transfer pears to platter. Strain wine mixture through sieve into bowl; pour back into Dutch oven. Heat to boiling over high heat; cook, uncovered, until liquid has reduced to 1½ cups, 15 to 30 minutes.
5 Cover pears and syrup separately and refrigerate until well chilled, at least 6 hours. To serve, spoon syrup over pears.

EACH SERVING About 352 calories, 1g protein, 76g carbohydrate, 1g total fat (0g saturated), 0mg cholesterol, 6mg sodium.

Cranberry-Poached Pears

A lovely autumn or winter dessert, the sweet pink pears are set off by the tart red syrup.

PREP 5 minutes • COOK 11 minutes
MAKES 4 servings.

4 firm ripe Bosc pears (8 ounces each)
1 cup cranberry-juice cocktail
¼ cup dried cranberries
1 tablespoon butter or margarine

1 With melon baller or small knife, remove cores from pears by cutting through blossom end (bottom), making sure to leave stems intact. Peel pears.
2 In 2-quart saucepan, heat juice and dried cranberries to boiling over high heat. Place pears on their sides in saucepan with juice mixture. Cover and cook over high heat, turning pears over once halfway through cooking, just until pears are very tender, 6 to 7 minutes, depending on ripeness of pears. With slotted spoon, transfer pears to serving dish; keep warm.
3 Boil juice mixture remaining in saucepan over high heat until mixture is reduced to ½ cup, about 3 minutes. Remove saucepan from heat.
4 To serve, stir butter into cranberry sauce. Spoon sauce and cranberries over pears.

EACH SERVING About 165 calories, 1g protein, 35g carbohydrate, 3g total fat (2g saturated), 8mg cholesterol, 31mg sodium.

Brown-Sugar Pear Shortcakes

Brown-Sugar Pear Shortcakes

Flavored with a hint of cinnamon and lemon peel, luscious pears are delicious when served over warm biscuits.

PREP 45 minutes • **BAKE** 12 minutes • **MAKES** 6 servings.

1 cup all-purpose flour
¾ cup cake flour (not self-rising)
3 tablespoons granulated sugar
2½ teaspoons baking powder
½ teaspoon salt
5 tablespoons cold butter, cut into pieces, plus 4 tablespoons butter
⅔ cup milk
2½ pounds ripe Bosc pears (about 6 medium), peeled, cored, and cut lengthwise into ¾-inch-thick wedges
¼ cup packed light brown sugar
¼ cup water
¼ teaspoon ground cinnamon
2 strips (2½" by ½" each) lemon peel
1 cup heavy or whipping cream, whipped

1 Prepare biscuits: Preheat oven to 425°F. In large bowl, with wire whisk, mix all-purpose flour, cake flour, granulated sugar, baking powder, and salt. With pastry blender or two knives used scissor-fashion, cut in 5 tablespoons cold butter until mixture resembles coarse crumbs. Add milk, stirring quickly just until mixture forms a soft dough that comes together (dough will be sticky).

2 Turn dough onto floured surface; gently knead 6 to 8 times until dough is of uniform consistency throughout. With floured hands, pat dough into 1-inch thickness. With floured 2½-inch round biscuit cutter, cut out as many biscuits as possible. With pancake turner, place biscuits, 1 inch apart, on ungreased cookie sheet. Press trimmings together; repeat as directed above to make 6 biscuits in all. Bake until golden, 12 to 15 minutes.

3 Meanwhile, prepare pears: In nonstick 12-inch skillet, melt remaining 4 tablespoons butter over medium-high heat. Add pears and cook, uncovered, stirring carefully with heat-safe rubber spatula, until browned and tender, 10 to 15 minutes. Stir in brown sugar, water, cinnamon, and lemon peel; cook 1 minute. Discard lemon peel.

4 To serve, with fork, split each warm biscuit horizontally in half. Spoon pear mixture onto bottom halves of biscuits; top with whipped cream, then biscuit tops.

EACH SERVING About 580 calories, 6g protein, 67g carbohydrate, 34g total fat (13g saturated), 58mg cholesterol, 590mg sodium.

QUICK PEAR DESSERTS

CHOCOLATE PEARS Microwave cored whole pears, covered, until tender, top with hot fudge sauce.

PEAR AND DRIED-CHERRY RICE PUDDING Cook diced pears in nonstick skillet until tender. Stir into deli rice pudding along with some dried cherries.

PEAR SMOOTHIES Peel very ripe pears; coarsely chop. Whirl in blender with milk, yogurt, honey, and ice until smooth.

Roasted Almond-Crusted Plums

Butter, brown sugar, and almonds turn tender plums into an elegant dessert. Serve them with scoops of vanilla ice cream.

PREP 15 minutes • BAKE 25 minutes
MAKES 6 servings.

6 large plums (4 to 5 ounces each),
   cut in half and pitted
3 tablespoons butter or margarine, softened
⅓ cup packed brown sugar
¼ cup all-purpose flour
⅓ cup sliced natural almonds

1 Preheat oven to 425°F. In shallow baking dish, arrange plums, cut side up, close together in one layer.

2 In medium bowl, with mixer at medium speed, beat butter and brown sugar until smooth. Stir in flour until blended. Stir in almonds. Sprinkle mixture evenly over plums. Bake until plums are tender, 25 to 35 minutes.

EACH SERVING About 204 calories, 2g protein, 31g carbohydrate, 9g total fat (4g saturated), 16mg cholesterol, 64mg sodium.

Broiled Amaretti Plums

The crunchy almond-flavored topping for the plums is made from crushed amaretti cookies. Just a couple of minutes under the broiler and the plums are ready to serve.

PREP 10 minutes • BROIL 2 minutes
MAKES 4 servings.

2 tablespoons brown sugar
2 tablespoons butter or margarine
½ cup crushed amaretti cookies
4 large firm, ripe plums, cut in half
   and pitted

1 Preheat broiler. In small microwave-safe bowl, heat sugar and butter in microwave oven on High until butter has melted, about 30 seconds; stir until blended. Add amaretti and stir just until coated.

2 Place plum halves, cut sides up, in 9" by 9" baking pan. Top each half with heaping teaspoon amaretti mixture. Place baking pan in broiler about 6 inches from source of heat and broil until tops are golden and plums are tender, 2 to 2½ minutes.

EACH SERVING About 190 calories, 2g protein, 32g carbohydrate, 7g total fat (4g saturated), 16mg cholesterol, 67mg sodium.

Perfect Plum Cobbler

A traditional biscuit-topped cobbler made with juicy plums.

PREP 25 minutes • **BAKE** 25 minutes • **MAKES** 8 servings.

PLUM FILLING

½ cup sugar

¼ cup cold water

2 tablespoons cornstarch

3 pounds plums, pitted and cut into
   1-inch chunks (about 8 cups)

BISCUITS

1½ cups all-purpose flour

2½ teaspoons baking powder

¼ teaspoon salt

¼ cup plus 2 teaspoons sugar

4 tablespoons cold butter or margarine,
   cut into pieces

¾ cup plus 1 tablespoon heavy or
   whipping cream

⅛ teaspoon ground cinnamon

1 Prepare filling: In 4-quart saucepan, stir sugar, water, and cornstarch until well blended and smooth. Add plums; cover and heat to boiling over high heat, stirring often. Reduce heat to medium-low; simmer 5 minutes.

2 Preheat oven to 400°F. Prepare biscuits: In large bowl, with wire whisk, mix flour, baking powder, salt, and ¼ cup sugar. With pastry blender or two knives used scissor-fashion, cut in butter until mixture resembles coarse crumbs. Add ¾ cup cream, stirring just until mixture forms soft dough that leaves side of bowl.

3 Turn dough onto lightly floured surface. Pat dough into 8" by 5" rectangle; brush with remaining 1 tablespoon cream and sprinkle with cinnamon and remaining 2 teaspoons sugar. Cut into 8 biscuits.

4 Pour hot filling into shallow 3½- to 4-quart baking dish; top with biscuits. Bake until biscuits are lightly browned and filling is bubbly, 25 to 30 minutes. Cool on wire rack 30 minutes. Serve warm.

EACH SERVING About 385 calories, 4g protein, 58g carbohydrate, 16g total fat (10g saturated), 50mg cholesterol, 270mg sodium.

Test Kitchen Tip

BUYING PLUMS

A plum's sweetness does not increase as the fruit softens, so be sure to purchase ripe fruit. Its color is determined by the variety. Plums should be plump, and evenly colored and yield gently to pressure. If the powdery bloom is still on the skin, it's a sign the plums haven't been overhandled. Avoid hard, shriveled, or cracked fruit.

Plum Compote with Ginger Syrup

Fresh ginger and orange add extra sparkle to summer fruits.

PREP 15 minutes plus chilling • COOK 15 minutes • MAKES about 5 cups or 6 servings.

½ cup white zinfandel or rosé wine
½ cup water
½ cup sugar
3 strips orange peel (3" by ¾" each)
3 slices unpeeled fresh ginger
   (¼ inch thick each)
4 whole black peppercorns
3 ripe medium plums (12 ounces), unpeeled
   and each cut into 8 wedges
3 ripe medium nectarines (1 pound), unpeeled
   and each cut into 8 wedges

1 In 3-quart saucepan, heat wine, water, sugar, orange peel, ginger, and peppercorns to boiling over high heat. Reduce heat to low and simmer 10 minutes.

2 Add plums to syrup and simmer 5 minutes. Transfer fruit mixture to medium bowl; stir in nectarines. Cover and refrigerate, stirring occasionally, at least 4 hours or overnight. Discard the orange peel, ginger, and peppercorns before serving.

EACH SERVING About 141 calories, 1g protein, 32g carbohydrate, 1g total fat (0g saturated), 0mg cholesterol, 1mg sodium.

Plum Compote with Ginger Syrup

Blueberry-Mango Compote

A summery duo that can't be beat.

PREP 15 minutes • **MAKES** 6 servings.

1 tablespoon dark Jamaican rum
1 tablespoon fresh lime juice
1 tablespoon sugar
2 large mangoes, peeled and cut into
   ¾-inch pieces
1 pint blueberries

In medium bowl, combine rum, lime juice, and sugar. Add mangoes and blueberries; toss to coat. Cover and refrigerate if not serving right away.

EACH SERVING About 97 calories, 1g protein, 24g carbohydrate, og total fat, omg cholesterol, 5mg sodium.

Test Kitchen Tip

CUTTING A MANGO

With a sharp knife, cut a lengthwise slice from each side of the long flat seed, as close to the seed as possible and set aside.

- Then, peel seed section; cut off as much flesh as possible. Discard seed. Cut the reserved mango pieces lengthwise into thick wedges. Use a knife to remove the peel from each wedge, cutting close to the peel.
- Or, for eating mango out of hand, score the flesh of each piece without cutting through the skin, and gently push it out to eat.

Dried Apricot, Prune, and Cherry Compote

This compote is made exclusively with dried fruits. It tastes great by itself but can also be served with crisp cookies or a generous dollop of vanilla yogurt.

PREP 15 minutes plus cooling
COOK 15 minutes • **MAKES** 8 servings.

1 cup dried apricots (8 ounces),
   each cut into thirds
¼ cup packed brown sugar
3 strips (3" by 1" each) lemon peel
1 cinnamon stick (3 inches)
4 cups apple cider or apple juice
1 cup pitted prunes (8 ounces), each cut in half
½ cup dried tart cherries (4 ounces)
½ teaspoon vanilla extract

1 In 3-quart saucepan, heat apricots, brown sugar, lemon peel, cinnamon stick, and apple cider to boiling over high heat. Reduce heat and simmer 5 minutes.
2 Spoon apricot mixture into large bowl; stir in prunes, cherries, and vanilla. Let cool to serve at room temperature, or cover and refrigerate. Store in refrigerator up to 1 week. Discard lemon peel and cinnamon stick before serving.

EACH SERVING About 257 calories, 2g protein, 67g carbohydrate, og total fat, omg cholesterol, 11mg sodium.

Fruit Compote with Spiced Vanilla Syrup

A fat-free dessert fragrant with dried peaches, plus fresh pears, apples, and cranberries bathed in an orange-scented vanilla syrup.

PREP 25 minutes plus chilling • **COOK** 25 minutes • **MAKES** about 14 cups or 20 servings.

1 navel orange
3½ cups water
1 cup sugar
2 cinnamon sticks (each 3 inches)
½ vanilla bean (3 inches), split
4 large firm but ripe Anjou or Bosc pears
    (2 pounds), peeled, cored, and each cut
    into 8 wedges
4 large Golden Delicious apples (about 2
    pounds), peeled, cored, and each cut
    into 12 wedges
2 cups cranberries
2 packages (6 ounces each) dried peaches,
    each cut in half

1 From orange, with vegetable peeler, remove 3 strips peel (about 1 inch wide each) and squeeze ½ cup juice.

2 In 5- to 6-quart saucepot, heat water, sugar, cinnamon sticks, vanilla bean, and orange peel to boiling over high heat, stirring frequently, until sugar has dissolved. Reduce heat to medium-low; cover and simmer, stirring occasionally, 10 minutes.

3 Add pears and apples to syrup, gently stirring to combine; heat to boiling over high heat. Reduce heat to medium-low; cover and simmer until pears and apples are tender, about 8 minutes. Stir in cranberries and peaches; cook 1 minute longer.

4 Pour fruit mixture into large heat-safe serving bowl; stir in orange juice. Cover and refrigerate at least 4 hours or up to 3 days to allow flavors to blend. Discard the orange peel, cinnamon sticks, and vanilla bean before serving.

EACH SERVING About 140 calories, 1g protein, 36g carbohydrate, 0g total fat, 0mg cholesterol, 2mg sodium.

Fruit Compote with Vanilla-Bean Syrup

Fruit Salad with Vanilla-Bean Syrup

Perfect alone or with a slice of Old-Fashioned Pound Cake (page 322).

PREP 30 minutes plus chilling
COOK 10 minutes • **MAKES** 12 servings.

2 large lemons
1 vanilla bean
¾ cup sugar
¾ cup water
3 ripe mangoes, peeled and cut into 1-inch chunks
2 pints strawberries, hulled and cut in half or into quarters if large
1 medium honeydew melon (about 3½ pounds), peeled and cut into 1-inch chunks

1 From 1 lemon, with vegetable peeler, remove 1 continuous strip of peel (about 1 inch wide); from lemons, squeeze ¼ cup juice. Cut vanilla bean lengthwise in half. With small knife, scrape seeds from vanilla bean, reserve seeds and pod.
2 In 1-quart saucepan, heat lemon peel, vanilla-bean seeds and pod, sugar, and water to boiling over high heat. Reduce heat to medium; cook, uncovered, until syrup is has thickened slightly, about 5 minutes. Pour syrup mixture through sieve into small bowl; discard solids. Stir in lemon juice. Cover and refrigerate syrup until chilled, about 2 hours.
3 Place mangoes, strawberries, and honeydew melon in large bowl; add chilled syrup and toss to coat fruit.

EACH SERVING About 120 calories, 1g protein, 31g carbohydrate, 0g total fat, 0mg cholesterol, 10mg sodium.

Sangria-Steeped Berries

This no-cook finale is a great warm weather treat.

PREP 10 minutes plus chilling
MAKES 4 servings

1 cup dry red wine
¼ cup orange-flavored liqueur or orange juice
2 tablespoons sugar
1 teaspoon freshly grated lemon peel
½ teaspoon freshly grated orange peel
4 cups assorted fresh berries, such as blackberries, blueberries, currants, raspberries, and sliced strawberries

1 In medium bowl, combine wine, liqueur, sugar, lemon peel, and orange peel. Add berries.
2 Cover and refrigerate 30 minutes or up to 4 hours to blend flavors.

EACH SERVING About 174 calories, 1g protein, 28g carbohydrate, 1g total fat (0g saturated), 0mg cholesterol, 6mg sodium.

Summary Fruit in Spiced Syrup

A light and lively make-ahead summer dessert.

PREP 15 minutes plus cooling and chilling • **COOK** 7 minutes • **MAKES** about 5 cups or 6 servings.

¾ cup water
½ cup sugar
3 whole cloves
1 cinnamon stick (3 inches)
1 star anise
1 strip (3" by ¾") fresh lemon peel
2 tablespoons fresh lemon juice
6 cups fresh fruit, such as sliced nectarines
  and plums, hulled strawberries, and
  blueberries and raspberries

1 In 1-quart saucepan, heat water, sugar, cloves, cinnamon, star anise, and lemon peel to boiling over medium-high heat, stirring frequently. Reduce heat to medium-low; simmer 5 minutes. Remove saucepan from heat; stir in lemon juice. Cool syrup to room temperature.

2 In large bowl, combine fruits and syrup. Cover and refrigerate, stirring occasionally, 2 hours. Remove cloves, cinnamon stick, star anise, and lemon peel before serving.

EACH SERVING About 125 calories, 1g protein, 32g carbohydrate, 1g total fat (0g saturated), 0mg cholesterol, 2mg sodium.

Summer Fruit in Spiced Syrup

Watermelon Bowl

For a great presentation, serve this colorful mixture of sweet summer fruits and minty syrup in the hollowed-out watermelon. It makes a very large quantity, so it's just right for casual summer get-togethers or family barbecues.

PREP 1 hour plus chilling • **COOK** 10 minutes • **MAKES** about 32 cups or 32 servings.

1½ cups water
1 cup sugar
1½ cups loosely packed fresh mint leaves
   and stems, chopped
3 tablespoons fresh lime juice
1 large watermelon (20 pounds), cut
   lengthwise in half
1 small cantaloupe
6 large plums, each cut in half and pitted
4 large nectarines, each cut in half and pitted
1 pound seedless green grapes

1 In 2-quart saucepan, heat water and sugar to boiling over medium heat, stirring occasionally, until sugar has dissolved. Boil 5 minutes. Stir in mint and lime juice and refrigerate until well chilled.

2 Meanwhile, cut watermelon flesh into bite-size pieces; discard seeds. Cut cantaloupe flesh into bite-size pieces. Cut plums and nectarines into wedges. In very large bowl or in shell of watermelon, combine cut-up fruit with grapes. Hold sieve over fruit and pour chilled syrup through. Gently toss to mix well. Cover and refrigerate, stirring occasionally, about 2 hours to blend flavors.

EACH SERVING About 111 calories, 2g protein, 26g carbohydrate, 1g total fat (0g saturated), 0mg cholesterol, 7mg sodium.

ANISE FRUIT BOWL
Prepare as directed above but substitute *2 tablespoons anise seeds* for mint.

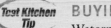 **BUYING WATERMELON**
Watermelons come in two sizes: icebox (around 8 pounds) and large (up to 20 pounds). The flesh can be the classic red or yellow, and some varieties are seedless. Watermelons should be firm and symmetrically shaped, either oblong or round, depending on the variety. The side of the melon that touched the soil should be yellowish or cream-colored, not pale green or white. The rind should have a velvety bloom, giving it a dull, not shiny, appearance.

To test a whole melon for ripeness, slap the side of the melon with the open palm of your hand; the sound should be deep and resonant. A dull thud indicates an underripe melon, and a hollow sounds means it is overripe and mushy.

Cut watermelon should have firm, deep red flesh with dark brown or black seeds. Avoid melons with white streak running through the flesh.

Rhubarb-Apple Crumble

A lowfat but irresistible homestyle dessert. The sweet oat topping is mixed with just a bit of butter for rich flavor.

PREP 20 minutes • **BAKE** 45 minutes
MAKES 6 servings.

⅓ cup granulated sugar
1 tablespoon cornstarch
1¼ pounds rhubarb, cut into ½-inch pieces
   (4 cups)
1¼ pounds Golden Delicious apples
   (3 medium), peeled, cored, and cut into
   1-inch pieces
½ cup packed brown sugar
2 tablespoons butter or margarine, softened
¼ teaspoon ground cinnamon
⅓ cup old-fashioned or quick-cooking oats,
   uncooked
¼ cup all-purpose flour

1 Preheat oven to 375°F. In large bowl, with fork, mix granulated sugar and cornstarch. Add rhubarb and apples and toss to coat. Spoon mixture into 11" by 7" baking dish or shallow 2-quart casserole.

2 In medium bowl, with fingertips, mix brown sugar, butter, and cinnamon until blended. Stir in oats and flour until combined; sprinkle mixture over fruit in baking dish.

3 Bake until filling is hot and bubbling and the topping has browned, about 45 minutes. Serve warm.

EACH SERVING About 252 calories, 2g protein, 53g carbohydrate, 5g total fat (2g saturated), 10mg cholesterol, 50mg sodium.

Chocolate Fondue with Fruit

A fun ending to any meal. Splurge on the best-quality chocolate you can find.

PREP 15 minutes • **COOK** 5 minutes
MAKES 8 servings.

6 squares (6 ounces) semisweet chocolate,
   coarsely chopped
½ cup half-and-half or light cream
½ teaspoon vanilla extract
4 small bananas, peeled and cut into
   ½-inch-thick slices
2 to 3 small pears, cored and cut into
   ½-inch-thick wedges
1 pint strawberries, hulled
½ cup finely chopped almonds, toasted
   (see page 13)

1 In heavy 1-quart saucepan, heat chocolate and half-and-half over low heat, stirring frequently, until chocolate has melted and mixture is smooth, about 5 minutes. Stir in vanilla; keep warm.

2 To serve, arrange bananas, pears, and strawberries on large platter. Spoon sauce into small bowl; place nuts in separate small bowl. With forks or sturdy canapé picks, have guests dip fruit into chocolate sauce, then into nuts.

EACH SERVING About 249 calories, 4g protein, 36g carbohydrate, 13g total fat (5g saturated), 6mg cholesterol, 10mg sodium.

Berry and Nectarine Oatmeal-Cookie Crisp

For this juicy fruit crisp, we've added pecans to the topping, making it reminiscent of old-fashioned oatmeal cookies.

PREP 20 minutes plus cooling • **BAKE** 40 minutes • **MAKES** 8 servings.

1 lemon
2 pounds nectarines (6 medium), unpeeled,
    pitted, and each cut into thick wedges
½ pint raspberries
1 cup blueberries
¼ cup granulated sugar
⅔ cup packed brown sugar
½ cup all-purpose flour
½ teaspoon ground nutmeg
6 tablespoons cold butter or margarine,
    cut into pieces
½ cup old-fashioned oats, uncooked
⅓ cup chopped pecans
vanilla ice cream (optional)

1 Preheat oven to 400°F. From lemon, grate ½ teaspoon peel and squeeze 2 teaspoons juice. In shallow 2-quart casserole or 8" by 8" baking dish, toss nectarines, raspberries, and blueberries with granulated sugar and lemon peel and juice until fruit is evenly coated.

2 In medium bowl, with wire whisk, mix brown sugar, flour, and nutmeg. With pastry blender or two knives used scissor-fashion, cut in butter until mixture resembles coarse crumbs. Stir in oats and pecans; sprinkle oat mixture evenly over fruit.

3 Bake crisp until top is golden and fruit is hot and bubbly, 40 to 45 minutes. Cool briefly on wire rack. Serve warm with ice cream, if you like.

EACH SERVING About 300 calories, 3g protein, 51g carbohydrate, 14g total fat (6g saturated), 25mg cholesterol, 100mg sodium.

Ambrosia

Some ambrosias have gotten away from the pure simplicity of the original recipe—not ours.

PREP 50 minutes • **BAKE** 15 minutes
MAKES 10 servings.

1 fresh coconut
1 ripe pineapple
6 large navel oranges

1 Preheat oven to 350°F. Prepare coconut: Using hammer and screwdriver or large nail, puncture two of the three eyes (indentations) in coconut. Drain liquid. Bake coconut 15 minutes. Remove from oven and wrap in kitchen towel. With hammer, hit coconut to break it into large pieces. With knife, pry coconut meat from shell. With vegetable peeler, peel brown outer skin from coconut meat. With vegetable peeler or on large holes of grater, shred 1 cup coconut. (Wrap and refrigerate remaining coconut up to 2 days for another use.)
2 Prepare pineapple: Cut crown and stem end from pineapple. Stand pineapple on cutting board, cut off rind, and remove eyes. Cut pineapple lengthwise into quarters. Cut out core. Cut quarters lengthwise in half, then crosswise into pieces. Place in large bowl.
3 Prepare oranges: Cut ends off oranges; stand oranges on cutting board and cut off peel and white pith. Holding oranges over bowl with pineapple to catch juice, cut out sections from between membranes, allowing sections to drop into bowl. Squeeze juice from membranes into bowl; discard membranes.
4 Add shredded coconut to bowl and toss gently to combine.

EACH SERVING About 240 calories, 3g protein, 31g carbohydrate, 14g total fat (12g saturated), 0mg cholesterol, 10mg sodium.

Mint Julep Cups

Bourbon and mint lend a gentle kick to fruit salad. It's just the thing to serve at a Kentucky Derby party.

PREP 25 minutes plus chilling
MAKES 6 servings.

¼ cup bourbon
¼ cup chopped fresh mint leaves
2 tablespoons sugar
1 pineapple
1 pint strawberries, hulled and thickly sliced

1 In large bowl, stir bourbon, mint, and sugar until blended.
2 Prepare pineapple as directed in Step 2 of recipe for Ambrosia (left). After coring quarters, cut them lengthwise in half, then crosswise into thin slices. Add to bowl with bourbon mixture.
3 Add strawberries; stir to combine. Refrigerate to blend flavors, about 2 hours.

EACH SERVING About 144 calories, 1g protein, 30g carbohydrate, 1g total fat (0g saturated), 0mg cholesterol, 4mg sodium.

FAST MINT MELON CUPS
Toss 1-inch chunks of honeydew and cantaloupe with fresh lime juice and honey. Garnish with a twist of lime peel.

Blueberry-Peach Shortcakes

Another fabulous take on everyone's favorite midsummer dessert. If you prefer, use a mix of peaches and raspberries, or try a combination of your favorite berries. It will be just as delicious.

PREP 30 minutes • COOK/BAKE 25 minutes • MAKES 8 servings.

2 tablespoons fresh lemon juice

1 tablespoon cornstarch

1½ pints blueberries (3¾ cups)

1 cup plus 3 tablespoons sugar

6 medium peaches (2 pounds), each peeled and cut into 8 wedges

3 cups all-purpose flour

4½ teaspoons baking powder

¾ teaspoon salt

9 tablespoons cold butter or margarine, cut into pieces, plus 1 tablespoon butter or margarine, melted

1 cup plus 2 tablespoons milk

1 cup heavy or whipping cream

1 Preheat oven to 425°F. Prepare fruit: In cup, with fork, blend lemon juice and cornstarch until smooth.

2 In 3-quart saucepan, heat blueberries, ⅔ cup sugar, and cornstarch mixture to boiling over medium-high heat, stirring. Reduce heat to medium; cook 1 minute. Stir in peaches; remove from heat.

3 Prepare biscuits: In large bowl, with wire whisk, mix flour, ⅓ cup sugar, baking powder, and salt. With pastry blender or two knives used scissor-fashion, cut in cold butter until mixture resembles coarse crumbs. Stir in milk just until mixture forms soft dough that leaves side of bowl.

4 On lightly floured surface, knead dough 6 to 8 times to mix thoroughly. With lightly floured hands, pat dough into 1-inch thickness. With floured 3-inch round biscuit cutter, cut out as many biscuits as possible. Place biscuits 1 inch apart on ungreased large cookie sheet. Press trimmings together; cut as directed above to make 8 biscuits in all.

5 With pastry brush, brush biscuits with melted butter; sprinkle with 1 tablespoon sugar. Bake biscuits until golden, 15 to 20 minutes.

6 In medium bowl, beat cream with remaining 2 tablespoons sugar until soft peaks form. With fork, split warm biscuits horizontally in half. Spoon some blueberry-peach mixture onto bottom halves of biscuits; top with whipped cream, then with more blueberry-peach mixture. Cover with biscuit tops.

EACH SERVING WITHOUT WHIPPED CREAM
About 613 calories, 8g protein, 91g carbohydrate, 26g total fat (16g saturated), 80mg cholesterol, 658mg sodium.

Nectarine and Blueberry Cobbler

The colorful sweet/tart combo of nectarines and blueberries is a luscious departure from the traditional peach version. No need to peel the nectarines, so prep is a cinch.

Prep 25 minutes plus cooling • **Cook/Bake** 20 minutes • **Makes** 8 servings.

FRUIT FILLING
8 firm but ripe medium nectarines
    (2½ pounds), pitted and cut into
    ½-inch wedges
1 pint blueberries
½ cup sugar
1 tablespoon plus 1 teaspoon cornstarch
1 tablespoon fresh lemon juice
½ cup water

BISCUITS
1¾ cups all-purpose flour
4 tablespoons sugar
1 tablespoon baking powder
¼ teaspoon salt
1 cup heavy or whipping cream

vanilla ice cream (optional)

1 Prepare filling: In 4-quart saucepan, heat nectarines, blueberries, sugar, cornstarch, lemon juice, and water to boiling over medium-high heat, stirring constantly. Reduce heat to low; simmer until fruit has softened, about 2 minutes. Remove saucepan from heat.

2 Preheat oven to 450°F. Prepare biscuits: In large bowl, with wire whisk, mix flour, 3 tablespoons sugar, baking powder, and salt. Reserve 1 tablespoon cream for brushing on biscuits later. In medium bowl, with mixer at medium speed, beat remaining cream just until stiff peaks form. With rubber spatula, stir whipped cream into flour mixture just until soft dough forms. With lightly floured hand, knead dough in bowl 3 or 4 times, just until it holds together. Do not overmix.

3 Turn dough onto lightly floured surface. With floured rolling pin, roll dough into ¾-inch thickness. With floured 2½-inch round biscuit cutter, cut out as many biscuits as possible. Press trimmings together; reroll and cut as directed to make 8 biscuits in all.

4 Reheat filling to boiling over medium heat. Pour into 11" by 7" baking dish or shallow 2½-quart casserole. Arrange biscuits on top of filling; brush with reserved 1 tablespoon cream and sprinkle with remaining 1 tablespoon sugar.

5 Bake cobbler until biscuits are browned and fruit mixture is bubbling, 15 to 17 minutes. Cool on wire rack 30 minutes to serve warm, or cool completely to serve later. Serve with ice cream, if you like.

Each serving About 355 calories, 5g protein, 60g carbohydrate, 12g total fat (7g saturated), 41mg cholesterol, 235mg sodium.

Nectarine and Blueberry Cobbler

Pies and Tarts

IT HAS BEEN SAID that the reputation of a home baker rests on his or her pies and tarts. When made from scratch, the flavorful, tender, and flaky crust and sweet filling of a just-from-the-oven pie or tart represents home baking at its best.

It's hard to select just one favorite pie or tart because there are so many to choose from. Do you lean toward fillings of ripe seasonal fruits or smooth custards and creams? Is your preference a sweet-tart citrus filling or one with rich ricotta or cream cheese? What about chocolate and nuts?

And let's not forget the crust! Whether it's a single- or double-crust pie, a cookie-crumb, shortbread, or buttery pastry crust, most pie and tart lovers agree that the perfect crust is as important as the filling. So that you'll never score a miss, we've matched nine of *Good Housekeeping*'s best piecrust recipes with the most sublime fillings, for a collection of more than fifty heavenly pies and tarts.

Here you'll find recipes for simple fruit pies that have been made in America since pioneer days. The abundance of summer's plump deep-hued berries and fragrant stone fruits have inspired generations of bakers to turn out such homespun desserts as Very Blueberry Pie (page 157), rustic Farm-Stand Cherry Pie (page 160), and Brown-Butter Peach Tart (page 170). As the cooler weather brings a bumper crop of autumn fruits, it's time for an Apple Galette (page 157), Cranberry-Pear Pie (page 164), or Pumpkin Pie with Pecan-Caramel Topping (page 184).

By the mid-twentieth century, when the refrigerator became a common accoutrement in American homes, refrigerator pies took hold. With smooth, creamy fillings everyone seemed to love, and since many were made with cookie-crumb crusts that required little baking, they had many advantages. Not only were they easy to prepare, they were left in the fridge to set well in advance of serving, which made them true time-savers. They still are. Our No-Bake Chocolate Fudge Tart (page 199) goes from prep to chilling in ten minutes! The rich Toasted Coconut Cream Pie (page 192) is just like Grandma's, only quicker and better. And in a fraction of the time it takes to make a classic cheesecake, you can be sitting down to a slice of Deluxe Cheese Pie (page 186), which is just as delicious.

Double Blueberry Pie and Peach and Raspberry Pie (page 158)

Pastry Dough for 2-Crust Pie

Our perfect from-scratch recipe gets its flavor from butter and its flakiness from vegetable shortening.

PREP 15 minutes plus chilling • **MAKES** enough dough for one 9-inch, 2-crust pie.

2¼ cups all-purpose flour
½ teaspoon salt
½ cup cold butter or margarine (1 stick),
   cut into pieces
¼ cup vegetable shortening
4 to 6 tablespoons ice water

1 In large bowl, with wire whisk, mix flour and salt. With pastry blender or two knives used scissor-fashion, cut in butter and shortening until mixture resembles coarse crumbs.

2 Sprinkle in ice water, 1 tablespoon at a time, mixing lightly with fork after each addition, until dough is just moist enough to hold together.

3 Shape dough into 2 disks, one slightly larger than the other. Wrap each disk in plastic wrap and refrigerate 30 minutes or up to overnight. (If chilled overnight, let stand 30 minutes at room temperature before rolling.)

4 On lightly floured surface, with floured rolling pin, roll larger disk of dough into 12-inch round. Gently roll dough round onto rolling pin and ease into pie plate, pressing dough against side of plate. Trim edge, leaving 1-inch overhang. Reserve trimmings for decorating pie, if you like. Spoon filling into crust.

5 Roll remaining disk of dough into 12-inch round. Cut ¾-inch circle out of center and cut 1-inch slits to allow steam to escape during baking; center dough over filling. Fold overhang under; make decorative edge. Bake as directed in recipe.

EACH ⅒ PASTRY About 235 calories, 3g protein, 23g carbohydrate, 15g total fat (7g saturated), 25mg cholesterol, 210mg sodium.

FOOD-PROCESSOR PASTRY DOUGH

In food processor with knife blade attached, pulse flour and salt to mix. Evenly distribute butter and shortening on top of flour mixture; pulse just until mixture resembles coarse crumbs. With processor running, pour 4 tablespoons ice water through feed tube. Immediately stop motor and pinch dough; it should be just moist enough to hold together. If not, with fork, stir in up to 2 tablespoons additional ice water. Refrigerate and roll as directed.

WHOLE-WHEAT PASTRY

Prepare dough as directed, but use *1½ cups all-purpose flour* and *¾ cup whole-wheat flour*.

EACH ⅒ PASTRY About 235 calories, 4g protein, 23g carbohydrate, 15g total fat (7g saturated), 25mg cholesterol, 210mg sodium.

FINISHING THE PIE EDGES

Decorative borders add a professional touch to homemade pies, whether they have one or two crusts or are to be filled with fruit, custard, or cream. In addition, a pretty edge helps keep the pie crust from shrinking by adhering it to the pie-plate rim. In some pies, a high edge keeps liquid fillings in and prevents juices from boiling out onto the oven floor. For best results, chill the pastry so it is firm (but not hard) enough to work with.

FORKED EDGE With kitchen shears, trim the edge of the dough even with the rim of the pie plate. With floured fork tines, press the dough edge at even intervals all around the rim.

SCALLOPED EDGE With kitchen shears, trim the edge of the dough, leaving a 1-inch overhang. Fold the overhang under to form a standing edge. Place your thumb and forefinger of one hand, 1 inch apart on the inner side of the pastry edge. With the forefinger of the other hand, gently pull the dough down toward the outer edge to form a scallop. Repeat all around.

CRIMPED EDGE (pictured at right) With kitchen shears, trim the edge of the dough, leaving a 1-inch overhang. Fold the overhang under to form a standing edge. Push one index finger against the inside of the rim. With your index finger and thumb of the other hand, pinch dough to crimp. Repeat all around, leaving ¼ inch between each crimp.

FLUTED EDGE With kitchen shears, trim the edge of the dough, leaving a 1-inch overhang. Fold the overhang under to form a standing edge. Place your thumb and forefinger of one hand ½ inch apart on the outside of the pastry edge; pinch the dough into a V shape. At the same time, with the forefinger of the other hand on the inner side of the pastry edge, push the dough to define the shape. Repeat all around.

ROPE EDGE With kitchen shears, trim the edge of the dough, leaving a 1-inch overhang. Fold the overhang under to form a standing edge. Pinch the dough edge at a 45° angle between your thumb and forefinger. At the same time, slightly twist the dough outward. Repeat all around at 1-inch intervals.

TURRET EDGE With kitchen shears, trim the edge of the dough, leaving a 1-inch overhang. With a knife, cut the dough at ½-inch intervals. Fold down the pieces of dough, alternating toward and away from the rim.

Pastry Dough for 1-Crust Pie

Chilling a piecrust before baking helps it retain its shape.

PREP 15 minutes plus chilling
MAKES enough dough for one 9-inch crust.

1¼ cups all-purpose flour
¼ teaspoon salt
4 tablespoons cold butter or margarine, cut into pieces
2 tablespoons vegetable shortening
3 to 5 tablespoons ice water

1 In large bowl, with wire whisk, mix flour and salt. With pastry blender or two knives used scissor-fashion, cut in butter and shortening until mixture resembles coarse crumbs.
2 Sprinkle in ice water, 1 tablespoon at a time, mixing lightly with fork after each addition, until dough is just moist enough to hold together.
3 Shape dough into disk; wrap in plastic wrap. Refrigerate 30 minutes or up to overnight. (If chilled overnight, let stand 30 minutes at room temperature before rolling.)
4 On lightly floured surface, with floured rolling pin, roll dough into 12-inch round. Ease into pie plate, gently pressing dough against side of plate.
5 Make decorative edge as desired. Refrigerate or freeze until firm, 10 to 15 minutes. Fill and bake as directed in recipe.

EACH 1/10 PASTRY About 123 calories, 2g protein, 13g carbohydrate, 7g total fat (4g saturated), 12mg cholesterol, 104mg sodium.

Pastry Dough for 9-Inch Tart

Tart pastry is a bit richer than pie pastry and bakes up crisper.

PREP 15 minutes plus chilling
MAKES enough dough for one 9-inch tart shell.

1 cup all-purpose flour
¼ teaspoon salt
6 tablespoons cold butter or margarine, cut into pieces
1 tablespoon vegetable shortening
2 to 3 tablespoons ice water

1 In large bowl, with wire whisk, mix flour and salt. With pastry blender or two knives used scissor-fashion, cut in butter and shortening until mixture resembles coarse crumbs.
2 Sprinkle in ice water, 1 tablespoon at a time, mixing lightly with fork after each addition, until dough is just moist enough to hold together.
3 Shape dough into disk; wrap in plastic wrap. Refrigerate 30 minutes or up to overnight. (If chilled overnight, let stand 30 minutes at room temperature before rolling.)
4 On lightly floured surface, with floured rolling pin, roll dough into 11-inch round. Ease dough into 9-inch tart pan with removable bottom. Fold overhang in and press dough against side of pan so it extends ⅛ inch above rim. Refrigerate or freeze until firm, 10 to 15 minutes. Fill and bake as directed in recipe.

EACH ⅛ PASTRY About 151 calories, 2g protein, 13g carbohydrate, 10g total fat (6g saturated), 23mg cholesterol, 160mg sodium.

Pastry Dough for 11-Inch Tart

When rolling pastry for a large tart, lift it and turn it occasionally to keep thickness even and prevent sticking.

PREP 15 minutes plus chilling
MAKES enough dough for one 11-inch tart shell.

1½ cups all-purpose flour
½ teaspoon salt
½ cup cold butter or margarine (1 stick), cut into pieces
2 tablespoons vegetable shortening
3 to 4 tablespoons ice water

1 In large bowl, with wire whisk, mix flour and salt. With pastry blender or two knives used scissor-fashion, cut in butter and shortening until mixture resembles coarse crumbs.

2 Sprinkle in ice water, 1 tablespoon at a time, mixing lightly with fork after each addition, until dough is just moist enough to hold together.

3 Shape dough into disk; wrap in plastic wrap. Refrigerate 30 minutes or up to overnight. (If chilled overnight, let stand 30 minutes at room temperature before rolling.)

4 On lightly floured surface, with floured rolling pin, roll dough into 14-inch round. Ease dough into 11-inch tart pan with removable bottom. Fold overhang in and press dough against side of pan so it extends ⅛ inch above rim. Refrigerate or freeze until firm, 10 to 15 minutes. Fill and bake as directed in recipe.

EACH ½2 PASTRY About 148 calories, 2g protein, 13g carbohydrate, 10g total fat (5g saturated), 21mg cholesterol, 175mg sodium.

Sweet Pastry Crust

A delicate crust that tastes just like a butter cookie! When rolled into a rectangle, it's perfect for our Berries-and-Jam Tart (page 177).

PREP 15 minutes plus cooling
BAKE about 20 minutes
MAKES one 14" by 8" crust.

¾ cup butter or margarine (1½ sticks), softened
⅓ cup sugar
1 large egg
2 teaspoons vanilla extract
2 cups all-purpose flour
¼ teaspoon salt

1 Preheat oven to 400°F. In large bowl, with mixer at low speed, beat butter and sugar until blended. Increase speed to high; beat until light and creamy, occasionally scraping bowl with rubber spatula. Reduce speed to medium; beat in egg and vanilla until blended. At low speed, gradually beat in flour and salt just until dough begins to form. With hands, press dough together; shape into small rectangle.

2 On large cookie sheet, with floured rolling pin, roll dough into 14" by 8" rectangle. (To make handling easier, place a damp towel under cookie sheet to prevent sheet from moving.) With fingers, gently crimp edges of rectangle to form decorative border. With fork, prick dough at ½-inch intervals to prevent puffing and shrinking during baking.

3 Bake crust until golden, about 20 minutes. Cool crust on cookie sheet on wire rack.

EACH ½2 CRUST About 205 calories, 3g protein, 21g carbohydrate, 12g total fat (7g saturated), 49mg cholesterol, 171mg sodium.

Pat-in-Pan Dough for 9-Inch Tart

With this handy no-roll dough, lack of counter space is no longer is an obstacle for bakers who like to make French-style pastry.

PREP 10 minutes plus chilling
MAKES enough dough for one 9-inch lattice-top tart.

¾ cup unsalted butter (1½ sticks), softened (do not use margarine or salted butter)
½ cup sugar
1 large egg
2 teaspoons vanilla extract
2 cups all-purpose flour
¼ teaspoon salt

1 In large bowl, with mixer at low speed, beat butter and sugar until blended. Increase speed to high; beat until light and creamy, scraping bowl occasionally with rubber spatula. Reduce speed to medium; beat in egg and vanilla until blended. With wooden spoon, stir in flour and salt until dough begins to form.

2 With hands, press dough together in bowl and knead a few times until flour is evenly moistened. Divide dough into 2 pieces, one slightly larger than the other; flatten into disks. Wrap each disk in plastic wrap and refrigerate 30 minutes, or until dough is firm enough to handle.

EACH ⅛ PASTRY About 310 calories, 4g protein, 32g carbohydrate, 18g total fat (11g saturated), 73mg cholesterol, 255mg sodium.

Pat-in-Pan Dough for 11-Inch Tart

For those who are skittish about rolling out dough, this crust is a perfect alternative; you just pat the dough in the pan with your hands.

PREP 10 minutes plus chilling
MAKES enough dough for one 11-inch lattice-top tart.

1 cup unsalted butter (2 sticks), softened (do not use margarine or salted butter)
½ cup sugar
1 large egg
1 tablespoon vanilla extract
3 cups all-purpose flour
¼ teaspoon salt

1 In large bowl, with mixer at low speed, beat butter and sugar until blended. Increase speed to high; beat until light and creamy, scraping bowl occasionally with rubber spatula. Reduce speed to medium; beat in egg and vanilla. With wooden spoon, stir in flour and salt until mixture is crumbly.

2 With hands, press dough together in bowl and knead a few times until flour is evenly moistened. Divide dough into 2 pieces, one slightly larger than the other; flatten into disks. Wrap each disk in plastic wrap and refrigerate 30 minutes, or until dough is firm enough to handle.

EACH 1/12 PASTRY About 290 calories, 4g protein, 32g carbohydrate, 16g total fat (10g saturated), 59mg cholesterol, 210mg sodium.

Graham Cracker–Crumb Crust

For the freshest flavor, make your own cookie crumbs. Personalize your crusts by using your favorite cookies to make the crumbs.

PREP 10 minutes • **BAKE** 10 minutes
MAKES one 9-inch crust.

1¼ cups graham-cracker crumbs
    (11 rectangular graham crackers)
4 tablespoons butter or margarine, melted
1 tablespoon sugar

1 Preheat oven to 375°F.
2 In 9-inch pie plate, with fork, mix crumbs, melted butter, and sugar until crumbs are evenly moistened.
3 With hand, press mixture firmly onto bottom and up side of pie plate, making small rim.
4 Bake 10 minutes; cool on wire rack. Fill as recipe directs.

EACH ⅟₁₀ CRUST About 105 calories, 1g protein, 12g carbohydrate, 6g total fat (3g saturated), 12mg cholesterol, 137mg sodium.

CHOCOLATE WAFER–CRUMB CRUST

Prepare as directed, but substitute *1¼ cups chocolate-wafer crumbs (24 cookies)* for graham-cracker crumbs.

EACH ⅟₁₀ CRUST About 108 calories, 1g protein, 12g carbohydrate, 7g total fat (3g saturated), 13mg cholesterol, 130mg sodium.

VANILLA WAFER–CRUMB CRUST

Prepare as directed, but substitute *1¼ cups vanilla-wafer crumbs (35 cookies)* for graham-cracker crumbs.

EACH ⅟₁₀ CRUST About 92 calories, 1g protein, 9g carbohydrate, 6g total fat (3g saturated), 12mg cholesterol, 80mg sodium.

Test Kitchen Tip

MAKING COOKIE CRUMBS

To make cookie crumbs, place the cookies in a heavy-duty zip-tight plastic bag and crush them with a rolling pin or meat mallet. Cookies can also be crushed in a food processor or blender. For about 1 cup of crumbs, use approximately twenty 2¼ inch chocolate wafers, 14 gingersnaps, 22 vanilla wafers, or 7 rectangular plain or chocolate graham crackers.

Shortbread Crust

Plenty of butter mixed with confectioners' sugar and cornstarch gives this crust a melt-in-your-mouth texture.

PREP 15 minutes • **BAKE** 30 minutes
MAKES one 9-inch crust.

¾ cup all-purpose flour
⅓ cup cornstarch
½ cup butter or margarine (1 stick), softened
⅓ cup confectioners' sugar
1 teaspoon vanilla extract

1 Preheat oven to 325°F. In medium bowl, with wire whisk, mix flour and cornstarch.
2 In large bowl, with mixer at medium speed, beat butter and confectioners' sugar until light and fluffy. Beat in vanilla. Reduce speed to low; beat in flour mixture until combined. Scrape dough into 9-inch tart pan with removable bottom.
3 To make handling easier, place sheet of plastic wrap over dough and smooth dough over bottom and up side of pan. Remove and discard plastic wrap. With fork, prick dough all over.
4 Bake until lightly golden, 27 to 30 minutes. Cool in pan on wire rack. Fill as directed in recipe.

EACH ⅛ CRUST About 185 calories, 1g protein, 19g carbohydrate, 12g total fat (7g saturated), 31mg cholesterol, 120mg sodium.

Prebaked Piecrust or Tart Shell

For the best flavor and texture, be sure to bake the piecrust until golden all over.

PREP 15 minutes plus chilling
BAKE 20 minutes
MAKES 1 piecrust or tart shell.

Pastry Dough for 1-Crust Pie, Pastry Dough for 9-Inch Tart, or Pastry Dough for 11-Inch Tart (page 136 and 137)

1 Prepare pastry dough as directed through chilling.
2 Preheat oven to 425°F. Use dough to line 9-inch pie plate, 9-inch tart pan with removable bottom, or 11-inch tart pan with removable bottom. If using pie plate, make decorative edge. Refrigerate or freeze until firm, 10 to 15 minutes.
3 Line pie or tart shell with foil; fill with pie weights or dry beans. Bake 15 minutes. Remove foil with weights; bake until golden, 5 to 10 minutes longer. If shell puffs up during baking, gently press it down with back of spoon. Cool on wire rack. Fill (and bake) as directed in recipe.

Apple Pie

Make with a combination of apples, such as Braeburn, Granny Smith, and Golden Delicious. You can also use half brown sugar and half granulated sugar.

PREP 45 minutes plus chilling • **BAKE** 1 hour 20 minutes • **MAKES** 10 servings.

Pastry Dough for 2-Crust Pie (page 134)
⅔ cup sugar
2 tablespoons all-purpose flour
½ teaspoon ground cinnamon
⅛ teaspoon salt
3 pounds cooking apples (9 medium), peeled,
    cored, and thinly sliced
1 tablespoon fresh lemon juice
1 tablespoon butter or margarine,
    cut into pieces

1 Prepare pastry dough as directed through chilling.

2 Preheat oven to 425°F. In large bowl, with wire whisk, mix sugar, flour, cinnamon, and salt. Add apples and lemon juice; gently toss to combine.

3 Use larger disk of dough to line 9-inch pie plate. Trim edge, leaving 1-inch overhang. Spoon apple filling into crust; dot with butter. Roll out remaining disk of dough; cut out center circle and 1-inch slits to allow steam to escape during baking. Center dough over filling. Fold overhang under and make decorative edge.

4 Place pie on foil-lined cookie sheet to catch any overflow during baking. Bake 20 minutes. Turn oven control to 375°F; bake until filling bubbles in center, about 1 hour longer. If necessary, cover pie loosely with foil during last 20 minutes of baking to prevent overbrowning. Cool on wire rack 1 hour to serve warm, or cool completely to serve later.

EACH SERVING About 369 calories, 3g protein, 55g carbohydrate, 16g total fat (8g saturated), 28mg cholesterol, 251mg sodium.

APPLE-SPICE PIE
Prepare dough and filling as directed, but in Step 2 whisk *1 teaspoon ground cinnamon, ½ teaspoon ground ginger, and ¼ teaspoon ground nutmeg* with other dry ingredients.

Upside-Down Apple Tart (Tarte Tatin)

This classic French dessert is simply a caramelized apple tart baked in an oven-safe skillet. Serve it warm with vanilla ice cream.

PREP 55 minutes plus chilling and cooling • **COOK/BAKE** 45 minutes • **MAKES** 10 servings.

Pastry Dough for 11-inch Tart (page 137)
1 cup sugar
6 tablespoons butter or margarine
1 tablespoon fresh lemon juice
3½ pounds Golden Delicious apples (about
    9 medium), peeled, cored, and cut
    in half

1 Preheat oven to 425°F. Prepare pastry as directed, but do not chill before rolling. On lightly floured surface, with floured rolling pin, roll dough into 12-inch round. Transfer to cookie sheet and refrigerate until ready to use.
2 In heavy 12-inch skillet with oven-safe handle (if skillet is not oven-safe, wrap handle in double layer of foil), heat sugar, butter, and lemon juice to boiling over medium-high heat. Place apples in skillet cut side down, overlapping them slightly if necessary. Cook 10 minutes. Carefully turn apples rounded side down; cook until syrup has thickened slightly and turned amber in color, 10 to 12 minutes longer. Remove from heat.
3 Remove dough from cookie sheet and place on top of apples in skillet. Carefully tuck edge of dough under to form rim around apples. With knife, cut six ½-inch-long slits in dough to allow steam to escape during baking. Bake until crust is golden, about 25 minutes. Remove from oven; cool on wire rack 10 minutes.
4 To unmold, place large round platter upside down over skillet. Grasping platter and skillet firmly together, very carefully and quickly flip skillet over to invert tart onto platter (do this over sink since tart may be extremely juicy). Cool 30 minutes to serve warm, or cool completely to serve later.

EACH SERVING About 380 calories, 2g protein, 51g carbohydrate, 20g total fat (11g saturated), 46mg cholesterol, 290mg sodium.

PEACH TARTE TATIN
Prepare dough and filling as directed, but substitute *3¾ pounds firm-ripe peaches (11 medium),* peeled, halved, and pitted, for apples. Bake and cool as directed.

EACH SERVING About 365 calories, 3g protein, 49g carbohydrate, 19g total fat (11g saturated), 43mg cholesterol, 280mg sodium.

PEAR TARTE TATIN
Prepare dough and filling as directed, but substitute *3¾ pounds firm-ripe Bosc pears (about 7),* peeled, cored, and halved lengthwise, for apples. Bake and cool as directed.

EACH SERVING About 405 calories, 3g protein, 58g carbohydrate, 19g total fat (11g saturated), 43mg cholesterol, 280mg sodium.

Upside-Down Apple Tart (Tarte Tatin)

Apple-Frangipane Tart

Frangipane is the French name for a rich pastry filling/topping whose principal ingredient is ground almonds or almond paste.

PREP 35 minutes plus chilling and cooling • **BAKE** 1 hour 20 minutes • **MAKES** 12 servings.

Pastry Dough for 11-inch Tart (page 137)

FRANGIPANE FILLING
1 tube or can (7 to 8 ounces) almond paste, crumbled
4 tablespoons butter or margarine, softened
½ cup sugar
¼ teaspoon salt
2 large eggs
¼ cup all-purpose flour

APPLE TOPPING
1¼ pounds Granny Smith apples (about 3 medium)
¼ cup apricot jam
1 tablespoon almond-flavored liqueur

1 Prepare pastry dough as directed through chilling.

2 Preheat oven to 425°F. Use dough to line 11-inch round tart pan with removable bottom. Fold overhang in and press dough against side of pan so it extends ⅛ inch above rim. Refrigerate 30 minutes, or freeze until firm, about 10 minutes.

3 Line tart shell with foil; fill with pie weights or dry beans. Bake 15 minutes. Remove foil with weights; bake until golden, 5 to 10 minutes longer. If shell puffs up during baking, gently press it down with back of spoon. Transfer tart shell in pan to wire rack. Turn oven control to 375°F.

4 Meanwhile, prepare filling: In food processor with knife blade attached, pulse almond paste, butter, sugar, and salt until mixture is crumbly. Add eggs and pulse until smooth, scraping bowl with rubber spatula if necessary. (There may be some tiny lumps.) Add flour and pulse just until combined.

5 Peel, halve, and core apples. Cut each half crosswise into very thin slices. Spoon almond filling into warm tart shell; spread evenly. Arrange apple slices in concentric circles over filling, closely overlapping them. Bake until apples are tender when pierced with tip of knife, 1 hour to 1 hour and 10 minutes. Cool slightly in pan on wire rack.

6 Meanwhile, in 1-quart saucepan, heat jam and liqueur over low heat until jam has melted, about 2 minutes. Press jam mixture through sieve into small bowl. Brush jam mixture over warm apple slices. Finish cooling tart on wire rack.

7 When cool, carefully remove side of pan. Serve tart at room temperature or refrigerate up to 1 day. If tart is refrigerated, let stand at room temperature at least 1 hour before serving.

EACH SERVING About 360 calories, 5g protein, 41g carbohydrate, 21g total fat (9g saturated), 68mg cholesterol, 285mg sodium.

OPPOSITE: Apple-Frangipane Tart

PEAR-FRANGIPANE TART

Prepare dough and filling as directed, but substitute *1½ pounds Bartlett or Anjou pears,* peeled, cored, and thinly sliced for the apples. Bake and cool as directed.

EACH SERVING About 340 calories, 5g protein, 37g carbohydrate, 20g total fat (8g saturated), 66mg cholesterol, 275mg sodium.

PEACH- OR NECTARINE-FRANGIPANE TART

Prepare dough and filling as directed, but substitute *1¼ pounds peaches (about 5),* peeled, pitted, and thinly sliced, or *1¼ pounds nectarines (about 5),* pitted and thinly sliced for the apples. Bake and cool as directed.

EACH SERVING About 330 calories, 5g protein, 34g carbohydrate, 19g total fat (8g saturated), 66mg cholesterol, 275mg sodium.

TART CHERRY-FRANGIPANE TART

Prepare dough and filling as directed, but substitute *1½ pounds tart cherries (1 quart),* pitted and drained for the apples. Bake and cool as directed.

EACH SERVING About 330 calories, 5g protein, 34g carbohydrate, 20g total fat (8g saturated), 66mg cholesterol, 275mg sodium.

APRICOT-FRANGIPANE TART

Prepare dough and filling as directed, but substitute *1 pound fresh apricots,* pitted and each cut into 4 wedges for the apples. Bake and cool as directed.

EACH SERVING About 330 calories, 6g protein, 34g carbohydrate, 20g total fat (8g saturated), 66mg cholesterol, 275mg sodium.

Apple Crumble Pie

This is simply a more elegant and richer version of a classic apple pie: A sour cream–enriched apple filling is topped with a sweet nutty crumb mixture.

PREP 30 minute plus chilling and cooling • **BAKE** 2 hours • **MAKES** 10 servings.

Prebaked Piecrust (page 140)

CRUMB TOPPING

½ cup all-purpose flour

½ cup packed brown sugar

½ teaspoon ground cinnamon

6 tablespoons cold butter or margarine, cut into pieces

½ cup chopped walnuts

APPLE FILLING

⅓ cup granulated sugar

2 tablespoons all-purpose flour

⅛ teaspoon ground nutmeg

⅛ teaspoon ground ginger

⅛ teaspoon salt

1 container (8 ounces) sour cream

2 teaspoons fresh lemon juice

1 teaspoon vanilla extract

2 pounds Granny Smith apples or other tart cooking apples (6 medium), peeled, cored, and cut into ½-inch-thick wedges

1 Prepare and baked piecrust as directed on page 140, but reduce baking time after removing foil with pie weights to 10 to 12 minutes. Cool in pan on wire rack. Turn oven control to 400°F.

2 Prepare topping: In medium bowl, with wire whisk, mix flour, brown sugar, and cinnamon. With pastry blender or two knives used scissor-fashion, cut in butter until mixture resembles coarse crumbs. Stir in walnuts; cover and refrigerate topping.

3 Prepare filling: In large bowl, mix granulated sugar, flour, nutmeg, ginger, and salt. Add sour cream, lemon juice, and vanilla; whisk until smooth. Stir in apples. Spoon filling into cooled pie shell. Sprinkle topping evenly over filling.

4 Place sheet of foil under pie plate; crimp foil edges to form rim to catch any overflow during baking. Bake pie 30 minutes. Turn oven control to 350°F. Bake pie until apples are tender when pierced with tip of sharp knife, 1 hour and 10 to 15 minutes longer. If necessary, cover pie loosely with foil during last 20 minutes of baking to prevent overbrowning. Cool pie on wire rack 1 hour to serve warm, or cool completely to serve later. Refrigerate any leftovers.

EACH SERVING About 420 calories, 5g protein, 47g carbohydrate, 25g total fat (12g saturated), 43mg cholesterol, 230mg sodium.

Apple Galette

This no-fuss free-form tart is baked on a cookie sheet instead of in a tart pan for a more casual look.

PREP 40 minutes plus chilling • **BAKE** 45 minutes • **MAKES** 8 servings.

Pastry Dough for 1-Crust Pie (page 136)
2 pounds Golden Delicious apples (6 medium)
¼ cup sugar
2 tablespoons butter or margarine,
    cut into pieces
2 tablespoons apricot preserves

1 Prepare pastry dough as directed through chilling.

2 Preheat oven to 425°F. On lightly floured surface, with floured rolling pin, roll dough into 15-inch round. Transfer to ungreased large cookie sheet; refrigerate.

3 Peel apples; cut in half. With melon baller, remove cores. Cut apples crosswise into ¼-inch-thick slices. Arrange apple slices on dough round in concentric circles, overlapping slices and leaving 1½-inch border. Sprinkle apples evenly with sugar and dot with butter. Fold border of dough over apples.

4 Place two sheets of foil under cookie sheet; crimp foil edges to form rim to catch any overflow during baking. Bake galette until apples are tender, about 45 minutes. Transfer cookie sheet to wire rack.

5 In small saucepan, heat apricot preserves over low heat until bubbling. Press preserves through sieve into small bowl. Brush preserves over apples. Cool galette slightly to serve warm.

EACH SERVING About 270 calories, 2g protein, 39g carbohydrate, 12g total fat (6g saturated), 23mg cholesterol, 162mg sodium.

Test Kitchen Tip

GALETTES GALORE
The French word *galette* is applied to many different foods—all of them round and flat. The French twelfth-night cake, called *Galette du Roi*, or King's Cake, is made of flaky pastry; a lucky bean (or small porcelain figurine) is baked into the cake. In Eastern Brittany, both flour crêpes and buckwheat crêpes are called galettes, while in burgundy, *Galettes Flamades* are orange-flavored hazelnut tartlets. A flat cake formed of thin potato slices is a *Galette de Pommes de Terre*.

Apple Turnovers

Steamed apple dumplings and fried apple pies appear in many nineteenth-century cookbooks. Small half-moon turnovers appear to be a twentieth-century creation, often called "children's pies," as they're just the right size for children to eat out of hand. Turnovers similar to ours are found in Charleston Receipts, *recipes collected by the Junior League of Charleston in 1950. Fannie Farmer does not include any turnovers in her 1923 cookbook. However, in the 1990* Fannie Farmer Baking Book, *by Marion Cunningham, there are six different turnovers. All are made with pastry rounds that are filled and folded in half, then crimped closed with fork tines.*

PREP 1 hour plus chilling and cooling • **COOK/BAKE** 45 minutes • **MAKES** 14 turnovers.

Pastry Dough for 2-Crust Pie (page 134)
3 tablespoons plus ⅓ cup granulated sugar
2 tablespoons butter or margarine
2 large Granny Smith apples (1½ pounds),
    peeled, cored, and chopped
1 tablespoon cornstarch
¼ teaspoon ground cinnamon
pinch salt
1 teaspoon fresh lemon juice
1 large egg, beaten
1 cup confectioners' sugar
2 tablespoons warm water
2 teaspoons light corn syrup
½ teaspoon vanilla extract

1 Prepare pastry dough as directed through chilling, but in Step 1, add 2 tablespoons granulated sugar along with flour.

2 In 10-inch skillet, melt butter over medium-high heat. Add apples, ⅓ cup granulated sugar, cornstarch, cinnamon, and salt; cook, stirring, until apples are tender, about 8 minutes. Add lemon juice; set aside to cool completely.

3 On lightly floured surface, with floured rolling pin, roll 1 disk of dough into round about ⅛ inch thick. Using 5-inch round plate as guide, cut out 5 dough rounds. Repeat with remaining dough; reroll trimmings. You should have 14 dough rounds in all.

4 Preheat oven to 400°F. Grease two large cookie sheets.

5 Onto half of each dough round, place 1 heaping tablespoon apple filling; fold dough over filling. With fork, firmly press edges together to seal. Place turnovers, 2 inches apart, on prepared cookie sheets. With pastry brush, brush turnovers with beaten egg and sprinkle with remaining 1 tablespoon granulated sugar. With small sharp knife, cut two 1-inch slits in top of each turnover to allow steam to escape during baking. Bake 15 minutes. Turn oven control to 350°F. Bake until golden brown, 20 to 25 minutes longer. Cool on wire racks.

6 Meanwhile, in small bowl, combine confectioners' sugar, water, corn syrup, and vanilla; stir until smooth and spreadable. Drizzle icing over cooled turnovers; let set before serving.

EACH TURNOVER About 290 calories, 3g protein, 41g carbohydrate, 13g total fat (6g saturated), 37mg cholesterol, 185mg sodium.

Apple Turnovers

Rustic Apricot Crostata

In Italy, desserts are a bit more straightforward than in the United States but no less delicious, as this lovely lattice-topped tart demonstrates. On a slight departure from the traditional, we've replaced some of the flour in the crust with ground toasted almonds for extra flavor.

PREP 45 minutes plus chilling • **BAKE** 40 minutes • **MAKES** 12 servings.

½ cup blanched almonds, toasted
   (see page 13)
3 tablespoons cornstarch
2½ cups all-purpose flour
¼ teaspoon salt
1 cup butter (2 sticks), softened
   (do not use margarine)
½ cup plus 2 teaspoons sugar
1 large egg plus 1 large egg yolk
2 teaspoons vanilla extract
1 jar (12 ounces) apricot preserves (1 cup)
1 tablespoon water

1 In food processor with knife blade attached, finely grind toasted almonds with cornstarch. In medium bowl, with wire whisk, mix almond mixture, flour, and salt.

2 In large bowl, with mixer at high speed, beat butter and ½ cup sugar until creamy. Add 1 egg and vanilla; beat until almost combined (mixture will look curdled). With wooden spoon, stir in flour mixture until dough begins to form. With hands, press dough together in bowl. Shape dough into 2 disks, one slightly larger than the other. Wrap each in plastic wrap and refrigerate 1 hour 30 minutes to 2 hours.

3 Preheat oven to 375°F. Remove both pieces of dough from refrigerator. On lightly floured surface, with floured rolling pin, roll out larger disk of dough into 14-inch round. Use dough to line 11-inch tart pan with removable bottom.

Fold overhang in and press dough against side of pan (so it extends ⅛ inch above rim).

4 On lightly floured waxed paper, roll remaining disk of dough into 12-inch round. With pastry wheel or knife, cut dough into twelve 1-inch-wide strips. Refrigerate 15 minutes.

5 Spread preserves evenly over dough in tart pan to within ½ inch of edge. Make lattice top: Place 5 dough strips, 1 inch apart, across tart, trimming ends even with side of tart pan; repeat with 5 more strips placed diagonally across first ones to make diamond lattice pattern. Trim ends and reserve trimmings.

6 Make rope edge for tart shell: With hands, roll trimmings and remaining 2 strips of dough into ¼ inch-thick ropes. Press ropes around edge of tart to create finished edge.

7 In cup, with fork, beat egg yolk and water. Brush egg-yolk mixture over lattice and edge of tart; sprinkle with remaining 2 teaspoons sugar. Bake until crust is deep golden, 40 to 45 minutes. Check tart occasionally during first 30 minutes of baking; if crust puffs up, prick with tip of knife. Cool on wire rack. Remove side of pan to serve.

EACH SERVING: About 390 calories, 5g protein, 50g carbohydrate, 20g total fat (10g saturated), 77mg cholesterol, 220mg sodium.

Rustic Apricot Crostata

Buttery Apricot Tart

The rich crust for this elegant fruit tart has a bit of extra sugar to balance the tartness of the fresh apricots.

PREP 20 minutes plus cooling • **BAKE** 1 hour 10 minutes • **MAKES** 8 servings.

SWEET PASTRY DOUGH
1¼ cups all-purpose flour
¼ cup sugar
¼ teaspoon salt
7 tablespoons butter or margarine,
    cut into pieces

APRICOT FILLING
¼ cup sugar
1½ teaspoons all-purpose flour
1½ pounds apricots (8 to 10 large),
    cut in half and pitted
2 tablespoons plain dried bread crumbs
confectioners' sugar
2 tablespoons chopped shelled pistachios

1 Preheat oven to 375°F.

2 Prepare dough: In medium bowl, with wire whisk, mix flour, sugar, and salt. With pastry blender or two knives used scissor-fashion, cut in butter until mixture resembles coarse crumbs. With hand, press dough together in bowl. Press dough onto bottom and up side of 11-inch fluted tart pan with removable bottom. Trim edge even with rim of pan. Bake tart shell 20 minutes.

3 Meanwhile, prepare filling: In medium bowl, with wire whisk, mix sugar and flour. Add apricots and toss to coat.

4 Sprinkle hot tart shell with bread crumbs. Arrange apricot halves, cut side down in shell. Bake until shell is golden and apricots are tender, 50 to 55 minutes. Cool tart in pan on wire rack.

5 To serve, carefully remove side of tart pan. Sprinkle edge of tart with confectioners' sugar. Sprinkle tart with pistachios.

EACH SERVING: About 265 calories, 4g protein, 37g carbohydrate, 12g total fat (7g saturated), 29mg cholesterol, 200mg sodium.

> **Test Kitchen Tip** This sweet pastry dough for Buttery Apricot Tart can be made in a food processor with knife blade attached. Combine all ingredients and pulse just until dough comes together.

Buttery Apricot Tart

Warm Banana-Pecan Tart

To keep last-minute preparation to a minimum, bake the crust up to two days ahead. Prepare the toasted pecan cream up to one day in advance and refrigerate. Then simply assemble the tart just before serving.

PREP 1 hour plus chilling • **BAKE/BROIL** 32 minutes • **MAKES** 12 servings.

Pastry Dough for 11-Inch Tart (page 137)
½ cup pecans, toasted (see page 13)
½ cup plus 1 tablespoon sugar
3 large egg yolks
1 tablespoon cornstarch
¾ cup half-and-half or light cream
2 tablespoons butter or margarine,
   cut into pieces
1 teaspoon vanilla extract
5 ripe medium bananas (2 pounds)

1 Prepare pastry dough as directed through chilling.

2 Prepare pecan cream: In blender or in food processor with knife blade attached, pulse pecans and ¼ cup sugar until pecans are very finely ground.

3 In small bowl, with wire whisk, mix egg yolks, ¼ cup sugar, and cornstarch until blended. In 2-quart saucepan, heat half-and-half to simmering over medium-high heat. While whisking constantly, gradually pour about half of simmering cream into egg-yolk mixture in bowl. Return egg-yolk mixture to saucepan and cook over low heat, whisking constantly, until mixture has thickened (do not boil), 4 to 5 minutes. Stir in pecan mixture, butter, and vanilla; cook, stirring, until butter has melted. Transfer pecan-cream mixture to medium bowl. Press plastic wrap directly onto surface and refrigerate at least 30 minutes or up to overnight.

4 Meanwhile, preheat oven to 425°F. Use dough to line 11-inch tart pan with removable bottom. Fold overhang in and press dough against side of pan so it extends ⅛ inch above rim. Refrigerate or freeze shell until firm, 10 to 15 minutes.

5 Line tart shell with foil; fill with pie weights or dry beans. Bake 15 minutes. Remove foil with weights; bake until golden, 5 to 10 minutes longer. If shell puffs up during baking, gently press it down with back of spoon. Transfer pan to wire rack. Turn oven control to broil.

6 Cut bananas on diagonal into thin slices. Arrange banana slices, overlapping slightly, in tart shell. Spoon chilled pecan-cream filling over bananas and sprinkle with remaining 1 tablespoon sugar. Cover edge of shell with foil to prevent overbrowning. Place at position closest to heat source and broil until top is lightly caramelized, 1 to 2 minutes. Carefully remove side of pan. Serve warm.

EACH SERVING About 315 calories, 4g protein, 36g carbohydrate, 18g total fat (8g saturated), 85mg cholesterol, 203mg sodium.

Blueberry-Almond Tart

Sweet summer blueberries and a buttery almond filling are a perfect combination in this heavenly tart!

PREP 45 minutes plus cooling • **BAKE** 1 hour 10 minutes • **MAKES** 12 servings.

Pastry Dough for 11-inch Tart (page 137)
1 tube or can (7 to 8 ounces) almond
     paste, broken into 1-inch pieces
4 tablespoons butter or margarine,
     softened
½ cup sugar
¼ teaspoon salt
2 large eggs
2 teaspoons vanilla extract
¼ cup all-purpose flour
1½ cups blueberries

1 Prepare pastry dough as directed through chilling.

2 Preheat oven to 375°F. Use dough to line 11-inch tart pan with removable bottom. Fold overhang in and press dough against side of pan so it extends ⅛ inch above rim.

3 Line tart shell with foil; fill with pie weights or dry beans. Bake 20 minutes. Remove foil with weights; bake until golden, 8 to 10 minutes longer. (If shell puffs up during baking, gently press it down with back of spoon.) Transfer pan to wire rack.

4 Meanwhile, prepare filling: In large bowl, with mixer at medium speed, beat almond paste, butter, sugar, and salt until evenly blended, scraping bowl frequently with rubber spatula (mixture will resemble coarse crumbs). Add eggs and vanilla. Increase speed to medium-high, and beat until blended. (There may be some tiny lumps.) With wooden spoon, stir in flour.

5 Pour almond-paste mixture into warm tart shell; spread evenly. Scatter blueberries evenly over filling. Bake until golden, 40 to 45 minutes. Cool in pan on wire rack. When cool, carefully remove side from pan.

EACH SERVING About 325 calories, 5g protein, 34g carbohydrate, 20g total fat (5g saturated), 48mg cholesterol, 295mg sodium.

Very Blueberry Pie

We like to serve this pie with cinnamon-scented whipped cream. Or, if you prefer, add a pinch of cinnamon or grated lemon peel to the filling.

PREP 25 minutes plus chilling • **BAKE** 1 hour 20 minutes • **MAKES** 10 servings.

Pastry Dough for 2-Crust Pie (page 134)
¾ cup sugar
¼ cup cornstarch
pinch salt
6 cups blueberries (3 pints)
1 tablespoon fresh lemon juice
2 tablespoons butter or margarine,
    cut into pieces

1 Prepare pastry dough as directed through chilling.

2 Preheat oven to 425°F.

3 In large bowl, with wire whisk, mix sugar, cornstarch, and salt. Add blueberries and lemon juice; toss to combine.

4 Use larger disk of dough to line 9-inch pie plate. Trim edge, leaving 1-inch overhang. Spoon blueberry filling into crust; dot with butter. Roll out remaining disk of dough; cut out ¾-inch center circle and cut 1-inch slits to allow steam to escape during baking. Center dough over filling. Fold overhang under and make decorative edge.

5 Place pie on foil-lined cookie sheet to catch any overflow during baking. Bake 20 minutes. Turn oven control to 375°F; bake until filling bubbles and crust is golden, about 1 hour longer.

If necessary, cover pie loosely with foil during last 20 minutes of baking to prevent overbrowning. Cool on wire rack 1 hour to serve warm, or cool completely to serve later.

EACH SERVING About 374 calories, 4g protein, 53g carbohydrate, 17g total fat (8g saturated), 31mg cholesterol, 253mg sodium.

 Test Kitchen Tip

FINISHING THE PIE TOP

When making a double-crust pie, the top crust should always have an opening for the steam to escape. It could be slits, a penny-size hole in the center, or tiny decorative cutouts. You can also glaze the crust before baking:

To brown the crust, brush with milk, half-and-half, or heavy cream.

For a shiny top crust, brush with lightly beaten egg white.

For a golden crust, brush with beaten whole egg or egg yolk.

To add sparkle, sprinkle lightly with granulated sugar.

Very Blueberry Pie

Double Blueberry Pie

In this old New England recipe, the blueberry flavor is maximized by stirring raw berries into the cooked filling. We like it with a simple gingersnap crust to make it especially easy for casual summer entertaining. The recipe has been so popular over the years that we have developed some delicious variations using other fresh fruits (below). See photo on page 132.

PREP 30 minutes plus cooling and chilling • **COOK/BAKE** 8 minutes • **MAKES** 10 servings.

1⅔ cups gingersnap cookie crumbs
   (25 cookies)
5 tablespoons butter or margarine, melted
2 tablespoons plus ½ cup sugar
2 tablespoons cornstarch
2 tablespoons cold water
3 pints blueberries
whipped cream (optional)

1 Preheat oven to 375°F. In 9-inch pie plate, with fork, mix cookie crumbs, melted butter, and 2 tablespoons sugar until crumbs are evenly moistened. With hand, press mixture firmly onto bottom and up side of pie plate. Bake 8 minutes. Cool on wire rack.

2 In 2-quart saucepan, blend cornstarch and water until smooth. Add half of blueberries and remaining ½ cup sugar to cornstarch mixture; heat to boiling over medium-high heat, pressing blueberries against side of saucepan with back of spoon. Boil, stirring constantly, 1 minute. Remove from heat; stir in remaining blueberries.

3 Pour blueberry filling into cooled crust. Press plastic wrap directly onto surface and refrigerate until thoroughly chilled, about 5 hours. Serve with whipped cream, if desired.

EACH SERVING About 241 calories, 2g protein, 42g carbohydrate, 8g total fat (4g saturated), 16mg cholesterol, 201mg sodium.

APRICOT AND BLACKBERRY PIE

Prepare as directed, but substitute *1¼ cups graham-cracker crumbs (11 rectangular graham crackers)* for gingersnap cookie crumbs in Step 1. Substitute *2 pounds ripe apricots,* halved, pitted, and each half cut into 4 wedges, and *½ pint blackberries (about 1½ cups)* for blueberries. Fill and bake as directed.

PEACH AND RASPBERRY PIE

Prepare as directed, but substitute *1¼ cups vanilla wafer crumbs (about 35 cookies)* for gingersnap cookie crumbs in Step 1. Substitute *2 pounds ripe peaches,* peeled, or *nectarines,* unpeeled, each halved and pitted, and each half cut into 4 wedges, and *1 pint raspberries (about 3 cups)* for blueberries. Fill and bake as directed.

Tart Cherry Pie

If you see tart (sour) cherries in your farmers' market, buy enough to make several desserts as well as some to freeze. Invest in a cherry pitter; it makes quick work of removing the pits.

PREP 1 hour plus chilling • **BAKE** 1 hour 20 minutes • **MAKES** 10 servings.

Pastry Dough for 2-Crust Pie (page 134)
1 cup sugar
¼ cup cornstarch
pinch salt
2¼ pounds tart (sour) cherries, pitted
   (4½ cups)
1 tablespoon butter or margarine,
   cut into pieces

EACH SERVING About 381 calories, 4g protein, 57g carbohydrate, 16g total fat (8g saturated), 28mg cholesterol, 239mg sodium.

1 Prepare pastry dough as directed through chilling.

2 Preheat oven to 425°F. In large bowl, with wire whisk, mix sugar, cornstarch, and salt. Add cherries and toss to combine.

3 Use larger disk of dough to line 9-inch pie plate. Trim edge, leaving 1-inch overhang. Spoon cherry filling into crust; dot with butter. Roll out remaining disk of dough; cut out ¾-inch center circle and cut 1-inch slits to allow steam to escape during baking. Center dough over filling. Fold overhang under and make decorative edge.

4 Place pie on foil-lined cookie sheet to catch any overflow during baking. Bake 20 minutes. Turn oven control to 375°F; bake until filling bubbles in center, 1 hour to 1 hour 10 minutes longer. If necessary, cover pie loosely with foil during last 20 minutes of baking to prevent overbrowning. Cool on wire rack 1 hour to serve warm, or cool completely to serve later.

FROZEN TART CHERRY PIE
Prepare as directed, but use *1¼ cups sugar, 1 bag (20 ounces) frozen tart cherries,* thawed (with their juice), and *⅓ cup cornstarch.*

CANNED CHERRY PIE
Prepare as directed, but use *2 cans (16 ounces each) pitted tart (sour) cherries packed in water.* Drain; reserve ½ cup cherry juice. In medium bowl, combine *¾ cup sugar, ¼ cup cornstarch, ⅛ teaspoon ground cinnamon,* and *pinch salt.* Add reserved cherry juice, cherries, and *½ teaspoon vanilla;* toss to combine.

Farm-Stand Cherry Pie

This beautiful pie is made with a cornmeal crust that adds both flavor and texture.

PREP 45 minutes plus chilling • **BAKE** 45 minutes • **MAKES** 6 servings.

1½ cups all-purpose flour
⅓ cup plus 1 tablespoon cornmeal
⅔ cup plus 1 teaspoon sugar
½ teaspoon plus ⅛ teaspoon salt
½ cup cold butter or margarine (1 stick),
    cut into pieces
4 to 5 tablespoons cold water
2 tablespoons plus 1 teaspoon cornstarch
1½ pounds dark sweet cherries, pitted
1 large egg white

1 Preheat oven to 425°F. In medium bowl, with wire whisk, mix flour, ⅓ cup cornmeal, ⅓ cup sugar, and ½ teaspoon salt. With pastry blender or two knives used scissor-fashion, cut in butter until mixture resembles coarse crumbs. Sprinkle water, 1 tablespoon at a time, into flour mixture, mixing with hands until dough comes together. (It will feel dry at first.) Shape dough into ball.
2 Sprinkle large cookie sheet with remaining 1 tablespoon cornmeal. Place dampened towel under cookie sheet to prevent it from slipping. On cookie sheet with floured rolling pin, roll dough into 13-inch round. With long metal spatula, gently loosen round from cookie sheet.
3 In large bowl, with wire whisk, mix ⅓ cup sugar and cornstarch. Sprinkle half of sugar mixture over center of dough round, leaving 2½-inch border. Add cherries and any cherry juice to sugar mixture remaining in bowl; toss well. With slotted spoon, spoon cherry mixture over sugared area on dough round (reserve any cherry-juice mixture in bowl). Fold dough up around cherries, leaving 4-inch opening in center. Pinch dough to seal any cracks.

4 In cup, beat egg white and remaining ⅛ teaspoon salt. Brush egg-white mixture over dough; sprinkle with remaining 1 teaspoon sugar. Pour cherry-juice mixture over cherries. Refrigerate until well chilled, about 30 minutes.
5 Bake pie until crust is golden brown and cherry mixture bubbles gently, 45 to 50 minutes. If necessary, cover pie loosely with foil during last 10 minutes of baking to prevent overbrowning.
6 As soon as pie is done, use long metal spatula to loosen it from cookie sheet to prevent sticking. Cool 15 minutes on cookie sheet, then slide onto wire rack to cool completely.

EACH SERVING About 460 calories, 6g protein, 74g carbohydrate, 17g total fat (10g saturated), 42mg cholesterol, 387mg sodium.

STARCHES IN FRUIT PIES

In fruit pies, starches thicken the juice that is released as the pie bakes. Which one you use is a matter of personal preference: How do you want the cooked pie filling to look? Flour produces an opaque gel filling, whereas cornstarch produces a clearer gel filling with a glossy appearance. Root starches such as arrowroot and tapioca produce an almost translucent gel filling. (You'll need about half as much cornstarch or root starch as flour for the same thickening power.) Be sure to store all starches in airtight containers in a dry place; otherwise, they can lose their potency.

Farm-Stand Cherry Pie

Cherry Hand Pies

These turnover-like mini pies are perfect to take on a summer picnic or to the beach—no messy cutting necessary. Just unwrap and eat!

PREP 1 hour plus chilling and cooling • **BAKE** 25 minutes • **MAKES** 14 pies.

CHERRY FILLING
1 pound tart cherries (3 cups), stems removed
½ cup sugar
1 tablespoon butter or margarine
pinch salt
2 tablespoons cornstarch
2 tablespoons water

SOUR-CREAM PASTRY
2¼ cups all-purpose flour
2 tablespoons sugar
½ teaspoon salt
½ cup cold butter or margarine (1 stick),
   cut into pieces
¼ cup vegetable shortening
⅓ cup sour cream
about 4 teaspoons cold water
1 large egg, lightly beaten
1 tablespoon sugar

1 Prepare filling: With cherry pitter, remove pits from cherries over 10-inch skillet to catch juice; discard pits. To same skillet, add cherries, sugar, butter, and salt; cook over medium-high heat, stirring frequently, until mixture simmers and sugar has dissolved, 3 minutes.

2 In cup, blend cornstarch with 2 tablespoons water until smooth; add to cherry mixture and cook, stirring frequently, until mixture thickens, 1 to 2 minutes longer. Transfer filling to medium bowl; cover and refrigerate until chilled, about 1 hour.

3 While filling is chilling, prepare pastry: In medium bowl, with wire whisk, mix flour, sugar, and salt. With pastry blender or two knives used scissor-fashion, cut in butter and shortening until mixture resembles coarse crumbs. Add sour cream and sprinkle about 4 teaspoons cold water, 1 teaspoon at a time, into flour mixture, mixing lightly with fork after each addition until dough is just moist enough to hold together. Shape dough into 2 disks. Wrap each disk in plastic wrap, and refrigerate until firm enough to roll, about 30 minutes.

4 Preheat oven to 375°F. Grease two large cookie sheets. On lightly floured surface, with floured rolling pin, roll 1 disk of dough into 12-inch round. Using 5-inch round plate as guide, cut out 4 rounds from dough; reserve trimmings. Repeat with remaining dough. Reroll trimmings to make 14 rounds in all.

5 Into center of each dough round, spoon 1 heaping tablespoon filling. With pastry brush, brush edge of each round with some beaten egg. Fold dough over filling. With fork, firmly press edges together to seal. With wide metal spatula, transfer pies to prepared cookie sheets. Brush tops of pies with beaten egg. With fork, poke several holes in tops of pies to allow steam to escape during baking; sprinkle with 1 tablespoon sugar. Bake pies until golden brown, about 25 minutes. Transfer pies to wire rack to cool.

EACH PIE About 240 calories, 3g protein, 30g carbohydrate, 13g total fat (6g saturated), 37mg cholesterol, 177mg sodium.

Cherry Hand Pies

Cranberry-Pear Pie

You'll need ripe, sweet pears to help balance the tartness of the cranberries, so be sure to buy the pears a few days ahead of time, as they'll likely need time to ripen.

PREP 45 minutes plus chilling • **BAKE** 1 hour 20 to 30 minutes • **MAKES** 10 servings.

Pastry Dough for 2-Crust Pie (page 134)
¾ cup plus 1 tablespoon sugar
3 tablespoons cornstarch
⅛ teaspoon ground cinnamon
1½ cups cranberries, coarsely chopped
3 pounds fully-ripe pears (6 large), peeled, cored, and sliced
2 tablespoons butter or margarine, cut into pieces
1 large egg white, lightly beaten

1 Prepare dough as directed through chilling.
2 Preheat oven to 425°F. In large bowl, with wire whisk, mix ¾ cup sugar, cornstarch, and cinnamon. Add cranberries and pears; toss to combine.
3 Use larger disk of dough to line 9-inch pie plate. Trim edge, leaving 1-inch overhang. Spoon filling into crust; dot with butter. Roll out remaining disk of dough; cut out ¾-inch center circle and cut 1-inch slits to allow steam to escape during baking. Center dough over filling. Fold overhang under and make decorative edge. Brush crust with beaten egg white; sprinkle with remaining 1 tablespoon sugar.
4 Place pie on foil-lined cookie sheet to catch any overflow during baking. Bake 20 minutes. Turn oven control to 375°F. Bake until filling bubbles in center, 60 to 70 minutes longer. If necessary, cover loosely with foil during last 20 minutes of baking to prevent overbrowning. Cool on wire rack 1 hour to serve warm, or cool completely to serve later.

EACH SERVING About 415 calories, 4g protein, 63g carbohydrate, 17g total fat (9g saturated), 31mg cholesterol, 240mg sodium.

CRANBERRY-APPLE PIE
Prepare dough and filling as directed, but substitute *3 pounds Golden Delicious or Gala apples,* peeled, cored, and sliced, for pears. Bake and cool as directed.

EACH SERVING About 410 calories, 4g protein, 62g carbohydrate, 17g total fat (9g saturated), 31mg cholesterol, 240mg sodium.

Test Kitchen Tip **PROTECTING EDGES OF PIECRUST**
To keep pie crust edges from overbrowning, fold a 12-inch square of foil into quarters. With scissors, cut out and discard an 8-inch round from middle. Unfold foil and place over the edges of the pie, folding foil edges around piecrust to cover it. Then, place a 12-inch square of foil over pie. Fold foil edges around piecrust to cover it.

Peach-Blueberry Galette

Blueberries and peaches are perfect for summer pastries such as this rustic-looking treat.

PREP 30 minutes plus chilling • BAKE 40 minutes • MAKES 8 servings.

Pastry Dough for 1-Crust Pie (page 136)
⅓ cup plus 2 tablespoons sugar
2 tablespoons cornstarch
2 pounds ripe peaches (6 large), peeled,
    pitted, and each cut into 6 wedges
1 cup blueberries
2 teaspoons fresh lemon juice
1 tablespoon butter or margarine, cut
    into pieces

1 Prepare pastry dough as directed through chilling.

2 Preheat oven to 425°F. In large bowl, with wire whisk, mix ⅓ cup sugar and cornstarch. Add peaches, blueberries, and lemon juice; toss to combine.

3 On lightly floured surface, with floured rolling pin, roll dough into 14-inch round. Trim edges even. Transfer dough to ungreased large cookie sheet. Spoon fruit filling onto dough, leaving 2-inch border; dot with butter. Fold uncovered border of dough over fruit.

4 Sprinkle dough and filling with remaining 2 tablespoons sugar. Place two sheets of foil under cookie sheet; crimp foil edges to form rim to catch any overflow. Bake until filling bubbles in center, about 40 minutes. Cool on wire rack 30 minutes to serve warm, or cool completely to serve later.

EACH SERVING About 266 calories, 3g protein, 41g carbohydrate, 11g total fat (5g saturated), 19mg cholesterol, 146mg sodium.

Jeweled Fruit Galettes

Use a mix of whatever fruit you love—peaches, nectarines, plums, apricots, berries, or cherries—for these free-form individual tarts.

PREP 1 hour plus chilling and cooling • BAKE 25 minutes • MAKES 8 galettes.

CRUST
1¾ cups all-purpose flour
2 tablespoons sugar
¼ teaspoon baking powder
½ cup cold butter or margarine (1 stick),
    cut into pieces
⅓ cup sour cream
1 large egg yolk
2 tablespoons water

FRUIT TOPPING
½ cup sugar
2 tablespoons all-purpose flour
½ teaspoon grated fresh lemon peel
pinch grated nutmeg
1½ pounds mixed fruit, such as nectarines,
    plums, peaches (peeled), apricots (all pitted
    and thinly sliced); raspberries, blackberries,
    blueberries, grapes; and/or cherries (stems
    removed, pitted, and cut in half)
2 tablespoons butter or margarine,
    cut into small pieces

1 Prepare crust: In large bowl, with wire whisk, mix flour, sugar, and baking powder. With pastry blender or two knives used scissor-fashion, cut in butter until mixture resembles coarse crumbs. In small bowl, with fork, beat sour cream, egg yolk, and water until blended. Drizzle sour-cream mixture over flour mixture and stir with fork until dough begins to hold together. Gather dough into ball; divide in half and shape each half into a rectangle. Wrap each rectangle separately in plastic wrap and refrigerate 30 minutes or freeze 15 minutes, until firm enough to roll.

2 On floured surface, with floured rolling pin, roll 1 rectangle into a 19" by 6½" strip. Using bowl or plate as guide, cut out three 6-inch rounds; reserve trimmings. With wide spatula, transfer rounds to large cookie sheet, leaving room for a fourth round; refrigerate. Repeat with remaining dough and another cookie sheet. Gather trimmings; wrap in plastic wrap and freeze 10 minutes. Reroll trimmings into a 12" by 6½" strip; cut out 2 more rounds; place 1 round on each cookie sheet and refrigerate. (Discard remaining trimmings.)

3 Preheat oven to 400°F. Prepare topping: In small bowl, with fork, mix ¼ cup sugar, flour, lemon peel, and nutmeg. Sprinkle about 2 teaspoons of the mixture on each dough round, leaving ¾-inch border. Arrange fruit on top of sugar mixture. Fold uncovered border of dough over fruit, pleating edges and pressing them together to keep fruit in place. Sprinkle remaining ¼ cup sugar over fruit and dot with butter.

4 Place cookie sheets on two oven racks and bake until crust is well browned and fruit is tender, 25 to 30 minutes, rotating cookie sheets between upper and lower oven racks halfway through baking. With wide spatula, transfer galettes to wire rack to cool.

EACH SERVING About 365 calories, 5g protein, 48g carbohydrate, 18g total fat (11g saturated), 71mg cholesterol, 175mg sodium.

Peach Pie

Don't let the summer go by without making at least one fresh peach pie!

PREP 35 minutes plus chilling • **BAKE** 1 hour 5 minutes • **MAKES** 10 servings.

Pastry Dough for 2-Crust Pie (page 134)
¾ cup sugar
¼ cup cornstarch
pinch salt
3 pounds ripe peaches (9 large), peeled,
    pitted, and sliced (7 cups)
1 tablespoon fresh lemon juice
1 tablespoon butter or margarine,
    cut into pieces

1 Prepare pastry dough as directed through chilling.

2 Preheat oven to 425°F. In large bowl, with wire whisk, mix sugar, cornstarch, and salt. Add peaches and lemon juice; gently toss to combine.

3 Use larger disk of dough to line 9-inch pie plate. Trim edge, leaving 1-inch overhang. Spoon peach filling into crust; dot with butter. Roll out remaining disk of dough; cut out ¾-inch center circle and cut 1-inch slits to allow steam to escape during baking. Center dough over filling. Fold overhang under and make decorative edge.

4 Place pie on foil-lined cookie sheet to catch any overflow during baking. Bake 20 minutes. Turn oven control to 375°F; bake until filling bubbles in center, 45 to 60 minutes longer. If necessary, cover pie loosely with foil during last 20 minutes of baking to prevent overbrowning. Cool on wire rack 1 hour to serve warm, or cool completely to serve later.

EACH SERVING About 360 calories, 4g protein, 52g carbohydrate, 16g total fat (8g saturated), 28mg cholesterol, 236mg sodium.

PLUM PIE
Prepare pie as directed but substitute *3 pounds tart plums (9 large),* pitted and sliced, for peaches and use *1 cup sugar.* Bake and cool as directed.

PEAR PIE
Prepare pie as directed but substitute *3 pounds ripe pears,* peeled, cored, and sliced, for peaches and add *⅛ teaspoon ground nutmeg* to sugar mixture. Bake and cool as directed.

Peach Pie

Brown-Butter Peach Tart

This beautiful dessert is a nice change from a traditional pie: A thin layer of sliced peaches is baked in a buttery egg filling. Be sure to use real butter; margarine or other substitutes don't do justice to the recipe.

PREP 40 minutes • **BAKE** 1 hour • **MAKES** 12 servings.

CRUST
7 tablespoons butter (do not use margarine),
    melted and cooled to room temperature
⅓ cup sugar
¼ teaspoon vanilla extract
1 cup all-purpose flour
pinch salt

BROWN-BUTTER FILLING
½ cup sugar
2 large eggs
¼ cup all-purpose flour
½ cup butter (1 stick; do not use margarine)
3 medium peaches (1 pound), peeled, pitted,
    and thinly sliced

1 Preheat oven to 375°F. Prepare crust: In medium bowl, stir melted butter, sugar, and vanilla until blended. Stir in flour and salt until dough just begins to come together. Press dough onto bottom and up sides of 9-inch tart pan with removable bottom. Trim edge even with rim of pan.

2 Line tart shell with foil; fill with pie weights or dry beans. Bake crust until golden brown, about 15 minutes. If shell puffs up during baking, gently press it down with back of spoon.

3 Meanwhile, prepare filling: In small bowl, with wire whisk, beat sugar and eggs until well mixed. Beat in flour until blended; set aside.

4 In 1-quart saucepan, heat butter over medium heat, stirring occasionally, until it has melted and turned a dark, nutty brown color (do not burn), about 5 minutes. Whisking constantly, pour hot butter in steady stream into egg mixture; whisk until blended.

5 Remove foil with weights from tart shell. Arrange peach slices decoratively in warm tart shell; pour in brown-butter mixture. Bake until puffed and golden, about 45 minutes. Cool completely on wire rack. Refrigerate leftovers.

EACH SERVING About 250 calories, 3g protein, 27g carbohydrate, 15g total fat (9g saturated), 74mg cholesterol, 165mg sodium.

Test Kitchen Tip

PEELING PEACHES
Our favorite method of peeling peaches, especially a lot of them, is to submerge them, a few at a time, in boiling water for about 20 seconds (not longer or they will start to cook). Remove them with a slotted spoon and plunge immediately into a large bowl of ice water. The skins should slip right off. Another method, if peaches are perfectly ripe: Put tip of paring knife into stem end and peel away skin in strips. Whatever you do, don't peel a ripe peach with a vegetable peeler—you'll bruise the delicate flesh.

Brown-Butter Peach Tart

Country Peach Pie

It's always a good idea to have an easy-to-make one-crust pie in your repertoire, particularly when it's filled with sweet juicy peaches bathed in a tangy sour-cream custard.

PREP 45 minutes plus chilling • **BAKE** 35 minutes • **MAKES** 10 servings.

Pastry Dough for 1-Crust Pie (page 136)
1 container (8 ounces) sour cream
2 large eggs
¾ cup sugar
¼ cup all-purpose flour
1 teaspoon vanilla extract
4 ripe large peaches (1¾ pounds), peeled,
    pitted, and cut into ¼-inch-thick slices

1 Prepare pastry dough as directed through chilling.

2 Preheat oven to 425°F. In medium bowl, with wire whisk, mix sour cream, eggs, sugar, flour, and vanilla until blended; set aside.

3 Use dough to line 9-inch pie plate. Trim edge, leaving 1-inch overhang. Fold overhang under; bring up over pie-plate rim and pinch to make high stand-up edge.

4 Spoon peaches into crust. Pour custard over peaches. Bake pie until edge of custard is golden brown and knife inserted in center of pie comes out clean, 35 to 40 minutes. Cool pie on wire rack 1 hour to serve warm, or cool completely to serve later.

EACH SERVING About 280 calories, 4g protein, 37g carbohydrate, 13g total fat (7g saturated), 66mg cholesterol, 135mg sodium.

Country Peach Pie

Pineapple Tart

The sweet and tangy tropical flavor of this tart would be a delicious finale for an Asian or Mexican dinner. Substitute lime juice for lemon juice if you like.

PREP 45 minutes plus chilling • **BAKE** 35 minutes • **MAKES** 10 servings.

Pat-in-Pan Dough for 9-inch Tart (page 138)
1 can (20 ounces) crushed pineapple in
    unsweetened pineapple juice
⅓ cup packed light brown sugar
2 tablespoons fresh lemon juice
1 tablespoon butter or margarine, softened
1 large egg yolk
1 tablespoon water
1 teaspoon granulated sugar

1 Prepare dough as directed through chilling.

2 Meanwhile, in 10-inch skillet, heat pineapple with its juice, brown sugar, and lemon juice to boiling over medium-high heat. Cook, stirring frequently, until liquid has evaporated, about 15 minutes; stir in butter. Spoon pineapple mixture into medium bowl; cover and refrigerate until cool.

3 Preheat oven to 375°F. Remove both pieces of dough from refrigerator. With floured hands, press larger disk of dough onto bottom and up side of 9-inch round tart pan with removable bottom. Refrigerate until chilled, at least 15 minutes.

4 Meanwhile, on sheet of lightly floured waxed paper, roll remaining disk of dough into 10-inch round. With pastry wheel or sharp knife, cut dough into ten ¾-inch-wide strips. Refrigerate 15 minutes.

5 Spread chilled pineapple filling over dough in tart pan to within ½ inch of edge. Make lattice top: Place 5 dough strips, about 1 inch apart, across top of tart, trimming ends even with side of tart pan. To complete lattice, place 5 more strips diagonally across first strips to make diamond lattice pattern. Trim ends and reserve trimmings.

6 Make rope edge for tart shell: with hands, roll trimmings and remaining 2 strips of dough into ¼-inch-thick ropes. Press ropes around edge of tart to create finished edge. (If rope pieces break, just press pieces together.)

7 In small cup, with fork, beat egg yolk and water. Brush egg-yolk mixture over lattice and edge of tart; sprinkle with granulated sugar. Bake until crust is golden, 35 to 40 minutes. Cover tart loosely with foil to prevent overbrowning during last 15 minutes of baking. Cool in pan on wire rack. Remove tart from pan to serve.

EACH SERVING About 335 calories, 4g protein, 44g carbohydrate, 16g total fat (10g saturated), 83mg cholesterol, 220mg sodium.

Plum-Frangipane Tart

Make this tart with red or black plums—it will be equally good either way.

PREP 30 minutes plus chilling • **BAKE** 1 hour 10 minutes • **MAKES** 12 servings.

Pastry Dough for 11-Inch Tart (page 137)
1 tube or can (7 to 8 ounces) almond paste, crumbled
4 tablespoons butter or margarine, softened
½ cup sugar
¼ teaspoon salt
2 large eggs
2 teaspoons vanilla extract
¼ cup all-purpose flour
1¼ pounds ripe plums (5 large), halved, pitted, and each cut into 6 wedges

1 Prepare pastry dough as directed through chilling.

2 Preheat oven to 425°F. Use dough to line 11-inch tart pan with removable bottom. Refrigerate or freeze until firm, 10 to 15 minutes.

3 Line tart shell with foil; fill with pie weights or dry beans. Bake 15 minutes. Remove foil with weights; bake until golden, 5 to 10 minutes longer. If shell puffs up during baking, gently press it down with back of spoon.

4 Meanwhile, in large bowl, with mixer at low speed, beat almond paste, butter, sugar, and salt until almond paste is crumbly. Increase speed to medium-high and beat until well blended, about 3 minutes, frequently scraping bowl with rubber spatula. (There may be some tiny lumps.) Add eggs and vanilla; beat until smooth. With wooden spoon, stir in flour.

5 Pour almond-paste mixture into warm tart shell. Arrange plums in concentric circles over filling. Bake until golden, 50 to 60 minutes. Cool in pan on wire rack. When cool, carefully remove side of pan.

EACH SERVING About 342 calories, 6g protein, 37g carbohydrate, 20g total fat (8g saturated), 66mg cholesterol, 274mg sodium.

CRANBERRY-ALMOND TART
Prepare as directed, but omit plums. Bake almond filling until golden, about 20 minutes. Cool in pan on wire rack. In 2-quart saucepan, heat *1 cup cranberries, ¾ cup sugar, ⅓ cup water,* and *½ teaspoon freshly grated orange peel* to boiling over high heat. Reduce heat; simmer until cranberries pop and mixture has thickened slightly, about 5 minutes. Stir in additional *2 cups cranberries.* Set aside to cool. When cool, carefully remove side of pan; spoon cranberry topping over almond filling.

Raspberry Tart

The unsurpassed flavor of fresh raspberries is glorified in this tangy tart. It's made in a springform pan to give it a handmade look, but you can use a tart pan if you prefer.

PREP 20 minutes plus chilling • **BAKE** 1 hour 5 minutes • **MAKES** 8 servings.

Pastry Dough for 9-Inch Tart (page 136)
⅔ cup sugar
¼ cup all-purpose flour
4 cups raspberries (4 half-pints)
1 cup heavy or whipping cream, whipped
  (optional)

1 Prepare pastry dough as directed through chilling.

2 Preheat oven to 425°F. Roll dough into 11-inch round; fold into quarters. Ease dough onto bottom and 1 inch up side of 9-inch springform pan. Refrigerate or freeze until firm, 10 to 15 minutes.

3 Line tart shell with foil; fill with pie weights or dry beans. Bake 15 minutes. Remove foil with weights; bake until golden, 5 to 10 minutes longer. If shell puffs up during baking, gently press it down with back of spoon. Remove from oven. Turn oven control to 375°F.

4 In large bowl, with wire whisk, mix sugar and flour. Add raspberries and gently toss to combine. Spoon raspberry filling into warm tart shell. Bake until filling bubbles in center, about 45 minutes.

5 Cool completely in pan on wire rack. When cool, carefully remove side of pan. Serve with whipped cream, if desired.

EACH SERVING About 260 calories, 3g protein, 39g carbohydrate, 11g total fat (6g saturated), 23mg cholesterol, 160mg sodium.

Raspberry-Ganache Tart

A rich, buttery crust that melts in your mouth like shortbread is topped with a decadent bittersweet-chocolate filling and a sprinkling of raspberries.

PREP 30 minutes plus chilling and cooling
BAKE 30 minutes • **MAKES** 12 servings.

Shortbread Crust (page 140)
½ cup heavy or whipping cream
3 tablespoons butter or margarine
7 squares (7 ounces) semisweet chocolate, coarsely chopped
1 square (1 ounce) unsweetened chocolate, coarsely chopped
½ teaspoon vanilla extract
1 cup raspberries (half-pint)

1 Prepare and bake crust as directed; cool.
2 In 2-quart saucepan, heat heavy cream and butter to boiling over medium-high heat. Remove from heat; add semisweet and unsweetened chocolates and whisk until melted and smooth. Whisk in vanilla.
3 Pour hot chocolate ganache into cooled crust and spread evenly. Sprinkle tart evenly with raspberries. Refrigerate until chilled and firm enough to slice, about 1 hour. If tart has been refrigerated more than 1 hour, let stand at room temperature 30 minutes before serving for best flavor and texture.

EACH SERVING About 290 calories, 3g protein, 25g carbohydrate, 21g total fat (13g saturated), 44mg cholesterol, 141mg sodium.

Berries-and-Jam Tart

A medley of three types of berries tops a delicious jam-glazed crust. Serve with a dollop of whipped cream or sour cream if you like.

PREP 30 minutes plus cooling
BAKE 20 minutes • **MAKES** 12 servings.

Sweet Pastry Crust (page 137)
⅔ cup seedless red raspberry or strawberry jam
2 tablespoons almond-flavored liqueur (optional)
1 pint strawberries (3¼ cups), hulled and cut lengthwise in half
½ pint blueberries (1¼ cups)
1 cup raspberries (half-pint)

1 Prepare and bake crust as directed; cool.
2 In small saucepan, heat jam over medium heat, stirring often, until melted. Remove from heat and stir in liqueur if using.
3 Reserve 2 tablespoons jam mixture; brush remaining mixture over cooled crust. Arrange berries decoratively over jam-glazed crust; drizzle with reserved jam mixture. Refrigerate up to 1 day if not serving right away.

EACH SERVING About 275 calories, 3g protein, 39g carbohydrate, 12g total fat (2g saturated), 18mg cholesterol, 215mg sodium.

Raspberry-Ganache Tart

Double Raspberry Pie

Raspberries are so delicate in texture and flavor that they really don't need much cooking, if any, to make a great pie. Here, an intense berry puree is made with frozen raspberries (less expensive than fresh), then a bountiful quantity of fresh berries is folded into the puree, and the filling is poured into a prebaked crust.

PREP 35 minutes plus chilling and cooling • **BAKE** 20 minutes • **MAKES** 10 servings.

Pastry Dough for 1-Crust Pie (page 136)
1 package (10 ounces) frozen raspberries
   in heavy syrup, thawed
½ cup plus 1 tablespoon sugar
2 tablespoons cornstarch
2 tablespoons butter or margarine
5 cups fresh raspberries
1 cup heavy or whipping cream
½ teaspoon vanilla extract

1 Prepare pastry dough as directed through chilling.

2 Preheat oven to 425°F. Use dough to line 9-inch pie plate. Trim edge, leaving 1-inch overhang; bring up over pie-plate rim and pinch to make decorative edge. Refrigerate or freeze until firm, 10 to 15 minutes.

3 Line pie shell with foil; fill with pie weights or dry beans. Bake 15 minutes. Remove foil with weights; bake until golden, 5 to 10 minutes longer. Cool on wire rack.

4 In food processor with knife blade attached, puree frozen raspberries and syrup until smooth. Strain puree through sieve set over small bowl; discard seeds.

5 In 2-quart saucepan, with wire whisk, mix ½ cup sugar and cornstarch until well blended. Add puree and stir until sugar has dissolved. Heat to boiling over medium heat, stirring constantly; boil, stirring, 2 minutes. Pour mixture into large bowl. Add butter; stir until melted. Let cool to room temperature.

6 Gently fold fresh raspberries into puree. Turn raspberry mixture into baked pie shell; spread evenly. Refrigerate until set, about 3 hours, or up to 6 hours.

7 In small bowl, with mixer on high speed, beat remaining 1 tablespoon sugar, cream, and vanilla until soft peaks form. Garnish top of pie with whipped cream.

EACH SERVING About 340 calories, 3g protein, 41g carbohydrate, 19g total fat (10g saturated), 51mg cholesterol, 135mg sodium.

Italian Triple-Berry Tart

Make the filling and crust early in the day, then just fold in the whipped cream and top with berries to serve.

PREP 30 minutes plus chilling and cooling • **BAKE** 20 minutes • **MAKES** 12 servings.

⅓ cup sugar

2 tablespoons cornstarch

3 large egg yolks

1 cup milk

2 tablespoons butter or margarine,
   cut into pieces

1 teaspoon vanilla extract

Pastry Dough for 11-Inch Tart (page 137)

½ cup heavy or whipping cream

2 cups blueberries (1 pint)

2 cups raspberries (1 pint)

2 cups blackberries (1 pint)

confectioners' sugar

1 In medium bowl, with wire whisk, mix sugar and cornstarch until blended. Add egg yolks and stir. In 2-quart saucepan, heat milk to simmering over medium-high heat. While whisking constantly, gradually pour about half of simmering milk into egg-yolk mixture. Return mixture to saucepan and cook, whisking constantly, until pastry cream has thickened and boils. Reduce heat and simmer, stirring, 1 minute. Remove from heat; add butter and vanilla, stirring until butter has melted. Transfer to bowl, press plastic wrap directly onto surface. Refrigerate until well chilled, at least 2 hours or up to 6 hours.

2 Prepare dough as directed through chilling.

3 Preheat oven to 425°F. Use dough to line 11-inch tart pan with removable bottom. Refrigerate or freeze until firm, 10 to 15 minutes.

4 Line tart shell with foil; fill with pie weights or dry beans. Bake 15 minutes. Remove foil with weights; bake until golden, 5 to 10 minutes longer. If shell puffs up, gently press it down with back of spoon. Cool in pan on wire rack.

5 Up to 2 hours before serving, in small bowl, with mixer at medium speed, beat cream until stiff peaks form. Whisk pastry cream until smooth; with rubber spatula, gently fold in whipped cream until blended. Spoon pastry-cream filling into tart shell.

6 In large bowl, gently toss blueberries, raspberries, and blackberries. Spoon berries over filling and dust with confectioners' sugar.

EACH SERVING About 290 calories, 4g protein, 30g carbohydrate, 18g total fat (10g saturated), 95mg cholesterol, 212mg sodium.

PUFF PASTRY VARIATION

Prepare tart as directed but instead of making a round tart shell, use prepared puff pastry to make a rectangular tart: Preheat oven to 400°F. Unfold *1 sheet (half 17¼-ounce package) frozen puff pastry*, thawed; place on ungreased large cookie sheet with dampened towel underneath to prevent it from slipping. With rolling pin, roll pastry into 12" by 9" rectangle. Cut a ¼-inch-wide strip from each long side. Lightly brush both long edges of pastry sheet with water; place strips on top to build up long edges. Press strips lightly to adhere. With fork, prick center portion of pastry all over. Bake until deep golden, 20 to 25 minutes; prick again halfway through baking. Cool completely on wire rack. Fill with pastry cream and top with berries as directed. Makes 10 servings.

EACH SERVING About 311 calories, 4g protein, 33g carbohydrate, 19g total fat (6g saturated), 90mg cholesterol, 105mg sodium.

Maple-Walnut Pie

The subtle flavor of maple is a perfect match for walnuts. For even more maple flavor, serve the pie with whipped cream sweetened with maple syrup.

PREP 25 minutes plus chilling • **BAKE** 1 hour 10 minutes • **MAKES** 10 servings.

Pastry Dough for 1-Crust Pie (page 136)
1 cup maple or maple-flavored syrup
4 tablespoons butter or margarine, melted
3 tablespoons sugar
¼ teaspoon salt
3 large eggs
2 cups walnuts (8 ounces)

1 Prepare pastry dough as directed through chilling.
2 Preheat oven to 425°F. Use dough to line 9-inch pie plate. Trim edge, leaving 1-inch overhang. Fold overhang under; bring up over pie-plate rim and pinch to make high stand-up edge. Refrigerate or freeze until firm, 10 to 15 minutes.
3 Line pie shell with foil; fill with pie weights or dry beans. Bake 15 minutes. Remove foil with weights; bake until golden, 5 to 10 minutes longer. If shell puffs up during baking, gently press it down with back of spoon. Turn oven control to 350°F.
4 In medium bowl, with wire whisk, mix maple syrup, butter, sugar, salt, and eggs until blended. Spread walnuts over bottom of pie shell; carefully pour egg mixture over walnuts. Bake until knife inserted 1 inch from edge comes out clean, 50 to 60 minutes. Cool on wire rack at least 1 hour for easier slicing.

EACH SERVING About 437 calories, 7g protein, 42g carbohydrate, 28g total fat (8g saturated), 89mg cholesterol, 233mg sodium.

Chocolate-Walnut Pie

Imagine an ultra-rich brownie baked in a shortbread crust. Sound good? Here's the recipe. All you have to decide is whether to serve it with whipped cream or a scoop of vanilla or coffee ice cream.

PREP 45 minutes plus cooling • **BAKE** 1 hour **MAKES** 12 servings.

Shortbread Crust (page 140)
8 tablespoons butter or margarine
3 squares (3 ounces) unsweetened chocolate, chopped
½ cup granulated sugar
½ cup packed light brown sugar
2 large eggs
¾ cup all-purpose flour
1 teaspoon vanilla extract
⅛ teaspoon salt
¾ cup walnuts (3 ounces), coarsely chopped

1 Prepare and bake crust as directed; cool.
2 Preheat oven to 325°F. In 3-quart saucepan, heat butter and chocolate over low heat, stirring occasionally, until melted. Remove from heat and stir in granulated and brown sugars. Add eggs, one at a time, stirring well after each addition. Stir in flour, vanilla, salt, and nuts until blended. Pour into cooled baked piecrust.
3 Bake 30 minutes or until top is just set. Cool on wire rack 1 hour to serve warm, or cool completely to serve later.

EACH SERVING About 385 calories, 5g protein, 39g carbohydrate, 25g total fat (13g saturated), 77mg cholesterol, 195mg sodium.

Georgia Chocolate Pecan Pie

Native Americans were probably the first to cultivate pecan trees. By the late 1700s, George Washington and Thomas Jefferson, among others, were planting them in their gardens. Surprisingly, it wasn't until the early twentieth century that recipes for pecan pie began to appear in print. Home economists in the Karo test kitchens most likely created the first pecan pie in the early 1900s, using a good amount of corn syrup—light or dark—in every pie. Today, it is a standard on traditional Southern menus—whether in classic form or embellished with chocolate.

PREP 45 minutes plus chilling • BAKE 1 hour 5 minutes • MAKES 12 servings.

Pastry Dough for 1-Crust Pie (page 136)
4 tablespoons butter or margarine
2 squares (2 ounces) unsweetened chocolate, chopped
1¾ cups pecan halves (7 ounces)
¾ cup packed dark brown sugar
¾ cup dark corn syrup
1 teaspoon vanilla extract
3 large eggs

1 Prepare pastry dough as directed through chilling.

2 Use dough to line 9-inch pie plate. Trim edge, leaving 1-inch overhang. Fold overhang under; bring up over pie-plate rim and pinch to make decorative edge. Refrigerate or freeze until firm, 10 to 15 minutes.

3 Preheat oven to 425°F. In heavy 1-quart saucepan, heat butter and chocolate over low heat, stirring frequently, until melted and smooth. Cool slightly.

4 Line pie shell with foil; fill with pie weights or dry beans. Bake 15 minutes. Remove foil with weights; bake until golden, 5 to 10 minutes longer. If shell puffs up during baking, gently press it down with back of spoon. Cool on wire rack. Turn oven control to 350°F.

5 Coarsely chop 1 cup pecans. In large bowl, with wire whisk, mix cooled chocolate mixture, brown sugar, corn syrup, vanilla, and eggs until blended. Stir in chopped pecans and remaining pecan halves.

6 Pour pecan mixture into pie shell. Bake until filling is set around edge but center jiggles slightly, 45 to 50 minutes. Cool on wire rack at least 1 hour for easier slicing.

EACH SERVING About 395 calories, 5g protein, 43g carbohydrate, 24g total fat (4g saturated), 53mg cholesterol, 225mg sodium.

CLASSIC PECAN PIE
Prepare as directed but omit unsweetened chocolate.

EACH SERVING About 374 calories, 4g protein, 42g carbohydrate, 22g total fat (7g saturated), 74mg cholesterol, 179mg sodium.

Double-Berry Linzer Tart

To give this Austrian tart holiday flair, we've added fresh cranberries to the traditional raspberry jam.

Prep 30 minutes plus chilling • **Cook/Bake:** 50 minutes • **Makes** 10 servings.

1 cup cranberries
¼ cup plus ⅓ cup packed brown sugar
¼ cup cranberry-juice cocktail
pinch plus ¼ teaspoon salt
¾ cup seedless raspberry jam
⅔ cup hazelnuts (filberts), toasted and skinned (page 256)
1¼ cups all-purpose flour
6 tablespoons butter or margarine, softened
1 large egg
½ teaspoon vanilla extract
¼ teaspoon baking powder
¼ teaspoon ground cinnamon
confectioners' sugar (optional)

1 In nonreactive 1-quart saucepan, heat cranberries, ¼ cup brown sugar, cranberry-juice cocktail, and pinch salt to boiling over medium-high heat. Reduce heat to medium and cook, stirring occasionally, until cranberries pop and mixture has thickened slightly, about 6 minutes. Stir in raspberry jam; refrigerate until cool, about 30 minutes.

2 Meanwhile in blender or in food processor with knife blade attached, pulse hazelnuts and ¼ cup flour until nuts are very finely ground.

3 In large bowl, with mixer at low speed, beat butter and remaining ⅓ cup brown sugar until blended. Increase speed to medium-high; beat until light and fluffy, about 3 minutes. With mixer at medium speed, beat in egg and vanilla until smooth, about 1 minute. Reduce speed to low. Add hazelnut mixture, remaining 1 cup flour, baking powder, cinnamon, and remaining ¼ teaspoon salt; beat just until combined.

4 With floured hands, press two-thirds of dough onto bottom and up side of 9-inch tart pan with removable bottom. Trim edge even with rim of pan. Shape remaining dough into a disk. Wrap tart shell and disk of dough separately in plastic wrap. Refrigerate until disk of dough is firm enough to shape, about 30 minutes.

5 Preheat oven to 400°F. Spoon cooled filling into tart shell. On lightly floured surface, divide remaining dough into 10 equal pieces. With floured hands, roll each piece into 8½-inch-long rope. Place 5 ropes, 1½ inches apart, across top of tart. Place remaining 5 ropes at right angles to first ropes to make lattice pattern. Or, if desired, weave dough ropes to create "fancy" lattice pattern. Trim ends of ropes even with edge of tart and press ends to seal. With hands, roll any dough trimmings into ¼-inch-thick ropes. Press ropes around edge of tart to make finished edge. If ropes break, press pieces together.

6 Bake until filling bubbles and crust is lightly browned, about 40 minutes. Cool in pan on wire rack at least 1 hour. When cool, carefully remove side of pan. Dust with confectioners' sugar, if desired.

Each serving About 290 calories, 4g protein, 43g carbohydrate, 12g total fat (5g saturated), 40mg cholesterol, 175mg sodium.

Double-Berry Linzer Tart

Pumpkin Pie with Pecan-Caramel Topping

Purists might consider the addition of a chewy-crunchy topping to pumpkin pie gilding the lily, but others will simply sit back and lick their lips.

PREP 1 hour plus cooling • **COOK/BAKE** 1 hour 30 minutes • **MAKES** 12 servings.

CRUST
½ cup pecans, toasted (page 13)
2 tablespoons granulated sugar
1¼ cups all-purpose flour
¼ teaspoon salt
4 tablespoons cold butter or margarine
2 tablespoons vegetable shortening
3 tablespoons ice water

PUMPKIN FILLING
1 can (15 ounces) solid-pack pumpkin
   (not pumpkin-pie mix)
¾ cup heavy or whipping cream
½ cup milk
½ cup packed light brown sugar
1½ teaspoons ground cinnamon
½ teaspoon salt
¼ teaspoon ground nutmeg
¼ teaspoon ground ginger
¼ teaspoon ground cloves
3 large eggs

PECAN-CARAMEL TOPPING
1 cup packed light brown sugar
¼ cup heavy or whipping cream
2 tablespoons light corn syrup
2 tablespoons butter or margarine
1 teaspoon distilled white vinegar
1 cup pecans, toasted (page 13)
   and broken
1 teaspoon vanilla extract

1 Prepare crust: In food processor with knife blade attached, pulse toasted pecans and granulated sugar until pecans are finely ground. Add flour and salt to nut mixture and pulse to blend. Add butter and shortening and pulse just until mixture resembles very coarse crumbs. With processor running, add water, stopping just before dough forms a ball. With hands, shape dough into a disk.

2 Between lightly floured sheets of paper, with rolling pin, roll dough into a 12 round. Dough will be very tender; refrigera too soft to roll. Gently ease dough into 9-i pie plate; trim edge, leaving 1-inch overhan Fold overhang under; bring up over pie-plate ri and pinch to make high decorative edge. With fork, prick bottom and side of pie shell at 1-inch intervals. Refrigerate about 30 minutes.

3 Preheat oven to 400°F. Line pie shell with foil; fill with pie weights or dry beans. Bake 20 minutes. Remove foil with weights; bake until lightly browned, about 10 minutes longer. If shell puffs up during baking, gently press it down with back of spoon. Cool on wire rack at least 15 minutes. Turn oven control to 350°F.

4 Prepare filling: In large bowl, with wire whisk, beat pumpkin, cream, milk, brown sugar, cinnamon, salt, nutmeg, ginger, cloves, and eggs until blended. Pour filling into cooled pie shell. Bake until knife inserted 1 inch from edge of pie comes out clean, 50 to 60 minutes. Cool on wire rack until filling is slightly firm, about 1 hour.

Almond Cheesecake Tart

Both the crust and the filling of this luscious cheesecake are flavored with almonds: ground almonds in the crust and almond extract in the filling.

PREP 30 minutes plus cooling and chilling • **BAKE** about 30 minutes • **MAKES** 12 servings.

GRAHAM-CRACKER CRUST
½ cup slivered almonds
1 tablespoon sugar
11 graham crackers (4¾" by 2¼" each)
6 tablespoons butter or margarine, melted

CHEESE FILLING
1½ packages (8 ounces each) cream cheese, softened
½ cup sugar
2 large eggs
¾ teaspoon almond extract
¼ teaspoon vanilla extract
raspberries and blueberries, for garnish

1 Preheat oven to 375°F. Prepare crust: In food processor with knife blade attached, pulse almonds and sugar until almonds are finely ground. Add graham crackers and pulse until fine crumbs form. Pour in melted butter; pulse until evenly moistened. With hand, press mixture firmly onto bottom and up side of 11-inch tart pan with removable bottom. Bake 10 minutes. Cool on wire rack.

2 Turn oven control to 350°F. Prepare filling: In medium bowl, with mixer at low speed, beat cream cheese and sugar until smooth, occasionally scraping bowl with rubber spatula. Add eggs and almond and vanilla extracts; beat just until combined.

3 Pour cheese mixture into cooled crust. Bake until set, about 20 minutes. Cool tart on wire rack. Cover and refrigerate at least 2 hours.

4 To serve, arrange raspberries and blueberries decoratively on top of tart.

EACH SERVING About 285 calories, 5g protein, 21g carbohydrates, 21g total fat (11g saturated), 83mg cholesterol, 235mg sodium.

Almond Cheesecake Tart

Buttermilk Pie

This variation on the chess pie—and there are many—boasts a mildly tangy flavor, not just from the buttermilk but from a few spoonfuls of lemon juice.

PREP 40 minutes plus chilling and cooling • **BAKE** 1 hour 10 minutes • **MAKES** 10 servings.

Pastry Dough for 1-Crust Pie (page 136)
1 cup sugar
3 tablespoons all-purpose flour
3 large eggs
1 large egg yolk
1¼ cups buttermilk
2 tablespoons butter or margarine, melted and cooled
2 teaspoons fresh lemon juice
1½ teaspoons vanilla extract
⅛ teaspoon ground nutmeg
pinch salt

1 Prepare pastry dough as directed through chilling. Use dough to line 9-inch pie plate. Trim edge, leaving 1-inch overhang. Fold overhang under; bring up over pie-plate rim and pinch to make decorative edge.

2 Preheat oven to 425°F. Line pie shell with foil; fill with pie weights or dry beans. Bake 20 minutes. Remove foil with weights; bake until golden, about 5 minutes longer. If crust puffs up during baking, gently press it down with back of spoon. Cool on wire rack at least 10 minutes. Turn oven control to 350°F.

3 In large bowl, with wire whisk, mix sugar and flour. In medium bowl, beat eggs and egg yolk. Add buttermilk, melted butter, lemon juice, vanilla, nutmeg, and salt and whisk until blended. Whisk egg mixture into sugar mixture until combined.

4 Pour filling into cooled piecrust. Bake until knife inserted halfway between edge and center comes out clean, about 45 minutes. Cool on wire rack 2 hours to serve warm.

EACH SERVING About 275 calories, 5g protein, 37g carbohydrate, 12g total fat (6g saturated), 105mg cholesterol, 195mg sodium.

Ricotta Pie

Italians particularly enjoy cheese pies and tarts at Easter time, but you can serve this one anytime—plain or with fresh fruit.

PREP 50 minutes plus chilling • **BAKE** 35 minutes • **MAKES** 20 servings.

Pat-in-Pan Dough for 9-inch Tart (page 138)
1 package (8 ounces) cream cheese, softened
¾ cup sugar
¼ teaspoon ground cinnamon
1 container (32 ounces) ricotta cheese
5 large egg whites, beaten

1 Prepare pastry dough as directed but shape dough into one disk. Wrap in plastic wrap and refrigerate until firm enough to handle, about 30 minutes.

2 Meanwhile, in large bowl, with mixer at low speed, beat cream cheese, sugar, and cinnamon until blended. Increase speed to high; beat until light and creamy. Reduce speed to medium. Add ricotta and all but 1 tablespoon egg whites and beat just until blended.

3 Preheat oven to 400°F. Lightly grease 13" by 9" glass baking dish.

4 With lightly floured hands, press dough evenly onto bottom and up sides of prepared baking dish. Brush reserved egg white over bottom and sides of dough. Pour in ricotta filling; spread evenly. With fingers, gently push edge of dough into scalloped design around top of filling.

5 Bake 25 minutes. Turn oven control to 350°F. Bake until center barely jiggles, 10 to 15 minutes longer. Cool completely in dish on wire rack. Cover and refrigerate until well chilled, at least 6 hours, or overnight.

EACH SERVING About 280 calories, 9g protein, 22g carbohydrate, 17g total fat (11g saturated), 65mg cholesterol, 190mg sodium.

Test Kitchen Tip

CRUST FOR CREAM PIES

When making crusts for cream pies, as soon as pie shell comes out of the oven, brush with lightly beaten egg white, making sure to cover areas pricked with fork. The heat from the hot pie shell will cook the egg white and form a protective seal that will prevent a soggy crust. Cool completely before filling.

Toasted Coconut Cream Pie

Good Housekeeping reader Mary Jane Ogilvie Silvia remembers her mother, Scottish-born Margaret Ogilvie, baking this pie every Thanksgiving in Lancaster, Pennsylvania.

PREP 35 minutes plus cooling and chilling • **COOK/BAKE** 35 minutes • **MAKES** 10 servings.

CRUST
1 cup all-purpose flour
½ cup sweetened shredded coconut, toasted
6 tablespoons cold butter or margarine,
    cut into small pieces
2 tablespoons sugar
1 tablespoon cold water

FILLING
2 cups milk
1 can (8 ½ ounces) cream of coconut
    (not coconut milk)
⅓ cup cornstarch
¼ teaspoon salt
4 large egg yolks
2 tablespoons butter or margarine
1 teaspoon vanilla extract

TOPPING
1 cup heavy or whipping cream
2 tablespoons sugar
½ teaspoon vanilla extract
2 tablespoons sweetened shredded coconut,
    toasted

1 Prepare crust: Preheat oven to 375°F. In food processor, with knife blade attached; pulse flour, coconut, butter, sugar, and water until dough just comes together.

2 Spray 9-inch pie plate with nonstick cooking spray. Press dough evenly onto bottom and up side of pie plate, making a short rim. Bake pie shell until golden, about 20 minutes. If necessary, cover edge with foil during last 10 minutes of baking to prevent overbrowning. Cool on wire rack.

3 Meanwhile, prepare filling: In 3-quart saucepan, with wire whisk, mix milk, cream of coconut, cornstarch, and salt until blended. Cook over medium heat, stirring constantly, until mixture has thickened and begins to bubble around side of pan, about 7 minutes. Boil 1 minute.

4 In small bowl, with wire whisk or fork, lightly beat egg yolks. Beat small amount of hot milk mixture into beaten egg yolks. Slowly pour egg-yolk mixture back into milk mixture, whisking rapidly to prevent curdling. Cook over low heat, whisking constantly, until very thick (mixture should be about 160°F), about 2 minutes.

5 Remove saucepan from heat; stir in butter and vanilla until butter has melted and mixture is smooth. Pour hot filling into cooled crust; press plastic wrap directly onto surface to prevent skin from forming. Refrigerate until filling is cold and set, about 4 hours.

6 To serve, prepare topping: In small bowl, with mixer at medium speed, beat cream and sugar until stiff peaks form when beaters are lifted. Beat in vanilla. Spread whipped cream over filling. Sprinkle with toasted coconut.

EACH SERVING About 425 calories, 5g protein, 40g carbohydrate, 28g total fat (16g saturated), 133mg cholesterol, 224mg sodium.

Grandma's Sweet Potato Pie

Christopher Columbus found the sweet potato growing in South and Central America. He took some of these new vegetables back to Spain, where they were soon under cultivation. Before long, other European countries followed suit. Although American colonists were also cultivating sweet potatoes by the 1650s, early cookbooks contain no mention of using them in pies. A precursor is found in Eliza Leslie's 1848 Directions for Cookery—*a pudding that is made from grated parboiled sweet potatoes, sugar, eggs, wine, and brandy.*

PREP 1 hour plus chilling and cooling • COOK/BAKE 1 hour 30 minutes • MAKES 10 servings.

Pastry Dough for 1-Crust Pie (page 136)
2 medium sweet potatoes (8 ounces each),
    not peeled, or 2 cans (16 to 17 ounces each)
    sweet potatoes, drained
1½ cups half-and-half or light cream
¾ cup packed dark brown sugar
1 teaspoon ground cinnamon
¾ teaspoon ground ginger
¼ teaspoon ground nutmeg
½ teaspoon salt
3 large eggs

1 Prepare pastry dough as directed through chilling.

2 Meanwhile, if using fresh sweet potatoes, in 3-quart saucepan, heat sweet potatoes and *enough water to cover* to boiling over high heat. Reduce heat; cover and simmer until tender, about 30 minutes. Drain.

3 Preheat oven to 425°F. Use dough to line 9-inch pie plate. Trim edge, leaving 1-inch overhang. Fold overhang under; bring up over pie-plate rim and pinch to make decorative edge. Refrigerate or freeze until firm, 10 to 15 minutes.

4 When cool enough to handle; peel sweet potatoes and cut into large pieces. In large bowl, with mixer at low speed, beat boiled or canned sweet potatoes until smooth. Add half-and-half, brown sugar, cinnamon, ginger, nutmeg, salt, and eggs; beat until well blended.

5 Line pie shell with foil; fill with pie weights or dry beans. Bake 10 minutes. Remove foil with weights; bake until golden, about 10 minutes longer. If shell puffs up during baking, gently press it down with back of spoon. Cool on wire rack at least 10 minutes. Turn oven control to 350°F.

6 Spoon sweet-potato filling into cooled pie shell. Bake until knife inserted 1 inch from edge comes out clean, about 40 minutes. Cool on wire rack 1 hour to serve warm, or cool slightly and refrigerate to serve later.

EACH SERVING About 295 calories, 5g protein, 39g carbohydrate, 13g total fat (7g saturated), 89mg cholesterol, 265mg sodium.

Lemon Meringue Pie

Here is our favorite recipe for this classic citrus masterpiece, crowned with billowing meringue.

PREP 45 minutes plus chilling and cooling • **COOK/BAKE** 40 minutes • **MAKES** 10 servings.

Pastry Dough for 1-Crust Pie (page 136)
4 to 6 lemons
1½ cups sugar
½ cup cornstarch
¼ teaspoon plus pinch salt
1½ cups water
3 large eggs, separated, plus 1 large egg white
2 tablespoons butter or margarine,
   cut into pieces
¼ teaspoon cream of tartar

1 Prepare pastry dough as directed through chilling.

2 Preheat oven to 425°F. Use dough to line 9-inch pie plate. Trim edge, leaving 1-inch overhang. Fold overhang under; bring up over pie-plate rim and pinch to make decorative edge. Refrigerate or freeze until firm, 10 to 15 minutes.

3 Line pie shell with foil; fill with pie weights or dry beans. Bake 15 minutes. Remove foil with weights; bake until golden, 5 to 10 minutes longer. If shell puffs up during baking, gently press it down with back of spoon. Cool completely on wire rack.

4 Meanwhile, from lemons, grate 1 tablespoon peel and squeeze ¾ cup juice; set aside.

5 In 2-quart saucepan, with wire whisk, mix 1 cup sugar, cornstarch, and ¼ teaspoon salt; stir in water. Cook over medium heat, whisking constantly, until mixture has thickened and boils; boil 1 minute. Remove from heat.

6 In small bowl, with wire whisk, beat egg yolks. Add ⅓ cup hot cornstarch mixture, whisking until blended; slowly pour egg-yolk mixture back into cornstarch mixture in saucepan, whisking rapidly to prevent curdling. Place saucepan over low heat and cook, whisking constantly, until filling is very thick (mixture should be about 160°F), about 4 minutes. Remove from heat. Add butter, whisking until melted, then gradually whisk in lemon peel and juice until blended. Pour into cooled pie shell.

7 Turn oven control to 400°F. In small bowl, with mixer at high speed, beat the 4 egg whites, cream of tartar, and remaining pinch salt until soft peaks form when beaters are lifted. Sprinkle in remaining ½ cup sugar, 2 tablespoons at a time, beating until sugar has completely dissolved and egg whites stand in stiff, glossy peaks when beaters are lifted.

8 Spread meringue over filling to edge of pie shell, sealing meringue to edge and swirling with spoon to make attractive top. Bake until meringue is golden, about 10 minutes. Cool on wire rack away from drafts. Refrigerate at least 3 hours for easier slicing or up to 2 days.

EACH SERVING About 321 calories, 4g protein, 52g carbohydrate, 11g total fat (5g saturated), 82mg cholesterol, 224 mg sodium.

LIME MERINGUE PIE

Prepare crust and filling as directed, but substitute *2 teaspoons freshly grated lime peel* for lemon peel and *½ cup fresh lime juice* for fresh lemon juice. Bake and cool as directed.

EACH SERVING About 305 calories, 4g protein, 48g carbohydrate, 11g total fat (5g saturated), 82mg cholesterol, 225mg sodium.

Lemon Tart

A piquant tart that can be served on its own or accented with fresh berries. Be sure to make a high pastry rim to contain all the delicious filling.

PREP 25 minutes plus chilling and cooling • **BAKE** 50 minutes • **MAKES** 8 servings.

Pastry Dough for 9-Inch Tart (page 136)
4 to 6 lemons
4 large eggs
1 cup granulated sugar
⅓ cup heavy or whipping cream
confectioners' sugar

1 Prepare pastry dough as directed through chilling.

2 Preheat oven to 425°F. Use dough to line 9-inch tart pan with removable bottom. Fold overhang in and press dough against side of pan so it extends ¼ inch above rim of pan. Refrigerate or freeze until firm, 10 to 15 minutes.

3 Line tart shell with foil; fill with pie weights or dry beans. Bake 15 minutes. Remove foil with weights; bake until golden, 5 to 10 minutes longer. If shell puffs up during baking, gently press it down with back of spoon. Cool in pan on wire rack. Turn oven control to 350°F.

4 From lemons, grate 1½ teaspoons peel and squeeze ⅔ cup juice. In medium bowl, with wire whisk, beat eggs, granulated sugar, and lemon peel and juice until well combined. Whisk in cream.

5 Carefully pour lemon filling into cooled tart shell. Place tart on foil-lined cookie sheet to catch any overflow during baking. Bake until filling has set but center still jiggles slightly, about 30 minutes. Cool completely on wire rack. Just before serving, dust with confectioners' sugar.

EACH SERVING About 324 calories, 5g protein, 40g carbohydrate, 17g total fat (9g saturated), 143mg cholesterol, 195mg sodium.

Test Kitchen Tip — **JUICING A LEMON** The juice flows more readily when the fruit is warm. Zap citrus whole in the microwave for 20 to 30 seconds. Squeeze as you like, either with an electric citrus juicer for big jobs or an old-fashioned reamer for a few tablespoons.

Chocolate Truffle Tart

Silky and decadent, all you'll need is one thin slice!

PREP 20 minutes plus chilling and cooling • **BAKE** 40 minutes • **MAKES** 12 servings.

Pastry Dough for 9-Inch Tart (page 136)
6 squares (6 ounces) semisweet chocolate,
    coarsely chopped
½ cup butter or margarine (1 stick)
¼ cup sugar
1 teaspoon vanilla extract
3 large eggs
½ cup heavy or whipping cream
softly whipped cream (optional)

1 Prepare pastry dough as directed through chilling.

2 Preheat oven to 425°F. Use dough to line 9-inch tart pan with removable bottom. Trim edge even with rim of pan. Refrigerate or freeze until firm, 10 to 15 minutes.

3 Line tart shell with foil; fill with pie weights or dry beans. Bake 15 minutes. Remove foil with weights; bake until golden, 5 to 10 minutes longer. If shell puffs up during baking, gently press it down with back of spoon. Cool in pan on wire rack. Turn oven control to 350°F.

4 Meanwhile, in heavy 2-quart saucepan, heat chocolate and butter over very low heat, stirring frequently, until melted and smooth. Add sugar and vanilla, stirring until sugar has dissolved. In small bowl, with wire whisk, lightly beat eggs and cream. Whisk ⅓ cup warm chocolate mixture into egg mixture; stir egg mixture back into chocolate mixture in saucepan until blended.

5 Pour warm chocolate filling into cooled tart shell. Bake until custard is set but center still jiggles slightly, about 20 minutes.

6 Cool in pan on wire rack. When cool, carefully remove side of pan. Refrigerate until chilled, about 4 hours. Serve with whipped cream, if desired.

EACH SERVING About 306 calories, 4g protein, 22g carbohydrate, 24g total fat (14g saturated), 103mg cholesterol, 206mg sodium.

No-Bake Chocolate Fudge Tart

This rich, elegant do-ahead dessert is perfect for those occasions when company is coming and time is limited.

PREP 10 minutes plus chilling • **MICROWAVE** 1½ minutes • **MAKES** 8 servings.

¾ cup half-and-half or light cream
3 tablespoons sugar
6 squares (6 ounces) semisweet chocolate, chopped
2 squares (2 ounces) unsweetened chocolate, chopped
1 teaspoon vanilla extract
1 (6-ounce) ready-to-use chocolate cookie piecrust
½ cup heavy or whipping cream
Chocolate Curls for garnish (page 362)

1 In microwave-safe medium bowl, stir half-and-half and 2 tablespoons sugar. Heat mixture in microwave oven on High until very hot, about 1½ minutes. Add semisweet and unsweetened chocolates and vanilla and stir until chocolates have melted. Pour mixture into piecrust. Cover and refrigerate at least 1 hour or up to 3 days.
2 To serve, in small bowl, with mixer at medium speed, beat heavy cream until soft peaks form. Add remaining 1 tablespoon sugar; beat until stiff peaks form. With spatula, spread whipped cream over chocolate filling. Garnish with Chocolate Curls.

EACH SERVING About 350 calories, 4g protein, 34g carbohydrate, 24g total fat (12g saturated), 29mg cholesterol, 115mg sodium.

No-Bake Chocolate Fudge Tart

Banana Cream Pie

If you love traditional piecrust with cream, bake up our 9-inch crust on page 140.

PREP 30 minutes plus cooling and chilling • **COOK/BAKE** 20 minutes • **MAKES** 10 servings.

Vanilla Wafer–Crumb Crust (page 139)
¾ cup sugar
⅓ cup cornstarch
¼ teaspoon salt
3¾ cups milk
5 large egg yolks
2 tablespoons butter or margarine,
   cut into pieces
1¾ teaspoons vanilla extract
3 ripe medium bananas
¾ cup heavy or whipping cream

1 Prepare and bake crust as directed; cool completely on wire rack.

2 Meanwhile, prepare filling: In 3-quart saucepan, stir sugar, cornstarch, and salt; stir in milk. Cook over medium heat, stirring constantly, until mixture has thickened and boils; boil 1 minute. In small bowl, with wire whisk, lightly beat egg yolks; beat in ½ cup hot milk mixture. Slowly pour egg-yolk mixture back into milk, stirring rapidly to prevent curdling. Cook over low heat, stirring constantly, until mixture has thickened, about 2 minutes. Remove from heat. Add butter and 1½ teaspoons vanilla; stir until butter has melted. Transfer to medium bowl. Press plastic wrap directly onto surface to prevent skin from forming. Refrigerate, stirring occasionally, until cool, about 1 hour.

3 Spoon half of filling into crust. Slice 2 bananas crosswise. Arrange sliced bananas on top; spoon remaining filling evenly over bananas. Press plastic wrap onto surface; refrigerate at least 4 hours or up to overnight.

4 To serve, prepare topping: In small bowl, with mixer at medium speed, beat cream and remaining ¼ teaspoon vanilla until stiff peaks form when beaters are lifted; spread over filling. Slice remaining banana; arrange around edge of pie.

EACH SERVING About 367 calories, 6g protein, 41g carbohydrate, 21g total fat (12g saturated), 162mg cholesterol, 216mg sodium.

COCONUT CREAM PIE
Prepare as directed but omit bananas. In Step 3, fold *¾ cup sweetened flaked coconut* into filling before spooning into crust. Refrigerate and top with whipped cream as directed. To serve, sprinkle with *¼ cup sweetened flaked coconut,* toasted.

Butterscotch Pie

Butterscotch, a blend of butter and brown sugar, is always a crowd-pleaser, especially when it comes in the form of a smooth, creamy pie filling.

PREP 35 minutes plus chilling and cooling • COOK/BAKE 35 minutes • MAKES 10 servings.

Prebaked Piecrust for 1-Crust Pie or 9-inch
   Tart Shell (page 140)
3 tablespoons butter (do not use margarine)
1 cup packed dark brown sugar
½ cup boiling water
¼ cup cornstarch
¼ teaspoon salt
1¾ cups whole milk
½ cup heavy or whipping cream
4 large egg yolks
1 teaspoon vanilla extract
whipped cream, for garnish

1 Prepare and bake crust as directed; cool on wire rack.

2 Meanwhile, prepare filling: In 12-inch skillet, heat butter over medium heat until butter has melted and turns deep golden brown, 6 to 7 minutes. (Do not burn.) Add brown sugar and stir until blended. Carefully stir in boiling water; boil, stirring constantly until smooth, about 1 minute. (There will be a few lumps of brown sugar.) Remove skillet from heat.

3 In 3-quart saucepan, with wire whisk, mix cornstarch and salt; whisk in milk, cream, and brown-sugar mixture. Cook over medium heat, whisking constantly, until mixture has thickened and boils; boil 1 minute. Remove from heat.

4 In small bowl, with wire whisk, lightly beat egg yolks. In thin steady stream, add about ½ cup hot milk mixture to yolks, whisking until blended. Gradually add yolk mixture back to milk mixture, whisking rapidly to prevent curdling. Cook over low heat, stirring constantly, until mixture is very thick and coats the back of a spoon (temperature should be 160°F). Stir in vanilla.

5 Pour hot filling into cooled pie shell; press plastic wrap directly onto surface. Refrigerate until filling has set, at least 4 hours or overnight. Garnish with whipped cream.

EACH SERVING About 355 calories, 5g protein, 39g carbohydrate, 20g total fat (11g saturated), 130mg cholesterol, 240mg sodium.

Peanut Butter Silk Pie

Peanut butter is not just for PB&Js. This pie is an easy-to-make dessert that is sophisticated enough for grown-ups. A baked crumb crust made with chopped peanuts is filled with a rich creamy peanut butter–based mixture and garnished with whipped cream and more chopped peanuts.

PREP 20 minutes plus cooling and chilling • **BAKE** 10 minutes • **MAKES** 10 servings.

PEANUT CRUMB CRUST
1 cup graham cracker crumbs
½ cup unsalted dry-roasted peanuts,
    finely chopped
4 tablespoons butter or margarine, melted
2 tablespoons brown sugar

PEANUT BUTTER FILLING
1 cup heavy or whipping cream
1 package (8 ounces) cream cheese, softened
1 cup granulated sugar
1 cup creamy peanut butter
1 teaspoon vanilla extract

whipped cream and chopped dry-roasted
    peanuts, for garnish

1 Preheat oven to 375°F. crust: In 9-inch glass pie plate, with fork, mix crumbs, peanuts, butter, and brown sugar until crumbs are evenly moistened. Press mixture firmly onto bottom and up side of pie plate, making a small rim. Bake 10 minutes. Cool in pan on wire rack.

2 Prepare filling: In small bowl, with mixer at medium speed, beat cream until stiff peaks form. In large bowl, with mixer at medium speed, beat cream cheese, granulated sugar, peanut butter, and vanilla until creamy, occasionally scraping bowl with rubber spatula. With rubber spatula, fold half of whipped cream into peanut butter mixture until blended, then fold in remaining whipped cream.

3 Scrape filling into cooled crust; spread evenly. Refrigerate until filling is firm, at least 4 hours or overnight. To serve, garnish with whipped cream and chopped peanuts.

EACH SERVING About 540 calories, 11g protein, 38g carbohydrate, 41g total fat (17g saturated), 71mg cholesterol, 295mg sodium.

White Russian Pie

An exquisite double coffee–flavored pie made with espresso and coffee liqueur.

PREP 45 minutes plus cooling and chilling • **COOK/BAKE** 15 minutes • **MAKES** 10 servings.

Chocolate Wafer–Crumb Crust (page 139)
1 envelope plus 1 teaspoon unflavored gelatin
¾ cup milk
1 cup espresso or very strong brewed coffee
1 cup sugar
3 tablespoons coffee-flavored liqueur
1½ cups heavy or whipping cream

1 Prepare and bake crust as directed, cool completely on wire rack.

2 In 1-quart saucepan, evenly sprinkle gelatin over ¼ cup milk; let stand 2 minutes to soften gelatin slightly.

3 Stir espresso into gelatin mixture. Cook over medium-low heat, stirring, until gelatin has dissolved. Stir in sugar and cook, stirring, just until sugar has dissolved. Stir in remaining ½ cup milk and coffee liqueur.

4 Pour coffee mixture into medium bowl. Place bowl in larger bowl of ice water and stir frequently until coffee mixture mounds when dropped from spoon, about 15 minutes. Remove from ice bath.

5 In small bowl, with mixer at medium speed, beat ¾ cup cream until stiff peaks form. With rubber spatula, fold whipped cream into coffee mixture until blended. Spoon coffee filling into cooled crust. Refrigerate until pie is well chilled and set, at least 3 hours or up to 24 hours.

6 Up to 2 hours before serving, beat remaining ¾ cup cream until stiff peaks form. Spoon whipped cream over pie.

EACH SERVING About 336 calories, 3g protein, 35g carbohydrate, 20g total fat (12g saturated), 64mg cholesterol, 155mg sodium.

 SERVING CRUMB-CRUST PIES

Serving a pie with a crumb crust can be difficult—the crust can stick to the pan and crumble. Here's the secret: Run a kitchen towel under hot water, squeeze out excess liquid, then open up the towel on a countertop. Set the pie plate on the towel and let stand briefly. The heat will soften the margarine or butter in the crust and make it easy to cut the pie into perfect slices.

Chocolate Walnut Caramel Tart

This creamy, nut-studded filling is flavored with bittersweet chocolate and enriched with caramel.

PREP about 50 minutes plus cooling, chilling, and standing • BAKE about 27 minutes
MAKES 16 servings.

SHORTBREAD CRUST

10 tablespoons butter (1¼ sticks), cut up
   and softened (no substitutions)
½ cup confectioners' sugar
1 teaspoon vanilla extract
1½ cups all-purpose flour

WALNUT-CARAMEL FILLING

2¼ cups granulated sugar
½ cup heavy or whipping cream
½ cup butter (1 stick), cut up (no substitutions)
2 cups walnuts

CHOCOLATE GANACHE

½ cup heavy or whipping cream
1 tablespoon granulated sugar
1 teaspoon butter or margarine
5 ounces semisweet chocolate, coarsely
   chopped
1 teaspoon vanilla extract

1 Prepare crust: Preheat oven to 325°F. In large bowl, with mixer on medium speed, beat butter and confectioners' sugar 2 minutes or until light and fluffy, occasionally scraping bowl with rubber spatula. Beat in vanilla. Reduce speed to low; beat in flour until combined. Transfer dough to ungreased 11-inch tart pan with removable bottom.

2 To prevent dough from sticking to fingertips, place sheet of plastic wrap over dough, then press dough over bottom and up side of pan. Remove and discard plastic wrap. Prick dough all over with fork. Bake crust 27 to 30 minutes or until golden. Cool in pan on wire rack.

3 Prepare filling: In 4-quart saucepan or 12-inch skillet, heat granulated sugar over medium-high heat until melted and amber in color, 8 to 9 minutes, swirling pan frequently. Remove pan from heat. Carefully add cream (mixture will boil rapidly) and stir with wire whisk until a smooth caramel forms. Stir in butter and walnuts. Remove pan from heat.

4 Place tart pan on cookie sheet for easier handling. Pour filling into cooled crust. Refrigerate tart to set filling while making ganache.

5 Prepare ganache: In 1-quart saucepan, combine cream, sugar, and butter, and heat to boiling over medium heat; remove saucepan from heat. Add chocolate to cream mixture and whisk until melted and smooth. Stir in vanilla.

6 Remove tart from refrigerator. Evenly spread ganache over filling. Return tart to refrigerator. Refrigerate at least 3 hours or until set. Remove side of pan. Let tart stand at room temperature 30 minutes to soften slightly before serving.

EACH SERVING About 480 calories, 4g protein, 48g carbohydrate, 32g total fat (15g saturated), 59mg cholesterol, 150mg sodium.

Chocolate Walnut Caramel Tart

Strawberry Mousse Pie

Make this recipe when you have sweet, tasty berries. We prefer a graham-cracker crust with the filling.

PREP 1 hour plus cooling and chilling • **COOK/BAKE** 15 minutes • **MAKES** 10 servings.

Graham Cracker–Crumb Crust (page 139)
1 envelope plus 1 teaspoon unflavored
   gelatin
⅓ cup water
2 pints strawberries (6 cups), hulled,
   plus additional, for garnish
¾ cup sugar
1 tablespoon fresh lemon juice
½ cup heavy or whipping cream

1 Prepare and bake crust as directed; cool completely on wire rack.

2 In 1-quart saucepan, evenly sprinkle gelatin over water; let stand 2 minutes to soften gelatin slightly.

3 Meanwhile, in medium bowl, mash 2 pints strawberries, leaving some lumps. Stir in sugar and lemon juice.

4 Heat gelatin mixture over medium-low heat, stirring frequently, until gelatin has completely dissolved. Stir gelatin mixture into strawberry mixture.

5 Place bowl with strawberry mixture in larger bowl of ice water and stir frequently until mixture mounds when dropped from spoon, 10 to 15 minutes. Remove bowl from ice bath. Reserve ice bath.

6 In small bowl, with mixer at medium speed, beat cream until stiff peaks form. With rubber spatula, fold whipped cream into strawberry mixture until blended. Return bowl with strawberry mixture to ice bath; stir occasionally until mixture mounds when dropped from spoon, about 3 minutes longer.

7 Spoon strawberry filling into cooled crust. Refrigerate until pie is chilled and set, at least 3 hours or up to 24 hours. To serve, top with whole strawberries.

EACH SERVING About 230 calories, 2g protein, 32g carbohydrate, 11g total fat (6g saturated), 29mg cholesterol, 138mg sodium.

Almond Tartlets

Serve these delightful morsels as soon as they are cool. They get soggy if they stand too long, especially in humid weather.

PREP 1 hour plus chilling • **BAKE** 15 minutes • **MAKES** 36 tartlets.

Pastry Dough for 1-Crust Pie (page 136)
1 cup blanched almonds, toasted
    (page 13)
1 cup confectioners' sugar, plus additional
    for sprinkling (optional)
1 large egg
3 tablespoons butter or margarine, softened
1 teaspoon vanilla extract

1 Prepare dough as directed through chilling.
2 Preheat oven to 400°F. In food processor with knife blade attached, pulse almonds and 1 cup confectioners' sugar until nuts are very finely ground. Add egg, butter, and vanilla; process until smooth. Set aside.
3 On lightly floured surface, roll dough paper-thin (thinner than $^{1}/_{16}$ inch thick). With 2½-inch round cutter, cut out 36 pastry rounds (if necessary, reroll scraps). Fit 1 round into each of 36 mini muffin-pan cups or 1¾-inch tartlet molds.

4 Spoon almond filling to within ¼ inch of rim of each tartlet shell. Bake until golden, about 15 minutes. Remove tartlets from pans; cool completely on wire racks. Sift confectioners' sugar over tartlets, if you like.

EACH TARTLET About 85 calories, 2g protein, 8g carbohydrate, 5g total fat (2g saturated), 12 mg cholesterol, 40mg sodium.

HAZELNUT TARTLETS
Prepare tartlet shells and filling as directed, but substitute *1 cup hazelnuts*, toasted and skinned (see page 256), for almonds. Bake and cool as directed.

EACH TARTLET About 80 calories, 1g protein, 8g carbohydrate, 5g total fat (2g saturated), 12mg cholesterol, 40mg sodium.

Lemon Curd and Fruit Tartlets

Lemon Curd and Fruit Tartlets

These tiny tarts, reminiscent of quaint French pastry shops, will evoke oohs *and* aahs *when you bring them to the table. A layer of lemon curd (which can be cooked and chilled well in advance) makes a lovely foil for a few perfect berries.*

PREP 35 minutes plus chilling
BAKE 15 minutes • MAKES 24 tartlets.

Pastry Dough for 9-Inch Tart (page 136)
Lemon Curd (page 236)
1½ pints berries, such as raspberries, blueberries, or hulled strawberries
¼ cup apricot jam

1 Prepare dough as directed through chilling.
2 Preheat oven to 425°F. Divide dough in half. Roll each half into 12-inch rope; cut each rope into twelve 1-inch pieces. Press 1 piece of dough evenly into bottom and up side of each of 24 mini muffin-pan cups (1¾" by 1"). With toothpick, prick each shell all over. Bake until golden, 15 minutes. Cool in pans on wire rack 5 minutes. Remove shells from pans; cool completely on wire rack.
3 Meanwhile, prepare Lemon Curd; chill as directed.
4 Fill each tartlet shell with about 2 teaspoons curd. Top with fresh berries of your choice.
5 In small saucepan, heat apricot jam over low heat just until melted. Press jam through sieve into small bowl. Drizzle warm jam over berries on each tartlet.

EACH TARTLET About 115 calories, 1g protein, 12g carbohydrate, 7g total fat (4g saturated), 42mg cholesterol, 85mg sodium.

Cream Cheese and Fruit Tartlets

You'll need mini muffin pans to make these dainty tarts. Use a different combination of fresh fruits for each tartlet.

PREP 45 minutes plus chilling and cooling
BAKE 15 minutes • MAKES 24 tartlets.

Pastry Dough for 9-Inch Tart (page 136)
1 container (8 ounces) cream cheese spread
3 tablespoons sugar
1 tablespoon milk
¾ teaspoon vanilla extract
mixed fruit: peeled, sliced kiwifruit; halved strawberries; drained canned mandarin-orange sections; and halved small seedless red and green grapes

1 Prepare pastry dough as directed through chilling.
2 Preheat oven to 425°F. Divide dough in half. Roll each half into 12-inch rope; cut each rope into twelve 1-inch pieces. Press 1 piece of dough evenly onto bottom and up side of each of 24 mini muffin-pan cups (1¾" by 1"). With toothpick, prick each shell all over. Bake until golden, about 15 minutes. Cool in pans on wire rack 5 minutes. Remove tart shells from pans; cool completely on rack.
3 Meanwhile, in small bowl, with whisk, beat cream cheese, sugar, milk, and vanilla until blended. Spoon filling into shells. Top each tartlet with some kiwifruit, strawberries, orange sections, and/or grapes. Refrigerate up to 1 hour.

EACH TARTLET WITHOUT FRUIT About 90 calories, 1g protein, 6g carbohydrate, 7g total fat (4g saturated), 18mg cholesterol, 89mg sodium.

Pastries

IF YOU'VE EVER GAZED LONGINGLY at a bakery display of golden cream-filled puffs, chocolate-glazed Éclairs (page 215); and sugary coiled Palmiers (page 222), you know the pull these pastries have. Not only are they a dessert lover's fantasy come true—luscious combinations of light, flaky puff pastry and rich cream filling drizzled or glazed with sweet icing—but they are also a vision of the pastry maker's artistry.

The secret to these and other specialty pastries, like honey-soaked Baklava (page 226) and elegant Crepes Suzette (page 231), is in the making and handling of the pastry doughs. While the ingredients for these doughs are basic and few, it's mastering the technique of incorporating them into a dough and the strict adherence to timing that will turn you into an accomplished pastry chef.

Cream puffs, profiteroles, and éclairs are some of the delicious desserts that are formed with *choux pastry*. This special puff pastry dough is made by combining flour with boiling water and butter, then beating eggs into the mixture until it becomes sticky. Sometimes referred to as "choux paste," the dough can be piped into shapes, which expand during baking into delectable, rich puffs that are crispy outside and hollow inside—perfect for filling.

True *puff pastry*, is made by placing pats of chilled butter on a layer of dough and repeatedly rolling and folding the dough to create more and more layers. When baked, the water in the butter turns to steam, causing the layers to rise to a nearly weightless flaky pastry that can be used in a variety of desserts, including Napoleons (page 235), an almond-paste–filled cake known as Pithiviers (page 220), and light cookies, such as Palmiers (page 222).

Phyllo dough, which is very similar to strudel dough, can be found packaged fresh or frozen. Meaning "leaf" in Greek, phyllo refers to the paper-thin, almost see-through sheets of dough. When brushed with melted butter, spread with chopped nuts and fruits, and layered, phyllo bakes into very fine, crisp multilayered sweets, like Baklava (page 226), or Pistachio Spirals (page 229), and custard-layered Galatoboureko (page 228), so popular throughout Greece and the Middle East.

Crepes are simply very thin pancakes made from a plain or sweetened batter. But when they're spread with jam or filled with fruit or flavored cream, then rolled or folded and bathed in syrup or flamed with liqueur, they become the ultimate in sophisticated desserts.

Without a luscious sweet filling to complete them, however, these specialty pastries would be only empty baked shells and sheets. The most versatile of all is Vanilla Pastry Cream (page 235), but try the Chocolate and Praline variations, too. If you're partial to citrus, you'll love our velvety Lemon Curd (page 236) or orange-and-cinnamon–infused Ricotta Filling (page 237).

Praline Cream-Puff Wreath (page 214)

Saint-Honoré

Saint-Honoré

This lavish creation is so-named in honor of Saint Honoré, the patron saint of French bakers: A glorious construct, it consists of a flaky pastry base ringed with cream-filled puffs, filled with rich pastry cream, then drizzled with caramel.

PREP 2 hours • **COOK/BAKE** 55 minutes • **MAKES** 16 servings.

Vanilla Pastry Cream (page 235)
Pastry Dough for 9-inch Tart (page 136)
Choux Pastry (page 212)
1 cup heavy or whipping cream
1½ cups sugar
¼ cup water

1 Prepare Vanilla Pastry Cream; cover and refrigerate until ready to use.

2 Prepare pastry dough as directed through chilling. On lightly floured surface, with floured rolling pin, roll dough into 12-inch circle; trim edges. Transfer dough to ungreased large cookie sheet; prick with fork and refrigerate.

3 Preheat oven to 400°F. Grease and flour large cookie sheet.

4 Prepare Choux Pastry. Spoon some of the batter into large pastry bag fitted with ½-inch round tip. Pipe batter into sixteen 1½-inch-wide and 1-inch-high mounds, 2 inches apart, onto prepared cookie sheet. With fingertip dipped in water, smooth any peaks. Fill pastry bag with remaining batter and pipe around edge of dough circle to form rim.

5 Bake puffs 40 minutes and pastry circle 25 minutes, until golden, rotating sheets between upper and lower racks after 20 minutes of baking. Transfer puffs to wire rack to cool. Cool pastry circle on cookie sheet on wire rack.

6 In small bowl, with mixer at high speed, beat cream until stiff peaks form. Spoon 1¼ cups pastry cream into large pastry bag fitted with a ¼-inch round tip. Fold whipped cream into remaining 1½ cups pastry cream; refrigerate.

7 Insert tip of pastry bag into side of each puff and pipe in pastry cream to fill halfway.

8 In 2-quart saucepan, heat sugar and water to boiling over medium-high heat. Boil until mixture turns amber in color. Immediately pour hot caramel into small bowl to stop cooking. Carefully dip bottom of each puff in caramel and attach to top of rim in ring around edge of pastry. Drizzle remaining caramel over puffs. Spread pastry-cream mixture evenly in center of circle. Refrigerate up to 6 hours before serving.

EACH SERVING About 390 calories, 6g protein, 46g carbohydrate, 20g total fat (11g saturated), 159mg cholesterol, 215mg sodium.

Pithiviers

Named for a town south of Paris, this impressive pastry "cake" has a rich almond-paste filling.

PREP 20 minutes plus chilling • **BAKE** 30 minutes • **MAKES** 12 servings.

½ recipe Puff Pastry (page 218), cut into
    2 pieces, or 1 package (17¼ ounces)
    frozen puff pastry, thawed
2 large eggs
1 tablespoon water
1 tube or can (7 to 8 ounces) almond paste
1 tablespoon vanilla extract
2 teaspoons sugar

1 Prepare fresh Puff Pastry, if using, as directed. In medium bowl, with fork, beat eggs. Transfer 1 tablespoon egg to cup. Add water; stir until blended. Set aside. In food processor with knife blade attached, pulse almond paste until fine crumbs form. Add almond paste and vanilla to eggs in bowl; with fork, mix until smooth.

2 Lightly flour large cookie sheet. Place damp towel under cookie sheet to prevent it from moving. Place 1 sheet puff pastry on cookie sheet. With floured rolling pin, roll puff pastry into 13-inch square.

3 Invert 11-inch round dish or bowl onto dough, lightly pressing on it to leave impression of circle. With pastry wheel or sharp knife, trim dough to 12-inch circle, leaving 1-inch border around dish; use trimmings for Palmiers (page 222), if desired.

4 With small spatula, cover circle with almond mixture, leaving 1-inch border. Lightly flour another large cookie sheet; on it, roll, mark, and trim remaining piece of puff pastry as directed in Steps 2 and 3. Refrigerate about 15 minutes, or until dough is chilled enough to move without losing its shape.

5 Preheat oven to 400°F. With pastry brush, brush some reserved egg mixture on border around almond mixture. Place chilled dough circle on top of almond mixture; press all around edge to seal. With tip of sharp knife, cut ½-inch triangles, 2 inches apart, from edge of dough; discard triangles. With tip of knife, lightly score top circle with curved lines, starting at center and working toward edge (do not cut all the way through). Brush circle with remaining egg mixture; sprinkle with sugar. (Dessert can be prepared to this point and refrigerated up to 4 hours before baking.)

6 Bake 10 minutes. Turn oven control to 350° F. Bake until no part of dough remains white, 20 to 25 minutes longer, covering pastry loosely with foil to prevent overbrowning. Cool on wire rack at least 30 minutes before serving.

EACH SERVING About 265 calories, 5g protein, 23g carbohydrate, 17g total fat (8g saturated), 66mg cholesterol, 85mg sodium.

APPLE-ALMOND PITHIVIERS

Prepare dough as directed for Pithiviers. Prepare filling as directed in Step 1 but use *1 large egg, ½ tube or can (7 to 8 ounces) almond paste,* and *2 teaspoons vanilla extract*; spread on dough. Top with *1 pound Golden Delicious apples (3 medium)*, peeled, cored, thinly sliced, and tossed with *2 teaspoons all-purpose flour.* Top filling with remaining dough circle. Cut triangles in edge; score top. Brush top with egg mixture and sprinkle with sugar. Bake and cool as directed. Makes 10 servings.

EACH SERVING About 265 calories, 4g protein, 23g carbohydrate, 17g total fat (9g saturated), 59mg cholesterol, 95mg sodium.

Pithiviers

Phyllo Tartlet Shells

Use these just like other pastry shells for desserts, or fill them with your favorite savory spread to serve as appetizers.

PREP 10 minutes • **BAKE** 15 minutes • **MAKES** 8 tartlet shells.

3 tablespoons butter or margarine, melted
6 sheets (16" by 12" each) fresh or frozen
 (thawed) phyllo

1 Preheat oven to 375°F. Lightly brush eight 2½-inch muffin-pan cups with melted butter.

2 Place 1 sheet of phyllo on work surface; brush with some melted butter. (To prevent phyllo from drying out, keep remaining sheets covered with plastic wrap and damp cloth as you work.) Place second sheet of phyllo on top; brush with melted butter. Repeat with third sheet. Cut layered phyllo into eight 4-inch squares. Place 1 phyllo square in each prepared muffin-pan cup, gently patting phyllo onto bottom and against side of cup. Repeat buttering and layering with remaining 3 sheets of phyllo; cut into 8 squares and place crosswise over phyllo in muffin-pan cups, patting into place.

3 Bake until golden, about 15 minutes. Cool in pan on wire rack 15 minutes; carefully remove phyllo shells from muffin-pan cups. Fill just before serving.

EACH SHELL About 81 calories, 1g protein, 7g carbohydrate, 5g total fat (3g saturated), 12mg cholesterol, 113mg sodium.

> **Test Kitchen Tip**
>
> **PHYLLO PASTRY** Fragile, tissue-thin, phyllo is similar to strudel dough. Layered and buttered, it can be used in place of puff pastry to make Napoleons and pastry cups.
>
> **STORING PHYLLO DOUGH** Fresh phyllo dough can be kept refrigerated, tightly wrapped, for 5 days or frozen up to 3 months. Store-bought frozen phyllo will keep 3 to 6 months in your freezer; thaw overnight in the refrigerator before using. Never refreeze thawed phyllo dough; it will become dry and crumbly.
>
> **KEEPING PHYLLO MOIST** Phyllo sheets dry out quickly and become unusable, so don't remove the wrapping until all the other ingredients are assembled. To keep the phyllo sheets you're not working with from drying out, cover them with waxed paper topped by a slightly damp cloth. Don't let the cloth touch the phyllo, or it will become soggy and unworkable.
>
> **SAVING TIME** Phyllo piecrusts and cups can be baked a day ahead and stored in airtight containers. Recrisp, if necessary, in the oven before filling and serving.

Phyllo Tartlet Shells

Baklava

Packaged phyllo makes this signature Greek pastry easy to prepare at home. Just layer the sheets of phyllo with the sweet, cinnamony walnut filling, bake, then soak the whole pan of pastry with warm honey. Food of the gods!

PREP 30 minutes • **BAKE** 1 hour 25 minutes • **MAKES** 24 servings.

4 cups walnuts (16 ounces), finely chopped
½ cup sugar
1 teaspoon ground cinnamon
1 package (16 ounces) fresh or frozen (thawed) phyllo (sixteen 16" by 12" sheets)
¾ cup butter or margarine (1½ sticks), melted
1 cup honey

1 Preheat oven to 300°F. Grease 13" by 9" glass or ceramic baking dish. In large bowl, mix walnuts, sugar, and cinnamon.

2 Trim phyllo sheets into 13" by 9" rectangles; reserve left-over phyllo strips. (To prevent phyllo from drying out, keep covered with plastic wrap and damp cloth as you work.) In prepared baking dish, place 1 phyllo sheet; brush with some melted butter. Repeat to make 5 more phyllo layers; sprinkle 1 cup walnut mixture over phyllo.

3 Place 1 phyllo sheet in baking dish over walnut mixture; brush lightly with melted butter. Repeat to make 5 more phyllo layers, overlapping reserved phyllo strips to make additional rectangles, if necessary. Sprinkle 1 cup walnut mixture over phyllo. Repeat layering two more times, ending with walnut mixture.

4 Place remaining phyllo sheets on top of walnut layer; brush lightly with melted butter. With sharp knife, cut lengthwise halfway through phyllo layers to make 3 equal strips; cut each strip crosswise halfway through layers into 4 rectangles; then cut each rectangle diagonally into 2 triangles. Bake until top is golden brown, about 1 hour 25 minutes.

5 Meanwhile, in 1-quart saucepan, heat honey over medium-low heat until hot but not boiling. Spoon hot honey evenly over hot baklava. Cool baklava in pan on wire rack at least 1 hour to absorb honey, then cover and let stand at room temperature up to 1 day. To serve, with sharp knife, cut all the way through layers.

EACH SERVING About 265 calories, 4g protein, 25g carbohydrate, 18g total fat (5g saturated), 16mg cholesterol, 115mg sodium.

> *Test Kitchen Tip*
> **MEASURING STICKY STUFF**
> To make honey, molasses, and corn syrup slip right out of a measuring cup or spoon, coat the cup with cooking spray before adding the sticky ingedient.

Strawberry Napoleons

These are easier to make than traditional napoleons and are a pleasant change from strawberry shortcake.

PREP 45 minutes plus cooling • **BAKE** 10 minutes • **MAKES** 8 servings.

1 large egg white
pinch salt
1 teaspoon water
4 sheets (16" by 12" each) fresh or frozen
  (thawed) phyllo
3 tablespoons butter or margarine, melted
⅓ cup plus 1 tablespoon sugar
½ cup sliced natural almonds
¾ cup heavy or whipping cream
½ teaspoon vanilla extract
1 pint strawberries, hulled and sliced

1 Preheat oven to 375° F. In small bowl, with fork, lightly beat egg white and salt with water. On work surface, place 1 phyllo sheet; brush with some melted butter and sprinkle with about 1 rounded tablespoon sugar. (To prevent phyllo from drying out, keep covered with plastic wrap and damp cloth as you work.) Top with second phyllo sheet; brush with some melted butter and sprinkle with 1 rounded tablespoon sugar. Repeat layering with third phyllo sheet, melted butter, and sugar. Top with remaining phyllo sheet and brush with egg-white mixture.

2 With sharp knife or pizza wheel, cut phyllo lengthwise into 3 equal strips, then cut each strip crosswise into 4 squares. Cut each square diagonally in half to make 24 triangles. Place phyllo triangles on two ungreased large cookie sheets; sprinkle with almonds and 1 rounded tablespoon sugar. Bake until golden, about 10 minutes. With wide spatula, transfer phyllo to wire racks to cool.

3 Just before serving, in small bowl, with mixer at medium speed, beat cream, vanilla, and remaining 1 tablespoon sugar until stiff peaks form.

4 To assemble napoleons, place 1 phyllo triangle in center of each of eight dessert plates. Top each with about 1 tablespoon whipped cream and about 1 rounded tablespoon sliced strawberries. Cover each with second phyllo triangle, rotating it so that points of second triangle are angled slightly away from points of first triangle. Top triangles with equal amounts of remaining whipped cream and remaining strawberries; top each with third triangle. Serve immediately.

EACH SERVING About 230 calories, 3g protein, 20g carbohydrate, 16g total fat (8g saturated), 42mg cholesterol, 125mg sodium.

Strawberry Napoleons

Galatoboureko

For this Greek dessert, a rich, thick vanilla custard is nestled between layers of phyllo, then soaked with lemon syrup while still warm. Serve warm or chilled.

PREP 50 minutes • **COOK/BAKE** 45 minutes • **MAKES** 24 servings.

6 cups milk
2 strips (3" by 1" each) orange peel
¾ cup quick-cooking enriched farina cereal
¾ cup sugar
4 large eggs
2 teaspoons vanilla extract
1 package (16 ounces) fresh or frozen (thawed) phyllo (sixteen 16" by 12" sheets)
½ cup butter or margarine (1 stick), melted
Lemon Syrup (below)

1 Preheat oven to 350°F. Grease 13" by 9" baking dish. In 3-quart saucepan, heat milk and orange peel to boiling over medium-high heat. In small bowl, with fork, mix farina and sugar. Gradually sprinkle farina mixture into hot milk mixture, stirring with wooden spoon; heat to boiling. Reduce heat to medium-low and simmer, stirring, until mixture has thickened slightly, about 5 minutes. Remove from heat. Discard orange peel.

2 In large bowl, with mixer at high speed, beat eggs and vanilla until well blended. Reduce speed to medium and gradually beat in hot farina mixture.

3 In prepared baking dish, place 1 phyllo sheet, allowing it to extend up sides of dish; brush with some melted butter. (To prevent phyllo from drying out, keep covered with plastic wrap and damp cloth as you work.) Repeat to make about 5 more layers, brushing each with melted butter. Pour farina mixture into phyllo-lined dish.

4 Cut remaining phyllo into approximately 13" by 9" rectangles, reserving left-over phyllo strips. Place 1 phyllo sheet on top of farina mixture; brush with some melted butter. Repeat to make about 6 layers with remaining phyllo and melted butter, overlapping reserved phyllo strips to make additional rectangles, if necessary. With sharp knife, cut lengthwise through top phyllo layers only to make 4 equal strips, then cut each strip crosswise into 6 pieces. Bake until top is golden and puffy, about 35 minutes.

5 Meanwhile, prepare Lemon Syrup. Pour hot syrup evenly over phyllo. Cool in pan on wire rack at least 2 hours before serving.

6 To serve, with sharp knife, cut all the way through layers. Serve warm, or cover and refrigerate up to 1 day to serve chilled.

EACH SERVING About 180 calories, 4g protein, 25g carbohydrate, 7g total fat (4g saturated), 54mg cholesterol, 140mg sodium.

LEMON SYRUP

In 1-quart saucepan, heat *¾ cup sugar, ⅓ cup water,* and *4 strips (3" by 1" each) lemon peel* to boiling over medium heat, stirring occasionally. Reduce heat; simmer until syrup has thickened slightly, about 8 minutes. Discard lemon peel and stir in *1 tablespoon fresh lemon juice.* Makes about ¾ cup.

EACH TABLESPOON About 24 calories, 0g protein, 6g carbohydrate, 0g total fat, 0mg cholesterol, 0mg sodium.

Pistachio Spirals

These snail-shaped pastries are very popular in the Middle East. If you like, prepare and refrigerate the syrup several days in advance.

PREP 1 hour plus cooling • **COOK/BAKE** 35 minutes • **MAKES:** 12 servings

LEMON SYRUP
1 lemon
⅔ cup sugar
1 cup water
1 teaspoon vanilla extract

PHYLLO SPIRALS
6 sheets (16" by 12" each) fresh or frozen
   (thawed) phyllo
6 tablespoons butter or margarine, melted
2 tablespoons sugar
⅔ cup shelled pistachios, finely chopped

1 Prepare syrup: From lemon, with vegetable peeler, remove peel; squeeze 1 tablespoon juice. In 1-quart saucepan, heat sugar, lemon peel, and water to boiling over medium-high heat; boil 15 minutes. Pour syrup into bowl; discard lemon peel. Stir in vanilla and lemon juice; cover and refrigerate.

2 Prepare spirals: Preheat oven to 350°F. Arrange phyllo sheets in stack. Cut stack lengthwise in half, then crosswise in half to make 24 rectangles, each about 8½" by 6". (To prevent phyllo from drying out, keep covered with plastic wrap and damp cloth as you work.)

3 On sheet of waxed paper, brush 1 phyllo rectangle with some melted butter. Place another rectangle on top and brush with some melted butter. Fold both layers crosswise in half. Brush top with more butter and sprinkle with ½ teaspoon sugar. Spoon 1½ teaspoons pistachios in a line down one long side of phyllo, leaving ½-inch border. Fold edges in over pistachios and roll up from long side. Coil phyllo roll tightly to make a snail shape. Transfer to cookie sheet. Repeat with remaining phyllo, butter, sugar, and pistachios, reserving leftover pistachios.

4 Bake until spirals are crisp and golden, about 20 minutes. With wide metal spatula, transfer spirals to a deep dish, such as a pie plate, that will hold them in single layer. Pour chilled lemon syrup over hot spirals and sprinkle with remaining pistachios. Cool to room temperature.

EACH SERVING About 175 calories, 2g protein, 21g carbohydrate, 10g total fat (5g saturated), 16mg cholesterol, 107mg sodium.

Basic Crepes

These delicate pancakes can be stuffed with one of our fillings or rolled up with some jam.
Crepes can be prepared up to one day ahead; wrap a stack tightly in plastic wrap and refrigerate.

PREP 5 minutes plus chilling • **COOK** 25 minutes • **MAKES** 12 crepes.

3 large eggs
1½ cups milk
4 tablespoons butter or margarine, melted
⅔ cup all-purpose flour
½ teaspoon salt

1 In blender, blend eggs, milk, 2 tablespoons butter, flour, and salt until smooth, scraping down sides of blender. Transfer batter to medium bowl; cover and refrigerate at least 1 hour or up to overnight to allow flour to absorb liquid.

2 Heat nonstick 10-inch skillet over medium-high heat. Brush bottom of skillet lightly with some remaining butter. With wire whisk, throughly mix batter to blend well. Pour scant ¼ cup batter into skillet; tilt pan to coat bottom completely with batter. Cook crepe until top is set and underside is lightly browned, about 1½ minutes.

3 With heat-safe rubber spatula, loosen edge of crepe; turn. Cook until second side has browned, about 30 seconds. Slip crepe onto waxed paper. Repeat with remaining batter, brushing pan lightly with butter before cooking each crepe and stacking crepes between layers of waxed paper.

EACH CREPE About 97 calories, 3g protein, 7g carbohydrate, 6g total fat (3g saturated), 68mg cholesterol, 166mg sodium.

Test Kitchen Tip

CREPE BATTER
These very thin French dessert pancakes can be made from plain or sweetened batter. Spread them with jam, a fruit mixture, or other sweet filling, then serve rolled or folded. They can be topped with a sweet sauce or confectioners' sugar and for a special occasion, set aflame with brandy or liqueur.

Crepes Suzette

For real table-side drama, you can flambé the crepes in a chafing dish, but they are just as enjoyable when prepared in the kitchen.

PREP 30 minutes plus chilling
COOK 10 minutes • **MAKES** 6 servings.

Basic Crepes (opposite)
1 orange
4 tablespoons butter or margarine
2 tablespoons sugar
¼ cup orange-flavored liqueur

1 Prepare Basic Crepes.
2 Prepare sauce: From orange, grate ½ teaspoon peel and squeeze ⅓ cup juice. In nonreactive 12-inch skillet, heat orange peel and juice, butter, and sugar over low heat, stirring until butter has melted.
3 Fold crepes into quarters; arrange in sauce, overlapping if necessary, and heat through, turning crepes once.
4 In very small saucepan, heat liqueur over medium heat until hot; remove from heat. Carefully ignite liqueur with long match; pour flaming liqueur over crepes. When flame dies down, transfer crepes to dessert plates.

EACH SERVING About 311 calories, 7g protein, 22g carbohydrate, 20g total fat (12g saturated), 156mg cholesterol, 411mg sodium.

Banana Crepes with Maple-Walnut Sauce

These scrumptious crepes are the perfect dessert for an elegant dinner party.

PREP 10 minutes • **COOK** 5 minutes
MAKES 4 servings.

½ cup walnuts
2 tablespoons butter or margarine
2 tablespoons brown sugar
2 tablespoons maple syrup
2 tablespoons heavy or whipping cream
⅛ teaspoon ground cinnamon
pinch salt
4 firm ripe bananas, each peeled and
    cut diagonally into ¾-inch-thick slices
4 (7-inch) crepes, refrigerated
vanilla ice cream (optional)

1 In nonstick 12-inch skillet, heat walnuts, butter, brown sugar, maple syrup, cream, cinnamon, and salt over medium heat, stirring frequently, until mixture has thickened and boils, 3 to 4 minutes. Stir in bananas and cook, gently stirring occasionally to coat with sauce, just until bananas are soft and heated through, 2 to 3 minutes longer.
2 Place 1 crepe in center of each of 4 dessert plates. Spoon one fourth of banana mixture lengthwise in center of each crepe. Fold sides of crepe over to enclose filling. Drizzle with any remaining sauce in skillet. Serve with vanilla ice cream, if you like.

EACH SERVING About 365 calories, 5g protein, 48g carbohydrate, 19g total fat (7g saturated), 31mg cholesterol, 117mg sodium.

Lemon-Sugar Crepes

These delicate crepes are perfect on a brunch menu or as a light (and do-ahead) dinner party finale.

PREP 10 minutes plus chilling • **COOK/BAKE** 35 minutes • **MAKES** 12 crepes or 6 servings.

3 lemons
3 large eggs
1½ cups whole milk
⅔ cup all-purpose flour
½ teaspoon salt
3 tablespoons butter or margarine, melted
¾ cup granulated sugar
candied lemon peel (optional)

1 From lemons, grate ½ teaspoon peel and squeeze ¼ cup juice. Cover and refrigerate juice.
2 In blender, blend eggs, milk, flour, salt, lemon peel, and 2 tablespoons melted butter until smooth, scraping down the sides of blender. Transfer batter to medium bowl; cover and refrigerate at least 1 hour or up to overnight to allow flour to absorb liquid.
3 Heat nonstick 10-inch skillet over medium-high heat. Brush bottom of skillet lightly with some remaining butter. Pour scant ¼ cup batter into skillet, tilt pan to coat bottom completely with batter. Cook crepe until top is set and underside is lightly browned, about 1½ minutes.
4 With heat-safe rubber spatula, loosen edge of crepe; turn. Cook until second side has browned, about 30 seconds. Slip crepe onto waxed paper. Repeat with remaining batter, brushing pan lightly with butter before cooking each crepe and stacking crepes between layers of waxed paper.

5 When ready to serve, preheat oven to 350°F. Grease 13" by 9" baking dish. Sprinkle each crepe with 1 tablespoon sugar and 1 tablespoon reserved lemon juice. Fold each crepe into quarters; place in baking dish, overlapping slightly. Cover dish with foil; heat crepes in oven until hot, about 12 minutes. If you like, top each crepe with candied lemon peel and serve.

EACH SERVING About 290 calories, 7g protein, 40g carbohydrate, 12g total fat (7g saturated), 136mg cholesterol, 340mg sodium.

> **Test Kitchen Tip**
> **MAKE AHEAD TIP**
> Crepes can be prepared and frozen up to 2 months ahead. To freeze, stack crepes, placing waxed paper between crepes. Wrap stacked crepes tightly in foil; label and freeze. To use, place wrapped, frozen crepes on cookie sheet and heat in preheated 350°F oven until heated through, about 20 minutes. To serve, follow step 4.

Lemon-Sugar Crepes

Apple-Calvados Crepes

These crepes can be filled with almost any seasonal fruits. Calvados is French apple brandy; applejack is the American version. If you prefer, substitute apple juice.

PREP 50 minutes plus chilling • **COOK/BAKE** 30 minutes • **MAKES** 6 servings.

12 Basic Crepes (page 230)
5 tablespoons butter or margarine
3 pounds Golden Delicious apples (6 large),
    peeled, cored, and finely chopped
½ cup plus 1 tablespoon sugar
¼ cup Calvados or applejack brandy

1 Prepare Basic Crepes.

2 Preheat oven to 400°F. In 12-inch skillet, melt 4 tablespoons butter over medium-high heat. Stir in apples and ½ cup sugar; cover and cook until apples are soft, about 10 minutes. Remove cover and cook, stirring occasionally, until apples begin to caramelize, about 10 minutes. Stir in Calvados and remove from heat.

3 Spread scant ¼ cup apple mixture down center of each crepe and roll up jelly-roll fashion. Arrange rolled crepes in single layer, seam side down, in shallow 3½- to 4-quart baking dish. Dot with remaining 1 tablespoon butter and sprinkle with remaining 1 tablespoon sugar. Bake until heated through, about 5 minutes.

EACH SERVING About 472 calories, 7g protein, 64g carbohydrate, 22g total fat (13g saturated), 161mg cholesterol, 430mg sodium.

PLUM FILLING

In 12-inch skillet, melt *3 tablespoons butter or margarine* over medium-high heat. Add *2½ pounds ripe plums (10 large),* quartered and pitted, *⅔ cup granulated sugar,* and *pinch ground cloves.* Cook, stirring occasionally, until plums are tender, 15 to 20 minutes. Fill crepes, dotting with butter and sprinkling with sugar, and bake as directed.

EACH SERVING About 428 calories, 8g protein, 59g carbohydrate, 19g total fat (10g saturated), 151mg cholesterol, 392mg sodium.

MIXED BERRY FILLING

In medium bowl, toss *1½ cups hulled and halved strawberries, 1½ cups blueberries, 1½ cups raspberries,* and *⅔ cup granulated sugar.* Fill crepes, dotting with butter and sprinkling with sugar, and bake as directed.

EACH SERVING About 326 calories, 7g protein, 47g carbohydrate, 13g total fat (7g saturated), 135mg cholesterol, 335mg sodium.

BANANA FILLING

In medium bowl, toss *2 large ripe bananas,* sliced, with *¼ cup packed brown sugar.* Fill crepes, dotting with butter and sprinkling with sugar, and bake as directed.

EACH SERVING About 267 calories, 7g protein, 3g carbohydrate, 13g total fat (7g saturated), 135mg cholesterol, 337mg sodium.

Vanilla Pastry Cream

This versatile cream is used to fill many classic desserts, such as Éclairs (page 215) and Napoleons (page 219). Be sure to cook the pastry cream for the full two minutes, or it may not set up.

PREP 5 minutes plus chilling • **COOK** 10 minutes • **MAKES** 2¾ cups.

2¼ cups milk
4 large egg yolks
⅔ cup sugar
¼ cup all-purpose flour
¼ cup cornstarch
1 tablespoon vanilla extract

1 In 3-quart saucepan, heat 2 cups milk over medium-high heat until bubbles form around edge. Meanwhile, in large bowl, with wire whisk, beat egg yolks, remaining ¼ cup milk, and sugar until combined; whisk in flour and cornstarch until blended. Gradually whisk hot milk into egg-yolk mixture.

2 Return milk mixture to saucepan; cook over medium-high heat, whisking constantly, until mixture has thickened and boils. Reduce heat to low and cook, stirring, 2 minutes.

3 Remove from heat and stir in vanilla. Pour pastry cream into shallow dish. Press plastic wrap directly onto surface of pastry cream to prevent skin from forming. Refrigerate at least 2 hours or up to overnight.

EACH TABLESPOON About 31 calories, 1g protein, 5g carbohydrate, 1g total fat (0g saturated), 21mg cholesterol, 7mg sodium.

CHOCOLATE PASTRY CREAM

Prepare pastry cream as directed, but in Step 3, stir in *3 squares (3 ounces) melted semisweet chocolate* and *1 square (1 ounce) melted unsweetened chocolate,* with vanilla. Makes about 3 cups.

EACH TABLESPOON About 44 calories, 1g protein, 3g carbohydrate, 3g total fat (2g saturated), 23mg cholesterol, 37mg sodium.

Praline Pastry Cream

Use this luscious pastry cream to fill Éclairs (page 215) and Strawberry Napoleons (page 227). It requires a little extra work, but when your guests take their first bite, you will be rewarded with lip-smacking praise.

PREP 15 minutes plus chilling
COOK 25 minutes • MAKES about 3¼ cups.

Vanilla Pastry Cream (page 235)
1 cup sugar
⅓ cup water
1 cup slivered blanched almonds, toasted
   (page 13)

1 Prepare Vanilla Pastry Cream and refrigerate until cold.
2 Grease jelly-roll pan. In 2-quart saucepan, heat sugar and water over low heat, stirring gently, until sugar has dissolved. Increase heat to medium and boil rapidly. With pastry brush dipped in water, occasionally wash down side of pan to prevent sugar from crystallizing. Cook, swirling pan occasionally, until syrup turns a light amber, about 7 minutes.
3 Working quickly, stir in almonds. Spread almond mixture in thin layer on prepared jelly-roll pan; cool until hardened. Break praline into small pieces.
4 In food processor with knife blade attached, process praline until finely ground. In medium bowl, combine pastry cream and praline powder until blended.

EACH TABLESPOON About 55 calories,
1g protein, 8g carbohydrate, 2g total fat
(og saturated), 18mg cholesterol, 5mg
sodium.

Lemon Curd

A British teatime tradition (where it is often served on toast), lemon curd is a velvety citrus custard that also makes a wonderful filling for tarts. Lemon Curd Cream is a super-rich variation.

PREP 5 minutes • COOK 12 minutes
MAKES about 1 cup.

2 lemons
½ cup sugar
6 tablespoons butter or margarine
3 large egg yolks

1 From lemons, grate 1½ teaspoons peel and squeeze ⅓ cup juice. In 1-quart saucepan, cook lemon peel and juice, sugar, butter, and yolks over low heat, stirring constantly with wooden spoon, until mixture thickens and coats back of spoon, or temperature on candy thermometer reads 140°F, about 5 minutes. (Do not boil or yolks will curdle.)
2 Pour mixture into medium bowl. Press plastic wrap directly onto surface of curd to keep skin from forming as it cools. Cool to room temperature. Refrigerate 1 hour, or up to 2 days.

EACH TABLESPOON About 75 calories,
1g protein, 7g carbohydrate, 5g total fat
(3g saturated), 52mg cholesterol, 45mg sodium.

LEMON CURD CREAM
Prepare and cool Lemon Curd as directed. In small bowl, with mixer at high speed, beat *¼ cup heavy or whipping cream* to soft peaks. Fold into curd. Makes about 1⅔ cups.

EACH TABLESPOON About 55 calories,
og protein, 4g carbohydrate, 4g total fat
(2g saturated), 35mg cholesterol,
30mg sodium.

Lemon Filling

This "sturdier" cornstarch-thickened version of lemon curd works as a filling for a layer cake or jelly roll.

PREP 15 minutes • COOK 8 minutes
MAKES about 1 cup.

3 large lemons
1 tablespoon cornstarch
6 tablespoons butter or margarine
¾ cup sugar
4 large egg yolks

1 From lemons, grate 1 tablespoon peel and squeeze ½ cup juice. In 2-quart saucepan, with wire whisk, mix cornstarch and lemon peel and juice until smooth. Add butter and sugar. Heat to boiling over medium heat; boil, stirring constantly, 1 minute.

2 In small bowl, with fork, beat egg yolks lightly. Into egg yolks, beat small amount of hot lemon mixture; pour egg mixture back into lemon mixture in saucepan, beating rapidly. Reduce heat to low; cook, stirring constantly, until thick, 5 minutes (do not boil).

3 Pour mixture into medium bowl. Press plastic directly wrap onto surface to keep skin from forming as it cools. Cool to room temperature. Refrigerate 3 hours, or up to 3 days.

EACH TABLESPOON About 95 calories, 1g protein, 11g carbohydrate, 6g total fat (3g saturated), 65mg cholesterol, 45mg sodium.

Ricotta Filling

Vary this quick filling by stirring in chopped dried fruit, finely chopped semisweet chocolate, or chocolate mini chips. Try it in Phyllo Tartlet Shells (page 224).

PREP 5 minutes • MAKES about 4 cups.

1 container (32 ounces) ricotta cheese
1⅓ cups confectioners' sugar
2 teaspoons vanilla extract
1 teaspoon freshly grated orange peel
⅛ teaspoon ground cinnamon

In food processor with knife blade attached, pulse ricotta until smooth. Add confectioners' sugar, vanilla, orange peel, and cinnamon; pulse until well blended.

EACH TABLESPOON About 35 calories, 2g protein, 3g carbohydrate, 2g total fat (1g saturated), 7mg cholesterol, 10mg sodium.

Special Desserts

THE DESSERTS IN THIS CHAPTER ARE INDEED SPECIAL. Although some might consider them old-fashioned, we think they'll never go out of style because of their simplicity, ease of preparation, and comfort factor. These friendly finales are special because they never fail to soothe with their sweetness. You know them as soufflés, custards, mousses, puddings, meringues, trifle, and tiramisu.

Warm, fluffy, high-topped *soufflés* are at once impressive enough for the most formal dinner and unpretentious enough for a casual get-together. Baked in individual ramekins or a large soufflé dish, our recipe picks for Chocolate, Orange, Ginger-Pear, Raspberry, and Amaretto-Chocolate soufflés (pages 240–247) are all about lightness and intensity of flavor.

Eggs and milk or cream are what give slow-cooked *custards* their silky, rich texture and enormous appeal. Crème Brûlée (page 248) and Crème Caramel (page 251) both sport a topping of caramelized sugar—on the former, it's brittle and crunchy, on the latter it forms a glaze and pools on the serving dish. Chocolate fanatics just might fight over the last of the Chocolate Pôts de Crème (page 249), the creamy baked custard traditionally served in tiny pot-shaped cups made for this purpose.

Steamed, boiled, or baked, *puddings* vary in texture from soft and spongy, like our three varieties of bread pudding, to thick and creamy, as represented by New England's corn meal-and-molasses Indian Pudding (page 254), Britain's caramel-topped Sticky Toffee Pudding (page 255), and that perennial favorite—rice pudding (page 253).

When you want a special dessert that's both light and guaranteed to make people smile, turn to *meringues*. These fat-free cloudlike confections, baked in the shape of nests, disks, or flat rectangles, can be used as the bases for a variety of easy, pretty, and delicious desserts. Crisp on the outside and melt-in-your-mouth inside, fill or layer them with custards or whipped cream and fruits. For extra make-ahead ease, prepare the fillings and meringues for a spectacular Coconut-Lime Dacquoise (page 266) or Lemon and Fresh Raspberry Dacquoise (page 268) several days ahead and layer them the day of the party.

The combination of cake and custard that comprise Tiramisu (page 271) or trifle is reason enough to get out your best large glass bowl. For the classic Italian sweet, alternating layers of ladyfingers soaked in coffee and brandy and a rich cream mixture are topped with a dusting of cocoa and decorated with Chocolate Curls (page 362). A beautiful bowl of Raspberry-Banana Trifle (page 273) shows off jam-sandwiched slices of pound cake surrounding layers of sliced bananas and custard.

These are desserts that will make everyday dinners special, special events memorable, and good times even better.

Baked Chocolate-Hazelnut Puddings (page 256)

Chocolate Soufflés

These are irresistible as individual soufflés and spectacular baked as one large soufflé.

PREP 20 minutes plus cooling • **BAKE** 25 minutes • **MAKES** 8 servings.

1¼ cups plus 3 tablespoons granulated sugar
¼ cup all-purpose flour
1 teaspoon instant espresso-coffee powder
1 cup milk
5 squares (5 ounces) unsweetened chocolate, chopped
3 tablespoons butter or margarine, softened
4 large eggs, separated
2 teaspoons vanilla extract
2 large egg whites
¼ teaspoon salt
confectioners' sugar

1 In 3-quart saucepan, whisk 1¼ cups granulated sugar, flour, and espresso powder. Gradually whisk in milk until blended. Cook over medium heat, stirring constantly with wooden spoon, until mixture has thickened and boils; boil, stirring, 1 minute. Remove from heat.

2 Stir in chocolate and butter until melted and smooth. With whisk, beat in egg yolks until well blended; stir in vanilla. Cool to lukewarm.

3 Meanwhile, preheat oven to 350°F. Grease eight 6-ounce custard cups or ramekins or a 2-quart soufflé dish; sprinkle lightly with remaining 3 tablespoons granulated sugar.

4 In large bowl, with mixer at high speed, beat the 6 egg whites and salt just until stiff peaks form when beaters are lifted. With rubber spatula, gently fold one-third of beaten egg whites into chocolate mixture, then fold back into remaining egg whites just until blended.

5 Spoon mixture into prepared custard cups or soufflé dish. (If using custard cups, place in jelly-roll pan for easier handling.) Bake until soufflés have puffed (centers will still be glossy), 25 to 30 minutes for individual soufflés, 30 to 35 minutes for large soufflé. Dust with confectioners' sugar. Serve immediately.

EACH SERVING About 356 calories, 7g protein, 44g carbohydrate, 19g total fat (10g saturated), 122mg cholesterol, 178mg sodium.

> **Test Kitchen Tip**
> **HOT SOUFFLÉS**
> *The secret to a high-rising soufflé is in the egg whites.* Separate eggs when cold, but let whites stand at room temperature for about 30 minutes before beating. Beat just until stiff but not dry; do not overbeat.
> *To create the "crown" effect* characteristic of a classic soufflé, when mixture is turned into the soufflé dish, use a spoon to make a 1-inch deep indentation around the top, 1 to 1½ inches from rim.
> *Soufflés need to be timed carefully.* They should be served as soon as they come out of the oven; otherwise they tend to collapse inward. Be sure oven is thoroughly preheated and don't open the door before the end of baking time; a rush of cold air could cause the soufflé to collapse.
> *If your soufflé does collapse* before you get it to the table, pretend that's the way it's supposed to be. Drizzle it with sauce or top with whipped cream or sliced fruit and call it a "baked pudding."

Chocolate Soufflés

Orange Liqueur Soufflé

Perhaps the most popular and elegant of all soufflés. Infuse it with your favorite orange liqueur: Grand Marnier, Curaçao, or Triple Sec.

PREP 20 minutes plus cooling • **BAKE** 30 minutes • **MAKES** 8 servings.

4 tablespoons butter or margarine
⅓ cup all-purpose flour
⅛ teaspoon salt
1½ cups milk, warmed
½ cup plus 2 tablespoons granulated sugar
4 large eggs, separated
⅓ cup orange-flavored liqueur
1 tablespoon freshly grated orange peel
2 large egg whites
confectioners' sugar
whipped cream (optional)

1 In heavy 2-quart saucepan, melt butter over low heat. Add flour and salt; cook, stirring, 1 minute. With wire whisk, gradually whisk in warm milk. Cook over medium heat, stirring with wooden spoon, until mixture has thickened and boils. Reduce heat and simmer 1 minute. Remove from heat.

2 With wire whisk, stir ½ cup granulated sugar into milk mixture. Gradually whisk in egg yolks, stirring rapidly to prevent curdling. Cool egg-yolk mixture to lukewarm, stirring occasionally. Stir in orange liqueur and orange peel.

3 Preheat oven to 375°F. Grease 2-quart soufflé dish with butter and evenly sprinkle with remaining 2 tablespoons granulated sugar.

4 In large bowl, with mixer at high speed, beat the 6 egg whites until stiff peaks form when beaters are lifted. With rubber spatula, gently fold one-third of beaten egg whites into egg-yolk mixture; fold back into remaining egg whites just until blended.

5 Spoon mixture into prepared soufflé dish. If desired, to create top-hat effect (center will rise higher than edge), with back of spoon, make 1-inch-deep indentation all around top of soufflé about 1 inch from edge of dish. Bake until soufflé has puffed, top is golden brown, and knife inserted 1 inch from edge comes out clean, 30 to 35 minutes. Dust with confectioners' sugar. Serve immediately. Pass whipped cream to spoon onto each serving if you like.

EACH SERVING About 214 calories, 6g protein, 26g carbohydrate, 10g total fat (5g saturated), 128mg cholesterol, 162mg sodium.

Orange Liqueur Soufflé

Individual Ginger-Pear Soufflés

Whipping up a soufflé has never been simpler: Just make one of our pureed fruit bases.

PREP 45 minutes plus cooling • **COOK/BAKE** 42 minutes • **MAKES** 6 servings.

4 cups peeled, cored, and coarsely chopped
    fully ripe pears (5 to 6 pears)
1 tablespoon fresh lemon juice
2 teaspoons minced, peeled fresh ginger
1 tablespoon butter or margarine, melted
2 tablespoons plus ¼ cup sugar
6 large egg whites
½ teaspoon cream of tartar
1 teaspoon vanilla extract

1 In nonreactive 2-quart saucepan, combine pears, lemon juice, and ginger. Cover and cook over medium-high heat until pears are very tender, about 15 minutes. Remove cover and cook, stirring occasionally, until mixture is almost dry and reduced to about 1 cup, 10 to 15 minutes.
2 In blender with center part of cover removed to let steam escape, or in food processor with knife blade, puree pear mixture until smooth. Cool to room temperature in large bowl.
3 Meanwhile, preheat oven to 425°F. Brush six 6-ounce custard cups or ramekins with melted butter and sprinkle with 2 tablespoons sugar.
4 In large bowl, with mixer at high speed, beat egg whites and cream of tartar until soft peaks form when beaters are lifted. Gradually sprinkle in remaining ¼ cup sugar, 1 tablespoon at a time, beating until sugar has dissolved. Add vanilla; continue beating until whites stand in stiff peaks when beaters are lifted. With rubber spatula, fold beaten egg whites, one-third at a time, into pear mixture just until blended.
5 Spoon mixture into prepared cups. Place cups in jelly-roll pan for easier handling. Bake until soufflés have puffed and tops begin to brown, 12 to 15 minutes. Serve immediately.

EACH SERVING: About 180 calories, 4g protein, 38g carbohydrate, 3g total fat (1g saturated), 5 mg cholesterol, 72mg sodium.

BANANA SOUFFLÉS

In blender or in food processor with knife blade attached, puree *3 very ripe, large bananas, 1 tablespoon fresh lemon juice,* and *¼ teaspoon ground cinnamon* until smooth. (You should have about 1 cup). Fold beaten egg whites into banana puree and bake as directed.

EACH SERVING About 150 calories, 4g protein, 30g carbohydrate, 2g total fat (2g saturated), 5 mg cholesterol, 72mg sodium.

PEACH OR APRICOT SOUFFLÉS

Drain *1 can (1 pound, 13 ounces) peaches in heavy syrup or 2 cans (16 ounces each) apricots in heavy syrup.* In blender or in food processor with knife blade attached, puree peaches or apricots until smooth. Transfer to 4-quart saucepan and heat to boiling over medium-high heat. Reduce heat to medium-low and cook, stirring occasionally, until puree is reduced to 1 cup, 15 to 20 minutes. Transfer fruit puree to large bowl; cool to room temperature. Stir in *1 tablespoon fresh lemon juice and ⅛ teaspoon almond extract.* Fold beaten egg whites into fruit puree and bake as directed.

EACH SERVING About 155 calories, 4g protein, 32g carbohydrate, 2g total fat (1g saturated), 5mg cholesterol, 77mg sodium.

Raspberry Soufflé

Here's an impressive fat-free dessert you can make in a snap: Fold store-bought raspberry fruit spread into beaten egg whites and bake. To do ahead, prepare and refrigerate soufflé mixture in soufflé dish up to three hours, then bake as directed just before serving.

PREP 20 minutes • **BAKE** 15 minutes • **MAKES** 6 servings.

⅔ cup seedless raspberry spreadable fruit
   (no-sugar-added jam)
1 tablespoon fresh lemon juice
4 large egg whites
½ teaspoon cream of tartar
2 tablespoons sugar
1 teaspoon vanilla extract

1 Preheat oven to 375°F. In large bowl, with wire whisk, beat raspberry fruit spread and lemon juice until blended; set aside.

2 In small bowl, with mixer at high speed, beat egg whites and cream of tartar until soft peaks form when beaters are lifted. Sprinkle in sugar, beating until sugar has dissolved. Add vanilla; continue beating until whites stand in stiff peaks when beaters are lifted.

3 With rubber spatula, fold one-third of whites into raspberry mixture until well blended, then fold in remaining whites. Spoon soufflé mixture into 1½-quart soufflé dish; gently spread evenly. Bake until puffed and lightly browned, 15 to 18 minutes. Serve immediately.

EACH SERVING About 75 calories, 3g protein, 16g carbohydrate, 0g total fat, 0mg cholesterol, 35mg sodium.

Raspberry Soufflé

Amaretto-Chocolate Soufflé

This irresistibly rich dessert is the kind of sublime treat you'd expect to find on the menu at an upscale restaurant—and you don't have to make reservations to enjoy it!

PREP 20 minutes plus cooling • COOK/BAKE 45 minutes • MAKES 10 servings.

1 cup plus 2 tablespoons granulated sugar
¼ cup all-purpose flour
1 teaspoon instant espresso-coffee powder
1 cup milk
5 squares (5 ounces) unsweetened chocolate, coarsely chopped
3 tablespoons butter or margarine
3 tablespoons almond-flavored liqueur
2 teaspoons vanilla extract
4 large **eggs**, separated
2 large egg whites
¼ teaspoon salt
confectioners' sugar

1 In 3-quart saucepan, with wire whisk, mix ½ cup granulated sugar, flour, and espresso powder; gradually whisk in milk, whisking until blended. Cook over medium heat, stirring constantly, until mixture thickens and boils. Boil, stirring, 1 minute. Remove saucepan from heat. Stir in chocolate and butter. With wire whisk, beat in liqueur and vanilla until mixture is smooth and creamy. Whisk in egg yolks. Cool to lukewarm, stirring occasionally.

2 Preheat oven to 350°F. Grease 2-quart soufflé dish; sprinkle with 2 tablespoons granulated sugar.

3 In large bowl, with mixer at high speed, beat the 6 egg whites and salt until foamy. Gradually beat in remaining ½ cup granulated sugar just until stiff peaks form when beaters are lifted. With rubber spatula, gently fold two-thirds of whites, one-third at a time, into chocolate mixture. Fold chocolate mixture back into remaining whites.

4 Pour chocolate mixture into soufflé dish; bake 40 minutes. When soufflé is done, sprinkle with confectioners' sugar. Serve immediately.

EACH SERVING About 270 calories, 6g protein, 33g carbohydrate, 14g total fat (6g saturated), 2g fiber, 88mg cholesterol, 155mg sodium.

> **Test Kitchen Tip** SERVING SOUFFLÉS
> To serve a soufflé, insert two serving forks, back-to-back, into the center. Gently divide the soufflé into portions, then serve with a large spoon.

Amaretto-Chocolate Soufflé

Crème Brûlée

With its brittle caramelized top, this velvety custard has risen from obscurity to become a megastar of the dessert world.

PREP 20 minutes plus cooling and chilling • **BAKE/BROIL** 38 minutes • **MAKES** 10 servings.

½ vanilla bean or 2 teaspoons vanilla extract
1½ cups heavy or whipping cream
1½ cups half-and-half or light cream
8 large egg yolks
⅔ cup granulated sugar
⅓ to ½ cup packed brown sugar

1 Preheat oven to 325°F. If using vanilla bean, with knife, cut lengthwise in half; scrape out seeds and reserve. In heavy 3-quart saucepan, heat cream, half-and-half, and vanilla bean and seeds over medium heat until bubbles form around edge. (If using vanilla extract, stir in after cream mixture in Step 2.) Remove from heat. With slotted spoon, remove vanilla bean.

2 Meanwhile, in large bowl, with wire whisk, beat egg yolks and granulated sugar until well blended. Slowly stir in hot cream mixture until well combined. Stir in vanilla extract, if using. Pour cream mixture into ten 4- to 5-ounce broiler-proof ramekins or a shallow 2½-quart casserole.

3 Place ramekins or casserole in large roasting pan (17" by 11½"); place pan in oven. Carefully pour enough very hot water into pan to come halfway up sides of ramekins or casserole. Bake just until set (mixture will still be slightly soft in center), 35 to 40 minutes. Transfer to wire rack to cool to room temperature. Cover and refrigerate until well chilled, at least 3 hours or up to overnight.

4 Up to 2 hours before serving, preheat broiler. Place brown sugar in small sieve; with spoon, press sugar through sieve to evenly cover tops of chilled custards.

5 Place ramekins in jelly-roll pan for easier handling. With broiler rack at closest position to heat source, broil crème brûlée just until brown sugar has melted, 3 to 4 minutes. Serve, or refrigerate up to 2 hours. The melted sugar will form a delicious brittle crust.

EACH SERVING About 307 calories, 4g protein, 25g carbohydrate, 21g total fat (12g saturated), 232mg cholesterol, 38mg sodium.

Chocolate Pôts de Crème

This old-fashioned dessert is sometimes served in porcelain cups specially made for the purpose (the cups themselves are also called pôts de crème). *If you have some pretty china teacups and saucers—a matching or not—they can be used instead.*

PREP 15 minutes plus chilling • **COOK/BAKE** 35 minutes • **MAKES** 6 servings.

3 squares (3 ounces) semisweet chocolate,
   chopped
2½ cups milk
2 large eggs
2 large egg yolks
¼ cup sugar
1 teaspoon vanilla extract

1 Preheat oven to 350°F. In 3-quart saucepan, heat chocolate and ¼ cup milk over low heat, stirring often, until chocolate has melted. Remove saucepan from heat.

2 In 2-quart saucepan, heat remaining 2¼ cups milk to boiling over medium-high heat; stir into chocolate mixture.

3 In large bowl, with wire whisk or fork, beat whole eggs, egg yolks, sugar, and vanilla until blended. Gradually whisk in chocolate mixture until well combined. Divide mixture evenly among six 6-ounce ramekins.

4 Place ramekins in 14" by 10" roasting pan; place pan in oven. Carefully pour boiling water into roasting pan to come halfway up sides of ramekins. Bake until knife inserted halfway between edge and center of custards comes out clean, 30 to 35 minutes. Transfer ramekins to wire rack to cool. Cover and refrigerate until well chilled, at least 3 hours.

EACH SERVING About 210 calories, 7g protein, 22g carbohydrate, 11g total fat (6g saturated), 156mg cholesterol, 75mg sodium.

MOCHA PÔTS DE CRÈME
Prepare as directed for Chocolate Pôts de Crème, but in Step 2 heat the 2¼ cups milk to boiling with *1 tablespoon instant coffee powder.* Bake, cool, and chill as directed.

EACH SERVING About 204 calories, 7g protein, 22g carbohydrate, 11g total fat (5g saturated), 155mg cholesterol, 70mg sodium.

Panna Cotta with Raspberry Sauce

Panna cotta *means "cooked cream" in Italian, even though it is barely cooked at all.*

PREP 20 minutes plus chilling • **COOK** 15 minutes • **MAKES** 8 servings.

1 envelope unflavored gelatin
1 cup milk
½ vanilla bean or 1½ teaspoons vanilla extract
1¾ cups heavy or whipping cream
¼ cup sugar
1 strip (3" by 1") lemon peel
1 cinnamon stick (3 inches)
Raspberry Sauce (page 95)
fresh raspberries

1 In 2-cup measuring cup, sprinkle gelatin evenly over milk; let stand 2 minutes to soften gelatin slightly. If using vanilla bean, with knife, cut lengthwise in half; scrape out seeds and reserve.
2 In 1-quart saucepan, combine cream, sugar, lemon peel, cinnamon stick, and vanilla bean halves and seeds. (If using vanilla extract, stir into cream mixture in step 3.) Heat to boiling over high heat, stirring occasionally. Reduce heat and simmer, stirring occasionally, 5 minutes. Stir in gelatin mixture; cook over low heat, stirring frequently, until gelatin has completely dissolved, 2 to 3 minutes.
3 Discard lemon peel, cinnamon stick, and vanilla bean from cream mixture. Stir in vanilla extract, if using. Pour cream mixture into medium bowl set in large bowl of ice water. With rubber spatula, stir mixture until it just begins to set, 10 to 12 minutes. Pour cream mixture into eight 4-ounce ramekins. Place ramekins in jelly-roll pan for easier handling. Cover and refrigerate panna cotta until well chilled and set, 4 hours or up to overnight.
4 Meanwhile, prepare Raspberry Sauce.

5 To unmold panna cotta, run tip of knife around edges. Tap side of each ramekin sharply to break seal. Invert onto plates. Spoon raspberry sauce around each panna cotta and sprinkle with raspberries.

EACH SERVING WITHOUT RASPBERRY SAUCE
About 228 calories, 3g protein, 9g carbohydrate, 20g total fat (13g saturated), 76mg cholesterol, 37mg sodium.

Test Kitchen Tip

CUSTARDS Soft, soothing custards, both stove-top and baked, are made from a sweetened mixture of milk and eggs that is slow-cooked to prevent curdling.
COOK IT! For silky stove-top custards, cook over low heat, stirring constantly to prevent boiling. Cook baked custards in a water bath—place baking dish or dishes in a larger pan of hot water—to insulate them from the direct heat of the oven so they bake evenly, without separating.
IS IT DONE YET? A *baked custard* is done when the center jiggles slightly; it will firm up as it cools. To check, insert a knife 1 inch up from the center; it should come out clean. A *stove-top custard* is ready when it coats a spoon well. Run a finger across the spoon; it should leave a track.
COOL IT! Remove *a baked custard* from its water bath immediately, otherwise it will continue to cook. Cool *stove-top custards* with a piece of plastic wrap placed directly on top so the custard doesn't form a "skin."

Perfect Crème Caramel

A classic do-ahead dessert that can tame the assertive flavors of a southwestern-style meal.

PREP 15 minutes plus chilling
BAKE 40 minutes • MAKES 8 servings.

1 cup sugar
5 large eggs
3 cups whole milk
2 teaspoons vanilla extract
¼ teaspoon salt

1 Preheat oven to 325°F. In heavy 1-quart saucepan, heat ½ cup sugar over medium heat, swirling pan occasionally, until melted and amber in color, 5 to 7 minutes. Into each of eight 6 ounce custard cups or ramekins, immediately spoon about 1 tablespoon caramel, tilting cup so that it coats bottom.
2 In large bowl, with wire whisk, mix eggs and remaining ½ cup sugar until well blended. Whisk in milk, vanilla, and salt until well combined. Pour milk mixture over caramel in cups.
3 Place cups in large roasting pan; place pan on oven rack. Carefully pour enough hot tap water into pan to come halfway up sides of cups.
4 Bake custard until knife inserted in center comes out clean, 40 to 45 minutes. Transfer cups to wire rack to cool to room temperature. Cover and refrigerate until well chilled, 4 hours or up to 2 days.
5 To unmold, run small metal spatula or thin knife around side of each cup. Invert each custard onto a dessert plate, allowing caramel syrup to drip from cup onto custard.

EACH SERVING About 202 calories, 7g protein, 30g carbohydrate, 6g total fat (3g saturated), 146mg cholesterol, 156mg sodium.

Mango Mousse

Sweet, thick cream of coconut is the secret behind this dessert—a luscious taste of the tropics.

PREP 20 minutes plus chilling
COOK 2 minutes • MAKES 8 servings.

1 envelope unflavored gelatin
¼ cup cold water
2 large ripe mangoes, peeled and coarsely chopped (3 cups)
1 can (15 ounces) cream of coconut
½ cup fresh lime juice (from 4 large limes)
fresh berries (optional)

1 In 1-quart saucepan, sprinkle gelatin evenly over water; let stand 2 minutes to soften gelatin slightly.
2 Meanwhile, in blender, combine mangoes, cream of coconut, and lime juice; puree until smooth.
3 Cook gelatin over low heat, stirring frequently, until it has completely dissolved, 2 to 3 minutes. Add to mango mixture and process until well blended. Pour into 8 custard cups. Cover and refrigerate until well chilled, 4 hours or up to overnight. Serve with berries, if you like.

EACH SERVING About 181 calories, 3g protein, 18g carbohydrate, 12g total fat (11g saturated), 0mg cholesterol, 38mg sodium.

> **Test Kitchen Tip** **CARAMEL**
> To remove hardened caramel from saucepan, fill pan with water and bring to a boil. Use a pastry brush to "wash" away caramel on sides of pan.

Cappuccino Mousse

For a fanciful presentation, serve this espresso-and-cream mousse in an assortment of coffee cups.

PREP 30 minutes plus chilling • **COOK** 2 minutes • **MAKES** 8 servings.

1 envelope plus 1 teaspoon unflavored gelatin
⅓ cup plus ½ cup milk
1 cup espresso or very strong brewed coffee
½ cup plus 1 teaspoon sugar
2 tablespoons coffee-flavored liqueur
1⅓ cups heavy or whipping cream
pinch ground cinnamon

1 In 1-quart saucepan, evenly sprinkle gelatin over ⅓ cup milk; let stand 5 minutes to soften gelatin slightly. Stir in espresso. Heat over low heat, stirring frequently, until gelatin has completely dissolved, 2 to 3 minutes. Remove from heat; add ½ cup sugar, stirring until dissolved. Stir in remaining ½ cup milk and liqueur. Transfer mixture to large bowl.

2 Place bowl in larger bowl of ice water. With rubber spatula, stir just until mixture mounds slightly when dropped from spoon, about 15 minutes. Remove from water bath.

3 Meanwhile, in medium bowl, with mixer at medium speed, beat 1 cup cream until soft peaks form. Fold one-third of cream into coffee mixture until well blended. Gently fold in remaining beaten cream. Spoon mixture into 8 coffee cups or 6-ounce custard cups. Cover and refrigerate until set, 4 hours or up to overnight.

4 Just before serving, in small bowl, beat remaining ⅓ cup cream, remaining 1 teaspoon sugar, and cinnamon until stiff peaks form. To serve, spoon dollop of whipped cream onto each mousse.

EACH SERVING About 217 calories, 3g protein, 17g carbohydrate, 15g total fat (10g saturated), 58mg cholesterol, 30mg sodium.

The Best Rice Pudding

Turn basic rice pudding into a sublime dessert by folding in some whipped cream before serving. If raisins are not your favorite omit them, or add an equal amount of another dried fruit instead.

PREP 5 minutes plus chilling • **COOK** 1 hour 15 minutes • **MAKES** 8 servings.

4 cups whole milk
½ cup long-grain white rice
½ cup sugar
¼ teaspoon salt
1 teaspoon vanilla extract
½ cup raisins (optional)
¼ cup heavy or whipping cream
⅛ teaspoon ground cinnamon (optional)

1 In 4-quart saucepan, combine milk, rice, sugar, and salt; heat to boiling over medium-high heat, stirring occasionally. Reduce heat to low; cover and simmer, stirring occasionally, until rice is very tender, about 1 hour. Remove pan from heat, stir in vanilla and raisins, if using.
2 Transfer pudding to medium serving bowl. Place plastic wrap directly on surface of pudding to prevent skin from forming. Refrigerate until well chilled, at least 4 hours.
3 When pudding is cold, in small bowl, with mixer at medium speed, beat cream until stiff peaks form. With rubber spatula, gently fold cream into pudding. If not serving pudding right away, cover and refrigerate up to 3 days. Sprinkle cinnamon over pudding just before serving, if you like.

EACH SERVING About 192 calories, 5g protein, 28g carbohydrate, 7g total fat (4g saturated), 27mg cholesterol, 135mg sodium.

Vanilla Rice Pudding with Dried Cherries

The starchy nature of short-grain Arborio rice gives this pudding its unsurpassed creaminess.

PREP 15 minutes plus cooling and chilling
COOK 1 hour 40 minutes • **MAKES** 12 servings.

½ vanilla bean or 1 tablespoon vanilla extract
6 cups milk
¾ cup sugar
¾ cup short-grain rice, preferably Arborio
½ cup dried cherries or raisins
2 tablespoons dark rum (optional)
¼ teaspoon salt
½ cup heavy or whipping cream

1 If using vanilla bean, with knife cut lengthwise in half; scrape out seeds and reserve.
2 In heavy 4-quart saucepan, combine milk, sugar, and vanilla bean halves and seeds; heat to boiling over medium-high heat, stirring occasionally (If using vanilla extract, stir in with rum in Step 3.) Stir in rice and heat to boiling. Reduce heat; cover and simmer, stirring occasionally, until mixture is very creamy and has thickened slightly, about 1 hour 25 minutes (pudding will firm up on chilling). Discard vanilla bean.
3 Spoon rice pudding into large bowl, stir in dried cherries, rum, if using, and salt. Cool slightly, then cover and refrigerate until well chilled, at least 6 hours or up to overnight.
4 Up to 2 hours before serving, in small bowl, with mixer at medium speed, beat cream until stiff peaks form. Using rubber spatula, fold half of whipped cream into rice pudding, then fold in remaining cream.

EACH SERVING About 212 calories, 5g protein, 31g carbohydrate, 8g total fat (5g saturated), 31mg cholesterol, 112mg sodium.

Indian Pudding

A baked cornmeal-and-molasses pudding that has been a New England favorite for many years. Top each serving with a scoop of vanilla ice cream.

PREP 30 minutes • **COOK/BAKE** 2 hours 25 minutes • **MAKES** 8 servings.

4 cups milk
⅔ cup cornmeal
½ cup light (mild) molasses
4 tablespoons butter or margarine,
   cut into pieces
¼ cup sugar
1 teaspoon ground ginger
1 teaspoon ground cinnamon
½ teaspoon salt
¼ teaspoon ground nutmeg
whipped cream or vanilla ice cream (optional)

1 Preheat oven to 350°F. Grease shallow 1½-quart baking dish.

2 In small bowl, combine 1 cup milk and cornmeal. In 4-quart saucepan, heat remaining 3 cups milk to boiling over high heat. With wire whisk, whisk in cornmeal mixture; heat to boiling. Reduce heat and simmer, stirring frequently with wooden spoon to prevent lumps, until mixture is very thick, about 20 minutes. Remove from heat; stir in molasses, butter, sugar, ginger, cinnamon, salt, and nutmeg until well blended.

3 Pour batter evenly into prepared baking dish. Place baking dish in large roasting pan; place pan in oven. Carefully pour enough very hot water into roasting pan to come halfway up sides of baking dish. Cover with foil and bake pudding 1 hour. Remove foil and bake until lightly browned and just set, about 1 hour longer.

4 Remove baking dish from water. Cool pudding in pan on wire rack 30 minutes. Serve pudding warm with whipped cream or vanilla ice cream, if you like.

EACH SERVING About 253 calories, 5g protein, 36g carbohydrate, 11g total fat (6g saturated), 33mg cholesterol, 271mg sodium.

Test Kitchen Tip

BAKED PUDDINGS
In England, puddings traditionally were the sweet course at the end of a meal, but over the years, a "pudding" came to mean any dessert. Technically, when we refer to a pudding we mean a combination of a custard (usually eggs, milk, and sugar) mixed with flavorings, (like fruits, jams, spices, and nuts), and cooked with a starch, such as bread, rice, flour, or cornmeal. A pudding is cooked until thickened, then cooled until set. It is frequently topped with a sweet sauce, meringue, or whipped cream. There are so many kinds of puddings—from sturdy and rich, to light and delicate—so it's a good idea to consider your whole meal and the season when deciding which pudding to make.

Sticky Toffee Pudding

This English pudding, with its sticky caramel topping, is outstanding when served warm with whipped cream.

PREP 20 minutes plus standing and cooling • **BAKE/BROIL** 35 minutes • **MAKES** 12 servings.

1 cup chopped pitted dates
1 teaspoon baking soda
1½ cups boiling water
10 tablespoons butter or margarine
　　(1¼ sticks), softened
1 cup granulated sugar
1 large egg
1 teaspoon vanilla extract
2 cups all-purpose flour
1 teaspoon baking powder
1 cup packed brown sugar
¼ cup heavy or whipping cream
whipped cream (optional)

1 Preheat oven to 350°F. Grease 13" by 9" baking pan. In medium bowl, combine dates, baking soda, and boiling water; let mixture stand 15 minutes.

2 In large bowl, with mixer at medium speed, beat 6 tablespoons butter until creamy. Beat in granulated sugar until light and fluffy. Add egg and vanilla; beat until blended. Reduce speed to low; add flour and baking powder, beating to combine. Add date mixture and beat until well combined (batter will be very thin). Pour batter into prepared pan. Bake until golden and toothpick inserted in center of pudding comes out clean, about 30 minutes.

3 Meanwhile, in 2-quart saucepan, heat brown sugar, cream, and remaining 4 tablespoons butter to boiling over medium-high heat. Boil 1 minute; remove saucepan from heat.

4 Turn oven control to broil. Spread brown-sugar mixture evenly over top of hot pudding. Broil at position closest to heat source until bubbling, about 30 seconds. Cool in pan on wire rack 15 minutes. Serve warm with whipped cream, if you like.

EACH SERVING About 362 calories, 3g protein, 62g carbohydrate, 12g total fat (7g saturated), 50mg cholesterol, 259mg sodium.

Baked Chocolate-Hazelnut Puddings

Bake this rich, soufflélike dessert in individual ramekins. If you like, substitute toasted blanched almonds for the hazelnuts. See photo on page 238.

PREP 30 minutes plus chilling • **BAKE** 25 minutes • **MAKES** 8 servings.

¾ cup hazelnuts, toasted (see below)
¾ cup sugar
4 tablespoons butter or margarine, softened
7 large eggs, separated
8 squares (8 ounces) semisweet chocolate,
    melted and cooled
¼ teaspoon salt
¾ cup heavy or whipping cream
1 teaspoon vanilla extract

1 Generously butter eight 6-ounce ramekins; set aside.

2 In food processor with knife blade attached, process hazelnuts and ¼ cup sugar until very finely ground.

3 In large bowl, with mixer at medium speed, beat butter until smooth. Gradually add ¼ cup sugar, beating until creamy. Add egg yolks, one at a time, beating after each addition. Beat in hazelnut mixture and chocolate until blended.

4 In another large bowl, with mixer at high speed, beat egg whites, salt, and remaining ¼ cup sugar until stiff peaks form when beaters are lifted. Stir one-fourth of beaten whites into chocolate mixture until well combined. Gently fold remaining whites into chocolate mixture. Spoon batter into prepared ramekins. Cover and refrigerate 4 hours or overnight.

5 Preheat oven to 350°F. Place ramekins in large roasting pan (17" by 11½"); place pan in oven. Carefully pour boiling water into roasting pan to come halfway up sides of ramekins. Bake until knife inserted in centers comes out with some fudgy batter stuck to it, about 25 minutes. Cool ramekins on wire rack 5 minutes.

6 Meanwhile, in small bowl, with mixer at medium speed, beat cream and vanilla until soft peaks form when beaters are lifted.

7 To serve, scoop out small amount of pudding from top of each dessert; fill with some whipped cream. Replace scooped-out pudding on top of cream. Serve puddings with remaining whipped cream on the side.

EACH SERVING About 500 calories, 10g protein, 37g carbohydrate, 37g total fat (17g saturated), 235mg cholesterol, 215mg sodium.

 TOASTING HAZELNUTS

Toasting nuts brings out their flavor, and in the case of nuts such as hazelnuts, allows the skins to be removed.

To toast almonds, pecans, walnuts, or hazelnuts, preheat the oven to 350°F. Spread the shelled nuts in a single layer on a cookie sheet. Bake, stirring occasionally, until lightly browned and fragrant, about 10 minutes. Toast hazelnuts until the skins begin to peel away. Let the nuts cool completely before chopping.

To skin hazelnuts, wrap the still-warm toasted nuts in a clean kitchen towel and let stand for about 10 minutes. Using the towel, rub off as much of the skins as possible (all of the skin may not come off).

Chocolate Bread Pudding

For this pudding, cubes of bread are steeped in chocolate custard and then layered with ribbons of melted semisweet chocolate.

PREP 25 minutes plus chilling • **BAKE** 50 minutes • **MAKES** 8 servings.

8 slices stale firm white bread
3 tablespoons plus ⅓ cup sugar
8 squares (8 ounces) semisweet chocolate,
    melted
3 cups milk
3 large eggs
1½ teaspoons vanilla extract

1 Grease 8" by 8" baking dish. Cut bread into 1-inch squares. Arrange one-third of bread squares in prepared dish in single layer; sprinkle with 1 tablespoon sugar and drizzle with 2 tablespoons melted chocolate. Repeat to make a second layer. Top with remaining bread.

2 In 2-quart saucepan, heat milk to boiling over medium-high heat. Meanwhile, in medium bowl, with wire whisk, combine eggs and ⅓ cup sugar. While whisking, slowly pour milk into egg mixture. Add remaining melted chocolate and vanilla; stir to combine.

3 Pour egg mixture over bread. Refrigerate, gently stirring mixture occasionally, until bread is soaked with chocolate mixture, about 3 hours.

4 Preheat oven to 325°F. Sprinkle pudding with remaining 1 tablespoon sugar. Place dish in 13" by 9" roasting pan; place pan in oven. Carefully pour boiling water into roasting pan to come halfway up sides of dish. Bake until knife inserted in center of pudding comes out clean, about 50 minutes. Transfer dish from roasting pan to wire rack to cool 15 minutes. Serve pudding warm, or cover and refrigerate to serve cold later.

EACH SERVING About 355 calories, 9g protein, 49g carbohydrate, 15g total fat (8g saturated), 93mg cholesterol, 225mg sodium.

Test Kitchen Tip

BREADS FOR BREAD PUDDING

Firm white bread is used for most of our bread puddings. If you're buying sliced bread in the supermarket, look for one with dense texture. Words like "hearty," "traditional," and "brick oven-baked" are cues to good texture. The bread need not be fresh, in fact, slightly stale bread is preferable. Excellent options for pudding are French or Italian bread, challah, brioche, and raisin bread.

Plum Pudding with Hard Sauce

Our holiday steamed pudding is the perfect prepare-ahead recipe because the flavor improves as the pudding ages. Hard Sauce, made with rum or brandy, is the classic accompaniment.

PREP 1 hour • **COOK** 2 hours • **MAKES** 2 puddings, or 16 servings.

2¼ cups all-purpose flour
1 cup fresh bread crumbs (2 slices firm
   white bread)
1 teaspoon baking powder
1 teaspoon ground cinnamon
½ teaspoon salt
¼ teaspoon ground nutmeg
¼ teaspoon ground cloves
1 cup pitted prunes, chopped
1 cup pitted dates, chopped
¾ cup dark seedless raisins
½ cup walnuts, toasted (page 13)
   and chopped
1 medium Granny Smith apple, peeled, cored,
   and shredded
1 teaspoon freshly grated lemon peel
1 cup butter or margarine (2 sticks), softened
1 cup packed light brown sugar
2 large eggs
⅔ cup buttermilk
½ cup dark molasses
⅓ cup dark rum or brandy
Hard Sauce (opposite)

1 Generously grease two 1-quart heat-safe bowls. Cut two pieces of foil 2 inches larger than tops of bowls. Grease dull side of each piece of foil.

2 In large bowl, with wire whisk, mix flour, bread crumbs, baking powder, cinnamon, salt, nutmeg, and cloves. Add prunes, dates, raisins, walnuts, apple, and lemon peel to flour mixture. With hands, thoroughly toss mixture until fruits are well coated and separate.

3 In separate large bowl, with mixer at low speed, beat butter and brown sugar until blended. Increase speed to high; beat until light and fluffy, about 1 minute. Reduce speed to medium; add eggs, one at a time, beating well after each addition. Beat in buttermilk, molasses, and rum (mixture will look curdled). With wooden spoon, stir butter mixture into flour mixture until well blended.

4 Divide batter equally between prepared bowls; cover tightly with foil, greased side down, pressing foil against sides of bowls. Tightly tie string under rims of bowls to keep foil in place and puddings from getting wet.

5 Place metal cookie cutter or small wire rack in each of two 5-quart saucepots. (Cookie cutters serve as steaming racks.) Pour in enough water to come 1½ inches up sides of pots. Set pudding bowls on top of cookie cutters. Cover and heat water to boiling over high heat. Reduce heat; simmer until toothpick inserted through foil in center of puddings comes out clean, about 2 hours.

6 Meanwhile, prepare Hard Sauce.

7 When puddings are done, cool in bowls on wire racks 5 minutes. Remove foil; run tip of small knife around edges of puddings. Invert onto serving plates. Serve hot with Hard Sauce. If making ahead, cool puddings completely in bowls, then wrap well in heavy-duty foil. Refrigerate up to 1 month, or freeze up to 3 months. To serve, cover and resteam pudding (thawed, if frozen) as directed in Step 5, 1 hour.

EACH SERVING WITHOUT HARD SAUCE About 378 calories, 5g protein, 57g carbohydrate, 16g total fat (8g saturated), 58mg cholesterol, 266mg sodium.

HARD SAUCE

The essential companion to any warm steamed pudding, but especially Christmas plum pudding.

PREP 10 minutes • **MAKES** about 2 cups.

1 cup butter (2 sticks), softened (do not use margarine)
2 cups confectioners' sugar
¼ cup dark rum or brandy
1 teaspoon vanilla extract

1 In small bowl, with mixer at medium speed, beat butter until creamy. Reduce speed to low and gradually beat in confectioners' sugar until light and fluffy. Beat in rum and vanilla.

2 Serve, or transfer to airtight containers and refrigerate up to 1 month. Let stand at room temperature until soft enough to spread, about 30 minutes.

EACH TABLESPOON About 84 calories, 0g protein, 7g carbohydrate, 6g total fat (4g saturated), 16mg cholesterol, 59mg sodium.

Bread-and-Butter Pudding

Cinnamon-raisin bread can be used in place of white bread for a tasty variation. Just reduce the ground cinnamon to one-half teaspoon.

PREP 10 minutes plus standing
BAKE 50 minutes • **MAKES** 8 servings.

½ cup sugar
¾ teaspoon ground cinnamon
4 tablespoons butter or margarine, softened
12 slices firm white bread
4 large eggs
3 cups milk
1½ teaspoons vanilla extract
whipped cream (optional)

1 Preheat oven to 325°F. Grease 8-inch square baking dish. In cup, with fork, mix 1 tablespoon sugar and cinnamon. Spread butter on one side of each bread slice. Arrange 4 bread slices in dish, overlapping slightly if necessary; lightly sprinkle with cinnamon mixture. Repeat to make two more layers.

2 In medium bowl, with wire whisk, beat eggs, milk, remaining sugar, and vanilla until well blended. Pour milk mixture over bread slices. Let stand 20 minutes, occasionally pressing bread down to absorb milk mixture.

3 Bake until knife inserted in center of pudding comes out clean, 50 to 60 minutes. Let stand 15 minutes to serve pudding warm, or cover and refrigerate to serve cold later. Top with whipped cream, if desired.

EACH SERVING About 313 calories, 10g protein, 38g carbohydrate, 13g total fat (7g saturated), 135mg cholesterol, 364mg sodium.

Black-and-White Bread Pudding with White-Chocolate Custard Sauce

For chocolate lovers: a sweet bread pudding with two kinds of chocolate. Serve it alone or with sinfully rich White-Chocolate Custard Sauce. (We love the pudding served warm and the sauce cold.)

PREP 40 minutes plus standing • **BAKE** 1 hour 15 minutes • **MAKES** 16 servings.

1 loaf (16 ounces) sliced firm white bread
9 large eggs
4 cups milk
½ cup sugar
1 tablespoon vanilla extract
½ teaspoon salt
3 ounces white chocolate or white baking bar, grated
3 squares (3 ounces) semisweet chocolate, grated
White-Chocolate Custard Sauce

1 Preheat oven to 325°F. Grease 13" by 9" baking dish. Place bread slices on large cookie sheet and bake, turning once, until lightly toasted, about 20 minutes. Place bread slices in prepared baking dish, overlapping slightly.

2 Meanwhile, in very large bowl, with wire whisk, beat eggs, milk, sugar, vanilla, and salt until well combined. Stir in grated white and semisweet chocolates. Pour milk mixture evenly over bread; let stand 20 minutes, occasionally pressing bread down to absorb milk mixture.

3 Cover baking dish with foil; bake 1 hour. Remove foil and bake until top is golden and knife inserted in center of pudding comes out clean, 15 to 20 minutes longer.

4 Meanwhile, prepare White-Chocolate Custard Sauce.

5 Serve bread pudding warm with custard sauce, or cover and refrigerate to serve cold later.

EACH SERVING WITHOUT WHITE-CHOCOLATE CUSTARD SAUCE: About 235 calories, 8g protein, 30g carbohydrate, 9g total fat, (4g saturated), 128mg cholesterol, 296 mg sodium.

WHITE-CHOCOLATE CUSTARD SAUCE

Finely chop *3 ounces white chocolate or white baking bar;* place in large bowl; set aside. In small bowl, with wire whisk, beat *4 large egg yolks* and *¼ cup sugar* until well blended. In heavy 2-quart saucepan, heat *1 cup milk* and *¾ cup heavy or whipping cream* over medium-high heat until bubbles form around edge. Into egg mixture, beat *⅓ cup hot milk mixture.* Slowly pour egg mixture back into milk mixture, stirring rapidly to prevent curdling. Reduce heat to low; cook, stirring constantly, until mixture has thickened slightly and coats back of spoon, about 5 minutes. (On thermometer, temperature should reach 160°F; do not boil, or sauce will curdle.) Pour milk mixture over white chocolate, stirring until chocolate melts and mixture is smooth. Serve custard sauce warm, or refrigerate to serve cold later. Makes about 2½ cups sauce.

EACH TABLESPOON About 41 calories, 1g protein, 3g carbohydrate, 3g total fat (2g saturated), 28mg cholesterol, 7mg sodium.

Black-and-White Bread Pudding with White-Chocolate Custard Sauce

Meringue Shells

Fill these versatile shells with whipped cream and berries or ice cream and chocolate sauce, or use to make Meringue Nests with Lemon Filling and Strawberries (opposite). Do not make meringues in humid weather: They will not stay crisp.

PREP 15 minutes plus cooling • **BAKE** 2 hours plus drying time • **MAKES** 6 servings.

3 large egg whites
⅛ teaspoon cream of tartar
¾ cup sugar
½ teaspoon vanilla extract

1 Preheat oven to 200°F. Line large cookie sheet with foil or parchment paper. In small bowl, with mixer at high speed, beat egg whites and cream of tartar until soft peaks form when beaters are lifted. Sprinkle in sugar, 2 tablespoons at a time, beating until sugar has dissolved. Add vanilla; continue beating until egg whites stand in stiff, glossy peaks when beaters are lifted.

2 Spoon meringue into 6 equal mounds on prepared cookie sheet, 4 inches apart. With back of tablespoon, spread each mound into 4-inch round. Make well in center of each round to form "nest."

3 Bake meringues until firm and just beginning to color, about 2 hours. Turn off oven; leave meringues in oven 1 hour or up to overnight to dry. If not leaving overnight, cool completely on cookie sheet on wire rack. Store meringue shells in airtight container.

EACH SERVING About 106 calories, 2g protein, 25g carbohydrate, og total fat, omg cholesterol, 28mg sodium.

MINIATURE MERINGUE SHELLS

Preheat oven to 200°F. Line 2 cookie sheets with foil or parchment paper. Prepare as directed in Step 1. Drop meringue by rounded teaspoons, 2 inches apart, on prepared cookie sheets. With back of teaspoon, make well in center of each mound to form "nest" about 1½ inches across. Bake until meringues are firm and just beginning to color, about 1 hour. Turn off oven; leave meringues in oven 1 hour or up to overnight to dry. If not leaving overnight, cool completely on cookie sheet on wire rack. Store as directed. Makes 20 miniature shells.

EACH SERVING: About 32 calories, og protein, 8g carbohydrate, og total fat, omg cholesterol, 8mg sodium.

Test Kitchen Tip

PERFECT MERINGUE SHELLS

For symmetrically shaped meringue shells, mark circles on the foil with a toothpick. Use a cake pan or saucer as a guide for large shells or a jar cap or cookie cutter for miniature shells.

Meringue Nests with Lemon Filling and Strawberries

Make the meringue nests and the lemon filling up to two days ahead, and assemble the dessert just before serving.

PREP 35 minutes plus chilling and cooling • **BAKE** 2 hours plus drying time • **MAKES** 6 servings.

Lemon Filling (page 237)
Meringue Shells (opposite)
½ cup heavy or whipping cream
1 pint strawberries, hulled and cut
    into quarters
2 tablespoons strawberry preserves
mint leaves

1 Prepare Lemon Filling. While lemon filling is chilling, prepare Meringue Shells.

2 In small bowl, with mixer at medium speed, beat cream until stiff peaks form. With rubber spatula, gently fold whipped cream into lemon filling until blended.

3 To serve, in medium bowl, toss strawberries with preserves until evenly coated. Spoon lemon filling into meringue shells, dividing evenly. Top with strawberry mixture and garnish with mint leaves; place on dessert plates.

EACH SERVING About 448 calories, 4g protein, 60g carbohydrate, 22g total fat (13g saturated), 200mg cholesterol, 150mg sodium.

Meringue Nests with Lemon Filling and Strawberries

Pavlova

Sometimes referred to as the "national dessert of Australia," this gorgeous dessert was created to honor prima ballerina Anna Pavlova, who was renowned for her leading role in Swan Lake. Swanlike in its enchanting delicacy and pristine whiteness, a meringue shell is filled with fresh fruit and whipped cream.

PREP 30 minutes • **BAKE** 2 hours plus drying time • **MAKES** 8 servings.

⅔ cup plus 2 tablespoons sugar
1 tablespoon cornstarch
4 large egg whites
¼ teaspoon salt
2 teaspoons distilled white vinegar
1½ teaspoons vanilla extract
1 cup heavy or whipping cream
3 kiwifruit, peeled, quartered lengthwise,
   and thickly sliced
½ pint raspberries
1 ripe passionfruit, pulp scooped out in
   small pieces (optional)

1 Preheat oven to 225°F. Line large cookie sheet with foil. Grease foil; dust with flour. Using bottom of 9-inch round plate or cake pan as a guide, with toothpick, trace a circle in center of foil on cookie sheet.

2 In small bowl, with wire whisk, mix ⅔ cup sugar and cornstarch.

3 In large bowl, with mixer at medium speed, beat egg whites and salt until foamy. Beat in sugar-cornstarch mixture, 1 tablespoon at a time, beating well after each addition, until sugar has completely dissolved and whites stand in stiff, glossy peaks when beaters are lifted. Beat in vinegar and 1 teaspoon vanilla. Spoon egg-white mixture into circle on foil. With spoon, spread mixture to edge of circle, forming 2-inch-high rim all around.

4 Bake until set, about 2 hours. Turn off oven; leave meringue in oven 2 hours or up to overnight to dry. If not leaving overnight, cool completely on cookie sheet on wire rack. Store in airtight container.

5 In small bowl, with mixer at medium speed, beat cream and remaining 2 tablespoons sugar to soft peaks. Beat in remaining ½ teaspoon vanilla.
6 To serve, transfer cooled meringue to cake plate. Spoon whipped cream into center and top with fruits.

EACH SERVING About 225 calories, 3g protein, 29g carbohydrate, 12g total fat (7g saturated), 41mg cholesterol, 110mg sodium.

Test Kitchen Tip

MERINGUES Don't make meringues on a humid or rainy day; they will absorb too much moisture and turn out soggy.

Make sure all sugar in the beaten meringue has dissolved. Test by rubbing a bit of the mixture between your fingers— it should feel smooth, not grainy.

To give meringues extra crispness and sparkle, sprinkle them with granulated sugar before baking.

Bake meringues at a low temperature (200° to 275°F) so they dry out thoroughly without overbrowning.

Let hard meringues dry completely in the turned-off oven for crisp results. They will have a gummy texture if removed too soon.

Serve meringue pies within a few hours after baking or up to 2 days. Hard meringues can be made ahead and stored up to a week in an airtight container.

Pavlova

Coconut-Lime Dacquoise

The ultimate do-ahead party dessert. Bake the crisp meringue layers up to two weeks ahead, then store in an airtight container. The filling needs to be made at least a day before serving to allow time for setting. To serve, assemble and refrigerate at least three hours before serving to soften the meringue layers.

PREP 1 hour plus cooling • **BAKE** 2 hours plus drying time • **MAKES** 12 servings.

MERINGUE LAYERS
1 cup sweetened flaked coconut
6 large egg whites
¼ teaspoon salt
¼ teaspoon cream of tartar
1½ cups confectioners' sugar

LIME FILLING
5 limes
1 can (14 ounces) lowfat sweetened
    condensed milk
1 container (8 ounces) plain lowfat yogurt
1 envelope unflavored gelatin
¼ cup cold water
2 cups raspberries (2 half-pints)
confectioners' sugar (optional)

1 One day before serving or up to 2 weeks ahead, prepare meringue layers: Preheat oven to 325°F. Spread coconut in even layer in 9" by 9" metal baking pan. Bake, stirring occasionally, until toasted, 12 to 15 minutes. Transfer coconut to wire rack to cool. Turn oven control to 250°F.

2 Line large cookie sheet (15" by 12") with foil. With toothpick, outline three 11" by 4" rectangles crosswise on foil, leaving ½ inch between rectangles.

3 In large bowl, with mixer at high speed, beat egg whites, salt, and cream of tartar until foamy. At high speed, gradually beat in sugar, 2 tablespoons at a time, beating well after each addition, until whites stand in stiff, glossy peaks when beaters are lifted. With hands, crush toasted coconut slightly; fold gently into egg whites.

4 With small metal spatula, spread one-third of egg-white mixture inside each rectangle on cookie sheet. Bake meringue layers 2 hours. Turn off oven; leave meringues in oven 2 hours or overnight to dry.

5 If meringues are still warm, cool on cookie sheet on wire rack 10 minutes. With metal spatula, carefully loosen and remove meringues from foil; cool completely.

6 At least 1 day before serving or up to 2 days ahead, prepare lime filling: From limes, finely grate 3 teaspoons peel and squeeze ½ cup juice. In medium bowl, with wire whisk, mix lime juice and 2 teaspoons lime peel with undiluted sweetened condensed milk and yogurt until blended. (Wrap remaining lime peel in plastic wrap and refrigerate for garnish.)

7 In 1-quart saucepan, evenly sprinkle gelatin over cold water; let stand 2 minutes to soften gelatin slightly. Cook over low heat, until gelatin has dissolved, stirring occasionally; with wire whisk, stir gelatin into lime mixture until blended. Cover surface of filling with plastic wrap and refrigerate until firm, at least 24 hours, before using.

8 Assemble dacquoise: At least 3 hours before serving, whisk lime filling to loosen. Place 1 meringue layer on serving plate; spread with 1 cup filling. Place some raspberries all around edge of lime-topped meringue. Repeat with another meringue layer, 1 cup filling, and some raspberries. Place remaining meringue layer over filling. Spoon remaining ½ cup filling in center of top layer of meringue; garnish filling with remaining raspberries and sprinkle with reserved lime peel. Refrigerate dacquoise 3 hours to soften meringue layers.

9 To serve, sprinkle top of dacquoise with confectioners' sugar, if desired. Use serrated knife for easier slicing.

EACH SERVING About 220 calories, 6g protein, 42g carbohydrate, 4g total fat (3g saturated), 8mg cholesterol, 130mg sodium.

Coconut-Lime Dacquoise

Lemon and Fresh Raspberry Dacquoise

Instead of the more traditional coffee and chocolate fillings, we use lemon and raspberry fillings between the crisp meringue layers for a fresh take on a classic French dessert.

PREP 55 minutes plus chilling • **COOK/BAKE** 55 minutes plus drying time • **MAKES** 12 servings.

MERINGUE LAYERS
6 large egg whites
¼ teaspoon cream of tartar
1¼ cups granulated sugar

LEMON AND RASPBERRY FILLINGS
3 large lemons
1 tablespoon cornstarch
6 tablespoons butter, cut into pieces
   (do not use margarine)
¾ cup granulated sugar
4 large egg yolks
1½ cups heavy or whipping cream
2 tablespoons confectioners' sugar
½ pint raspberries

1 Prepare meringue layers: Preheat oven to 300°F. Line 2 large cookie sheets with foil. Using 8-inch round plate or cake pan as guide, with toothpick, outline 4 circles on foil (two on each cookie sheet).

2 In large bowl, with mixer at high speed, beat egg whites and cream of tartar until soft peaks form. Sprinkle in sugar, 2 tablespoons at a time, beating until whites stand in stiff, glossy peaks when beaters are lifted.

3 Spoon one-fourth of meringue (about 1½ cups) inside each circle on prepared cookie sheets. With narrow metal spatula, spread meringue evenly to fill circles. Bake meringues 45 minutes. Turn off oven; leave meringues in oven 1 hour to dry. Cool meringues on cookie sheets on wire racks 10 minutes. With metal spatula, carefully loosen and remove meringues from foil; cool completely. Store in airtight container at room temperature up to 1 week.

4 While meringues bake, prepare lemon and raspberry fillings: From lemons, grate 1 tablespoon peel and squeeze ½ cup juice. In 2-quart saucepan, with wire whisk, mix cornstarch and lemon peel and juice until blended. Add butter and granulated sugar. Heat to boiling over medium-high heat, stirring constantly; boil 1 minute.

5 In small bowl, with wire whisk, lightly beat egg yolks. Into egg yolks, gradually beat ¼ cup hot lemon mixture; pour egg mixture back into lemon mixture in saucepan, beating rapidly to prevent curdling. Reduce heat to low; cook, stirring constantly, until mixture thickens (do not boil), about 5 minutes. Pour into medium bowl. Press plastic wrap directly onto surface of custard. Refrigerate until chilled, about 3 hours or up to 3 days.

6 When ready to assemble dacquoise, in medium bowl, with mixer at high speed, beat cream and confectioners' sugar until stiff peaks form. Fold 1 cup whipped cream into cold lemon filling. Reserve 10 raspberries in cup and ¾ cup whipped cream in small bowl; cover and refrigerate to use for garnish later. Fold remaining raspberries into remaining cream in bowl.

7 Assemble dacquoise: Place 1 meringue layer on cake plate or round platter. Spread with half of lemon filling. Top with another meringue layer and spread with raspberry filling. Top with another meringue layer and spread with remaining lemon filling. Top with remaining meringue layer. Loosely cover dacquoise with plastic wrap and refrigerate 5 hours or up to overnight to soften layers slightly.

8 To serve, with whisk, beat reserved whipped cream (cream may have separated slightly) to stiffen. Spoon cream onto center of dacquoise; sprinkle with reserved raspberries.

EACH SERVING About 325 calories, 4g protein, 37g carbohydrate, 19g total fat (11g saturated), 128mg cholesterol, 105mg sodium.

Lemon and Fresh Raspberry Dacquoise

Hazelnut Dacquoise

An exquisite combination of crunchy hazelnut meringue and coffee and chocolate fillings.

PREP 1 hour 30 minutes plus cooling and chilling • **BAKE** 45 minutes plus drying time
MAKES 12 servings.

1 cup hazelnuts (filberts), toasted and
    skinned (page 256)
1½ cups plus 4 tablespoons
    confectioners' sugar
2 tablespoons cornstarch
6 large egg whites
½ teaspoon cream of tartar
3 squares (3 ounces) semisweet chocolate,
    chopped
3 cups heavy or whipping cream
1 teaspoon vanilla extract
1 tablespoon instant espresso-coffee powder
Chocolate Curls (page 362)

1 Preheat oven to 300°F. Line 2 large cookie sheets with foil. Using 8-inch round cake pan as guide, with toothpick, outline 4 circles on foil (two on each cookie sheet).

2 In food processor with knife blade attached, process hazelnuts, ¾ cup confectioners' sugar, and cornstarch until hazelnuts are finely ground.

3 In large bowl, with mixer at high speed, beat egg whites and cream of tartar until soft peaks form when beaters are lifted. Sprinkle in ¾ cup confectioners' sugar, 2 tablespoons at a time, beating until sugar has completely dissolved and egg whites stand in stiff, glossy peaks when beaters are lifted.

4 With rubber spatula, gently fold hazelnut mixture into beaten egg whites just until blended. Spoon one-fourth of meringue mixture (about 1¼ cups) inside each circle on prepared cookie sheets. With narrow metal spatula, spread meringue evenly to fill circles.

5 Bake meringues 45 minutes. Turn off oven; leave meringues in oven 1 hour to dry. Cool meringues on cookie sheets on wire racks 10 minutes. Carefully peel foil from meringues and cool completely. Store in airtight container at room temperature up to 1 week.

6 Assemble dacquoise: In heavy 1-quart saucepan, melt chocolate over low heat, stirring frequently, until smooth; cool. In small bowl, with mixer at medium speed, beat 1½ cups cream, 1 tablespoon confectioners' sugar, and ½ teaspoon vanilla until soft peaks form. With rubber spatula, fold half of cream mixture into cooled melted chocolate just until blended (do not overfold); fold in remaining whipped cream.

7 In cup, dissolve espresso powder in 2 tablespoons cream; set aside. In small bowl, with mixer at medium speed, beat remaining cream, remaining 3 tablespoons confectioners' sugar, and remaining ½ teaspoon vanilla until soft peaks form. Add espresso mixture and beat until stiff peaks form.

8 Reserve ¼ cup chocolate cream. Place 1 meringue layer on platter; with narrow metal spatula, spread with half of chocolate cream. Top with another meringue layer and spread with half of coffee cream. Repeat with remaining meringue layers and remaining cream fillings. Mound reserved chocolate cream on top. Refrigerate dacquoise 5 hours or up to overnight to soften layers slightly. To serve, arrange Chocolate Curls on top of dacquoise.

EACH SERVING About 383 calories, 5g protein, 27g carbohydrate, 30g total fat (15g saturated), 82mg cholesterol, 52mg sodium.

Tiramisù

This classic sweet is a favorite afternoon treat in Italy; literally, it means "pick me up."

PREP 35 minutes plus chilling • **MAKES** 12 servings.

1 cup hot espresso or very strong brewed
   coffee
3 tablespoons brandy
2 tablespoons plus ½ cup sugar
18 crisp Italian ladyfingers (savoiardi;
   5 ounces)
½ cup milk
1 container (16 to 17½ ounces)
   mascarpone cheese
¾ cup heavy or whipping cream
Chocolate Curls (page 362)
unsweetened cocoa

1 In 9-inch pie plate, stir coffee, brandy, and 2 tablespoons sugar until sugar has dissolved; cool to room temperature. Dip both sides of 9 ladyfingers into coffee mixture, one at a time, to soak completely. Arrange soaked ladyfingers in single layer in 8-inch square baking dish.
2 In large bowl, stir milk and remaining ½ cup sugar until sugar has dissolved. Stir in mascarpone until blended.
3 In small bowl, with mixer at high speed, beat cream until soft peaks form. With rubber spatula, gently fold whipped cream into mascarpone mixture until blended. Spread half of mixture over ladyfingers in baking dish.

4 Dip remaining 9 ladyfingers into coffee mixture and arrange on top of mascarpone mixture. Spread with remaining mascarpone mixture. Refrigerate 3 hours or up to overnight.
5 Meanwhile, prepare Chocolate Curls.
6 Just before serving, dust with cocoa. Cut into squares and spoon into goblets or dessert dishes. Garnish with chocolate curls.

EACH SERVING About 323 calories, 4g protein, 22g carbohydrate, 23g total fat (15g saturated), 55mg cholesterol, 59mg sodium.

Test Kitchen Tip **PRETTY SLICES** To serve delicate layered desserts like tiramisù, use a serrated knife. Cut with a gentle sawing motion. Some people prefer to hold the knife vertically, either horizontal or vertical works.

Raspberry-Banana Trifle

Raspberry-Banana Trifle

This beautiful dessert is easier to make than you think, thanks to store-bought pound cake. To make ahead, fill and slice the cake the day before assembling the trifle; wrap and refrigerate until ready to use.

PREP 1 hour plus chilling • **COOK** 5 minutes • **MAKES** 24 servings.

CAKE
1 frozen pound cake (1 pound), thawed
6 tablespoons seedless red-raspberry jam

CUSTARD
6 large eggs
¾ cup sugar
⅓ cup cornstarch
4 cups milk
4 tablespoons butter or margarine
2 tablespoons vanilla extract
3 large ripe bananas (1½ pounds), sliced

TOPPING
1 cup heavy or whipping cream
2 tablespoons sugar
fresh raspberries and fresh mint leaves,
    for garnish

1 Prepare cake: With serrated knife, cut crust from pound cake. Place cake on one long side; cut lengthwise into 4 equal slices. With small spatula, spread 2 tablespoons jam on top of 1 cake slice; top with another cake slice. Repeat with remaining jam and cake, ending with cake. Slice jam-layered cake crosswise into ¼-inch-thick slices, keeping slices together, then cut cake lengthwise in half down center. (You should have about 26 jam-layered cake slices cut in half to make 52 half slices.)

2 Prepare custard: In medium bowl, with wire whisk, beat eggs, sugar, and cornstarch; set aside. In 4-quart saucepan, heat milk just to boiling.

While constantly beating with whisk, gradually pour about half of hot milk into egg mixture. Pour egg mixture back into milk in saucepan and cook over medium-low heat, whisking constantly, until mixture has thickened and begins to bubble around edge of pan (mixture will not boil vigorously). Simmer custard, whisking constantly, until it reaches a temperature of at least 160°F, about a minute. Remove saucepan from heat; stir in butter and vanilla.

3 Assemble trifle: In 4-quart glass trifle dish or deep glass bowl, place 2 rows of cake slices around side of bowl, alternating horizontal and vertical placement of cake slices to make a checkerboard design. Place some cake slices in a single layer to cover bottom of bowl; top with one-third of sliced bananas. Spoon one-third of warm custard on top of bananas. Top with half of remaining bananas and half of remaining custard. Top with remaining cake, bananas, and custard. Press plastic wrap directly onto surface of custard to prevent skin from forming. Refrigerate 6 hours or overnight.

4 Before serving, prepare topping. In small bowl, with mixer at medium speed, beat cream and sugar until stiff peaks form. Remove plastic wrap from trifle; top trifle with whipped cream and garnish with raspberries and mint.

EACH SERVING About 240 calories, 4g protein, 28g carbohydrate, 12g total fat (6g saturated), 77mg cholesterol, 112mg sodium.

New England Maple-Walnut Cake

Three moist cake layers are flavored with maple syrup and robed in luscious homemade frosting.

PREP 50 minutes plus cooling • BAKE 25 minutes • MAKES 16 servings.

⅔ cup walnuts
1 cup sugar
2¼ cups cake flour (not self-rising)
2 teaspoons baking powder
½ teaspoon salt
¼ teaspoon baking soda
¾ cup maple syrup or maple-flavored syrup
½ cup milk
½ teaspoon imitation maple flavor
¾ cup butter or margarine (1½ sticks),
   softened
3 large eggs
Maple Buttercream (page 353)
walnut halves (optional)

1 Preheat oven to 350°F. Grease three 8-inch round cake pans. Line bottoms with waxed paper; grease paper. Dust pans with flour.

2 In food processor with knife blade attached, pulse walnuts and 2 tablespoons sugar until walnuts are finely ground.

3 In medium bowl, with wire whisk, mix flour, baking powder, salt, and baking soda. In 2-cup measuring cup, with fork, mix maple syrup, milk, and maple flavor until blended.

4 In large bowl, with mixer at low speed, beat butter and remaining sugar until blended. Increase speed to high; beat until mixture has a sandy appearance, about 2 minutes, occasionally scraping bowl with rubber spatula. With mixer at medium-low speed, add eggs, one at a time, beating well after each addition. Reduce speed to low; add flour mixture alternately with maple-syrup mixture, beginning and ending with flour mixture. Beat just until smooth, occasionally scraping bowl with rubber spatula. Fold in ground-walnut mixture.

5 Divide batter evenly among prepared pans; spread evenly. Place two pans on upper oven rack and one pan on lower oven rack, so that pans are not directly above one another. Bake until toothpick inserted in center comes out clean, 25 to 30 minutes.

6 Cool in pans on wire racks 10 minutes. Run thin knife around edges to loosen layers from sides of pans. Invert onto wire racks. Remove wax paper; cool completely.

7 Meanwhile, prepare Maple Buttercream.

8 Place 1 layer, rounded side down, on cake plate. With narrow metal spatula, spread ⅔ cup buttercream over layer. Top with second layer, rounded side up, and spread with another ⅔ cup buttercream. Top with remaining cake layer, rounded side up. Spread remaining buttercream over top and side. Garnish with walnut halves, if you like. Refrigerate if not serving right away.

EACH SERVING WITH MAPLE BUTTERCREAM
About 440 calories, 4g protein,
52g carbohydrate, 25g total fat (9g saturated),
66mg cholesterol, 398mg sodium.

> **Test Kitchen Tip** **BUTTER CAKES**
> The rich flavor and moist texture of butter-based cakes, such as layer cakes, chocolate cakes, and pound cakes make them the royalty of the cake world. Beating the butter with the sugar until the mixture is light and fluffy is crucial to a successful result. When the butter and sugar are well creamed, beat in the eggs one at a time.

Banana Cake

Banana and chocolate are always a winning combination. This time, we've baked up three tender cake layers studded with mini chips and stacked them with a doubly rich frosting.

PREP 1 hour plus cooling • **BAKE** 25 minutes • **MAKES** 16 servings.

2 cups cake flour (not self-rising)
1 teaspoon baking powder
½ teaspoon baking soda
¼ teaspoon salt
1 cup mashed ripe bananas (2 to 3 medium)
¼ cup buttermilk or sour cream
1 teaspoon vanilla extract
½ cup butter or margarine (1 stick), softened
1¼ cups sugar
2 large eggs
½ cup semisweet-chocolate mini chips (optional)
Fudge Frosting (page 352)

1 Preheat oven to 350°F. Grease three 8-inch round cake pans. Line bottoms with waxed paper; grease paper. Dust pans with flour.

2 In medium bowl, with wire whisk, mix flour, baking powder, baking soda, and salt. In small bowl, with fork, mix bananas, buttermilk, and vanilla.

3 In large bowl, with mixer at medium speed, beat butter and sugar until light and creamy, about 5 minutes, occasionally scraping bowl with rubber spatula. Add eggs, one at a time, beating well after each addition. Reduce speed to low, add flour mixture alternately with banana mixture, beginning and ending with flour mixture. Beat just until blended, occasionally scraping bowl. With wooden spoon, stir in chocolate chips, if using.

4 Divide batter evenly among prepared pans; spread evenly. Place two pans on upper oven rack and one pan on lower over rack, so that pans are not directly above one another. Bake until toothpick inserted in center comes out clean, 25 to 30 minutes.

5 Cool layers in pans on wire racks 10 minutes. Run thin knife around edges to loosen layers from sides of pans. Invert onto wire racks. Remove waxed paper; cool completely.

6 Meanwhile, prepare Fudge Frosting.

7 Place 1 layer, rounded side down, on cake plate. With narrow metal spatula, spread ½ cup frosting over layer. Top with second layer, rounded side up, and spread with another ½ cup frosting. Top with remaining cake layer, rounded side up. Spread remaining frosting over top and side of cake. Refrigerate if not serving right away. If cake is very cold, let stand at room temperature 20 minutes before serving.

EACH SERVING WITH FUDGE FROSTING About 385 calories, 4g protein, 49g carbohydrate, 20g total fat (7g saturated), 45mg cholesterol, 332mg sodium.

> **Test Kitchen Tip** **DUSTING PAN WITH FLOUR**
> Using a piece of folded paper towel or waxed paper, spread a thin layer of shortening inside baking pan. Sprinkle about 1 tablespoon flour into pan. Tilt to coat bottom and side with flour, then invert pan and tap out excess flour.

Banana Cake

Spice Layer Cake

This recipe makes a triple-layer cake that you'll want to serve again and again. The unusual but easy-to-make Brown-Butter Frosting complements the aromatic spices beautifully.

PREP 50 minutes plus cooling • **BAKE** 25 minutes • **MAKES** 16 servings.

2⅔ cups all-purpose flour
2½ teaspoons baking powder
2 teaspoons ground cinnamon
1 teaspoon ground ginger
½ teaspoon salt
½ teaspoon ground nutmeg
¼ teaspoon ground cloves
1 cup butter or margarine (2 sticks), softened
1 cup granulated sugar
1 cup packed dark brown sugar
5 large eggs
1 cup milk
Brown-Butter Frosting (page 353) or
     other frosting

1 Preheat oven to 350°F. Grease three 8-inch round cake pans. Line bottoms with waxed paper; grease paper. Dust pans with flour.
2 In medium bowl, with wire whisk, mix flour, baking powder, cinnamon, ginger, salt, nutmeg, and cloves; set aside.
3 In large bowl, with mixer at low speed, beat butter and granulated and brown sugars until blended. Increase speed to medium; beat until light and fluffy, about 5 minutes, frequently scraping bowl with rubber spatula. Add eggs, one at a time, beating well after each addition. Reduce speed to low; add flour mixture alternately with milk, beginning and ending with flour mixture. Beat just until blended, occasionally scraping bowl.
4 Divide batter evenly among prepared pans; spread evenly. Place two pans on upper oven rack and one pan on lower oven rack so that pans are not directly above one another. Bake until toothpick inserted in center comes out clean, 25 to 30 minutes.
5 Cool layers in pans on wire racks 10 minutes. Run thin knife around edges to loosen layers from sides of pans. Invert onto wire racks. Remove waxed paper; cool completely.
6 Meanwhile, prepare Brown-Butter Frosting.
7 Place 1 layer, rounded side down, on cake plate. With narrow metal spatula, spread ½ cup frosting over layer. Top with second layer, rounded side up, and spread with another ½ cup frosting. Top with remaining layer, rounded side up. Spread remaining frosting over top and side of cake.

EACH SERVING WITH BROWN-BUTTER FROSTING
About 490 calories, 5g protein,
73g carbohydrate, 20g total fat (12g saturated),
116mg cholesterol, 360 mg sodium.

Spice Layer Cake

Test Kitchen Tip
STORING BUTTER CAKES
Unfrosted butter cakes stay moist and fresh tasting for two or three days because of their high fat content; store them at room termperature. Always refrigerate cakes with fillings or frostings made with whipped cream, cream cheese, sour cream, or eggs. Cake layers with butter or margarine will harden in the fridge, so let the cake stand at room temperature about 30 minutes before serving.

Applesauce Spice Cake

For a quick snack, make this easy cake. You may already have all of the ingredients on hand.

PREP 20 minutes • **BAKE** 40 minutes • **MAKES** 9 servings.

2 cups all-purpose flour
1½ teaspoons ground cinnamon
1 teaspoon baking powder
½ teaspoon baking soda
½ teaspoon ground ginger
¼ teaspoon ground nutmeg
½ teaspoon salt
½ cup butter or margarine (1 stick), softened
¼ cup granulated sugar
1 cup packed dark brown sugar
2 large eggs
1 ¼ cups unsweetened applesauce
½ cup dark seedless raisins
confectioners' sugar

1 Preheat oven to 350°F. Grease and flour 9-inch square baking pan.

2 In medium bowl, with wire whisk, mix flour, cinnamon, baking powder, baking soda, ginger, nutmeg, and salt; set aside.

3 In large bowl, with mixer at low speed, beat butter and granulated and brown sugars until blended. Increase speed to medium-high; beat until light and fluffy, about 3 minutes. Add eggs, one at a time, beating well after each addition. Reduce speed to low; beat in applesauce. Mixture may appear curdled. Beat in flour mixture until smooth, occasionally scraping bowl with rubber spatula. Stir in raisins.

4 Scrape batter into prepared pan; spread evenly. Bake until toothpick inserted in center comes out clean, about 40 minutes.

5 Cool cake completely in pan on wire rack. To serve, dust with confectioners' sugar.

EACH SERVING About 369 calories, 5g protein, 62g carbohydrate, 12g total fat (7g saturated), 75mg cholesterol, 383mg sodium.

Test Kitchen Tip

BROWN SUGAR Exposure to air causes brown sugar to dry out, but adding a slice of apple or bread to the box will soften it. Because air can get trapped between its coarse crystals, brown sugar should be firmly packed when measured.

Lemon Upside-Down Cake

Sweet brown sugar and tangy lemons combine to make a deliciously different upside-down cake. We also added a touch of cornmeal to the batter for down-home appeal.

PREP 30 minutes • **BAKE** 45 minutes • **MAKES** 12 servings.

¾ cup butter or margarine (1½ sticks), softened
1 cup packed light brown sugar
6 lemons
1 ⅓ cups all-purpose flour
¼ cup yellow cornmeal
2 teaspoons baking powder
½ teaspoon salt
¾ cup granulated sugar
2 large eggs
1 teaspoon vanilla extract
½ cup whole milk

1 Preheat oven to 350°F. In nonstick 10-inch skillet with oven-safe handle (if skillet is not oven-safe, wrap handle of skillet with double layer of foil), melt 4 tablespoons butter and brown sugar over medium heat, stirring often, until smooth, about 2 minutes. Remove from heat.
2 From lemons, grate 2 teaspoons peel. With knife, remove peel and white pith from lemons. Slice lemons crosswise into ¼-inch-thick slices. With tip of knife, remove seeds. Arrange lemon slices in skillet.

3 In medium bowl, with wire whisk, mix flour, cornmeal, baking powder, and salt; set aside.
4 In large bowl, with mixer at medium speed, beat remaining ½ cup butter and granulated sugar until creamy. Add eggs, one at a time, beating well after each addition until blended. Beat in vanilla and lemon peel. Reduce speed to low; add flour mixture alternately with milk, beginning and ending with flour mixture. Beat just until blended.
5 Spoon batter over lemons; spread evenly. Bake until toothpick inserted in center comes out clean, 45 to 50 minutes.
6 Cool cake in skillet on wire rack 10 minutes. Run thin knife around edge to loosen cake from side of skillet. Invert cake onto serving plate. Cool 30 minutes to serve warm, or cool completely to serve later.

EACH SERVING About 315 calories, 4g protein, 46g carbohydrate, 14g total fat (8g saturated), 70mg cholesterol, 310mg sodium.

Pineapple Upside-Down Cake

We cut the pineapple slices in half to fit more fruit into the pan.

PREP 30 minutes • **BAKE** 40 minutes • **MAKES** 8 servings.

2 cans (8 ounces each) pineapple slices in juice
8 tablespoons butter or margarine (1 stick),
    softened
⅓ cup packed brown sugar
1 cup cake flour (not self-rising)
1 teaspoon baking powder
¼ teaspoon salt
⅔ cup granulated sugar
1 large egg
1 teaspoon vanilla extract
⅓ cup milk

1 Preheat oven to 325°F. Drain pineapple slices in sieve set over bowl. Reserve 2 tablespoons juice. Cut 8 slices in half and drain on paper towels. Refrigerate remaining slices for another use.

2 In 10-inch oven-safe skillet (if skillet is not oven-safe, wrap handle of skillet with double layer of foil), melt 2 tablespoons butter and brown sugar over medium heat, stirring until smooth. Stir in reserved pineapple juice and heat to boiling; boil 1 minute. Remove skillet from heat. Decoratively arrange pineapple in skillet, overlapping slices slightly to fit.

3 In small bowl, with fork, mix flour, baking powder, and salt; set aside.

4 In large bowl, with mixer at high speed, beat remaining 6 tablespoons butter and granulated sugar until fluffy, frequently scraping bowl with rubber spatula. Reduce speed to low; beat in egg and vanilla until well blended. Add flour mixture alternately with milk, beginning and ending with flour mixture. Beat just until blended.

5 Spoon batter over pineapple; spread evenly. Bake until toothpick inserted in center comes out clean, 40 to 45 minutes.

6 Immediately run thin knife around edges to loosen cake from side of skillet. Invert cake onto serving plate. (If any pineapple slices stick to skillet, remove and replace on cake.) Cool 30 minutes to serve warm, or cool completely to serve later.

EACH SERVING About 302 calories, 3g protein, 46g carbohydrate, 13g total fat (8g saturated), 59mg cholesterol, 267mg sodium.

PLUM UPSIDE-DOWN CAKE

Prepare as directed but substitute *1 pound pitted plums* for pineapple and juice. Cut plums into ½-inch-thick wedges. In oven-safe skillet, stir 2 tablespoons butter and brown sugar over medium heat until smooth. Add plums; cook over high heat, stirring, until plums are glazed, about 1 minute.

EACH SERVING About 309 calories, 3g protein, 47g carbohydrate, 13g total fat (8g saturated), 59mg cholesterol, 267mg sodium.

APPLE UPSIDE-DOWN CAKE

Prepare as directed but substitute *3 large Golden Delicious apples* (1½ pounds) for pineapple and juice. Peel, core, and cut apples into ¼-inch-thick wedges. In oven-safe skillet, stir 2 tablespoons butter and brown sugar over medium heat, until smooth. Add apples; cook over high heat until apples are fork-tender and begin to brown, 7 to 8 minutes.

EACH SERVING About 321 calories, 3g protein, 50g carbohydrate, 13g total fat (8g saturated), 59mg cholesterol, 267mg sodium.

Gingerbread

Because it's mixed by hand, this gingerbread has a dense, chewy texture. For a more cakelike consistency, beat the batter with an electric mixer for two full minutes. (Important tip: Measure the water after it comes to a boil.)

PREP 15 minutes • **BAKE** 45 minutes • **MAKES** 9 servings.

2 cups all-purpose flour
½ cup sugar
2 teaspoons ground ginger
1 teaspoon ground cinnamon
½ teaspoon baking soda
½ teaspoon salt
1 cup light (mild) molasses
½ cup butter or margarine (1 stick),
    cut into 4 pieces
¾ cup boiling water
1 large egg, lightly beaten

1 Preheat oven to 350°F. Grease and flour 9-inch square baking pan.

2 In large bowl, with wire whisk, mix flour, sugar, ginger, cinnamon, baking soda, and salt until blended; set aside.

3 In small bowl, with fork, mix molasses and butter. Add boiling water (measure water after it comes to a boil) and stir until butter has melted. Add molasses mixture and beaten egg to flour mixture; whisk until smooth.

4 With rubber spatula, scrape batter into prepared pan. Bake until toothpick inserted in center comes out clean, 45 to 50 minutes. Cool in pan on wire rack. Serve gingerbread warm or at room temperature.

EACH SERVING About 349 calories, 4g protein, 59g carbohydrate, 12g total fat (7g saturated), 51mg cholesterol, 324mg sodium.

Test Kitchen Tip GINGER

Ground ginger differs in flavor from fresh ginger—it's not as heady and strong. So fresh ginger should not be substituted. Ground ginger is ideal for gingerbread, spice cakes, and that cookie-jar staple, gingersnaps.

Greek Walnut Cake

Toasted walnuts enrich this simple sheet cake, which is soaked with a warm lemon-honey syrup after it's baked. Serve with fresh fruit—figs if you can find them—and hot or iced tea.

PREP 25 minutes • **BAKE** 30 minutes • **MAKES** 16 servings.

CAKE

1 cup walnuts (4 ounces), toasted (page 13)
1 cup sugar
2 cups all-purpose flour
1½ teaspoons baking powder
½ teaspoon baking soda
½ teaspoon salt
½ teaspoon ground cinnamon
¼ teaspoon ground cloves
1 cup butter or margarine (2 sticks), softened
6 large eggs
1 tablespoon freshly grated lemon peel
1 container (8 ounces) plain lowfat yogurt

LEMON SYRUP

2 large lemons
⅔ cup sugar
⅓ cup honey
¾ cup water

1 Preheat oven to 350°F. Grease 13" by 9" baking pan.

2 Prepare cake: In blender or in food processor with knife blade attached, pulse walnuts and ¼ cup sugar until walnuts are finely ground.

3 In medium bowl, with wire whisk, mix flour, baking powder, baking soda, salt, cinnamon, and cloves; set aside.

4 In large bowl, with mixer at medium speed, beat butter and remaining ¾ cup sugar until creamy. Add eggs, one at a time, beating well after each addition. Beat in lemon peel. Reduce speed to low; alternately add flour mixture and yogurt, beginning and ending with flour mixture. Beat just until batter is smooth, occasionally scraping bowl with rubber spatula. Fold in walnut mixture.

5 Spoon batter into prepared pan, spread evenly. Bake until toothpick inserted in center comes out clean, 30 to 35 minutes.

6 Meanwhile, prepare syrup: From lemons, grate 1 tablespoon peel and squeeze 3 tablespoons juice. In 1-quart saucepan, heat sugar, honey, lemon peel, and water to boiling over high heat, stirring. Reduce heat to medium and simmer 2 minutes. Remove from heat and stir in lemon juice; cool slightly.

7 When cake is done, transfer cake in pan to wire rack. With toothpick, poke holes all over top of cake. Spoon warm syrup over cake. Cool cake completely in pan. When cool, cut cake lengthwise in half. Cut each half crosswise into 4 pieces, then cut each piece diagonally in half to form 2 triangles.

EACH SERVING About 345 calories, 6g protein, 41g carbohydrate, 18g total fat (3g saturated), 81mg cholesterol, 335mg sodium.

Pumpkin-Spice Cake

Canned solid-pack pumpkin isn't just for pies; you can use it in muffins, cookies, and this luscious glazed Bundt cake. The pumpkin makes the cake exceptionally moist, and pumpkin-pie spice adds that familiar autumnal note.

PREP 25 minutes plus cooling • **BAKE** 55 minutes • **MAKES** 20 servings.

3½ cups all-purpose flour
1 tablespoon pumpkin-pie spice
2 teaspoons baking powder
1 teaspoon baking soda
½ teaspoon salt
1 can (16 ounces) solid-pack pumpkin
   (not pumpkin-pie mix)
¼ cup milk
2 teaspoons vanilla extract
1 cup butter or margarine (2 sticks), softened
1¾ cups sugar
4 large eggs
Brown-Butter Glaze (page 359)

1 Preheat oven to 350°F. Grease and flour 10-inch Bundt pan.

2 In medium bowl, with wire whisk, mix flour, pumpkin-pie spice, baking powder, baking soda, and salt. In small bowl, with fork, mix pumpkin, milk, and vanilla.

3 In large bowl, with mixer at low speed, beat butter and sugar until blended, scraping bowl frequently with rubber spatula. Increase speed to high; beat until creamy, about 5 minutes, scraping bowl occasionally. Reduce speed to low; add eggs, one at a time, beating well after each addition. Add flour mixture alternately with pumpkin mixture, beginning and ending with flour mixture. Beat just until smooth, scraping bowl occasionally.

4 Pour batter into prepared pan. Bake until toothpick inserted in center comes out almost clean, 55 to 60 minutes.

5 Cool cake in pan on wire rack 15 minutes. Run tip of thin knife around edges to loosen cake from side and center tube of pan. Invert onto wire rack. Cool completely.

6 When cake is cool, prepare Brown-Butter Glaze.

7 Place cake on cake plate; pour glaze over cake, letting glaze drip down sides.

EACH SERVING WITH BROWN-BUTTER GLAZE About 340 calories, 4g protein, 49g carbohydrate, 15g total fat (8g saturated), 77mg cholesterol, 320mg sodium.

Test Kitchen Tip

PUMPKIN-PIE SPICE A ready-made blend of "warm" spices for baking, pumpkin-pie spice is sold in most supermarkets. But you can also mix up your own: Combine 1½ teaspoons ground cinnamon, 1 teaspoon ground ginger, ¼ teaspoon ground nutmeg, and ⅛ teaspoon ground cloves. Stir to combine. This makes roughly 1 tablespoon, enough for the Pumpkin-Spice Cake recipe.

Banana–Chocolate Chip Cake

Think of the world's best banana bread baked in a ring shape and dotted with chocolate. Yum! It's also delicious without the chocolate.

PREP 30 minutes • **BAKE** 40 minutes • **MAKES** 24 servings.

3 cups all-purpose flour
1½ teaspoons baking powder
¾ teaspoon baking soda
¾ teaspoon salt
¼ teaspoon ground cinnamon
1⅔ cups mashed fully ripe bananas
   (about 5 medium)
4 teaspoons fresh lemon juice
1 tablespoon vanilla extract
¾ cup butter or margarine (1½ sticks),
   softened
1 cup packed brown sugar
¾ cup granulated sugar
3 large eggs
¾ cup semi-sweet chocolate mini chips
confectioners' sugar (optional)

1 Preheat oven to 350°F. Grease 10-inch tube pan or 10-inch Bundt pan; dust with flour.

2 In medium bowl, with wire whisk, mix flour, baking powder, baking soda, salt, and cinnamon. In separate medium bowl, with fork, mix bananas, lemon juice, and vanilla.

3 In large bowl, with mixer at low speed, beat butter and brown and granulated sugars until blended, scraping bowl often with rubber spatula. Increase speed to medium-high; beat until creamy, about 3 minutes, occasionally scraping bowl. Reduce speed to low; add eggs, one at a time, beating well after each addition. Alternately add flour mixture and banana mixture, beginning and ending with flour mixture. Beat just until smooth. Stir in chocolate chips.

4 Spoon batter into prepared pan; spread evenly. Bake until toothpick inserted in center comes out clean, 40 to 50 minutes.

5 Cool cake in pan on wire rack 15 minutes. Run thin knife around edges to loosen cake from sides and center tube of pan. Invert cake onto serving plate; immediately invert again onto wire rack to cool completely. For fluted pan, invert cake directly onto wire rack. Sprinkle with confectioners' sugar before serving, if you like.

EACH SERVING About 215 calories, 3g protein, 33g carbohydrate, 9g total fat (5g saturated), 43mg cholesterol, 210mg sodium.

Toasted Coconut Cake

Cream of coconut and coconut flakes add a tropical note to this homespun butter cake. For a special dessert, try it toasted and served with cut-up pineapple splashed with dark rum.

PREP 30 minutes • **BAKE** 50 minutes • **MAKES** 16 servings.

3 cups all-purpose flour
2 teaspoons baking powder
¾ teaspoon salt
¾ cup butter or margarine (1½ sticks), softened
1¼ cups sugar
4 large eggs
1 teaspoon vanilla extract
1 can (8½ to 9 ounces) cream of coconut (not coconut milk), well stirred (¾ cup)
¾ cup flaked sweetened coconut, toasted

1 Preheat oven to 350°F. Grease 10-inch tube pan; dust pan with flour.

2 In medium bowl, with wire whisk, mix flour, baking powder, and salt; set aside.

3 In large bowl, with mixer at low speed, beat butter and sugar until blended, frequently scraping bowl with rubber spatula. Increase speed to medium-high; beat until creamy, about 3 minutes, occasionally scraping bowl. Reduce speed to low; add eggs, one at a time, beating well after each addition. Beat in vanilla. Alternately add flour mixture and cream of coconut, beginning and ending with flour mixture. Beat just until smooth. Stir in ½ cup coconut.

4 Spoon batter into prepared pan; spread evenly. Sprinkle remaining ¼ cup coconut over top. Bake until toothpick inserted in center of cake comes out clean, 50 to 55 minutes.

5 Cool cake in pan on wire rack 15 minutes. Run tip of thin knife around cake to loosen from side and center tube of pan; lift tube to separate cake from pan side. Invert cake onto cake plate. Turn cake, right side up, onto wire rack to cool completely.

EACH SERVING About 315 calories, 4g protein, 43g carbohydrate, 14g total fat (9g saturated), 78mg cholesterol, 275mg sodium.

Test Kitchen Tip **KNOW YOUR ELECTRIC MIXER**

If your mixer is on the powerful side, you might not want to mix the ingredients for the full amount of time indicated in the recipe (most of our recipes describe what the mixture should look like when it's fully mixed). If your model is sluggish, you might need to mix longer.

Peanut Butter–Cup Cake

Brown sugar and peanut butter keep this one moist for a week; slice as you need it for lunch-box desserts and after-school snacks. We love the cake with Rich Chocolate Glaze (page 358), but it's delicious unadorned too.

PREP 30 minutes plus cooling • **BAKE** 1 hour • **MAKES** 16 servings.

2 cups all-purpose flour

2 teaspoons baking powder

¾ cup creamy peanut butter

½ cup butter or margarine (1 stick), softened

1 cup granulated sugar

½ cup packed brown sugar

2 large eggs

2 teaspoons vanilla extract

⅔ cup whole milk

Rich Chocolate Glaze (page 358, optional)

1 Preheat oven to 325°F. Grease decorative 10-cup metal loaf pan or 10-cup Bundt pan; dust pan with flour.

2 In medium bowl, with wire whisk, mix flour and baking powder; set aside.

3 In large bowl, with mixer at low speed, beat peanut butter, butter, and granulated and brown sugars until blended, frequently scraping bowl with rubber spatula. Increase speed to medium-high; beat until creamy, about 3 minutes, occasionally scraping bowl. Reduce speed to low; add eggs, one at a time, beating well after each addition. Beat in vanilla. Alternately add flour mixture and milk, beginning and ending with flour mixture. Beat just until smooth.

4 Spoon batter into prepared pan; spread evenly. Bake until toothpick inserted in center comes out clean, 60 to 65 minutes.

5 Cool cake in pan on wire rack 15 minutes. Run thin knife around edge to loosen cake from side of pan. Invert cake directly onto wire rack to cool completely.

6 Prepare Rich Chocolate Glaze if you like. Glaze cooled cake with glaze.

EACH SERVING WITHOUT GLAZE About 270 calories, 6g protein, 34g carbohydrate, 13g total fat (6g saturated), 44mg cholesterol, 185mg sodium.

EACH SERVING WITH GLAZE About 325 calories, 6g protein, 38g carbohydrate, 17g total fat (7g saturated), 52mg cholesterol, 215mg sodium.

Black-and-White Cupcakes

Arrange these imaginative chocolate-and-vanilla–frosted treats on a pretty platter or tiered cake stand for a fun dessert; they're perfect for kids and adults! To make one dramatic "black-eyed Susan" cupcake, stir yellow food coloring into about one-quarter cup vanilla frosting until it's tinted bright yellow; use a star tip to pipe on petals, then finish with a chocolate center.

PREP 1 hour 30 minutes plus cooling and decorating • **BAKE** 25 minutes • **MAKES** 24 cupcakes.

SPECIAL EQUIPMENT
2 decorating bags
2 couplers
2 writing tips (each ¼-inch opening)
2 star tips (each ¼-inch opening)
2 small basketweave tips (each ⅛-inch opening)

Yellow Cake (page 276) or Chocolate
    Buttermilk Cake (page 300)
Vanilla Buttercream Frosting (page 350)
2 squares (2 ounces) unsweetened chocolate,
    melted and cooled
1 square (1 ounce) semisweet chocolate,
    melted and cooled

1 Prepare Yellow Cake or Chocolate Buttermilk Cake as recipe directs for cupcakes. Bake and cool as directed.

2 Prepare Vanilla Buttercream Frosting. Remove 1¼ cups frosting to a small bowl and set aside. To frosting remaining in bowl, beat in melted unsweetened and semisweet chocolates until blended. (You'll have slightly more chocolate frosting.) Spoon vanilla frosting into decorating bag fitted with a coupler. Spoon chocolate frosting into another decorating bag fitted with another coupler.

3 Using vanilla and chocolate frostings with suggested decorating tips, and small spatula, decorate tops of cupcakes as desired with black-and-white designs.

> **EACH CUPCAKE** About 290 calories, 3g protein, 34g carbohydrate, 16g total fat (8g saturated), 66mg cholesterol, 193mg sodium.

Black-and-White Cupcakes

Peanut-Butter Cupcakes

These cupcakes are great for kids' parties. If you prefer, omit the chocolate topping and use your favorite frosting instead.

PREP 10 minutes • **BAKE** 18 minutes • **MAKES** 18 cupcakes.

1¾ cups all-purpose flour

1 tablespoon baking powder

½ teaspoon salt

½ cup creamy or chunky peanut butter

¼ cup vegetable shortening

¾ cup sugar

2 large eggs

¾ teaspoon vanilla extract

1 cup milk

1 bar (4 ounces) semisweet or milk chocolate, cut into 18 pieces

1 Preheat oven to 350°F. Line eighteen 2½-inch muffin-pan cups with paper baking liners.

2 In medium bowl, with wire whisk, mix flour, baking powder, and salt; set aside.

3 In large bowl, with mixer at medium speed, beat peanut butter and shortening until blended. Add sugar and beat until light and fluffy, about 3 minutes. Add eggs, one at a time, beating well after each addition. Beat in vanilla. Reduce speed to low; add flour mixture alternately with milk, beginning and ending with flour mixture. Beat just until blended, occasionally scraping bowl with rubber spatula.

4 Divide batter evenly among cups. Bake until toothpick inserted in center of cupcakes comes out clean, about 18 minutes. Place 1 piece of chocolate on top of each cupcake; return to oven until chocolate melts, about 1 minute.

5 With small metal spatula, spread chocolate over tops of cupcakes. Remove from pans and cool on wire rack.

EACH CUPCAKE About 192 calories, 5g protein, 23g carbohydrate, 10g total fat (3g saturated), 26mg cholesterol, 193mg sodium.

Test Kitchen Tip

CUPCAKE CARRIER
Cupcakes are perfect for bake sales and school birthdays. But how can you get them to the party without squashing them? An 11" by 17" cookie pan with 1-inch-high sides holds 2 dozen cupcakes nicely. To keep cupcakes from sliding, line bottom of pan with several layers of paper towels and pad space with crumpled waxed paper. Cover with plastic wrap.

Peanut Butter Cupcakes

Almond Petits Fours

Almond Petits Fours

Present these rich morsels on your prettiest serving dish or dessert tray at a formal luncheon or afternoon tea.

PREP 15 minutes plus cooling, glazing, and decorating • **BAKE** 15 minutes
MAKES 2 dozen petits fours.

ALMOND CAKE

½ (7-ounce) tube almond paste
½ cup granulated sugar
½ cup butter or margarine (1 stick), softened
3 large eggs
½ cup all-purpose flour
¼ teaspoon baking powder
¼ teaspoon salt

FONDANT GLAZE

4 tablespoons butter or margarine, cut up
5 tablespoons milk
2 tablespoons light corn syrup
pinch salt
1 box (16 ounces) confectioners' sugar
blue, pink, green, and/or yellow paste
    food coloring

1 Prepare cake: Preheat oven to 350°F. Grease and flour 24 mini muffin-pan cups.

2 Crumble almond paste into food processor bowl with knife blade attached. Add granulated sugar and pulse until almond paste is finely ground. Add butter and process until smooth. Add eggs and process until blended, occasionally stopping processor and scraping side of bowl with rubber spatula. Add flour, baking powder, and salt and process until blended.

3 Spoon batter into muffin-pan cups, filling almost to top. Bake until golden brown and tops spring back when lightly touched with finger, 15 to 18 minutes. Cool cakes in pans on wire rack 10 minutes. Invert cakes onto wire rack to cool completely.

4 Meanwhile, prepare glaze: In microwave-safe medium bowl, heat butter in microwave oven on High until melted, about 30 seconds. Stir in milk, corn syrup, and salt, then stir in confectioners' sugar until mixture is smooth. Reserve 2 tablespoons white glaze for decorating tops of petits fours; cover with plastic wrap. Divide remaining glaze into desired number of custard cups; tint with choice of food coloring.

5 Decorate petits fours: If necessary, trim rounded sides of cakes so they will sit flat. Set cakes, still on wire rack, over waxed paper. Spoon tinted glazes over cakes as desired, allowing glaze to run down sides and drip onto waxed paper. If necessary, use small metal spatula to spread glaze evenly over tops and sides of cakes. Allow glaze to set, about 25 minutes.

6 When glaze has set, spoon reserved white glaze and remaining tinted glazes into separate heavy duty self-sealing plastic bags. Snip corner of each bag on diagonal to make ⅛-inch opening; use to pipe dots, lines, pretty designs, and/or letters on top of cakes. Allow designs to dry completely.

EACH PETIT FOUR About 155 calories, 2g protein, 22g carbohydrate, 7g total fat (4g saturated), 41mg cholesterol, 100mg sodium.

Chocolate Buttermilk Cake

The classic celebration cake—from birthday cake to bake sale cupcakes, it's always a hit. This recipe makes a 2-layer cake but a sheet cake, 3-layer cake, or cupcakes would be just as delicious. See photo on page 274.

PREP 45 minutes plus cooling • **BAKE** about 30 minutes • **MAKES** 16 servings.

2 cups all-purpose flour
1 cup unsweetened cocoa
1½ teaspoons baking soda
salt
1½ cups buttermilk
2 teaspoons vanilla extract
1¾ cups granulated sugar
¾ cup butter or margarine (1½ sticks),
    softened
3 large eggs
choice of frosting

1 Preheat oven to 350°F. Grease two 9-inch round cake pans. Line bottoms of pans with waxed paper. Grease waxed paper; dust with cocoa, shaking out excess.

2 On sheet of waxed paper, combine flour, cocoa, baking soda, and ¾ teaspoon salt. In 2-cup liquid measuring cup, mix buttermilk and vanilla; set aside.

3 In large bowl, with mixer on low speed, beat sugar and butter until blended. Increase speed to high; beat 3 minutes or until creamy, occasionally scraping bowl with rubber spatula. Reduce speed to low; add eggs, 1 at a time, beating well after each addition.

4 Beat in flour mixture alternately with buttermilk mixture just until blended, beginning and ending with flour mixture, scraping bowl occasionally.

5 Pour batter into prepared pans. Bake until toothpick inserted in center of cake comes out clean, 30 to 35 minutes. Cool in pans on wire racks 10 minutes. Invert cakes onto racks to cool completely. Carefully remove and discard waxed paper.

6 Prepare choice of frosting.

7 Assemble cake: Place 1 cake layer, rounded side down, on cake plate. With narrow metal spatula, spread ⅔ cup frosting over layer. Top with second layer, rounded side up. Spread remaining frosting over side and top of cake.

EACH SERVING WITHOUT FROSTING About 255 calories, 5g protein, 37g carbohydrate, 11g total fat (7g saturated), 65mg cholesterol, 360mg sodium.

 Test Kitchen Tip
DELICIOUS IN ANY SHAPE

Grease three 8-inch round cake pans or one 13"by 9" metal baking pan. Line with waxed paper, grease again; dust with cocoa, shaking out excess. Or, line 24 standard muffin-pan cups with paper baking liners. Bake 8-inch layers 25 to 30 minutes; 13"by 9" cake, 35 to 40 minutes; 13" by 9" cake, 35 to 40 minutes; and cupcakes, 20 to 25 minutes.

Reine de Saba

Named for the darkly beautiful Queen of Sheba—Reine de Saba in French—this intense chocolate-almond torte is equally tempting made with hazelnuts.

PREP 1 hour plus cooling • **BAKE** 25 minutes • **MAKES** 12 servings.

6 squares (6 ounces) semisweet chocolate
1 square (1 ounce) unsweetened chocolate
⅔ cup blanched almonds, toasted (page 13)
½ cup cake flour (not self-rising)
½ cup butter or margarine (1 stick), slightly softened
⅓ cup plus 4 tablespoons sugar
3 large eggs, separated
1 teaspoon vanilla extract
¼ teaspoon cream of tartar
⅓ cup heavy or whipping cream
1 teaspoon light corn syrup

1 Preheat oven to 325° F. Grease and flour 8-inch round cake pan.

2 Chop 3 squares of semisweet chocolate and the unsweetened chocolate. In small heavy saucepan, heat the chopped chocolates over low heat, stirring frequently, until melted and smooth. Remove saucepan from heat; cool.

3 In food processor with knife blade attached, pulse ¼ cup toasted nuts and flour until nuts are very finely ground (reserve remaining nuts for garnish).

4 In large bowl, with mixer at low speed, beat butter and ⅓ cup sugar just until blended. Increase speed to high; beat until light and fluffy, about 2 minutes. Reduce speed to low; beat in egg yolks, vanilla, and melted chocolate mixture until blended, about 1 minute, scraping bowl often with rubber spatula.

5 In small bowl, with clean beaters and mixer at high speed, beat egg whites and cream of tartar until soft peaks form. Gradually sprinkle in remaining 4 tablespoons sugar and beat until whites hold stiff, glossy peaks when beaters are lifted.

6 With rubber spatula, fold nut mixture into yolk mixture just until blended. Gently fold in beaten egg whites, one-third at a time.

7 Spread batter evenly in prepared pan. Bake until toothpick inserted in cake about 2 inches from edge comes out clean, 25 to 28 minutes. (Center of cake will still be slightly soft.)

8 Cool cake in pan on wire rack 15 minutes. Run thin knife around edges to loosen cake from side of pan. Invert onto wire rack to cool completely. (The recipe can be prepared up to this point 2 days in advance. If not using cake right away, wrap well with plastic wrap and refrigerate.)

9 Coarsely chop remaining 3 squares semisweet chocolate; place in small bowl. In small saucepan, heat cream just to boiling over low heat. Pour hot cream over chopped chocolate; let stand 1 minute. Gently stir until chocolate has melted; stir in corn syrup. Let stand at room temperature until glaze begins to thicken, about 5 minutes.

10 Meanwhile, coarsely chop reserved nuts.

11 Place cake on cake plate. Tuck strips of waxed paper under edge of cake to keep plate clean when glazing. Pour chocolate glaze over cake. With metal spatula, spread glaze to completely cover top and side of cake. Sprinkle chopped nuts around top edge of cake. Chill cake 20 minutes to set glaze. Remove and discard waxed-paper strips. Refrigerate cake if not serving right away.

EACH SERVING About 285 calories, 4g protein, 24g carbohydrate, 21g total fat (10g saturated), 83mg cholesterol, 100mg sodium.

Molten Chocolate Cakes

When you cut into these warm cakes, their delectable molten centers flow out. You can assemble them up to twenty-four hours ahead and refrigerate, or you can freeze them up to two weeks. If you refrigerate the cakes, bake them for ten minutes; if they are frozen, bake for sixteen minutes. Serve with whipped cream or vanilla ice cream.

PREP 20 minutes • **BAKE** 8 minutes • **MAKES** 8 servings.

4 squares (4 ounces) semisweet chocolate, chopped
½ cup butter or margarine (1 stick), cut into pieces
¼ cup heavy or whipping cream
½ teaspoon vanilla extract
¼ cup all-purpose flour
¼ cup granulated sugar
2 large eggs
2 large egg yolks
confectioners' sugar
whipped cream or vanilla ice cream (optional)

1 Preheat oven to 400°F. Grease eight 6-ounce custard cups. Dust with sugar.

2 In heavy 3-quart saucepan, heat chocolate, butter, and cream over low heat, stirring occasionally, until butter and chocolate have melted and mixture is smooth. Remove pan from heat. Add vanilla. With wire whisk, stir in flour just until mixture is smooth.

3 In medium bowl, with mixer at high speed, beat granulated sugar, eggs, and yolks until thick and lemon-colored, about 10 minutes. Fold egg mixture, one-third at a time, into chocolate mixture until blended.

4 Divide batter evenly among prepared custard cups. Place cups in jelly-roll pan for easier handling. Bake until edges of cakes are set but centers still jiggle, 8 to 9 minutes.

5 Cool in pan on wire rack 3 minutes. Run thin knife around edges to loosen cakes from sides of cups; invert onto dessert plates. Dust with confectioners' sugar. Serve immediately with whipped cream or ice cream, if desired.

EACH SERVING About 281 calories, 4g protein, 20g carbohydrate, 22g total fat (12g saturated), 148mg cholesterol, 139mg sodium.

Molten Chocolate Cakes

Brownie Pudding Cake

Two desserts for the price of one! The batter separates during baking into a fudgy brownie on top of a silky chocolate pudding.

PREP 20 minutes • **BAKE** 30 minutes • **MAKES** 8 servings.

2 teaspoons instant-coffee powder (optional)
2 tablespoons plus 1¾ cups boiling water
1 cup all-purpose flour
¾ cup unsweetened cocoa
½ cup granulated sugar
2 teaspoons baking powder
¼ teaspoon salt
½ cup milk
4 tablespoons butter or margarine, melted
1 teaspoon vanilla extract
½ cup packed brown sugar
whipped cream or vanilla ice cream (optional)

1 Preheat oven to 350°F. In cup, dissolve coffee powder in 2 tablespoons boiling water, if using.
2 In medium bowl, with wire whisk, mix flour, ½ cup cocoa, granulated sugar, baking powder, and salt. In 2-cup measuring cup, with fork, mix milk, melted butter, vanilla, and coffee, if using. With wooden spoon, stir milk mixture into flour mixture until just blended. Pour into ungreased 8-inch square baking dish.

3 In small bowl, with fork, mix brown sugar and remaining ¼ cup cocoa until well blended; sprinkle evenly over batter. Carefully pour remaining 1¾ cups boiling water evenly over mixture in baking dish; do not stir.
4 Bake 30 minutes (batter will separate into cake and pudding layers). Cool in pan on wire rack 10 minutes. Serve hot with whipped cream, if you like.

EACH SERVING About 238 calories, 4g protein, 43g carbohydrate, 7g total fat (5g saturated), 18mg cholesterol, 267mg sodium.

Brownie Pudding Cake

Classic Devil's Food Cake

Classic Devil's Food Cake

Devil's food cake is a twentieth-century creation. No one knows for sure how the cake got its name, but many believe it was due to its being rich and dark; the opposite of light and delicate angel food cake.

PREP 35 minutes plus cooling • BAKE 30 minutes • MAKES 16 servings.

2 cups all-purpose flour
1 cup unsweetened cocoa
1½ teaspoons baking soda
½ teaspoon salt
½ cup butter or margarine (1 stick), softened
1 cup packed light brown sugar
1 cup granulated sugar
3 large eggs
1½ teaspoons vanilla extract
1½ cups buttermilk
Chocolate Butter Frosting (page 351) or Fluffy
    White Frosting (page 350)

1 Preheat oven to 350°F. Grease three 8-inch round cake pans. Line bottoms with waxed paper; grease paper. Dust pans with flour.

2 In medium bowl, with wire whisk, mix flour, cocoa, baking soda, and salt, set aside.

3 In large bowl, with mixer at low speed, beat butter and brown and granulated sugars until blended. Increase speed to high; beat until light and fluffy, about 5 minutes. Reduce speed to medium-low; add eggs, one at a time, beating well after each addition. Beat in vanilla. Add flour mixture alternately with buttermilk, beginning and ending with flour mixture. Beat just until batter is smooth, occasionally scraping bowl with rubber spatula.

4 Divide batter equally among prepared pans; spread evenly. Place two pans on upper oven rack and one pan on lower oven rack so pans are not directly above one another. Bake until toothpick inserted in center comes out clean, 30 to 35 minutes.

5 Cool layers in pans on wire rack 10 minutes. Run thin knife around edges to loosen layers from sides of pans. Invert onto wire racks. Remove waxed paper; cool completely.

6 Meanwhile, prepare choice of frosting.

7 Place 1 cake layer, rounded side down, on cake plate. With narrow metal spatula, spread ⅓ cup frosting over layer. Top with second layer, rounded side up, and spread ⅓ cup frosting over layer. Place remaining layer, rounded side up, on top. Spread remaining frosting over top and side of cake.

EACH SERVING WITH CHOCOLATE BUTTER FROSTING About 450 calories, 5g protein, 74g carbohydrate, 17g total fat (10g saturated), 72mg cholesterol, 355mg sodium.

 CAKE CARRYING SUGGESTIONS

- Wrap a large cutting board or heavyweight cardboard with foil to provide a surface to serve large cakes.
- A few dollops of frosting on cake plate before placing cake on surface will keep cake from slipping.
- If covering a cake with plastic wrap, chill cake first to set frosting, then stick toothpicks into it to keep wrap from touching surface.
- When transporting a filled layer cake, insert a few pieces of dry spaghetti straight down through layers to keep them from shifting.

Blackout Cake

The renowned (now closed) Ebinger's Bakery of Brooklyn made this locally famous devil's food cake for years. Our version is heaven for chocolate lovers: rich chocolate cake layered with chocolate pudding and covered with chocolate cake crumbs. You can get a big head start on this recipe by baking and freezing the cake layers up to two months ahead. The pudding, however, should be made no earlier than several days before using and stored, well covered, in the refrigerator. When ready to assemble the cake, split the layers, using a serrated knife, while still frozen; they will be firm and easy to handle.

PREP 1 hour plus cooling • BAKE 25 minutes • MAKES 16 servings.

CHOCOLATE PUDDING

2 tablespoons butter or margarine

3 squares (3 ounces) semisweet chocolate, chopped

2 squares (2 ounces) unsweetened chocolate, chopped

⅔ cup sugar

6 tablespoons cornstarch

3 tablespoons unsweetened cocoa

2¼ cups whole milk

2 large eggs

2 teaspoons vanilla extract

CHOCOLATE CAKE

1½ cups all-purpose flour

about ⅔ cup unsweetened cocoa

1½ teaspoons baking powder

½ teaspoon baking soda

¼ teaspoon salt

¾ cup whole milk

1½ teaspoons vanilla extract

¾ cup butter or margarine (1½ sticks), softened

1½ cups sugar

3 large eggs

1 Prepare pudding: In 1-quart saucepan, heat butter and semisweet and unsweetened chocolates over low heat, stirring frequently, until melted and smooth; set aside.

2 In 3-quart saucepan, with wire whisk, mix sugar, cornstarch, and cocoa. Gradually add milk, whisking until blended (mixture will not be smooth). Cook over medium heat, whisking constantly, until mixture has thickened and boils; boil, stirring, 1 minute.

3 In small bowl, with wire whisk, beat eggs slightly. Whisk small amount of hot milk mixture into eggs until smooth. Gradually pour egg mixture back into milk mixture in saucepan, whisking rapidly to prevent lumping. Cook over medium heat, stirring constantly, until very thick, 2 minutes.

4 Remove saucepan from heat; stir in chocolate mixture and vanilla. Pour pudding into bowl; cover surface directly with plastic wrap to prevent skin from forming. Refrigerate until cool and set, at least 3 hours. Makes about 3 cups.

5 Meanwhile, prepare cake: Preheat oven to 350°F. Grease two 9-inch round cake pans. Line bottoms with waxed paper; grease paper. Dust pans with cocoa.

6 In small bowl, with wire whisk, mix flour, ⅔ cup cocoa, baking powder, baking soda, and salt. In 1-cup measuring cup, with fork, mix milk and vanilla.

7 In large bowl, with mixer at low speed, beat butter and sugar until blended. Increase speed to high; beat 2 minutes. Reduce speed to medium-low; add eggs, one at a time, beating well after each addition. With mixer at low speed, alternately add flour mixture and milk mixture, beginning and ending with flour mixture. Beat until batter is smooth, occasionally scraping bowl with rubber spatula.

8 Pour batter into prepared pans; spread evenly. Bake until toothpick inserted in center comes out clean, 25 to 30 minutes.

9 Cool cakes in pans on wire racks 10 minutes. Run thin knife around edges to loosen layers from sides of pans. Invert onto wire racks. Remove waxed paper; cool completely.

10 Assemble cake: With serrated knife, cut each cake horizontally in half to make 4 layers in all. With knife, trim about ¼ inch off side of cakes to make crumbs for decorating. With hand, crumble cake trimmings into small bowl (you should have about 1½ cups crumbs).

11 Place 1 cake layer on cake plate. With wire whisk, gently stir cooled pudding in bowl to loosen slightly for easier spreading. Spread ⅔ cup pudding over layer. Repeat with remaining 3 layers, using ⅔ cup pudding on each layer, ending with pudding. Use remaining pudding to lightly frost side of cake. Sprinkle some reserved cake crumbs on top of cake; press remaining crumbs onto pudding on side of cake. If not serving cake after 1 hour, cover and refrigerate up to 2 days.

EACH SERVING About 350 calories, 6g protein, 47g carbohydrate, 17g total fat (6g saturated), 73mg cholesterol, 290mg sodium.

Test Kitchen Tip **COCOA CONFUSION** Both natural and Dutch-process cocoas have rich chocolate flavor and contain only 8 to 24 percent fat, but there is a difference between the two cocoas.

In our kitchens, we usually use natural cocoa because it is readily available. Its acidity works in tandem with the baking soda in a batter to create carbon dioxide gas bubbles, which leaven cakes. Dutch-process cocoa (also called European-sytle) is treated with an alkali agent that neutralizes it and removes some of the cocoa's acidity (the process was developed in the Netherlands in the mid-1800s, hence the name). This procedure changes the cocoa's chemical composition, so it doesn't need to be combined with baking soda. You'll find Dutch-process cocoa at specialty food stores and most supermarkets. Look closely at the label; some cocoas are alkalized even when the label clearly doesn't state it.

As a rule, don't swap cocoas; use what is recommended.

Sacher Torte

This decadent Viennese chocolate dessert features two layers of apricot preserves and a chocolate glaze. Be traditional and serve the cake with schlag *(whipped cream). And, of course, for the best results, use butter, not margarine.*

PREP 45 minutes plus cooling • **BAKE** 40 minutes • **MAKES** 10 servings.

CAKE

¾ cup butter (1½ sticks), softened
¾ cup confectioners' sugar
6 large eggs, separated
1 teaspoon vanilla extract
3 squares (3 ounces) unsweetened chocolate, chopped
3 squares (3 ounces) semisweet chocolate, chopped
¼ teaspoon salt
¼ teaspoon cream of tartar
½ cup granulated sugar
¾ cup all-purpose flour
1 cup apricot preserves

CHOCOLATE GLAZE

3 squares (3 ounces) semisweet chocolate, chopped
2 tablespoons butter
1 teaspoon light corn syrup

1 Preheat oven to 350°F. Grease 9-inch springform pan. Line bottom of pan with waxed paper; grease paper. Dust pan with flour.

2 In large bowl, with mixer at medium speed, beat butter and confectioners' sugar until light and fluffy, about 3 minutes. Beat in egg yolks and vanilla until well blended.

3 In heavy 1-quart saucepan, heat unsweetened and semisweet chocolates over low heat, stirring frequently, until melted and smooth. With mixer at medium speed, immediately beat melted chocolate into egg-yolk mixture until well blended; set aside. (Chocolate must be warm, about 130°F, when added to egg-yolk mixture, or batter will be too stiff.)

4 In medium bowl, with clean beaters and with mixer at high speed, beat egg whites, salt, and cream of tartar until soft peaks form when beaters are lifted. Sprinkle in granulated sugar, 2 tablespoons at a time, beating until sugar has dissolved and egg whites stand in glossy, stiff peaks when beaters are lifted (do not overbeat). With rubber spatula, gently fold beaten egg whites, one-third at a time, into chocolate mixture. Sprinkle flour, about ¼ cup at a time, over chocolate mixture; gently fold in just until blended.

5 Scrape batter into prepared pan; spread evenly. Bake until toothpick inserted in center comes out clean, 40 to 45 minutes.

6 Cool in pan on wire rack 10 minutes. Run thin knife around cake to loosen from side of pan; remove pan side. Invert cake onto rack. Slip knife under cake to separate it from bottom of pan; remove pan bottom. Remove waxed paper; cool cake completely on rack.

7 When cake is cool, cut horizontally into 2 layers. Place bottom layer, cut side up, on cake plate. In 1-quart saucepan, heat apricot preserves over medium-high heat until melted and bubbling. Strain through sieve set over small bowl. With pastry brush, brush half of preserves evenly over layer; replace top layer, cut side down, and spread evenly with remaining preserves. Let stand 10 minutes to set preserves slightly.

8 Prepare glaze: In heavy 1-quart saucepan, heat chocolate, butter, and corn syrup over low heat, stirring frequently, until chocolate and butter have melted and mixture is smooth. Remove from heat and cool slightly, about 5 minutes.

9 Pour chocolate glaze over cake. With narrow metal spatula, spread glaze, allowing some to drip down side of cake; completely cover top and side of cake. Let stand until glaze has set, about 30 minutes. If not serving right away, refrigerate cake up to 4 hours. Let cake stand 20 minutes at room temperature before serving.

EACH SERVING About 505 calories, 7g protein, 61g carbohydrate, 29g total fat (17g saturated), 171mg cholesterol, 276mg sodium.

German's Chocolate Cake

Contrary to what most people think, this beloved chocolate cake is not a creation of Germany. The correct name is German's—the brand name of an American baking chocolate used in the cake.

PREP 45 minutes plus cooling • BAKE 30 minutes • MAKES 16 servings.

2 cups all-purpose flour
1 teaspoon baking soda
¼ teaspoon salt
1¼ cups buttermilk
1 teaspoon vanilla extract
3 large eggs, separated
1½ cups sugar
¾ cup butter or margarine (1½ sticks), softened
4 squares (4 ounces) sweet baking chocolate, melted
Coconut-Pecan Frosting (page 355)

1 Preheat oven to 350°F. Grease three 8-inch round cake pans. Line bottoms with waxed paper; grease paper. Dust pans with flour.

2 In medium bowl, with wire whisk, mix flour, baking soda, and salt. In 2-cup measuring cup, with fork, mix buttermilk and vanilla.

3 In medium bowl, with mixer at medium-high speed, beat egg whites until frothy. Sprinkle in ¾ cup sugar, 1 tablespoon at a time, beating until soft peaks form when beaters are lifted.

4 In large bowl, with mixer at medium speed, beat butter until light and fluffy. Add remaining ¾ cup sugar and beat until well blended. Reduce speed to medium-low; add egg yolks, one at a time, beating well after each addition. Beat in melted chocolate.

Reduce speed to low; add flour mixture alternately with buttermilk mixture, beginning and ending with flour mixture. Beat until smooth, occasionally scraping bowl. With rubber spatula, fold half of beaten egg whites into batter; gently fold in remaining egg whites.

5 Divide batter evenly among prepared pans; spread evenly. Place two pans on upper oven rack and one pan on lower oven rack so pans are not directly above one another. Bake until toothpick inserted in center comes out almost clean, about 30 minutes.

6 Cool in pans on wire racks 10 minutes. Run thin knife around edges to loosen layers from sides of pans. Invert onto racks. Remove waxed paper; cool completely.

7 Meanwhile, prepare Coconut-Pecan Frosting.

8 Place 1 layer, rounded side down, on cake plate. With narrow metal spatula, spread 1 cup frosting over layer. Top with second cake layer, rounded side up, and spread with 1 cup frosting. Place remaining layer, rounded side up, on top. Spread remaining frosting over top and side of cake.

EACH SERVING WITH FROSTING About 505 calories, 5g protein, 53g carbohydrate, 31g total fat (16g saturated), 140mg cholesterol, 320mg sodium.

Black Forest Cake

A standout among special-occasion cakes. The flavors blend best if you assemble it a day ahead.

PREP 1 hour plus chilling • **BAKE** 25 minutes • **MAKES** 16 servings.

CHOCOLATE CAKE
2 cups all-purpose flour
1 cup unsweetened cocoa
2 teaspoons baking powder
1 teaspoon baking soda
½ teaspoon salt
1⅓ cups milk
2 teaspoons vanilla extract
1 cup butter or margarine (2 sticks), softened
2 cups granulated sugar
4 large eggs

CHERRY FILLING
2 cans (16½ ounces each) pitted dark sweet
    cherries (Bing) in heavy syrup
⅓ cup kirsch (cherry brandy)

CREAM FILLING
1½ cups heavy or whipping cream
½ cup confectioners' sugar
2 tablespoons kirsch (cherry brandy)
1 teaspoon vanilla extract
Chocolate Curls (page 362)

1 Preheat oven to 350°F. Grease three 9-inch round cake pans. Line bottoms with waxed paper; grease paper. Dust pans with flour.

2 Prepare cake: In medium bowl, whisk flour, cocoa, baking powder, baking soda, and salt. In small bowl, with fork, mix milk and vanilla.

3 In large bowl, with mixer at low speed, beat butter and granulated sugar until blended. Increase speed to high; beat until creamy, about 2 minutes. Reduce speed to medium-low; add eggs, one at a time, beating well after each addition. With mixer at low speed, add flour mixture alternately with milk mixture, beginning and end-ing with flour mixture. Beat until batter is smooth, occasionally scraping bowl with rubber spatula.

4 Divide batter evenly among prepared pans; spread evenly. Place two pans on upper oven rack and one pan on lower oven rack, so that pans are not directly above one another. Bake until toothpick inserted in center comes out almost clean, about 25 minutes.

5 Cool in pans on wire racks 10 minutes. Run thin knife around edges to loosen layers from sides of pans. Invert onto wire racks. Remove and discard waxed paper; cool layers completely.

6 Meanwhile, prepare fillings: In sieve set over bowl, drain cherries well. Reserve ½ cup syrup; stir in ⅓ cup kirsch. Set syrup mixture aside. In small bowl, with mixer at medium speed, beat cream, confectioners' sugar, 2 tablespoons kirsch, and vanilla until stiff peaks form when beaters are lifted.

7 Assemble cake: Prepare Chocolate Curls as directed. Place 1 layer on serving plate; brush with one-third syrup mixture. Spread with one-third whipped-cream mixture, then top with half of cherries. Place second layer on top of cherries. Brush with half of remaining syrup mixture, spread with half of remaining cream mixture, and top with all of remaining cherries. Top with third layer; brush with remaining syrup mixture. Spoon remaining cream mixture onto center of top, leaving a border of cake around edge. Pile chocolate curls on top of whipped cream in center of cake. Cover and refrigerate cake overnight.

EACH SERVING About 450 calories, 6g protein, 58g carbohydrate, 22g total fat (8g saturated), 87mg cholesterol, 380mg sodium.

Black Forest Cake

Chocolate Truffle Cake

Bake this exceptionally rich dessert a day ahead for best flavor and texture. To serve, dip the knife in hot water before cutting each slice.

PREP 1 hour • **BAKE** 35 minutes • **MAKES** 24 servings.

1 cup butter (2 sticks) (do not use margarine)
14 squares (14 ounces) semisweet chocolate, chopped
2 squares (2 ounces) unsweetened chocolate, chopped
9 large eggs, separated
½ cup granulated sugar
¼ teaspoon cream of tartar
confectioners' sugar (optional)

1 Preheat oven to 300°F. Remove bottom from 9" by 3" springform pan and cover with foil, wrapping foil around to underside (to make it easier to remove cake). Replace pan bottom. Grease and flour foil bottom and side of pan.

2 In large microwave-safe glass bowl, combine butter and semisweet and unsweetened chocolates. In microwave oven, heat, uncovered, on Medium (50%), 2½ minutes; stir. Return chocolate mixture to microwave oven; heat until almost melted, 2 to 2½ minutes longer. Stir until smooth. (Or, in heavy 2-quart saucepan, heat butter and semisweet and unsweetened chocolates over low heat, stirring frequently, until melted. Pour chocolate mixture into large bowl.)

3 In small bowl, with mixer at high speed, beat egg yolks and granulated sugar until very thick and lemon-colored, about 5 minutes. Add egg-yolk mixture to chocolate mixture, stirring with rubber spatula until blended.

4 In another large bowl, with clean beaters and with mixer at high speed, beat egg whites and cream of tartar until soft peaks form when beaters are lifted. With rubber spatula or wire whisk, gently fold one-third of beaten egg whites into chocolate mixture. Fold in remaining whites, just until blended.

5 Pour batter into prepared pan; spread evenly. Bake 35 minutes. (Do not overbake; the cake will firm up on standing and chilling.) Cool cake completely in pan on wire rack; refrigerate overnight in pan.

6 To remove cake from pan, run thin knife that has been rinsed under very hot water and dried around edge to loosen cake from side of pan; remove side of pan. Invert onto cake plate; unwrap foil from pan bottom and remove bottom. Carefully peel foil away from cake.

7 Let cake stand 1 hour at room temperature before serving. If you like, just before serving, sprinkle cake with confectioners' sugar (see Tip, below).

EACH SERVING WITHOUT CONFECTIONERS' SUGAR About 200 calories, 4g protein, 17g carbohydrate, 14g total fat (6g saturated), 100mg cholesterol, 110mg sodium.

> **Test Kitchen Tip**
> **SIMPLE STENCILS** To decorate a cake with stars or other simple shapes, make a stencil by cutting the desired shape or shapes from a square of lightweight cardboard (a manila file folder works well). Hold stencil over top of cake and sift unsweetened cocoa, confectioners' sugar, or cinnamon sugar over it. Repeat for desired pattern.

Chocolate Truffle Cake

Light Chocolate–Buttermilk Bundt Cake

Satisfy your chocolate cravings with this lowfat treat. If you skip the Mocha Glaze, you'll save forty-five calories per serving.

PREP 30 minutes plus cooling • **BAKE** 45 minutes • **MAKES** 16 servings.

2¼ cups all-purpose flour
1½ teaspoons baking soda
½ teaspoon baking powder
½ teaspoon salt
¾ cup unsweetened cocoa
1 teaspoon instant espresso-coffee powder
¾ cup hot water
2 cups sugar
⅓ cup vegetable oil
2 large egg whites
1 large egg
1 square (1 ounce) unsweetened chocolate, melted
2 teaspoons vanilla extract
½ cup buttermilk
Mocha Glaze (page 358)

1 Preheat oven to 350°F. Grease the 10-inch Bundt pan.

2 In medium bowl, with wire whisk, mix flour, baking soda, baking powder, and salt. In 2-cup measuring cup, with fork, mix cocoa, espresso-coffee powder, and hot water until blended.

3 In large bowl, with mixer at low speed, beat sugar, oil, egg whites, and egg until blended. Increase speed to high; beat until creamy, about 2 minutes. Reduce speed to low; beat in cocoa mixture, melted chocolate, and vanilla. Add flour mixture alternately with buttermilk, beginning and ending with flour mixture. Beat just until blended, occasionally scraping bowl with rubber spatula.

4 Scrape batter into prepared pan; spread evenly with rubber spatula. Bake until toothpick inserted in center of cake comes out clean, about 45 minutes.

5 Cool cake in pan on wire rack 10 minutes. Run tip of thin knife around edge of cake to loosen from side and center tube of pan. Invert onto rack to cool completely.

6 Meanwhile, prepare Mocha Glaze. Place cake on cake plate; pour glaze over cooled cake.

EACH SERVING WITH GLAZE About 280 calories, 4g protein, 53g carbohydrate, 7g total fat (2g saturated), 14mg cholesterol, 232mg sodium.

EACH SERVING WITHOUT GLAZE About 235 calories, 4g protein, 42g carbohydrate, 7g total fat (2g saturated), 14mg cholesterol, 226mg sodium.

Walnut Torte

A torte (German for "cake") is a dense, moist cake in which ground nuts replace some of the flour.

PREP 25 minutes plus cooling • **BAKE** 25 minutes • **MAKES** 16 servings.

3 cups walnuts (12 ounces)
1 cup sugar
3 tablespoons all-purpose flour
1 teaspoon baking powder
¼ teaspoon salt
6 large eggs, separated
1 cup heavy or whipping cream

1 Preheat oven to 350°F. Grease two 9-inch round cake pans. Line bottoms of pans with waxed paper; grease paper.

2 Chop 2 tablespoons walnuts and reserve for garnish. In blender or in food processor with knife blade attached, working in batches if necessary, finely grind remaining walnuts and ¼ cup sugar. In medium bowl, with wire whisk, mix ground walnut mixture, flour, baking powder, and salt until blended; set aside.

3 In large bowl, with mixer on medium-high, beat egg whites until soft peaks form when beaters are lifted. Sprinkle in ¼ cup sugar, 1 tablespoon at a time, beating until soft peaks form.

4 In small bowl, with same beaters and with mixer at high speed, beat egg yolks and remaining ½ cup sugar until thick and lemon-colored, about 3 minutes. With rubber spatula, gently fold half of walnut mixture and half of egg yolks into beaten egg whites just until blended. Repeat with remaining walnut mixture and yolks, folding just until blended. Do not overmix.

5 Scrape batter into prepared pans; spread evenly. Bake until cake springs back when lightly pressed, 25 to 30 minutes.

6 Cool in pans on wire racks 5 minutes. Run thin knife around edges to loosen layers from sides of pans. Invert onto rack. Remove waxed paper; cool completely.

7 In small bowl, with mixer at medium-high speed, beat cream until soft peaks form. Place 1 cake layer, rounded side down, on cake plate. With narrow metal spatula, spread about half of whipped cream over cake layer. Top with second layer, rounded side up. Spread remaining whipped cream over top of cake; sprinkle with reserved chopped walnuts. Refrigerate until ready to serve, up to 4 hours.

EACH SERVING About 282 calories, 6g protein, 18g carbohydrate, 22g total fat (5g saturated), 100mg cholesterol, 98mg sodium.

Chocolate Pound Cake with Irish Whiskey–Cream Sauce

Bake this dense, decadent chocolate cake in a Bundt pan and serve with a big dollop of flavored whipped cream. The topping won't keep as well as the cake, so finish up the cream sauce while it's fresh, but enjoy the cake for the rest of the week.

PREP 30 minutes • **BAKE** 1 hour 15 minutes • **MAKES** 20 servings.

CHOCOLATE CAKE

3 cups all-purpose flour

1 cup unsweetened cocoa

½ teaspoon baking powder

1½ cups milk

2 teaspoons vanilla extract

1½ cups butter or margarine (3 sticks), softened

2¾ cups granulated sugar

5 large eggs

2 squares (2 ounces) bittersweet or semisweet chocolate, grated

IRISH WHISKEY–CREAM SAUCE

1 cup heavy or whipping cream

⅓ cup confectioners' sugar

¼ cup brewed coffee

2 tablespoons Irish whiskey or Bourbon

confectioners' sugar for garnish

1 Prepare cake: Preheat oven to 350°F. Grease and flour 12-cup Bundt pan. In medium bowl, with wire whisk, mix flour, cocoa, and baking powder. In small bowl, with fork, mix milk and vanilla.

2 In large bowl, with mixer at medium speed, beat butter until creamy. Gradually add granulated sugar, beating until well blended, occasionally scraping bowl with rubber spatula. Increase speed to medium-high; beat until creamy, about 3 minutes, frequently scraping bowl. Reduce speed to low; add eggs, one at a time, beating well after each addition. With mixer at low speed, alternately add flour mixture and milk mixture, beginning and ending with flour mixture. Beat until blended, occasionally scraping bowl. Stir in grated chocolate.

3 Spoon batter into prepared pan; spread evenly. Bake until toothpick inserted in center of cake comes out clean, about 1 hour 15 minutes.

4 Cool cake in pan on wire rack 10 minutes. Invert cake onto wire rack to cool completely.

5 Meanwhile, prepare sauce: In small bowl, with mixer at low speed, beat cream until frothy. Increase speed to medium; add confectioners' sugar and beat until stiff peaks form. With rubber spatula or wire whisk, fold in coffee and whiskey until blended. Cover and refrigerate up to 4 hours. Makes about 2 cups.

6 To serve, sprinkle cake with confectioners' sugar. Cut into wedges and pass cream sauce to spoon over each serving.

EACH SERVING WITHOUT SAUCE About 350 calories, 5g protein, 47g carbohydrate, 17g total fat (4g saturated), 56mg cholesterol, 220mg sodium.

EACH TABLESPOON SAUCE About 35 calories, 0g protein, 1g carbohydrate, 3g total fat (2g saturated), 10mg cholesterol, 5mg sodium.

Pound Cake

Everything you ever wanted in a pound cake. It's moist, rich, and toothsome.

PREP 25 minutes • **BAKE** 1 hour • **MAKES** 20 servings.

3 cups all-purpose flour
1½ teaspoons baking powder
¾ teaspoon salt
½ cup whole milk
4 teaspoons vanilla extract
1½ cups butter (3 sticks), softened
  (do not use margarine)
2 cups granulated sugar
5 large eggs
confectioners' sugar

1 Preheat oven to 325°F. Grease and flour 10-inch Bundt pan.

2 In medium bowl, with wire whisk, mix flour, baking powder, and salt. In small bowl, with fork, mix milk and vanilla.

3 In large bowl, with mixer at low speed, beat butter and granulated sugar until blended. Increase speed to medium-high; beat until creamy, about 3 minutes, occasionally scraping bowl with rubber spatula. Reduce speed to low; add eggs, one at a time, beating well after each addition. Alternately beat in flour mixture and milk mixture, beginning and ending with flour mixture. Beat just until smooth.

4 Spoon batter into prepared pan; spread evenly. Bake until toothpick inserted in center comes out clean, about 1 hour.

5 Cool cake in pan on wire rack 15 minutes. Run tip of thin knife around edges to loosen cake from sides and center tube of pan. Invert cake onto wire rack to cool completely. Dust with confectioners' sugar.

EACH SERVING About 302 calories, 4g protein, 36g carbohydrate, 16g total fat (9g saturated), 91mg cholesterol, 284mg sodium.

Test Kitchen Tip

TO BAKE 2 LOAVES Prepare recipe as directed in Steps 1 through 3, except in Step 1 grease and flour two 8½" by 4½" loaf pans. In Step 4, spread batter evenly in pans and bake as directed. Cool as directed in Step 5, except after inverting loaves onto rack, quickly invert again so they are top side up.

Cranberry Almond Pound Cake

The sweetness of almond paste is balanced by both fresh and dried cranberries for an unusually rich and flavorful version of one of our all-time favorites—pound cake.

PREP 35 minutes • **BAKE** 1 hour 30 minutes • **MAKES** 24 servings.

1 cup dried cranberries

2 tablespoons almond-flavor liqueur or orange juice

3 cups all-purpose flour

1 teaspoon baking powder

¾ teaspoon salt

½ teaspoon baking soda

1 tube or can (7 to 8 ounces) almond paste

1 cup butter or margarine (2 sticks), softened

2 cups sugar

½ teaspoon almond extract

5 large eggs

1 container (8 ounces) sour cream

2 cups cranberries, picked over

1 Preheat oven to 325°F. Grease 10-inch tube pan with removable bottom. Dust pan with flour. In small bowl, combine dried cranberries and liqueur; set aside.

2 In medium bowl, with wire whisk, mix flour, baking powder, salt, and baking soda. Onto sheet of waxed paper, grate almond paste.

3 In large bowl, with mixer at medium speed, beat butter until creamy. Gradually add sugar, 2 tablespoons at a time, beating until light and fluffy, about 3 minutes, occasionally scraping bowl with rubber spatula. Beat in almond paste and extract. Add eggs, one at a time, beating well after each addition. Reduce speed to low; add flour mixture alternately with sour cream, beginning and ending with flour mixture. Beat just until blended. With wooden spoon, stir in dried cranberries with liqueur and fresh cranberries.

4 Spoon batter into prepared pan. Bake until toothpick inserted in center comes out clean, 1 hour 30 minutes to 1 hour 40 minutes.

5 Cool cake in pan on wire rack 1 hour. Run thin knife around cake to loosen from side and center tube of pan; lift tube to separate from pan side. Invert cake onto wire rack; slide knife under cake to separate from bottom of pan. Turn cake, right side up; cool completely on wire rack.

EACH SERVING About 290 calories, 4g protein, 39g carbohydrate, 14g total fat (7g saturated), 70mg cholesterol, 220mg sodium.

 POUND CAKES
In the old days—when it wasn't worth firing up the oven unless you baked several cakes—pound cake recipes called for one pound each of butter, sugar, flour, and eggs. The butter and sugar, then the eggs, had to be laboriously creamed until perfectly smooth, light, and fluffy, because the beaten eggs had to serve as leavening (baking soda and powder were not used), and the batter had to be as light as possible to enable the eggs to do their work. Today, most folks are happy to bake one pound cake at a time and electric mixers, baking soda, baking powder, and other modern conveniences make whipping up a pound cake almost effortless. Still, you do want to cream the butter and sugar for a good long time, until it feels smooth, not grainy, between your fingers.

Lemon–Poppy Seed Pound Cake

This tangy-sweet cake keeps well. Store any leftover poppy seeds in the refrigerator. They turn rancid quickly at room temperature.

PREP 25 minutes • **BAKE** 1 hour 20 minutes • **MAKES** 16 servings.

2 cups all-purpose flour
2 tablespoons poppy seeds
½ teaspoon baking powder
¼ teaspoon baking soda
¼ teaspoon salt
2 large lemons
¾ cup butter or margarine (1½ sticks), softened
1½ cups plus ⅓ cup sugar
4 large eggs
1 teaspoon vanilla extract
½ cup sour cream

1 Preheat oven to 325°F. Grease and flour 9" by 5" metal loaf pan.

2 In medium bowl, with wire whisk, mix flour, poppy seeds, baking powder, baking soda, and salt. From lemons, grate 1 tablespoon peel and squeeze 3 tablespoons juice.

3 In large bowl, with mixer at low speed, beat butter and 1½ cups sugar until blended. Increase speed to high; beat until light and fluffy, about 5 minutes. Add eggs, one at a time, beating well after each addition, frequently scraping bowl with rubber spatula. Beat in lemon peel and vanilla. Reduce speed to low; add flour mixture alternately with sour cream, beginning and ending with flour mixture. Beat just until smooth.

4 Spoon batter into prepared pan; spread evenly. Bake until toothpick inserted in center comes out clean, about 1 hour 20 minutes.

5 Cool in pan on wire rack 10 minutes. Run thin knife around edges to loosen cake from sides of pan. Remove from pan; place on rack set over waxed paper.

6 In small bowl, combine lemon juice and remaining ⅓ cup sugar. With pastry brush, brush mixture over top and sides of warm cake. Cool completely.

EACH SERVING About 267 calories, 4g protein, 36g carbohydrate, 12g total fat (7g saturated), 80mg cholesterol, 178mg sodium.

Angel Food Cake

Angel food cake, beloved for its clean flavor and light texture, has an added attraction: It's lowfat.

PREP 30 minutes • **BAKE** 35 minutes • **MAKES** 16 servings.

1 cup cake flour (not self-rising)
½ cup confectioners' sugar
1⅔ cups egg whites (12 to 14 large egg whites)
1½ teaspoons cream of tartar
½ teaspoon salt
1¼ cups granulated sugar
2 teaspoons vanilla extract
½ teaspoon almond extract

1 Preheat oven to 375°F. Sift flour and confectioners' sugar through sieve set over small bowl.
2 In large bowl, with mixer at medium speed, beat egg whites, cream of tartar, and salt until foamy. Increase speed to medium-high; beat until soft peaks form when beaters are lifted. Sprinkle in granulated sugar, 2 tablespoons at a time, beating until sugar has dissolved and egg whites stand in stiff, glossy peaks when beaters are lifted. Beat in vanilla and almond extracts.
3 Sift flour mixture, one-third at a time, over beaten egg whites; fold in with rubber spatula just until flour mixture is no longer visible. Do not overmix.
4 Scrape batter into ungreased 9- to 10-inch tube pan; spread evenly. Bake until cake springs back when lightly pressed, 35 to 40 minutes.
5 Invert cake in pan onto large metal funnel or bottle; cool completely in pan. Run tip of thin knife around edges to loosen cake from side and center tube of pan. Remove from pan and place on cake plate.

EACH SERVING About 115 calories, 3g protein, 25g carbohydrate, 0g total fat, 0mg cholesterol, 114mg sodium.

CAPPUCCINO ANGEL FOOD CAKE
Prepare as directed but add *4 teaspoons instant espresso-coffee powder* and *½ teaspoon ground cinnamon* to egg whites before beating; use *1½ teaspoons vanilla extract* and omit almond extract. In cup, mix *1 tablespoon confectioners' sugar* and *⅛ teaspoon ground cinnamon*; sprinkle evenly over cooled cake.

Chocolate Angel Food Cake

Cocoa gives this angel food cake rich, satisfying chocolate flavor.

PREP 30 minutes • **BAKE** 35 minutes • **MAKES** 16 servings.

¾ cup cake flour (not self-rising)
½ cup unsweetened cocoa
1½ cups sugar
1⅔ cups egg whites (12 to 14 large egg whites)
1½ teaspoons cream of tartar
½ teaspoon salt
1½ teaspoons vanilla extract

1 Preheat oven to 375°F. Sift the flour, cocoa, and ¾ cup sugar through sieve set over a medium bowl.

2 In large bowl, with mixer at medium speed, beat egg whites, cream of tartar, and salt until foamy. Increase speed to medium-high; beat until soft peaks form when beaters are lifted. Sprinkle in remaining ¾ cup sugar, 2 tablespoons at a time, beating until sugar has dissolved and egg whites stand in stiff, glossy peaks when beaters are lifted. Beat in vanilla.

3 Sift cocoa mixture, one-third at a time, over beaten egg whites; fold in with rubber spatula just until cocoa mixture is no longer visible. Do not overmix.

4 Scrape batter into ungreased 9- to 10-inch tube pan; spread evenly. Bake until cake springs back when lightly pressed, 35 to 40 minutes.

5 Invert cake in pan onto large metal funnel or bottle; cool completely in pan. Run tip of thin knife around edges to loosen cake from side and center tube of pan. Remove from pan and place cake on plate.

EACH SERVING About 118 calories, 4g protein, 25g carbohydrate, 0g total fat, 0mg cholesterol, 115mg sodium.

 Test Kitchen Tip

WHY ANGEL FOOD CAKES COOL UPSIDE DOWN

Angel food cake, which is leavened only with beaten egg whites, doesn't have the stability of cake leavened with baking powder or soda. Cooling it thoroughly in an upside-down position before removing it from the pan allows the cake's very light and delicate structure to firm up. If cooled without inverting, the cake will lose volume. If removed from pan too early, it will collapse. If your tube pan does not have legs for support, it can be set upside down on an inverted large funnel or on the neck of a sturdy bottle for easy cooling

Strawberry Angel Food Layer Cake

Unlike the classic angel food cake, this one is baked in a jelly-roll pan, cut into strips, and then layered with a luscious filling of fresh whipped cream and sliced strawberries.

PREP 30 minutes • **BAKE** 25 minutes • **MAKES** 8 servings.

⅔ cup cake flour (not self-rising)
⅔ cup confectioners' sugar
8 large egg whites
¼ teaspoon salt
⅔ cup plus 2 tablespoons granulated sugar
2 teaspoons vanilla extract
3¼ cups strawberries (1 pint)
1 cup heavy or whipping cream

1 Preheat oven to 350°F. Grease 15½" by 10½" jelly-roll pan. Line pan with waxed paper; grease paper. Into small bowl, sift flour and confectioners' sugar.

2 In large bowl, with mixer at high speed, beat egg whites and salt until soft peaks form. Sprinkle in ⅔ cup granulated sugar, 2 tablespoons at a time, beating just until whites stand in stiff, glossy peaks when beaters are lifted. Beat in vanilla.

3 Sift flour mixture, one-third at a time, over beaten egg whites; fold in with rubber spatula just until flour mixture is no longer visible.

4 Scrape batter into prepared pan; spread evenly. Bake until cake springs back when lightly touched, 25 to 30 minutes.

5 Cool completely in pan on wire rack. Invert cake onto cutting board; carefully peel off waxed paper.

6 While cake cools, prepare strawberries and whipped cream: Reserve 5 or 6 smaller berries for garnish; hull and slice remaining strawberries. In large bowl, with mixer at medium speed, beat cream and remaining 2 tablespoons granulated sugar until soft peaks form. Reserve ¾ cup whipped cream. Fold sliced strawberries into whipped cream remaining in bowl.

7 Assemble cake: With serrated knife, cut cake into 3 equal strips, about 10" by 5" each. Place 1 cake strip on platter; spread with half of strawberry whipped cream. Top with another cake strip, then with remaining strawberry whipped cream. Top with remaining strip. Spread reserved whipped cream on top of cake. Cut each reserved strawberry in half; use to garnish top of cake. Refrigerate if not serving right away.

EACH SERVING About 285 calories, 5g protein, 41g carbohydrate, 11g total fat (7g saturated), 41mg cholesterol, 140mg sodium.

> **Test Kitchen Tip**
> ## FOAM CAKES
> Foam cakes depend on beaten whole eggs or egg whites for their volume and airy texture. Angel food cake is so light because it contains no fat, whereas sponge and chiffon cakes contain egg yolks in addition to whites plus vegetable oil or melted butter for additional moisture. Many recipes call for adding cream of tartar to the egg whites to give them more stability. When combining ingredients for a foam-cake batter, gently fold them together with a large rubber spatula so the batter doesn't deflate. Since foam cakes contain little or no fat, they dry out quickly; store them at room temperature no longer than two days.

Strawberry Angel Food Layer Cake

Hot-Water Sponge Cake

This fail-safe cake is traditionally baked in a tube pan, but you can also use two 9-inch round pans. Fill with Lemon Filling (page 237) and dust the top with confectioners' sugar. Also, try Whipped Cream Frosting (page 354), and serve with fresh berries.

PREP 20 minutes • **BAKE** 35 minutes • **MAKES** 16 servings.

6 large eggs
1¾ cups all-purpose flour
2 teaspoons baking powder
½ teaspoon salt
½ cup water
4 tablespoons butter or margarine,
   cut into 4 pieces
1 cup sugar
1½ teaspoons vanilla extract

1 Preheat oven to 350°F. Place eggs in bowl of warm water; let stand 10 minutes. Grease bottom of 9- to 10-inch tube pan without removable bottom. Or grease bottoms of two 9-inch round cake pans; line bottoms with waxed paper, and grease paper.

2 Sift flour, baking powder, and salt onto sheet of waxed paper.

3 In large bowl, with mixer at high speed, beat eggs until very foamy and doubled in volume, about 5 minutes. While beating eggs, combine water and butter in small saucepan and heat to boiling; remove from heat. Gradually sprinkle sugar into eggs, 2 tablespoons at a time, beating until eggs thicken slightly, about 2 minutes. Reduce mixer speed to low. Sift flour mixture over eggs and beat until blended and no lumps of flour remain, scraping bowl frequently with rubber spatula. Add hot-water mixture and vanilla; beat until blended, scraping bowl frequently.

4 Pour batter into prepared pan. Bake until toothpick inserted in center of cake comes out clean, 35 to 40 minutes for tube cake, or about 25 minutes for 9-inch layers.

5 Invert cake in tube pan onto large metal funnel or bottle; cool completely. For 9-inch layers, remove from pans immediately to cool on wire racks. Run tip of thin knife around edges to loosen tube cake from side and center tube of pan. Remove cake from pan and place on cake plate.

EACH SERVING About 155 calories, 4g protein, 23g carbohydrate, 5g total fat (3g saturated), 87mg cholesterol, 185mg sodium.

Double-Citrus Sponge Cake

This moist perfect-for-Passover cake is subtly flavored with lemon and orange peel. The cake is especially light and fluffy because egg whites and yolks are beaten separately, then folded together.

PREP 25 minutes • **BAKE** 40 minutes • **MAKES** 12 servings.

1 cup unsalted matzoh meal
¼ teaspoon salt
2 tablespoons plus 1 cup granulated sugar
9 large eggs, separated
2 teaspoons freshly grated lemon peel
1 teaspoon freshly grated orange peel
1 tablespoon confectioners' sugar (optional)

1 Preheat oven to 375°F. In blender or in food processor with knife blade attached, grind matzoh meal, salt, and 2 tablespoons granulated sugar until very fine (consistency will resemble that of flour).

2 In large bowl, with mixer at high speed, beat egg yolks and ⅓ cup granulated sugar until thick and lemon-colored and mixture forms ribbons when beaters are lifted, about 5 minutes, occasionally scraping bowl with rubber spatula. Beat in lemon and orange peels. Fold in matzoh-meal mixture until blended. Set yolk mixture aside (mixture will stiffen upon standing). Wash and dry beaters.

3 In another large bowl, with clean beaters and with mixer at high speed, beat egg whites until foamy. Gradually sprinkle in remaining ⅔ cup granulated sugar, 2 tablespoons at a time, beating until sugar has dissolved and whites stand in stiff peaks when beaters are lifted. (Do not overbeat whites.) With rubber spatula, stir about one-fourth of beaten whites into yolk mixture to loosen mixture. Fold in remaining whites, one-third at a time, just until blended.

4 Spoon batter into ungreased 10-inch tube pan with removable bottom. With metal spatula, cut though batter to break large air bubbles. Bake until top springs back when lightly touched with finger, about 40 minutes.

5 Invert cake in pan onto large metal funnel or bottle; cool completely in pan. Run tip of thin knife around edges to loosen cake from side and center tube of pan; lift tube to separate cake from pan side. Invert cake onto cake plate; slide knife under cake to separate from bottom of pan. Remove cake from pan and, if you like, sprinkle with confectioners' sugar before serving.

EACH SERVING About 170 calories, 6g protein, 28g carbohydrate, 4g total fat (1g saturated), 159mg cholesterol, 100mg sodium.

Boston Cream Pie

Some historians believe that this dessert, which is not a pie at all, dates back to a confection known as pudding-cake-pie. An early example is Washington Pie (also called Mrs. Washington's Pie), a "filled" cake sandwiched with raspberry jam and dusted with confectioners' sugar. As the story goes, in 1855, in Boston's famous Parker House Hotel, the German pastry chef decided to spruce up the hotel's Boston Pie (a sponge cake filled with vanilla custard and dusted with confectioners' sugar) by adding a rich chocolate glaze. His creation was called Parker House Chocolate Pie and Parker House Cream Pie. Over the years, this dessert came to be known by other names, including Boston Cream Cake and Boston Cream Pie, but little else has changed. It's still a cake (now a golden sponge) that's called a pie, filled with a dense vanilla custard and blanketed with a thick chocolate glaze. It remains the signature dessert at the Parker House and is also the official state dessert of Massachusetts.

PREP 40 minutes • **BAKE** 20 minutes • **MAKES** 12 servings.

1½ cups all-purpose flour
1½ teaspoons baking powder
¼ teaspoon salt
3 large eggs
½ cup water
3 tablespoons butter or margarine
1½ teaspoons vanilla extract
1⅓ cups sugar
Pastry Cream (page 331)
Chocolate Glaze (page 358)

1 Preheat oven to 350°F. Grease two 8-inch round cake pans. Line bottoms with waxed paper; grease and flour paper.

2 In medium bowl, with wire whisk, mix flour, baking powder, and salt; set aside.

3 In large bowl, with mixer at high speed, beat eggs until light and tripled in volume, about 5 minutes.

4 Meanwhile, in small saucepan, heat water and butter to boiling. Remove from heat; add vanilla.

5 With mixer at high speed, gradually add sugar to eggs, beating until thick and lemon-colored and mixture forms ribbon when beaters are lifted, 5 to 8 minutes, occasionally scraping bowl with rubber spatula. In two additions, fold in flour mixture just until blended. Pour in water mixture; stir gently until blended.

6 Divide batter evenly between prepared pans. Bake until toothpick inserted in center comes out clean, about 20 minutes.

7 Run thin knife around edges to loosen layers from sides of pans. Invert onto wire racks. Remove waxed paper; cool completely.

8 Meanwhile, prepare Pastry Cream.

9 When cake is cool, prepare Chocolate Glaze.

10 Place 1 layer, rounded side down, on cake plate; top with pastry cream. Top with second cake layer, rounded side up. Pour glaze over top. With narrow metal spatula, spread glaze evenly to edge, allowing it to drip down side of cake. Let glaze set.

EACH SERVING WITH CHOCOLATE GLAZE AND PASTRY CREAM About 325 calories, 5g protein, 50g carbohydrate, 12g total fat (7g saturated), 110mg cholesterol, 210mg sodium.

PASTRY CREAM

This rich-tasting pastry cream makes a great filling for a variety of layer cakes, éclairs, cream puffs, and other pastries.

PREP 8 minutes plus cooling and chilling
COOK 10 minutes • **MAKES** about 1½ cups.

¾ cup plus 6 tablespoons milk
2 large egg yolks
⅓ cup sugar
2 tablespoons all-purpose flour
2 tablespoons cornstarch
1 tablespoon butter or margarine
1 teaspoon vanilla extract

1 In 1-quart heavy saucepan, heat ¾ cup milk to boiling over medium heat.

2 Meanwhile, in large bowl, with wire whisk, beat egg yolks, remaining 6 tablespoons milk, and sugar until smooth. Add flour and cornstarch, whisking until blended. Gradually add hot milk, whisking until blended.

3 Return mixture to saucepan; cook over medium heat, whisking constantly, until mixture has thickened and boils, about 4 minutes. Reduce heat to low; cook, whisking constantly, 2 minutes. Remove saucepan from heat; stir in butter and vanilla.

4 Pour pastry cream into shallow dish. Press plastic wrap directly onto surface to keep skin from forming as it cools. Cool to room temperature. Refrigerate at least 2 hours, or up to overnight.

Boston Cream Pie

Vanilla Chiffon Cake

If you like, dust this tall, handsome cake with confectioners' sugar and serve some fresh berries on the side. The citrus variation is tart, so if you prefer your desserts on the sweet side, use three-quarters cup orange juice and omit the lemon juice.

PREP 20 minutes • **BAKE** 1 hour 15 minutes • **MAKES** 16 servings.

2¼ cups cake flour (not self-rising)
1½ cups sugar
1 tablespoon baking powder
1 teaspoon salt
¾ cup cold water
½ cup vegetable oil
5 large eggs, separated
2 large egg whites
1 tablespoon vanilla extract
½ teaspoon cream of tartar

1 Preheat oven to 325°F. In large bowl, with wire whisk, mix flour, 1 cup sugar, baking powder, and salt. Make well in center; add cold water, oil, egg yolks, and vanilla to well. With whisk, stir until smooth.

2 In separate large bowl, with mixer at high speed, beat the 7 egg whites and cream of tartar until soft peaks form when beaters are lifted. Sprinkle in remaining ½ cup sugar, 2 tablespoons at a time, beating until sugar has dissolved and egg whites stand in stiff, glossy peaks when beaters are lifted. With rubber spatula, fold one-third of beaten egg whites into egg-yolk mixture, then fold in remaining egg whites until blended.

3 Scrape batter into ungreased 9- to 10-inch tube pan; spread evenly. Bake until cake springs back when lightly pressed, about 1 hour 15 minutes.

4 Invert cake in pan onto large metal funnel or bottle; cool completely in pan. Run tip of thin knife around edges to loosen cake from side and center tube of pan; lift tube to separate from pan side. Invert cake onto plate; slide knife under cake to separate from bottom of pan. Remove cake from pan and place on serving plate.

EACH SERVING About 217 calories, 4g protein, 31g carbohydrate, 9g total fat (1g saturated), 66mg cholesterol, 264mg sodium.

CITRUS CHIFFON CAKE

Prepare as directed but substitute *1 tablespoon freshly grated orange peel* and *½ teaspoon freshly grated lemon peel* for vanilla, and substitute *¼ cup fresh orange juice* and *¼ cup fresh lemon juice* for cold water. In small bowl, combine *1 cup confectioners' sugar, 1 teaspoon freshly grated lemon peel, ¼ teaspoon vanilla extract,* and about *5 teaspoons orange juice* to make a smooth glaze; spoon over cooled cake.

Vanilla Chiffon Cake

Jelly Roll

Jelly rolls are easy to make and look sensational on a decorative platter. Fill with your favorite jam or Lemon Filling (page 237).

PREP 20 minutes plus cooling • **BAKE** 10 minutes • **MAKES** 10 servings.

5 large eggs, separated
½ cup granulated sugar
1 teaspoon vanilla extract
½ cup all-purpose flour
confectioners' sugar
⅔ cup strawberry jam

1 Preheat oven to 350°F. Grease 15½" by 10½" jelly-roll pan. Line with waxed paper; grease paper.

2 In large bowl, with mixer at high speed, beat egg whites until soft peaks form when beaters are lifted. Sprinkle in ¼ cup granulated sugar, 1 tablespoon at a time, beating until egg whites stand in stiff, glossy peaks when beaters are lifted. Do not overbeat.

3 In small bowl, with mixer at high speed, beat egg yolks, remaining ¼ cup granulated sugar, and vanilla until very thick and lemon colored, 8 to 10 minutes. Reduce speed to low; beat in flour until blended. With rubber spatula, gently fold egg-yolk mixture into beaten egg whites just until blended.

4 Scrape batter into prepared pan; spread evenly. Bake until cake springs back when lightly pressed, 10 to 15 minutes.

5 Meanwhile, sift confectioners' sugar onto clean kitchen towel. Run thin knife around edges to loosen cake from sides of pan; invert onto towel. Carefully remove waxed paper. Trim ¼ inch from edges of cake. From a short side, roll cake up with towel jelly-roll fashion. Place rolled cake, seam side down, on wire rack; cool completely.

6 Unroll cooled cake. With narrow metal spatula, spread evenly with jam. Starting from same short side, roll cake up (without towel). Place rolled cake, seam side down, on platter and dust with confectioners' sugar.

EACH SERVING About 163 calories, 4g protein, 30g carbohydrate, 3g total fat (1g saturated), 106mg cholesterol, 40mg sodium.

Jelly Roll

Brandied Bûche de Noël

This is our variation on the traditional French Yule Log. Instead of using all chocolate buttercream, we've chosen our Two-Tone Brandied Butter Frosting, which is actually two frostings: vanilla and chocolate.

PREP 1 hour 30 minutes plus cooling • **BAKE** 10 minutes • **MAKES** 14 servings.

⅓ cup all-purpose flour
¼ cup unsweetened cocoa
1 teaspoon ground cinnamon
¾ teaspoon ground ginger
pinch ground cloves
pinch salt
5 large eggs, separated
¼ teaspoon cream of tartar
½ cup granulated sugar
2 tablespoons butter or margarine,
    melted and cooled slightly
confectioners' sugar
Two-Tone Brandied Butter Frosting (page 355)
Meringue Mushrooms (optional, page 360)

1 Preheat oven to 375°F. Grease 15½" by 10½" jelly-roll pan. Line with waxed paper; grease and flour paper.
2 In small bowl, with wire whisk, mix flour, cocoa, cinnamon, ginger, cloves, and salt; set aside.
3 In large bowl, with mixer at high speed, beat egg whites and cream of tartar until soft peaks form when beaters are lifted. Gradually sprinkle in ¼ cup granulated sugar, 1 tablespoon at a time, beating until egg whites hold stiff peaks.
4 In separate large bowl, using same beaters and with mixer at high speed, beat egg yolks and remaining ¼ cup granulated sugar until very thick and lemon-colored, 5 to 10 minutes. With rubber spatula, gently fold beaten whites into beaten yolks, one-third at a time. Gently fold flour mixture, one-third at a time, into egg mixture. Fold in melted butter just until combined.

5 Scrape batter into prepared pan; spread evenly. Bake until top of cake springs back when lightly touched with finger, about 10 minutes.
6 Meanwhile, sprinkle clean kitchen towel with confectioners' sugar. Immediately invert cake onto sugared towel. Carefully peel off waxed paper. Starting from one long side, roll up cake, jelly-roll fashion, with towel. Transfer roll, seam side down, to wire rack and cool completely, about 1 hour.
7 Prepare Two-Tone Brandied Butter Frosting.
8 Gently unroll cooled cake. With metal spatula, spread vanilla frosting almost to edges. Starting from same long side, roll up cake without towel. Cut 1½-inch-thick diagonal slice off each end of roll. Place cake, seam side down, on platter. Spread chocolate frosting over roll. Place each end piece on sides of roll to resemble branches. Spread remaining chocolate frosting over roll and branches. Swirl frosting to resemble bark of tree. Refrigerate cake at least 2 hours before serving. Garnish platter with Meringue Mushrooms, if desired, and sprinkle lightly with confectioners' sugar.

EACH SERVING About 190 calories, 3g protein, 20g carbohydrate, 11g total fat (6g saturated), 99mg cholesterol, 120mg sodium.

Brandied Bûche de Noël

Fallen Chocolate Soufflé Roll

A flourless confection with the texture and taste of a rich chocolate soufflé but without the worry of collapse! Unlike other jelly-roll cakes, this one is not rolled up while still hot. If any cracks appear after the cake is rolled, a generous dusting of confectioners' sugar will mask them.

PREP 30 minutes plus cooling • **BAKE** 15 minutes • **MAKES** 16 servings.

1 teaspoon instant espresso-coffee powder
3 tablespoons hot water
5 squares (5 ounces) semisweet chocolate, chopped
1 square (1 ounce) unsweetened chocolate, chopped
6 large eggs, separated
¾ cup granulated sugar
1 teaspoon vanilla extract
¾ teaspoon ground cinnamon
¼ teaspoon salt
⅛ teaspoon ground cloves
1½ cups heavy or whipping cream
⅓ cup coffee-flavored liqueur
5 tablespoons confectioners' sugar plus additional for dusting

1 Preheat oven to 350°F. Grease 15½" by 10½" jelly-roll pan. Line with waxed paper; grease paper. Dust pan with flour.

2 In cup, dissolve espresso powder in hot water. In top of double boiler set over simmering water, heat semisweet and unsweetened chocolates with espresso mixture, stirring frequently, until chocolates have melted and mixture is smooth.

3 In large bowl, with mixer at high speed, beat egg whites until soft peaks form when beaters are lifted. Sprinkle in ¼ cup granulated sugar, 1 tablespoon at a time, beating until sugar has dissolved and egg whites stand in stiff, glossy peaks when beaters are lifted.

4 In small bowl, with mixer at high speed, beat egg yolks and remaining ½ cup granulated sugar until very thick and lemon-colored, about 10 minutes. Reduce speed to low; beat in vanilla, cinnamon, salt, and cloves. With rubber spatula, fold chocolate mixture into yolk mixture until blended. Gently fold one-third of beaten egg whites into chocolate mixture; fold chocolate mixture into remaining egg whites.

5 Spread batter evenly in prepared pan. Bake until firm to the touch, about 15 minutes. Cover cake with clean, damp kitchen towel; cool in pan on wire rack 30 minutes.

6 In large bowl, with mixer at medium speed, beat cream until soft peaks form. Add coffee liqueur and 3 tablespoons confectioners' sugar; beat until stiff peaks form.

7 Remove towel from cake; sift 2 tablespoons confectioners' sugar over cake. Run thin knife around edges to loosen cake from sides of pan. Cover cake with sheet of foil and a large cookie sheet; invert cake onto cookie sheet. Carefully remove waxed paper. With narrow metal spatula, spread whipped cream over cake, leaving ½-inch border. Starting from a long side and using foil to help lift cake, roll up cake jelly-roll fashion (cake may crack). Place, seam side down, on long platter. Refrigerate at least 1 hour, or until ready to serve. Just before serving, dust with confectioners' sugar.

EACH SERVING About 215 calories, 4g protein, 21g carbohydrate, 14g total fat (8g saturated), 110mg cholesterol, 65mg sodium.

Fruit-and-Nut Cake

This buttery cake, studded with sweet raisins and dried apricots and plums, might remind you of the holiday classic, but the flavor won't (we skipped the candied citron and glacéed cherries). You can replace these dried fruits with any of your favorites; try cherries, dates, or figs.

PREP 40 minutes • BAKE 1 hour 50 minutes • MAKES 20 servings.

2 cups all-purpose flour
1 teaspoon baking powder
¼ teaspoon ground allspice
¼ teaspoon ground cinnamon
¼ teaspoon salt
1 cup blanched whole almonds or walnuts
1 cup sugar
1 cup dried apricots, cut into ¼-inch pieces
1 cup golden raisins
¾ cup pitted dried plums (prunes), cut into
    ¼-inch pieces
1 cup butter or margarine (2 sticks), softened
4 large eggs
1½ teaspoons vanilla extract

1 Preheat oven to 300°F. Grease 8-inch spring-form pan; dust pan with flour.

2 In medium bowl, with wire whisk, mix flour, baking powder, allspice, cinnamon, and salt; set aside.

3 In food processor with knife blade attached, pulse ⅔ cup nuts and ¼ cup sugar until nuts are very finely ground. In medium bowl, combine nut mixture, apricots, raisins, and dried plums.

4 In large bowl, with mixer at low speed, beat butter and remaining ¾ cup sugar until blended, frequently scraping bowl with rubber spatula. Increase speed to medium-high; beat until creamy, about 3 minutes, occasionally scraping bowl. Reduce speed to low; add eggs, one at a time, beating well after each addition. Beat in vanilla. Gradually beat in flour mixture just until smooth (batter will be thick). Stir in fruit mixture.

5 Spoon batter into prepared pan; spread evenly. Arrange remaining ⅓ cup nuts decoratively on top of batter. Bake until toothpick inserted in center of cake comes out clean, 1 hour and 50 minutes to 2 hours. After baking 1 hour and 20 minutes, cover pan loosely with foil to prevent top from overbrowning.

6 Cool cake in pan on wire rack 20 minutes. Run thin knife around edges to gently loosen cake from side of pan. Remove pan side; cool completely on wire rack.

EACH SERVING About 275 calories, 4g protein, 35g carbohydrate, 14g total fat (7g saturated), 69mg cholesterol, 165mg sodium.

Brandy-Spice Dark Fruitcake

By using only dried fruits and adding molasses we came up with a moist, rich, flavor-packed fruitcake without the cloying sweetness of more traditional cakes with candied fruits.

PREP 45 minutes plus standing and cooling • **BAKE** 1 hour 35 minutes
MAKES 1 (3½-pound) fruitcake or 30 servings.

1 package (10 to 11 ounces) dried Mission or
    Calimyrna figs (about 2 cups)
1 package (9 to 10 ounces) dried dates
    (about 2 cups)
1 package (10 ounces) currants (about 2 cups)
2 cups dark raisins
1 cup brandy
2 cups all-purpose flour
1½ teaspoons ground ginger
1 teaspoon ground cinnamon
½ teaspoon baking soda
¼ teaspoon ground black pepper
¼ teaspoon ground nutmeg
⅛ teaspoon ground cloves
1 cup butter or margarine (2 sticks), softened
1 cup packed dark brown sugar
3 large eggs
½ cup dark molasses
2 teaspoons vanilla extract
1 cup walnuts, coarsely chopped

1 Remove and discard stems from figs. Coarsely chop figs and dates. In large bowl, combine figs, dates, currants, raisins, and brandy. Cover and let stand at room temperature, stirring occasionally, 2 hours, or up to overnight.

2 Preheat oven to 325°F. Generously grease 12-cup fluted baking pan (such as a Bundt pan); dust with flour.

3 In medium bowl, with wire whisk, mix flour, ginger, cinnamon, baking soda, pepper, nutmeg, and cloves; set aside.

4 In large bowl, with mixer at low speed, beat butter and brown sugar until blended. Increase speed to medium-high; beat until creamy, about 3 minutes, occasionally scraping bowl with rubber spatula. Reduce speed to medium; beat in eggs, one at a time, beating well after each addition (batter may look curdled). Beat in molasses and vanilla. Reduce speed to low; beat in flour mixture. With spoon, stir in nuts and dried-fruit mixture.

5 Spoon batter into prepared pan; spread evenly. Bake 1 hour. Cover fruitcake loosely with foil and bake until wooden skewer inserted in center of cake comes out clean, 35 to 55 minutes longer.

6 Cool cake in pan on wire rack 15 minutes. Run tip of thin knife around edges to loosen cake from side of pan. Invert cake onto wire rack to cool completely. Wrap fruitcake tightly with plastic wrap or foil; refrigerate overnight so cake will be firm enough to slice. Store in refrigerator up to 4 months.

EACH SERVING About 280 calories, 3g protein, 46g carbohydrate, 10g total fat (5g saturated), 39mg cholesterol, 105mg sodium.

New York–Style Cheesecake

Purists will insist on devouring this cake unadorned, while the more adventurous will enjoy our variations (page 342). A garnish of fresh berries on top of the cake always makes it look festive. See photo on page 343.

PREP 20 minutes plus cooling and chilling • **BAKE** 1 hour 5 minutes • **MAKES** 16 servings.

Graham Cracker–Crumb Crust (page 139), unbaked

3 packages (8 ounces each) cream cheese, softened

¾ cup sugar

1 tablespoon all-purpose flour

1½ teaspoons vanilla extract

3 large eggs

1 large egg yolk

¼ cup milk

fresh fruits for garnish (optional)

1 Preheat oven to 375°F. Prepare Crumb Crust as directed through step 2 in 8½- to 9-inch springform pan. With hand, press crumb mixture firmly onto bottom and up side of pan. Bake 10 minutes; cool crust in pan on wire rack. Turn oven control to 300°F.

2 In large bowl, with mixer at medium speed, beat cream cheese and sugar until smooth and fluffy. Beat in flour and vanilla until well combined. Reduce speed to low and beat in eggs and egg yolk, one at a time, beating well after each addition. Beat in milk just until blended.

3 Pour batter into prepared crust. Bake until set but still slightly wet 3 inches from center and lightly golden, 55 to 60 minutes.

4 Cool completely in pan on wire rack. Refrigerate overnight before serving. To serve, remove side of pan. Place cake on plate; garnish with fresh fruits, if you like.

EACH SERVING About 275 calories, 5g protein, 19g carbohydrate, 20g total fat (12g saturated), 108mg cholesterol, 230mg sodium.

Test Kitchen Tip **CHEESECAKES** Luscious and decadently rich, cheesecakes are of two basic types: those made with cream cheese and those made with curd cheese, such as ricotta or cottage cheese. For the perfect cheesecake, let the cream cheese stand at room temperature for at least 1 hour; it must be soft. Cheesecakes are baked until the center jiggles slightly; they will firm up during cooling and chilling. To prevent cracking during cooling, run a thin knife around the edge of the cheesecake as soon as it comes out of the oven.

APRICOT SWIRL CHEESECAKE

Prepare Graham Cracker–Crumb Crust (page 139) as directed. In 1-quart saucepan, heat ¾ *cup (5 ounces) dried apricots, ¾ cup water*, and *2 tablespoons sugar* to boiling over medium heat. Reduce heat; cover and simmer until apricots are very soft, 15 to 20 minutes. In food processor with knife blade attached, puree apricot mixture until smooth. Prepare batter as directed for New York–Style Cheesecake but omit milk. Spoon batter into prepared crust; spoon apricot mixture on top in several dollops. Using knife, swirl apricot mixture through cheesecake batter. Bake, cool, and chill as directed.

EACH SERVING About 300 calories, 6 g protein, 26 g carbohydrate, 20 g total fat (12 g saturated), 108 mg cholesterol, 225 mg sodium.

GINGER CHEESECAKE

Prepare Graham Cracker–Crumb Crust (page 139), but substitute *9 ounces gingersnaps,* crushed, for graham crackers; bake as directed in Step 1. Prepare batter as directed for New York–Style Cheesecake, adding *⅓ cup minced crystallized ginger* and *1 teaspoon freshly grated lemon peel* after milk in Step 2. Bake, cool, and chill as directed.

EACH SERVING About 320 calories, 6 g protein, 29 g carbohydrate, 21 g total fat (12 g saturated), 108 mg cholesterol, 280 mg sodium.

AMARETTO CHEESECAKE

Prepare Graham Cracker–Crumb Crust (page 139), but substitute *6 ounces amaretti cookies,* crushed, for graham crackers and omit sugar; bake as directed in Step 1. Prepare batter as directed for New York–Style Cheesecake, but use only *2 tablespoons milk* and add *2 tablespoons amaretto* (almond-flavored liqueur) in Step 2. Bake, cool, and chill as directed.

EACH SERVING About 280 calories, 5 g protein, 20 g carbohydrate, 20 g total fat (12 g saturated), 110 mg cholesterol, 175 mg sodium.

CHOCOLATE MARBLE CHEESECAKE

Prepare Chocolate Wafer–Crumb Crust (page 139) and bake as directed. Prepare batter as directed for New York–Style Cheesecake but omit milk. Melt *2 squares (2 ounces) semisweet chocolate.* In small bowl, stir together melted chocolate and 1 cup cheesecake batter. Pour remaining plain cheesecake batter into crust. Spoon chocolate batter over top in several dollops. Using knife, swirl chocolate batter through plain batter. Bake, cool, and chill as directed.

EACH SERVING About 290 calories, 5 g protein, 21 g carbohydrate, 21 g total fat (12 g saturated), 108 mg cholesterol, 220 mg sodium.

New York–Style Cheesecake (page 341)

Chocolate Cheesecake

Calling all chocoholics! Here's a triple chocolate treat: chocolate wafers, semisweet chocolate, and cocoa.

PREP 25 minutes plus cooling and chilling • **BAKE** 1 hour • **MAKES** 16 servings.

1½ cups chocolate-wafer cookie crumbs
    (part of 9-ounce package)
3 tablespoons butter or margarine, melted
2 tablespoons plus 1 cup sugar
3 packages (8 ounces each) cream cheese,
    softened
¼ cup unsweetened cocoa
4 large eggs
¾ cup sour cream
1½ teaspoons vanilla extract
8 squares (8 ounces) semisweet chocolate,
    melted and cooled

1 Preheat oven to 325°F. In 9" by 3" spring-form pan, combine chocolate-wafer crumbs, melted butter, and 2 tablespoons sugar; stir with fork until evenly moistened. With hand, press mixture firmly onto bottom of pan. Bake 10 minutes. Cool crust completely in pan on wire rack.

2 In large bowl, with mixer at low speed, beat cream cheese until smooth. Beat in remaining 1 cup sugar and cocoa until blended, occasionally scraping bowl with rubber spatula. Reduce speed to low. Add eggs, one at a time, beating just until blended, scraping bowl. Beat in sour cream and vanilla. Add melted chocolate and beat until well blended.

3 Pour chocolate mixture into prepared crust. Bake until set 2 inches from edge but center still jiggles, 50 to 55 minutes. Turn off oven; let cheesecake remain in oven with door ajar 1 hour.

4 Remove cake from oven; run tip of thin knife around edge to prevent cheesecake from cracking during cooling. Cool completely on wire rack. Cover loosely and refrigerate until well chilled, at least 6 hours or up to overnight. Remove side of pan to serve.

EACH SERVING About 384 calories, 7g protein, 34g carbohydrate, 26g total fat (15g saturated), 111mg cholesterol, 237mg sodium.

Test Kitchen Tip

SERVING CHEESECAKE

For a bakery-perfect cheesecake presentation, chill the cake thoroughly, preferably overnight. Tightly wrap it so the filling does not pick up aromas from other foods in the refrigerator. At serving time, place the pan on a cake plate. Carefully open the clasp and remove the side of the pan. Brush away any crumbs that fall onto the platter. Use a large, sharp knife to slice the cake into wedges. Wipe the blade clean after making each cut, then dip the blade in hot water, dry it off quickly, and cut the next slice.

Pumpkin Cheesecake

Pumpkin pie, move over. Here's a deliciously creamy dessert that is bound to be a hit at your next Thanksgiving dinner.

PREP 30 minutes plus cooling and chilling • **BAKE** 1 hour 25 minutes • **MAKES** 16 servings.

CRUMB CRUST

1 cup graham-cracker crumbs (8 rectangular graham crackers)

3 tablespoons butter or margarine, melted

2 tablespoons sugar

PUMPKIN FILLING

2 packages (8 ounces each) cream cheese, softened

1¼ cups sugar

1 can (15 ounces) solid pack pumpkin (not pumpkin pie filling)

¾ cup sour cream

2 tablespoons bourbon or 2 teaspoons vanilla extract

1 teaspoon ground cinnamon

½ teaspoon ground allspice

¼ teaspoon salt

4 large eggs

SOUR-CREAM TOPPING

1 cup sour cream

3 tablespoons sugar

1 teaspoon vanilla extract

1 Preheat oven to 350°F. Tightly wrap outside of 9" by 3" springform pan with heavy-duty foil. In pan, with fork, stir graham-cracker crumbs, melted butter, and sugar until crumbs are evenly moistened. Press crumb mixture firmly onto bottom of pan. Bake 10 minutes. Cool completely in pan on wire rack.

2 Prepare filling: In large bowl, with mixer at medium speed, beat cream cheese until smooth. Gradually add in sugar, beating until blended, about 1 minute, frequently scraping bowl with rubber spatula. Reduce speed to low. Beat in pumpkin, sour cream, bourbon, cinnamon, allspice, and salt. Add eggs, one at time, beating after each addition, just until blended.

3 Scrape pumpkin mixture into prepared crust and place in large roasting pan. Place pan on oven rack. Carefully pour enough boiling water into roasting pan to come 1 inch up side of springform pan. Bake until center of cake barely jiggles, about 1 hour 10 minutes.

4 Prepare topping: In small bowl, with wire whisk, beat sour cream, sugar, and vanilla until smooth. Remove cheesecake from water bath (leave water bath in oven); spread sour-cream mixture evenly over top. Return cake to water bath and bake 5 minutes longer.

5 Remove cheesecake from water bath and transfer to wire rack; remove foil. Run tip of thin knife around edge to prevent cheesecake from cracking during cooling. Cool completely in pan on wire rack. Cover and refrigerate until well chilled, at least 6 hours or up to overnight. Remove side of pan to serve.

EACH SERVING About 307 calories, 5g protein, 29g carbohydrate, 19g total fat (11g saturated), 101mg cholesterol, 217mg sodium.

Lemon-Ricotta Cheesecake

Ricotta cheese gives this cheesecake a lighter texture.

PREP 20 minutes plus cooling and chilling • **BAKE** 1 hour 25 minutes • **MAKES** 16 servings.

4 large lemons
1 cup vanilla-wafer crumbs (about 30 cookies)
4 tablespoons butter or margarine, melted
1¼ cups sugar
¼ cup cornstarch
2 packages (8 ounces each) cream cheese, softened
1 container (15 ounces) ricotta cheese
4 large eggs
2 cups half-and-half or light cream
2 teaspoons vanilla extract

1 Preheat oven to 375°F. From lemons, grate 4 teaspoons peel and squeeze ⅓ cup juice.

2 In 9" by 3" springform pan, combine cookie crumbs, melted butter, and 1 teaspoon lemon peel; stir with fork until evenly moistened. Press mixture firmly onto bottom of pan. Tightly wrap outside of pan with heavy-duty foil. Bake until crust is deep golden, about 10 minutes. Cool completely in pan on wire rack.

3 Turn oven control to 325°F. In small bowl, with fork, mix sugar and cornstarch until well blended.

4 In large bowl, with mixer at medium speed, beat cream cheese and ricotta until very smooth, about 5 minutes; gradually add sugar mixture, beating just until blended. Reduce mixer speed to low; beat in eggs, half-and-half, lemon juice, vanilla, and remaining 3 teaspoons lemon peel just until blended, frequently scraping bowl with rubber spatula.

5 Scrape cream-cheese mixture into prepared crust. Bake 1 hour 15 minutes. Turn off oven; let cheesecake remain in oven 1 hour longer.

6 Remove cake from oven and transfer to wire rack; remove foil. Run tip of thin knife around edge to prevent cheesecake from cracking during cooling. Cool completely in pan on wire rack. Cover and refrigerate cheesecake until well chilled, at least 6 hours or up to overnight. Remove side of pan to serve.

EACH SERVING About 324 calories, 8g protein, 25g carbohydrate, 22g total fat (13g saturated), 117mg cholesterol, 182mg sodium.

Lemon-Ricotta Cheesecake

Margarita Cheesecake

An excellent dessert for a southwestern-style meal; it will help tame those spicy flavors and refresh the palate.

PREP 35 minutes plus cooling and chilling • **BAKE** 1 hour • **MAKES** 20 servings.

7 tablespoons butter or margarine,
  cut into pieces
4 to 5 limes
1 orange
8 ounces vanilla wafer cookies (65 wafers)
4 packages (8 ounces each) cream cheese,
  softened
1¼ cups sugar
¼ teaspoon salt
4 large eggs
1 container (8 ounces) sour cream
¼ cup orange-flavor liqueur or orange juice
orange and lime slices for garnish

1 Preheat oven to 350°F. Tightly wrap outside of 10" by 2½" springform pan with heavy-duty foil. While oven preheats, melt butter in springform pan in oven.

2 Meanwhile, from limes, grate 1 tablespoon plus 2 teaspoons peel and squeeze ½ cup juice. From orange, grate ½ teaspoon peel. In food processor with knife blade attached, grind vanilla wafers and 2 teaspoons lime peel to make fine crumbs (you should have about 2½ cups crumbs). Stir crumbs into melted butter in springform pan, then press onto bottom and 2 inches up side of pan to form crust. Bake crust 15 minutes. Cool completely in pan on wire rack.

3 In large bowl, with mixer at medium speed, beat cream cheese until smooth, occasionally scraping bowl with rubber spatula. Gradually add sugar and salt, beating until blended. Reduce speed to low. Add eggs, one at a time, just until blended. Beat in sour cream, liqueur, orange peel, lime juice, and remaining 1 tablespoon lime peel; beat just until blended and smooth.

4 Pour cream-cheese mixture into prepared crust, making sure to scrape any peel remaining on beaters into batter. Bake 45 minutes (cheesecake will still jiggle slightly in center). Turn off oven and leave cheesecake in oven 1 hour to cool slightly and set.

5 Remove cheesecake from oven and cool completely in pan on wire rack. Cover and refrigerate cheesecake until well chilled, at least 6 hours, or up to 2 days.

6 To serve, carefully remove side of springform pan. Let cheesecake stand at room temperature 30 minutes for better flavor. If you like, arrange orange and lime slices on top of cake for garnish.

EACH SERVING About 335 calories, 6g protein, 23g carbohydrate, 25g total fat (15g saturated), 111mg cholesterol, 265mg sodium.

Margarita Cheesecake

Vanilla Buttercream Frosting

Use this satiny-smooth confection to decorate our Black-and-White Cupcakes (page 295).

PREP 15 minutes plus chilling
COOK 5 minutes • MAKES about 3¼ cups.

1 cup sugar
½ cup all-purpose flour
1⅓ cups milk
1 cup butter (2 sticks), softened
1 tablespoon vanilla extract

1 In 2-quart saucepan, with wire whisk, mix sugar and flour. Gradually whisk in milk until smooth. Cook over medium-high heat, stirring frequently, until mixture has thickened and boils. Reduce heat to low; cook, stirring constantly, 2 minutes.
2 Transfer mixture to bowl. Cover surface of mixture with plastic wrap; refrigerate and cool completely, 4 hours or overnight. Or, place in freezer 20 to 25 minutes, stirring once.
3 In large bowl, with mixer at medium speed, beat butter until creamy. Gradually beat in cooled milk mixture until blended. Add vanilla and beat until frosting is fluffy.

EACH TABLESPOON About 55 calories, 0g protein, 5 g carbohydrate, 6g total fat (3g saturated), 11mg cholesterol, 39mg sodium.

Fluffy White Frosting

This irresistible marshmallowlike frosting is best enjoyed the day it is made. If you're planning on frosting a chocolate cake, omit the lemon juice.

PREP 15 minutes • COOK 7 minutes
MAKES about 3 cups.

2 large egg whites
1 cup sugar
¼ cup water
2 teaspoons fresh lemon juice (optional)
1 teaspoon light corn syrup
¼ teaspoon cream of tartar

1 In medium bowl set over 3- to 4-quart saucepan filled with 1 inch simmering water (bowl should sit about 2 inches above water), with hand-held mixer at high speed, beat egg whites, sugar, water, lemon juice, if using, corn syrup, and cream of tartar until soft peaks form and mixture reaches 160°F on candy thermometer, about 7 minutes.
2 Remove bowl from pan; and beat egg-white mixture until stiff, glossy peaks form, 5 to 10 minutes longer.

EACH TABLESPOON About 17 calories, 0g protein, 4g carbohydrate, 0g total fat, 0mg cholesterol, 2mg sodium.

FLUFFY HARVEST MOON FROSTING
Prepare as directed above but substitute *1 cup packed dark brown sugar* for granulated sugar and omit lemon juice.

EACH TABLESPOON: About 18 calories, 0g protein, 5g carbohydrate, 0g total fat, 0mg cholesterol, 4mg sodium.

Chocolate Butter Frosting

The perfect partner for our old-fashioned Yellow Cake (page 276).

PREP 10 minutes • **MAKES** about 2 ½ cups.

¾ cup butter or margarine (1½ sticks),
    softened
2 cups confectioners' sugar
1 teaspoon vanilla extract
4 squares (4 ounces) semisweet chocolate,
    melted and cooled
2 squares (2 ounces) unsweetened chocolate,
    melted and cooled

In large bowl, with mixer at low speed, beat butter, confectioners' sugar, and vanilla until almost blended. Add semisweet and unsweetened chocolates. Increase speed to high; beat frosting until light and fluffy, about 1 minute.

EACH TABLESPOON About 75 calories,
0g protein, 8g carbohydrate, 5g total fat
(3g saturated), 9mg cholesterol, 36mg sodium.

 FROSTING KNOW-HOW

Before frosting or filling, let the cake cool, and brush off all loose crumbs. Cover the edges of the cake plate with strips of waxed paper to keep the plate clean; after frosting, slide out the strips and touch up the base of the cake with frosting if necessary.

LAYER CAKE Center one cake layer, top side down, on cake plate. Spread layer with frosting almost to the edge. Place second layer, top side up, on filling. (If there is a third layer, spread top of second layer with frosting and add final layer top side up). Frost sides thinly to set any loose crumbs, then apply second, more generous layer of frosting, swirling it up ½ inch above rim of cake. Lastly, frost top of cake, swirling frosting or leaving it smooth. Decorate as desired.

OBLONG CAKE Frost sides and top of cake as for layer cake, or leave cake in pan and frost just top.

TUBE OR RING CAKE Frost sides, then top and inside center as for layer cake.

CUPCAKES Dip top of each cupcake in frosting, turning it slightly to coat evenly.

GLAZING Brush crumbs from cake. Spoon glaze onto top of cake, letting it drip down sides. Spread thick glazes over top and sides of cake with metal spatula.

DRIZZLING Pour thin icing or glaze from spoon, quickly moving spoon back and forth or 'round and 'round over cake to form a decorative pattern.

Fudge Frosting

Chocolate lovers will put this at the top of their list. It's a great all-purpose frosting that enhances a variety of cakes and is especially tasty with layer cakes.

PREP 10 minutes plus cooling
COOK 8 minutes • **MAKES** 3 cups.

¾ cup sugar
¼ cup all-purpose flour
3 tablespoons unsweetened cocoa
1 cup milk
1 cup butter or margarine (2 sticks), softened
4 squares (4 ounces) semisweet chocolate, melted and cooled
1 tablespoon vanilla extract

1 In 2-quart saucepan, with wire whisk, mix sugar, flour, and cocoa. Gradually whisk in milk until smooth. Cook over medium heat, stirring frequently, until mixture has thickened and boils. Reduce heat to low; cook, stirring constantly, 2 minutes. Remove from heat; cool completely.
2 In medium bowl, with mixer at medium speed, beat butter until creamy. Gradually beat in milk mixture, melted chocolate, and vanilla.

EACH TABLESPOON About 64 calories, 0g protein, 6g carbohydrate, 5g total fat (3g saturated), 11mg cholesterol, 42mg sodium.

White Chocolate Butter Frosting

You can't tell that this is a chocolate frosting until you taste it. But oh, what a scrumptious surprise! Use this frosting on your favorite chocolate cake.

PREP 15 minutes plus cooling
MAKES about 3½ cups.

1 cup butter (2 sticks), softened (do not use margarine)
2 cups confectioners' sugar
6 ounces white chocolate, Swiss confectionery bars, or white baking bars, melted and cooled
3 tablespoons milk

1 In large bowl, with mixer at low speed, beat butter, confectioners' sugar, melted white chocolate, and milk just until combined. Increase speed to high; beat until light and fluffy, about 2 minutes, frequently scraping bowl with rubber spatula.

EACH TABLESPOON About 62 calories, 0g protein, 6g carbohydrate, 4g total fat (3g saturated), 9mg cholesterol, 37mg sodium.

Test Kitchen Tip **FIGURING FROSTING** Here's how much frosting you'll need for various cake sizes:

8-inch round, two layers	2¼ cups	9-inch square, one layer	2 cups
8-inch round, three layers	2¾ cups	13- by 9-inch, one layer	2⅓ cups
9-inch round, two layers	2⅔ cups	10-inch tube cake	2¼ cups
8-inch square, one layer	1⅓ cups	24 cupcakes	2¼ cups

Maple Buttercream

This is the frosting of choice for our New England Maple-Walnut Cake (page 277) but it would also pair well with our Spice Layer Cake (page 281).

PREP 10 minutes plus cooling
COOK 5 minutes • **MAKES** about 3½ cups.

½ cup all-purpose flour
⅓ cup sugar
1 cup milk
⅔ cup maple syrup or maple-flavor syrup
1 cup butter or margarine (2 sticks), softened
¼ teaspoon imitation maple flavor

1 In 2-quart saucepan, with wire whisk, mix flour and sugar until blended. Gradually whisk in milk and maple syrup until smooth. Cook over medium-high heat, stirring often, until mixture has thickened and boils. Reduce heat to low and cook, stirring constantly, 2 minutes. Remove from heat and cool completely.
2 In large bowl, with mixer at medium speed, beat butter until creamy. Gradually beat in cooled milk mixture and maple flavor. Increase speed to medium-high; beat until smooth.

EACH TABLESPOON 15 calories, 0g protein, 5g carbohydrate, 3g total fat (1g saturated), 1mg cholesterol, 41mg sodium.

Brown-Butter Frosting

An excellent foil for the spices in our Spice Layer Cake (page 281), this elegant frosting can be used to dress up any plain vanilla-flavored cake, especially pound cake.

PREP 10 minutes plus cooling
COOK 5 minutes • **MAKES** about 2⅓ cups.

½ cup butter (1 stick), cut into pieces (do not use margarine)
1 package (16 ounces) confectioners' sugar
about 3 tablespoons milk, half-and-half, or light cream
1½ teaspoons vanilla extract

1 In small skillet, heat butter over medium heat until melted and golden brown; let cool.
2 In large bowl, with mixer at medium-low speed, beat butter, confectioners' sugar, 3 tablespoons milk, and vanilla until smooth and blended. Beat in additional milk as needed for easy spreading consistency. Increase speed to medium-high; beat until light and fluffy, about 1 minute.

EACH TABLESPOON About 71 calories, 0g protein, 12g carbohydrate, 3g total fat (2g saturated), 7mg cholesterol, 26mg sodium.

Cream Cheese Frosting

The classic frosting for our classic version of Carrot Cake (page 286).

PREP 5 minutes • **MAKES** about 2½ cups.

2 packages (3 ounces each) cream cheese,
    slightly softened
6 tablespoons butter or margarine, softened
3 cups confectioners' sugar
1½ teaspoons vanilla extract

In large bowl, with mixer at low speed, beat cream cheese, butter, confectioners' sugar, and vanilla just until blended. Increase speed to medium. Beat until smooth and fluffy, about 1 minute, frequently scraping bowl with rubber spatula.

EACH SERVING 66 calories, 0g protein, 9g carbohydrate, 3g total fat (2g saturated), 30mg cholesterol, 9mg sodium.

Test Kitchen Tip

COLORING YOUR CAKES

For tinting frostings and icings, the pros prefer paste food colors (also called icing colors), which do not dilute the frosting as liquid colors can. Add paste coloring a tiny bit at a time, using the tip of a toothpick: The colors are extremely intense.

Whipped Cream Frosting

This quick and easy recipe tastes great with Hot-Water Sponge Cake (page 328) and fresh berries.

PREP 5 minutes • **MAKES** about 4 cups.

2 cups heavy or whipping cream
¼ cup confectioners' sugar
1 teaspoon vanilla extract

In large bowl, with mixer at medium speed, beat cream, confectioners' sugar, and vanilla until stiff peaks form.

EACH TABLESPOON About 30 calories, 0g protein, 1g carbohydrate, 3g total fat (2g saturated), 10mg cholesterol, 5mg sodium.

COFFEE WHIPPED CREAM FROSTING

Prepare as directed above but dissolve *2 teaspoons instant coffee powder* in *2 teaspoons hot water;* cool. Beat into whipped cream.

EACH TABLESPOON: About 30 calories, 0g protein, 1g carbohydrate, 3g total fat (2g saturated), 10mg cholesterol, 5mg sodium.

COCOA WHIPPED CREAM FROSTING

Prepare as directed above but use *½ cup confectioners' sugar* and add *½ cup unsweetened cocoa.*

EACH TABLESPOON: About 30 calories, 0g protein, 1g carbohydrate, 3g total fat (2g saturated), 10mg cholesterol, 5mg sodium.

Two-Tone Brandied Butter Frosting

This rich frosting creates two frostings: chocolate and vanilla. We use both to give our Brandied Bûche de Noël (page 337) a realistic look.

PREP 15 minutes plus cooling
COOK 10 minutes
MAKES 1½ cups of each flavor.

1 cup sugar
½ cup all-purpose flour
1 cup milk
1 square (1 ounce) semisweet chocolate, chopped
1 square (1 ounce) unsweetened chocolate, chopped
1 cup butter or margarine (2 sticks), softened
2 tablespoons brandy
1 teaspoon vanilla extract

1 In 2-quart saucepan, with wire whisk, mix sugar and flour. Add milk, whisking until smooth. Cook over medium-high heat, stirring often, until mixture has thickened and boils. Reduce heat to low and cook, stirring constantly, 2 minutes. Remove from heat and cool completely, about 45 minutes.

2 Meanwhile, melt semisweet and unsweetened chocolates over low heat, stirring frequently; cool slightly.

3 In large bowl, with mixer at medium speed, beat butter until creamy. Gradually beat in cooled milk mixture. When mixture is smooth, beat in brandy and vanilla until blended. Spoon half of frosting into small bowl; stir cooled chocolate into frosting remaining in large bowl.

EACH TABLESPOON (VANILLA) About 60 calories, 0g protein, 5g carbohydrate, 4g total fat (2g saturated), 11mg cholesterol, 40mg sodium.

EACH TABLESPOON (CHOCOLATE) About 70 calories, 0g protein, 6g carbohydrate, 5g total fat (3g saturated), 11mg cholesterol, 40mg sodium.

Coconut-Pecan Frosting

This unique cooked frosting is an absolute must for German's Chocolate Cake (page 311). You can also spread it on any chocolate or vanilla layer or sheet cake.

PREP 5 minutes plus cooling
COOK 15 minutes • **MAKES** about 3 cups.

½ cup butter or margarine (1 stick), cut into pieces
1 cup heavy or whipping cream
1 cup packed light brown sugar
3 large egg yolks
1 cup flaked sweetened coconut
1 cup pecans (4 ounces), chopped
1 teaspoon vanilla extract

1 In 2-quart saucepan, heat butter, cream, and brown sugar almost to boiling over medium-high heat, stirring occasionally.

2 Place egg yolks in medium bowl. Slowly pour about ½ cup hot butter mixture into egg yolks, whisking constantly. Reduce heat to medium-low. Add egg-yolk mixture to saucepan; whisk until mixture has thickened (do not boil). Remove from heat. Stir in coconut, pecans, and vanilla. Cool to room temperature.

EACH TABLESPOON About 80 calories, 1g protein, 6g carbohydrate, 6g total fat (3g saturated), 25mg cholesterol, 30mg sodium.

Amaretto Buttercream

This meringue-based buttercream is flavored with almond liqueur (substitute almond extract if you'd rather not use alcohol). Try it on a chocolate cake or any layer cake made with nuts.

PREP 35 minutes plus cooling • **COOK** 5 minutes • **MAKES** about 4 cups.

1 cup sugar
⅓ cup water
4 large egg whites
2 cups unsalted butter (4 sticks), softened
    (do not use salted butter or margarine)
¼ cup amaretto (almond-flavored liqueur)
    or ½ teaspoon almond extract
pinch salt

1 In 1-quart saucepan, heat ¾ cup sugar and water to boiling over high heat, without stirring. Cover and cook 2 minutes. Remove cover; set candy thermometer in place and continue cooking, without stirring, until temperature reaches 248° to 250°F, or hard-ball stage (when small amount of syrup can be formed into a hard ball that holds its shape). Remove saucepan from heat.
2 Just before syrup is ready (temperature will be about 220°F), in large bowl, with mixer at high speed, beat egg whites until foamy. Gradually beat in remaining ¼ cup sugar and continue beating until soft peaks form.

3 With mixer at low speed, slowly pour hot syrup in thin stream into beaten egg-white mixture. Increase speed to high; beat until meringue forms stiff peaks and mixture is cool to the touch, about 15 minutes.
4 When meringue is cool, reduce speed to medium. Gradually add softened butter, 1 tablespoon at a time, beating after each addition. (If buttercream appears to curdle, increase speed to high and beat until mixture comes together, then reduce speed to medium and continue adding softened butter, 1 tablespoon at a time.) When buttercream is smooth, reduce speed to low; beat in amaretto and salt until incorporated.

EACH TABLESPOON About 65 calories, 0g protein, 3g carbohydrate, 6g total fat (4g saturated), 16mg cholesterol, 5mg sodium.

Small-Batch Butter Frosting

The variations below offer four different frosting flavors to complement your cake.

PREP 10 minutes • **MAKES** about 2⅓ cups.

1 package (16 ounces) confectioners' sugar
½ cup butter or margarine (1 stick), softened
4 to 6 tablespoons milk or half-and-half
1½ teaspoons vanilla extract

In large bowl, with mixer at medium-low speed, beat confectioners' sugar, softened butter, and 3 tablespoons milk until smooth and blended. Beat in additional milk as needed for easy spreading consistency. Increase speed to medium-high; beat until light and fluffy.

EACH TABLESPOON About 70 calories, 0g protein, 12g carbohydrate, 3g total fat (2g saturated), 7mg cholesterol, 25mg sodium.

LEMON BUTTER FROSTING

Prepare as directed for Small-Batch Butter Frosting, but use *2 tablespoons milk, 2 tablespoons fresh lemon juice,* and *1 teaspoon grated lemon peel.* Use only *1 to 2 tablespoons additional milk* as needed for easy spreading consistency. Makes about 2⅓ cups.

EACH TABLESPOON About 70 calories, 0g protein, 12g carbohydrate, 3g total fat (2g saturated), 7mg cholesterol, 25mg sodium.

ORANGE BUTTER FROSTING

Prepare as directed for Lemon Butter Frosting, but substitute *2 tablespoons orange juice* for lemon juice and *1 teaspoon grated orange peel* for lemon peel. Makes about 2⅓ cups.

EACH TABLESPOON About 70 calories, 0g protein, 12g carbohydrate, 3g total fat (2g saturated), 7mg cholesterol, 25mg sodium.

CHOCOLATE BUTTER FROSTING

Prepare as directed for Small-Batch Butter Frosting, but beat in either *4 squares (4 ounces) bittersweet chocolate,* melted and cooled, or *3 squares (3 ounces) semisweet chocolate plus 1 square (1 ounce) unsweetened chocolate,* melted and cooled. Makes about 2¾ cups.

EACH TABLESPOON: About 75 calories, 0g protein, 12g carbohydrate, 3g total fat (2g saturated), 6mg cholesterol, 20mg sodium.

Chocolate Glaze

Pour or spread the warm (not hot) glaze over Boston Cream Pie (page 330) and Éclairs (page 215). The glaze will thicken and set as it cools.

PREP 5 minutes • COOK 3 minutes
MAKES about ½ cup.

3 squares (3 ounces) semisweet chocolate,
   coarsely chopped
3 tablespoons butter
1 tablespoon light corn syrup
1 tablespoon milk

In heavy 1-quart saucepan, heat chocolate, butter, corn syrup, and milk over low heat, stirring occasionally, until smooth.

EACH TABLESPOON About 100 calories, 1g protein, 9g carbohydrate, 8g total fat (5g saturated), 12mg cholesterol, 50mg sodium.

Rich Chocolate Glaze

Immediately pour glaze over top of cooled Peanut Butter–Cup Cake (page 293), allowing it to run down sides. Let cake stand at least 30 minutes to allow glaze to set before serving.

PREP 5 minutes • COOK 2 minutes
MAKES about ½ cup.

3 ounces milk chocolate, broken into pieces
3 tablespoons butter or margarine
1 tablespoon light corn syrup
1 tablespoon milk

In microwave-safe 1-quart measuring cup, heat chocolate, butter, corn syrup, and milk in microwave on High, stirring twice, until smooth, 1½ to 2 minutes.

EACH ½ TABLESPOON About 55 calories, 1g protein, 4g carbohydrate, 4g total fat (1g saturated), 8mg cholesterol, 30mg sodium.

Mocha Glaze

We use this tasty glaze to finish our Light Chocolate–Buttermilk Bundt Cake (page 316), but it would work equally well with our Walnut Torte (page 317).

PREP 5 minutes • MAKES about 1½ cups.

¼ teaspoon instant espresso-coffee powder
2 tablespoons hot water
3 tablespoons unsweetened cocoa
3 tablespoons dark corn syrup
1 tablespoon coffee-flavored liqueur
1 cup confectioners' sugar

In medium bowl, stir espresso-coffee powder and hot water until dissolved. Stir in cocoa, corn syrup, and coffee-flavored liqueur until blended. Add confectioners' sugar; stir until smooth.

EACH TABLESPOON 31 calories, 0g protein, 8g carbohydrate, 0g total fat, 0mg cholesterol, 4mg sodium.

Brown-Butter Glaze

This glaze gives our Pumpkin-Spice Cake (page 290) a rich flavor boost, but it is versatile enough to enhance any Bundt or tube cake.

PREP 5 minutes plus cooling
COOK 5 minutes • MAKES about 2 cups.

6 tablespoons butter or margarine
½ cup packed light brown sugar
2 tablespoons milk
1 teaspoon vanilla extract
1 cup confectioners' sugar

1 In 2-quart saucepan, heat butter over medium heat, stirring occasionally, until melted and golden brown, about 3 to 5 minutes. Reduce heat to low. Add brown sugar and milk and whisk until sugar has dissolved, about 2 minutes.
2 Remove saucepan from heat; whisk in vanilla. Gradually add confectioners' sugar, whisking until smooth, about 3 minutes. Cool glaze, whisking occasionally, until slightly thickened, about 5 minutes.

EACH TABLESPOON 47 calories, 0g protein, 7g carbohydrate, 2g total fat (1g saturated), 6mg cholesterol, 24mg sodium.

Ganache

Ganache is a thick, creamy chocolate filling meant to be slathered between layers of your favorite cake.

PREP 15 minutes plus chilling
COOK 5 minutes • MAKES 2 cups.

1 cup heavy or whipping cream
2 tablespoons sugar
2 teaspoons butter or margarine
10 squares (10 ounces) semisweet chocolate, chopped
1 teaspoon vanilla extract
1 to 2 tablespoons brandy or orange- or almond-flavored liqueur (optional)

1 In 2-quart saucepan, heat cream, sugar, and butter to boiling over medium-high heat. Remove saucepan from heat.
2 Add chocolate to cream mixture and whisk until chocolate has melted and mixture is smooth. Stir in vanilla and brandy, if using. Pour into jelly-roll pan and refrigerate until spreadable, at least 30 minutes.

EACH TABLESPOON About 74 calories, 1g protein, 6g carbohydrate, 6g total fat (3g saturated), 11mg cholesterol, 6mg sodium.

Meringue Mushrooms

Charming meringue mushrooms are a traditional finishing touch on our Brandied Bûche de Noël (page 337). You can make them well in advance, saving a bit of last-minute fuss at holiday time.

PREP 45 minutes • **BAKE** 1 hour 45 minutes plus drying • **MAKES** 30 mushrooms.

4 large egg whites
¼ teaspoon cream of tartar
¾ cup sugar
¼ teaspoon almond extract
2 squares (2 ounces) semisweet chocolate, melted
unsweetened cocoa

1 Preheat oven to 200°F. Line large cookie sheet with foil or parchment paper.

2 In medium bowl, with mixer at high speed, beat egg whites and cream of tartar until soft peaks form when beaters are lifted. Gradually sprinkle in sugar, 2 tablespoons at a time, beating well after each addition, until sugar has completely dissolved and whites stand in stiff, glossy peaks when beaters are lifted. Beat in almond extract.

3 Spoon meringue into large pastry bag with ½-inch plain tip. Pipe meringue onto cookie sheet in 30 mounds, each about 1½ inches in diameter, to resemble mushroom caps. Pipe remaining meringue upright in thirty 1¼-inch lengths to resemble mushroom stems. (If there is extra meringue, pipe additional stems in case of breakage.)

4 Bake 1 hour 45 minutes. Turn off oven; leave meringues in oven 30 minutes to dry. Cool completely on cookie sheet on wire rack.

5 With tip of small knife, cut small hollow in center of underside of each mushroom cap. Place small amount of melted chocolate in hollow; spread underside of cap with chocolate. Attach stem to cap by inserting pointed end of stem into hollow in underside of cap. Repeat with remaining stems, caps, and chocolate. Let chocolate set, about 1 hour.

6 Store meringue mushrooms in airtight container at room temperature up to 1 month. Just before serving, sprinkle lightly with unsweetened cocoa.

EACH MUSHROOM About 30 calories, 1g protein, 6g carbohydrate, 1g total fat (0g saturated), 0mg cholesterol, 10mg sodium.

Stabilized Whipped Cream

Adding gelatin to whipped cream stabilizes the mixture so that it does not break down and "weep."

PREP 10 minutes • **COOK** 5 minutes
MAKES about 4 cups.

2 cups heavy or whipping cream
1 teaspoon vanilla extract
1¼ teaspoons unflavored gelatin
2 tablespoons cold water
⅓ cup confectioners' sugar

1 In large bowl, stir cream and vanilla. In small saucepan, evenly sprinkle gelatin over cold water; let stand 1 minute to soften. Cook over medium-low heat, stirring frequently, until gelatin has completely dissolved, about 2 minutes (do not boil). Remove saucepan from heat.
2 With mixer at medium-high speed, immediately begin beating cream mixture. Beat until thickened and soft peaks just begin to form, about 1 minute. Beat in confectioners' sugar. Add dissolved gelatin in a thin steady stream, beating until stiff peaks form but mixture is still soft and smooth; do not overbeat.

EACH TABLESPOON: About 30 calories, 0g protein, 1g carbohydrate, 3g total fat (2g saturated), 10mg cholesterol, 5mg sodium.

Test Kitchen Tip

WORKING WITH WHIPPED CREAM

Chill cream, bowl, and beaters before beating. Start mixer on Slow to incorporate small air bubbles. Continue beating at on Medium until stiff peaks form.

If you accidentally overbeat the cream and it begins to turn to butter, gently whisk in more cream 1 tablespoon at a time. Don't beat the cream again, or you'll end up with a bowl of butter.

White Chocolate Hearts

These open designs are very striking when used on Chocolate Truffle Cake (page 315). They are also appropriate, especially on Valentine's Day, on any special chocolate cake.

PREP 15 minutes • **COOK** 3 minutes
MAKES 12 hearts.

1½ ounces white chocolate, coarsely chopped

1 With pencil, draw outline of 12 hearts, each about 1½" by 1½", on piece of waxed paper. Place waxed paper, pencil-side down, on cookie sheet, tape to cookie sheet.
2 In top of double boiler over simmering water, melt white chocolate, stirring, until smooth. Spoon warm chocolate into small decorating bag fitted with small writing tube; use to pipe heart-shaped outlines on waxed paper. Let hearts stand until set.

Chocolate Curls

For a professional look, use these curls to garnish ice cream, cakes, and pies.

PREP 15 minutes plus chilling

1 package (6 ounces) semisweet
   chocolate chips
2 tablespoons vegetable shortening

1 In heavy 1-quart saucepan, heat chocolate chips and shortening over low heat, stirring frequently, until melted and smooth.
2 Pour chocolate mixture into foil-lined or disposable 5¾" by 3¾" loaf pan. Refrigerate until chocolate has set, about 2 hours.
3 Remove chocolate from pan. Using vegetable peeler and working over waxed paper, draw blade across surface of chocolate to make large curls. If chocolate is too cold and curls break, let chocolate stand about 30 minutes at room temperature until slightly softened. To avoid breaking curls, use toothpick or wooden skewer to transfer.

Chocolate Wedges

A spectacular way to dress up cakes, ice cream, and pies.

PREP 15 minutes plus chilling

1 package (6 ounces) semisweet
   chocolate chips
2 tablespoons vegetable shortening

1 In heavy 1-quart saucepan, heat chocolate chips and shortening over low heat, stirring frequently, until melted and smooth.
2 On waxed paper, with toothpick, trace circle using bottom of 9-inch round cake pan as guide; cut out circle. Invert cake pan; moisten bottom with water. Place waxed-paper circle on bottom of pan (water will prevent paper from moving).
3 With narrow metal spatula, spread melted chocolate mixture evenly over waxed paper. Refrigerate until chocolate is firm, about 30 minutes.
4 Heat blade of long thin knife with hot water; wipe dry. Quickly but gently, cut chocolate into wedges.

WORKING WITH CHOCOLATE

Beautiful, chocolate garnishes, such as chocolate curls, wedges, and leaves, will make a dessert look as though it came right out of a professional's kitchen. Working with melted chocolate can be tricky, but these pointers should help.

Melt chocolate one of three ways: in the top of a double boiler over hot, not boiling, water; in a heat-safe measuring cup set in a pan of hot water; in a small, heavy saucepan over low heat.

To speed melting, break the chocolate into small pieces and stir often. Don't overheat; when heated too long, chocolate can become grainy.

When making chocolate garnishes, work with chocolate as soon as it is melted and smooth.

Chocolate Leaves

Only use nontoxic leaves, available at florist shops, such as lemon, gardenia, grape, magnolia, nasturtium, rose, and violet.

PREP 30 minutes plus chilling

12 lemon leaves
1 package (6 ounces) semisweet
    chocolate chips
¼ cup vegetable shortening

1 Wash leaves in warm soapy water; pat thoroughly dry with paper towels.
2 In heavy 1-quart saucepan, heat chocolate chips and shortening over low heat, stirring frequently, until melted and smooth.
3 With pastry brush or small metal spatula, spread layer of melted chocolate mixture on underside (back) of each leaf (underside will give more distinct leaf design). Place chocolate-coated leaves, chocolate side up, on waxed paper–lined cookie sheet. Refrigerate until chocolate is firm, about 30 minutes.
4 With cool hands, carefully and gently peel each leaf away from chocolate.

Photo Credits

Sang An: pages 74, 79, 81, 82, 232, and 321.

James Baigrie: pages 131 and 153.

Mary Ellen Bartley: page 25.

Brian Hagiwara: pages 37, 57, 70, 72, 86, 90, 93, 94, 120, 124, 133, 162, 167, 176, 188, 272, and 313.

Lisa Hubbard: page 274.

Rita Maas: pages 19, 31, and 346.

Steven Mark Needham: pages 21, 27, 32, 39, 42, 60, 116, 149, 150, 161, 208, 216, 221, 225, 227, 241, 261, 265, 306, 331, 336-37, 343, 360, 362, and 363.

Alison Miksch: page 279.

Alan Richardson: pages 69, 122, 145, 199, 205, 245, 267, 269, and 294.

Ann Stratton: pages 2, 48, 58, 62, 64, 67, 76, 96, 99, 100, 111, 114, 134-35, 140, 143, 156, 169, 170, 182, 185, 187, 210, 212, 214, 219, 223, 242-43, 248, 252, 263, and 305.

Mark Thomas: pages 16, 28, 43, 46, 51, 53, 54, 65, 222, 238, 246, 280, 287, 297, 302, 314, 324, 332, 334-35, and 351.

Wendell Webber: pages 298, 326, and 349.

Index

Metric Conversion Chart

The recipes that appear in this cookbook use the standard United States method for measuring liquid and dry or solid ingredients (teaspoons, tablespoons, and cups). The information on this chart is provided to help cooks outside the U.S. successfully use these recipes. All equivalents are approximate.

METRIC EQUIVALENTS FOR DIFFERENT TYPES OF INGREDIENTS

A standard cup measure of a dry or solid ingredient will vary in weight depending on the type of ingredient. A standard cup of liquid is the same volume for any type of liquid. Use the following chart when converting standard cup measures to grams (weight) or milliliters (volume).

Standard Cup	Fine Powder (ex flour)	Grain (ex.rice)	Granular (ex. sugar)	Liquid Solids (ex. butter)	Liquid (ex. milk)
1	140 g	150 g	190 g	200 g	240 ml
3/4	105 g	113 g	143 g	150 g	180 ml
2/3	93 g	100 g	125 g	133 g	160 ml
1/2	70 g	75 g	95 g	100 g	120 ml
1/3	47 g	50 g	63 g	67 g	80 ml
1/4	35 g	38 g	48 g	50 g	60 ml
1/8	18 g	19 g	24 g	25 g	30 ml

USEFUL EQUIVALENTS FOR LIQUID INGREDIENTS BY VOLUME

1/4 tsp	=						1 ml
1/2 tsp	=						2 ml
1 tsp	=						5 ml
3 tsp	=	1 tbls	=		1/2 fl oz	=	15 ml
		2 tbls	=	1/8 cup =	1 fl oz	=	30 ml
		4 tbls	=	1/4 cup =	2 fl oz	=	60 ml
		5 1/3 tbls	=	1/3 cup =	3 fl oz	=	80 ml
		8 tbls	=	1/2 cup =	4 fl oz	=	120 ml
		10 2/3 tbls	=	2/3 cup =	5 fl oz	=	160 ml
		12 tbls	=	3/4 cup =	6 fl oz	=	180 ml
		16 tbls	=	1 cup =	8 fl oz	=	240 ml
		1 pt	=	2 cups =	16 fl oz	=	480 ml
		1 qt	=	4 cups =	32 fl oz	=	960 ml
					33 fl oz	=	1000 ml = 1 l

USEFUL EQUIVALENTS FOR DRY INGREDIENTS BY WEIGHT

(To convert ounces to grams, multiply the number of ounces by 30.)

1 oz	=	1/16 lb	=	30 g
4 oz	=	1/4 lb	=	120 g
8 oz	=	1/2 lb	=	240 g
12 oz	=	3/4 lb	=	360 g
16 oz	=	1 lb	=	480 g

USEFUL EQUIVALENTS FOR COOKING/OVEN TEMPERATURES

	Fahrenheit	Celsius	Gas Mark
Freeze Water	32° F	0° C	
Room Temperature	68° F	20° C	
Boil Water	212° F	100° C	
Bake	325° F	160° C	3
	350° F	180° C	4
	375° F	190° C	5
	400° F	200° C	6
	425° F	220° C	7
	450° F	230° C	8
Broil			Grill

USEFUL EQUIVALENTS FOR LENGTH

(To convert inches to centimeters, multiply the number of inches by 2.5.)

1 in	=				2.5 cm
6 in	=	1/2 ft	=		15 cm
12 in	=	1 ft	=		30 cm
36 in	=	3 ft	=	1 yd =	90 cm
40 in	=				100 cm = 1 m